Understanding Indian Politics

C.P. Bhambhri

SHIPRA

(First Published in India in 2018)

Rs. 1800; US$ 72

ISBN: 978-93-86262-86-8

2022 Impression

Understanding Indian Politics

Published by:
SHIPRA PUBLICATIONS
LG 18-19, Pankaj Central Market
I.P. Ext., Patparganj, Delhi 110092, India
Tel.: +91 11 2223 5152/6152
E-mail: info@shiprapublication.com
www.shiprapublication.com

Preface

An effort has been made to understand, interpret and explain Indian politics by applying scientific theory of 'class analysis'of Karl Marx. Marx alerted us that observable or apparent is not real and the study of politics requires a theoretical and methodological approach to understand the nature of real social forces which shape politics of a society. Politics is not just a mere 'reflection' of social class power relations which exist in society, politics has its own 'autonomy' and it plays great role in the making and shaping of society. This 'dual' character of politics has to be kept in focus while understanding its complexities. If on one hand, politics is an instrument in the hands of exploiting propertied classes in every class-divided society, on the other, political managers of the state and politically elected Chief Executive exercise power to guide and control the exploiting classes. This theoretical and methodological perspective has been applied in this study of concrete politics of post-Independence India.

Part I of this study deals with politics of India and it has been narrated around Prime Ministers beginning with Jawaharlal Nehru [1947-1964] to Narendra Modi [2014 -]. The focus is not on the personality of individual Prime Ministers of India but important political events have been described around these Prime Ministers. Politics of India can be studied, explained and understood on the basis of "continuities and changes" which have taken place during the last seventy years of post-independence India. If Nehru's model of the state-led economic development continued to be followed by his successors like Indira Gandhi, Morarji Desai, Rajiv Gandhi et al, a fundamental rupture occurred in this path of economic development with Narasimha Rao in 1991 who launched New Economic Policy model based on 'liberalisation, privatization and globalization' and this model has been followed by successors of Narasimha Rao upto Narendra Modi. This is just one illustration to highlight the argument that the study of last seventy years may be studied around "continuity and change".

Part II of the book is focused on findings "explanations" around landmark issues of Indian politics like globalization or the growth of BJP. These two parts are interrelated because 'description' and 'explanation' are two sides of the same coin because the focus is to understand politics of India. The greatest challenge to Indian society and politics in the coming decades of 21st Century is the deepening of social cleavages because of the rising levels of 'social and economic inequalities' India is one country and one nation is a mere slogan because many India's have emerged and disparities of income and wealth among different social classes and strata are growing and the governing powerful groups are busy only in achieving the targets of the rate of economic growth and none of the dominant social group is thinking about 're-distribution' of social wealth with a view to establish socially equitable society. How can equality become the agenda of elected representatives in the Lok Sabha or state legislative assemblies who are themselves "multi-millionaire"? These are some of the major issues of Indian politics which have been discussed and described in this study. Social dialectics of India is at work and powerful social status-quoistforces are faced with the growing challenge of forces committed to change the existing exploitative and unequal social order and replace it with an 'alternative' equitable social order. It is difficult to predict the direction of future developments of politics.

Acknowledgements

Thanks are to *Pioneer, Tribune, People's Democracy*, et al where some contributions of the author were published. Thanks are also to Mr. D Kumar, enterprising publisher of Shipra, Delhi.

Chander Prakash Bhambhri
Jawaharlal Nehru University
New Delhi
July, 2018

Contents

1

Jawaharlal Nehru: The Foundational Phase

The retreating colonial state partitioned the country and transferred power to the leaders of all-India national Congress in India and the Muslim League in Pakistan, and these two countries emerged on the international map with Dominion Status on August 15, 1947. The Indian nationalist leadership recognised this fact of Dominion Status and Jawaharlal Nehru, the first Prime Minister of free India, clearly stated that the real journey for the establishment of Sovereign Democratic Republican state has just begun and many more steps will have to be taken to achieve the goal of 'Purna Swaraj' or complete Independence of the country. Nehru, in his famous speech 'Tryst with Destiny', stated that "Now the time comes when we shall redeem our pledge, not wholly or in full measure but substantially." The reference by Nehru in his 'speech' was to the ongoing process of Constitution making for India. The Constituent Assembly had held its first session on 9 December 1946, and the Draft Constitution, as prepared by the Drafting Committee, was presented to the Assembly President on 21 February 1948. Dr. B.R. Ambedkar moved a resolution that the 'Constitution' as settled by the Assembly, be passed. The Constitution was adopted on November 26, 1949 and after signatures of the members of the Constituent Assembly, the new Republic's Constitution was proclaimed on January 26, 1950. The Dominion Status of India ended with the adoption of the Constitution and the challenging task of laying the firm foundations of a modern, democratic, secular, federal Republic of India was undertaken in right earnest by the nationalist leadership. It deserves to be clearly understood that the task of laying down 'foundations' of a modern independent state is never an easy one and this has the reason that Jawaharlal Nehru faced many difficulties and problems in dealing with issues of state-formation in India. Nehru had to shoulder major responsibilities of sate-formation because he was much more than 'first among equals' while performing his obligations as Prime Minister. Nehru was not only one of the tallest leaders of anti-colonial struggle for independence, as Prime Minister from August 15, 1947 to May 27, 1964, he remained in full command of his government and the Congress party. It is essential to catalogue the major steps taken by the Nehru government during his fourteen years of power for dealing with the complex issues that faced the country after independence.

(a) Partition of India and the challenges which emerged during the early years of partition.
(b) Integration and Democratisation of more than 560 princely states into the Union of India.
(c) The holding of first Lok Sabha and State Assembly elections in 1951-52 on the basis of universal adult franchise.
(d) India-Pakistan war on Jammu and Kashmir from 1947-48 and post-ceasefire problems in the Security Council of the United Nations.
(e) Appointment of Fazal Ali Commission on the Reorganisation of States and discussions and decisions in 1955-56.
(f) The launching of Five-Year Plans for Economic Development of the country.
(g) Foreign policy of Non-Alignment and friendship with all countries and in keeping away from two power blocs of the cold war phase of politics. Nehru had emerged as the real leader after the Lok Sabha elections of 1952, 1957 and 1962.
(h) Nehru received set back: India-China Border Dispute 1962.
(i) Nehru breathed his last on May 27, 1964.

Nehru provided the framework for the domestic and foreign policies with a goal to create a 'relatively autonomous state' on the basis of policies of economic planning and non-alignment and peaceful co-existence with every country. Economic Planning was launched to accelerate the rate of growth of Indian economy to overcome inherited backwardness and poverty of the country. Nehru preferred the system of state-led and state-directed strategy of economic growth by following a model of 'mixed economy' with commanding heights for the public sector enterprises. The system of economic planning was equated with socialism and in reality Nehru laid down the foundations of state capitalism where private sector enterprises co-existed with enterprises controlled by the State and in Nehru's words "public sector occupying the commanding heights."

Nehru should be studied in a proper historical context because his contribution to the making of a modern, democratic, federal, secular and welfare state can be analysed and evaluated only by keeping in mind the challenges faced by every newly decolonised and liberated country from the colonial rule. Nehru laid down the foundations of a "relatively autonomous state which was based on democratic legitimacy" and he took great pains to spread the message of democracy during his extensive election campaigns; during the Lok Sabha elections of 1952, 1957 and 1962. Nehru could attempt to establish a relatively autonomous state and dominate over powerful social class forces because he mobilised the Indian voters and got his political strength from voters of India. Democracy acted as a countervailing force for restraining the desire of powerful social class forces which wanted to control and dominate over the state. This is the real meaning of Nehru's contribution to Indian democracy.

Only one illustration about Nehru's firm commitment to democracy can be provided by narrating the story of Reorganisation of States which was piloted by him. The post-Independence national leadership was faced with a Herculean task of creating a new political map for providing a shape to the completely shapeless British Provinces and 562 princely states, which had agreed to sign an Instrument of Accession in favour of India.

People's representatives have to speak and understand the language of their own voters and unlike the alien British rulers, elected representatives have to be accountable to their electorate and furthermore a common language of the elected and the voter is the only bond which provides a link between the parliament and the people. The implementation of the principle of language-based democracy in a multilingual country was a gigantic task and the author of *'The Discovery of India'* knew it quite well that unifying factors, in a highly diverse society, could never be imposed from above and any consensus-making on the accommodation of 'diversities' was Herculean task; especially for a country which had suffered wounds of partition. It would be wrong to say that the post-Independence Congress had abandoned its own pledge of linguistic reorganisation of India because the author of *'Unity in Diversity'* clearly understood the sensitivities of people and communities based on 'diverse identities' and the unfolding of events around the linguistic reorganisation of states proved that Nehru's 'caution' on the opening of Pandora's box was based on correct understanding of the politics of identity. India was partitioned on the basis of politics of clash of religion-based identity and Nehru could not have been insulated from the tragic events of post-Partition India. Context determines the text and actions of the makers of history. Nehru was doubly troubled because his commitment to diverse pluralism of India seemed to be coming into conflict with his firm belief that democratic consensus is the prime mover of governance in a country of diversities and pluralities. Nehru's handling of the emotive issue of linguistic reorganisation of India, especially after the tragic events for separate Andhra from Madras Presidency Province. He piloted the issue of language politics without sacrificing the basic principle of consensus-based democracy.

The deft political handling of the States Reorganisation by Nehru and keeping democratic sensitivities intact can be understood only by narrating the main events around the exercise of reorganisation. The State Re-organisation Commission was set up on December 22, 1953 with Syed Fazal Ali as Chairman, and Sardar K.M. Panikkar and H.N. Kunzru as members. The Commission submitted its 250 page report to the Government of India on September 30, 1955 together with summary of recommendations which was the result of 21 months of hard work by the Commission. The present political map of India is completely different from the recommendations for the creation of 16 new states by the Fazal Ali Commission.The process of decision-making by the Nehru government and the Congress party is illustrative of the fact that Nehru's government did not push the recommendations from 'above' and the Chief Ministers and various parties and groups were actively involved with the recommendations of the Commission. The Home Ministry acted as a 'nodal agency' beginning from October 19, 1955 for processing the report. The Congress Working Committee was immediately seized of the ticklish problems relating to the reorganisation and on November 9, 1955 it took important decisions. They were:

(a) greater Bombay, Maharashtra, including Vidarbha, and Gujarat should be formed into three separate states;
(b) subject to the wishes of the people concerned, the Telangana area to be merged with the Andhra state;
(c) accepted the proposal of the States Reorganisation Commission for the creation of a new state comprising Maha Koshal, Vindhya Pradesh, Madhya Bharat and Bhopal.

A sub-committee was also constituted with U.N. Dhebar, Jawaharlal Nehru, Maulana Azad and Govindvallabh Pant to 'consider, in consultation with the people concerned, the question of Punjab, PEPSU and Himachal Pradesh and also regarding the proposed Karnataka State, including Mysore and various border issues arising out of Commission's report'. Further, Uttar Pradesh was to remain 'as at present.' Nehru, while speaking in the Lok Sabha on December 21, 1955, stated that "Whatever be the decision Parliament might take on the report, he would suggest the division of India into zones, north, south, east and west with the Centre including and each zone having a Zonal Council to function as an advisory body to tackle the economic problems…." Nehru further said that "these zones might have a common Governor or High Court but above all they must work for a common economy" and Nehru concluded that "these were his personal views on the recommendations."

> Nehru was not only leading and guiding but encouraging full debate on contentious issues arising out of the recommendations of the States Reorganisation Commission's report. Nehru pursued his recommendation on Zonal Councils and stated on December 26, 1955: "If each state plans without reference to its neighbour-States, then it would not be a good plan....And in that way also help in lessening, in mitigating and controlling this narrow minded state-consciousness, a tendency which goes against the unity of India." Nehru's concern for the unification of a highly diverse society is reflected repeatedly, but in achieving this goal, he never abandoned his commitment to the role of public opinion in a democracy. Many new Fronts were opened by political parties and groups which were making claims and counter-claims, regarding the new shape of reorganised India. B.C. Roy, the Chief Minister of West Bengal, proposed a 'reunion' of West Bengal

> and Bihar, and on February 22, 1956, while responding to the opposition parties' criticism of his 'reunion proposals' in the State Assembly, he not only stated that "You (the opposition) betrayed West Bengal", he also declared that "in the demarcation of States, though it was an important point, "linguism could not be the dominating factor". B.C. Roy was going against the mainstream of political thinking which believed that "language is the basis of territorial identity and plays the role of a link between rulers and ruled in a democracy". Every claim and counter-claim on issues raised by the recommendations of the States Reorganisation Commission was justified and opposed on the basis of the meaning and substance of democracy, in a multi-lingual country where the alien rulers had ruled with the help of foreign language namely the English.

This demand for the reunification of West Bengal and Bihar found a legitimacy on January 24,1956 when it was endorsed in a 'joint statement' by the Chief Ministers of West Bengal and Bihar. This 'joint statement' by the two Chief Ministers led to resentment in both the States and the United Front of Bengal Leftist parties formed the West Bengal Linguistic State Reorganisation Committee and also decided to launch a civil disobedience movement from February 24, 1956 and it also called "for a general strike to protest against the Bengal-Bihar union move. "The United Front of all Leftist parties in West Bengal jumped into the fray and mobilised people against 're-union' move of two states. U.N. Dhebar chaired Congress Working Committee's sub-committee meeting on February 19, 1956, on the ticklish issue of merger of Andhra state and Telangana, and discussions were held with the "representatives of these two areas jointly to consider what safeguards, if any, should be provided to secure the development and the needs of the comparatively backward Telangana". In spite of the attempts by the leadership, separate Telangana demand refused to die. The 61st session of the Indian National Congress ended on February 12, 1956 by passing a resolution which favoured "the formation of bilingual states wherever possible and said unilinguialism should not be made a fetish." The Congress party was compelled to abandon its idea of 'bilingual states' in the face of stiff resistance from the majority of areas which were affected by such proposal. The government of India took decision on SRC on January 17, 1956 and decided to circulate a draft bill to the states and bring a law before Parliament after this.

Nehru had known that each and every proposal for the merger or unification of areas on the basis of Parliament's Legislation, in spite of popular participation of the concerned groups, will lead to controversies including violence because politics of language-based identity is both a uniting and a dividing social force in a multilingual society. The government decided on January 17, 1956 that Bombay city should be constituted as a centrally-administered area and two proposed states of Maharashtra and Gujarat were to create on the basis of law to be passed Parliament. A hell broke out on the issue of the status of Bombay city and the Congress Working Committee, in its meeting on January 23, 1956, admonished Maharashtra PCC which demanded Congress Ministers to resign and Bihar and Odisha PCCs were also warned against passing such resolutions because PCC "was not competent to ask for such reorganisation." It is not only that the Congress party was facing 'turmoil' in it own rank and file, every political party like the Praja Socialists, Communist, Akali Dal et al. were involved in struggle against one or the other proposal of the government on the implementation of the SRC recommendations. The only exception to this general rule was M.S. Golwalkar's RSS, Jan Sangh/BJP because the ideologies of religion-based identity of Hindutva had never accepted language-based pluralism of India. Not only this, Linguistic pluralism is considered a 'divisive force' by the believers of homogeneous and hegemonic Hindu Rashtra.

The reorganisation of the states in the 1990s leading to the creation of Chhattisgarh, Jharkhand and Uttaranchal has been possible because the BJP had emerged as a significant factor in Indian politics and the Congress party of the 1990s had no historical memory of its own past. It is not only Nehru but Indira Gandhi also had resisted the demand for the creation of Punjabi Suba of the Akali Dal and she conceded it only when issue became very emotive because Sant Fateh Singh announced self-immolation and separate states of Punjab, Haryana and Himachal Pradesh were created by reorganising Punjab State.

The above narrative is helpful in the understanding of complex democratic process during the founding period of the Indian Republic from 1947-64. It also deserves to be stated that Nehru was imposing neither his ideas and opinions on his own party nor on the profile of India. The journey of State's Reorganisation is a testimony to the fact that pressure groups were always active in democratic India. Nehru's phase of democracy witnessed a lot of democratic dissent and recognised opposition parties and non-political groups which were very active in moulding public opinion against government's decisions and policies. The Samyukta Maharashtra Samiti, the Maha Gujarat Samiti, the United Front of Leftist parties and Morchas by Akali Dal were a common practice followed by political and non-political formations which agitated against government's decisions. Nehru altered his government's decisions under public pressure. The adventurism of Bombay city, as centrally administered area, led to mass protests and the protestors compelled the government to abandon its plan. It also deserves to be stated that Nehru was aware about the pitfalls and dangers of 'linguistic chauvinism' and in his famous '*Letters to the Chief Ministers*' he continuously reminded them of that 'reorganisation of states' should be handled with great care and sensitivity. Democracy-at-work was witnessed during Nehru's phase of politics while dealing with the emotions of people on public issues.

The ruling class of every country, including India, wish to use the state as an instrument and an agency for their own class interests, and Nehru established a system of balance of power between the state and the pressures of the ruling classes and in the process, states during Nehru's phase of power from 1947 to 1964 (May 27) maintained there relative autonomy from the attempts of the ruling classes to dominate over the state. The Industrial Policy Resolution provided a framework for the private corporate sector and this framework was decided and implemented by India. Such illustrations can be multiplied to substantiate the argument that Nehru recognised the power of the dominant and exploiting classes and he evolved strategies for checkmating the unlimited desires of the ruling classes to dominate over the state.

Nehru made every effort to maintain relative autonomy of the Indian state while dealing with powerful countries during the vicious period of the Cold War politics. Nehru's framework of non-alignment and peaceful co-existence, during the cold war era of international politics, provided an opportunity to "take decisions on difficult issues on merits of the case" and policy decisions on foreign policy were taken on its own by the Government of India. India decided about her friends and opponents (or not so friendly) in international politics. Nehru played an activist's role in international politics, and friends and opponents were decided on the merits of the case.

Further, Nehru opposed and contested the forces represented by parties and groups which practiced religion-based politics. For Nehru, secular state along with democracy was considered as the real protector of 'unity in diversity'. Nehru considered secularism as an integral part of democratic governance in India.

The multidimensionality of Nehru can be understood by keeping in mind a fact that India had embarked on a difficult journey of establishing a democratic state in an extremely hostile social milieu and the only redeeming feature was that modern India was a product of democratic struggles independence. The Indian leadership had learnt their lessons of democracy during struggle for Independence and such a lesson was learnt in a very hard way and immense sacrifices were made to achieve independence through democratic movements. Nehru nurtured and nourished the tender plant of democracy. An important lesson from Nehru Era is that democracy in India cannot be taken for granted and it has to be defended because it is our great national inheritance. If Nehru's socialism was attacked, both by the supporters of free enterprise and also the Communists, his foreign policy of non-alignment was attacked by the Western countries for its tilt toward the Communist bloc in the Cold War. Nehru stood in the middle and his domestic policies could be described as left-of-Centre and his foreign policy as an assertion of national independence vis-a-vis both the Communist and the capitalist blocs during the Cold War. How do we evaluate a leader who remained Prime Minister for fourteen years? What was Nehru's contribution to the building of modern, democratic Republic of India? This narrative will help us to understand his contribution by keeping in mind the historical period of 1947 to 1964.

Nehru: A Critical Study

In assessing Jawaharlal Nehru's contribution to modern India one should examine the various influences, both of ideas and persons, that shaped and moulded his thought and personality.

Nehru's education and early training brought him into contact with scientific and technological advancement in the West, and the working of democratic institutions in England. This impact of Western science and liberalism made Nehru a life-long believer in democracy, individual freedom and the power of science and technology for social transformation of backward societies. The most precious thing for Nehru was individual freedom, and he strove hard to establish a social order which would guarantee, preserve and maximise the area of freedom. The impact of western liberalism is writ large on his personality and way of thinking. He was convinced that technological advancement will liberate Indians from the 'shackles of medievalism and feudalism.' Nehru's rationalism, humanism, agnosticism, concern for individual freedom (he believed that the content of liberty is equality), belief in democracy and science were the result of his early training and education. While in England, he came under the influence of Fabian Socialists who believed in 'gradualism' and the importance of the State as an instrument for the establishment of socialism.

Soviet Impact

During his visit to Europe and Soviet Russia in 1926-27, he was greatly influenced by the achievements of the Soviet Union in the field of economic development. During the freedom movement, he developed socialist ideas and later tried to practise and implement these ideas through 'economic planning' in independent India. The influence of Marx is clearly seen in his *Glimpses of World History* where he employs Marxist terminology and tools of analysis to understand historical processes. While he did not accept all the fundamentals of Marxism, he did believe that there are class antagonisms and exploitation of workers and peasants by property-owners in a capitalist society. He also accepted that social organisation on socialist principles is better than the exploitative capitalist social order.

Method

But the question was how to transform an acquisitive society into a socialist one, and what should be the method of social revolution in India. Nehru was in quest of replies to these questions, and was dissatisfied with the violent methods advocated by the Communists. His attitude to Communists first found expression when he attended the Brussels Congress of Oppressed Nationalities in February 1927. At that Congress, as well as at subsequent committee meetings of the League, he came into contact with the Communists who were strong in the Congress.

> He writes: 'So I turned inevitably with goodwill towards Communism, for, whatever its faults, it was at least not hypocritical and not imperialistic... These attracted me, as also the tremendous changes taking place in Russia. But Communists often irritated me by their dictatorial ways, their aggressive and rather vulgar methods, their habit of denouncing everybody who did not agree with them. This reaction was no doubt due, as they would say, to my own bourgeois education and upbringing.'

He found the answer to the question of methods for social revolution in Gandhi's philosophy of 'Ends and Means'. One of the most important influences in the making of Nehru's thought and philosophy of action was Gandhi. Though fundamentally opposed to each other in their approaches to the problems of life and society, Gandhi and Nehru worked together with the true spirit of comradeship; and Gandhi exercised great *influence* over the value-pattern and thought-processes of Nehru. Nehru had great faith in Gandhi.

Gandhi's Influence and Congress Party

Gandhian leadership and the nature of the Indian national movement had its impact on the making of Nehru's philosophy. India did not achieve freedom through violent revolution. If a leader comes to power after a successful violent revolution, he can afford to have a complete break with the past and construct a society according to the ideology of the revolution. Nehru's position was different. He had grown within the Congress and had been making efforts to mould and change the Congress according to his beliefs. After independence the leadership of the party fell on him. The nature of the Congress Party, the character of its membership, the intra-party pulls and pressures—all these factors have to be examined to assess the personality of Nehru and his contribution.

The character of the Congress Party is best described by Nehru himself. Writing about the pre-1920 Congress, Nehru wrote:

> "My politics had been those of my class, bourgeoisie. Indeed all vocal politics then (and to a great extent even now) were those of the middle classes, and Moderate and Extremist alike represented them and, in different ways, sought their betterment...."

Nehru describes the post-1920 Congress as the 'New Congress'. About the Congress of the Gandhi era, he writes: "The whole look of the Congress changed, European clothes vanished and soon only Khadi was to be seen; a new class of delegate, chiefly drawn from the lower middle classes became the type of Congressman...." But even this 'new Congress' had not been convinced of Socialism. Nehru complains repeatedly that Congress was not aware of social objectives to be achieved after freedom. "Yet I felt that, bourgeois as the outlook of the National Congress was, it did represent the only effective revolutionary force in the country."

Nehru was not the leader of a socialist or ideological nationalist movement. The Congress had all sorts of people in its fold. An active and articulate proletariat was not the vanguard of the nationalist movement. Thus, Nehru's formative influences, the values that were dear to him, the method of social revolution that he developed, the character of the national movement, the nature of the Congress and above all the country in which he was working and living—all these aspects have to be considered.

Practical

A serious charge levelled against Nehru is that he failed to create an appropriate organisational and institutional structure for the proper implementation of ideas which he sincerely believed in and stood for. He talked of social and economic planning, but never cared to work out the detailed implications in the light of its conceptual bearings.

Two observations of Gandhi are worth noting regarding the personality traits of Nehru. Gandhi observed that he (Nehru) "is undoubtedly an extremist, thinking far ahead of his surroundings. But he is humble enough and practical enough not to force the peace to the breaking point." Gandhi's saying that Nehru was 'practical enough' not to create acute crises may help us in understanding the so-called 'grand failures' of Nehru. An idea may be excellent but the fact of its acceptance by the people has also to be taken into account by the leader. Moreover, Nehru, as Gandhi said, "does not feel happy if he is bogged down by the smallness of the task immediately on hand." Nehru needed a 'broader canvas to work upon'; he gave 'big ideas' to the nation and the world. When it came to execution, his performance perhaps could not be described as remarkable. There may be valid explanations for these deficiencies. Perhaps the social and cultural setting of the country was not congenial for a 'breakthrough', or the ideas were far in advance of his times. Perhaps the tools he employed, i.e., the state apparatus, the bureaucracy and the Congress Party were defective and inadequate for the gigantic tasks.

Educator

Keeping in mind this total background in which Nehru was functioning, let us study some specific aspects of Nehru's political and social ideas. According to Nehru, the first step to awaken the exploited masses was the establishment of democracy. Universal adult franchise was a revolutionary step in the Indian context. The teeming millions living in the far-flung villages, with different stages of socio-economic development were for the First time, made partners in shaping the nation's destiny. These destiny makers participated in general elections and exercised their right to elect and reject leaders, and in the process the consciousness of the importance of the 'ballot' as an instrument of socio-economic transformation of the country gradually developed in the minds of the people.

Many had apprehensions about the success of democracy in India. They doubted whether democracy could succeed in a country of mass illiteracy, economic backwardness and social inequality. But Nehru was active in nurturing the plant of democracy in India. He not only provided political stability to India, but also showed the path to the 'emerging social forces' and taught them the manner of struggle against entrenched vested interests. Instead of taking any radical steps, such as the confiscation of property, and creating an acute class crisis, he concentrated on educating and preparing the people for the struggle to divest the vested interests. In his whirlwind election tour, Nehru put across his ideas of secularism, socialism, economic planning and democracy before the masses, and thereby tried to wake up the sleeping giant that was India. In a country where the majority of the masses were illiterate, Nehru acted as a great teacher. Through the spoken word, he made efforts to educate the masses in the problems of poverty, its causes and remedies, and also on the role that the common man should play in moulding the destiny of India. He made people realise the importance of their being sovereign, and urged them to exercise sovereignty against entrenched exploitative social forces and liberate themselves from the shackles of poverty and ignorance.

He also made the common man to realise the value of Parliament as an instrument of social change. As a leader of the majority party, he always tried to act on the basis of 'consensus'. During his Prime Ministership, he never allowed the army to meddle with civilian affairs. Nehru's refusal to nominate or even indicate his successors, and his supreme confidence that 17 years of his labour would not prove worthless, and that a successor would be found in a democratic manner, proves his faith in democratic values and in the democratic destiny of the country.

Step by Step

During the freedom movement, Nehru's socialist ideas influenced the youth and the intelligentsia. In 1929, at the Lahore session of the Congress, Nehru, as a President declared: "The philosophy of socialism has gradually permeated the entire structure of society the world over. And almost the only point in dispute is the pace and methods of advance to its full realisation. India will have to go that way too if she seeks to end her poverty and inequality, though she may evolve her own methods and may adopt the ideal to the genius of her race."

In 1931, at the Karachi session the Congress passed an important resolution of Swaraj, indicating fundamental rights, and its economic programme. Nehru writes: "In the Karachi resolution it (Congress) took a step, a very short step, in a socialist direction by advocating nationalisation of key industries and services, and various other measures to lessen the burden on the poor and increase it on the rich. This was not socialism at all, and a capitalist State could easily accept almost everything contained in that resolution."

At the Lucknow session in 1936, he said: "I am convinced that the only key to the solution of..India's problems lies in socialism....I see no way of ending the poverty, the vast unemployment, the degradation and the subjection of the Indian people except by changes in our political and social structure, ending vested interests in land and industry, as well as the feudal and autocratic Indian States system. That means the ending of private property except in a restricted sense, and the replacement of the present profit system by a higher ideal of cooperative service... the present order has reached the evening of its day, and it is upto usto try to mould the future as we would like it to be...." He reiterated his belief in socialism in his Presidential address to the Faizpur session in 1936.

In 1938, Subhash Chandra Bose, as President of the Congress, appointed Nehru as the Chairman of the National Planning Committee. Nehru said, 'For me this has been fascinating work and I have learnt much from it.... It is also clear that any effective planning must involve a socialisation of the economic structure.'

Nehru's Approach

When this believer in Socialism and economic planning became Prime Minister, it was expected that there would be radical changes in existing property relationships. The question to be discussed is: What is Nehru's contribution to the establishment of Socialism in India?

The socialists outside the Congress Party were greatly disappointed and were very vocal in their criticism of Nehru who according to them, had betrayed the cause of socialism.

Before any assessment of the failures and the contribution of Nehru to the building of socialism is made, one fact should be stated clearly: Nehru was concerned with evolving a set of principles and ideas to achieve a socialist reconstruction of society with democratic means rather than with a violent revolution. His conviction was that socialism without democracy would mean tyranny in the Indian context. Further, his assessment of the existing Indian situation was that radical transformation was not possible because of the compulsions of the objective situation. The masses were deep-rooted in superstition, fatalism and ignorance. Class distinctions had not yet crystallised. A revolutionary working class movement, ready to fight me entrenched vested interests, did not exist. In Nehru's opinion, in such a social context, the journey to socialism should be slow. These thought processes influenced his activities as a Prime Minister.

To achieve socialism, Nehru believed that public sector should occupy the commanding heights in the Indian economy. He believed that the major sectors of the Indian economy should be under public ownership. He believed in large-scale industrialisation which he considered essential for the eradication of poverty. As a chairman of the Planning Commission; he piloted Five-Year Plans for economic growth. The pillars of this economic planning were industrialisation, agrarian reform, community development, education and social welfare. It has been estimated that the rate of economic growth achieved in India since 1950-51 is 2 to 3 times as high as the rate recorded under British administration. As a result, the percentage increase in national income, in the 13 years till Nehru died, was higher than the percentage increase realised in India over the preceding half century.

'Mixed Economy'

But is this Socialism? The abolition of landlordism and emphasis on the public sector were steps towards the building of a socialist society. But Nehru's concept of a 'mixed economy' encouraged and strengthened capitalism in spite of the 'public sector'. The monopoly power of the capitalists increased during the 17 years of Nehru's socialism. He did not bring any radical change in property relationships, and as such, the foundations of the 'acquisitive society' remained intact. He was so obsessed with increase in production that he could not realise that the benefits of economic development would go more to the already well-of sections. His rejection of a ceiling on wealth and nationalisation of banks as doctrinaire beliefs made him blind to the direction of development of capitalism in his scheme of 'mixed economy', and a socialist Prime Minister had to appoint the Mahalanobis Committee to report on concentration of wealth during the period of planning. Neither land reforms nor economic planning benefited the common man to an appreciable extent. Thus, in the evolution of Nehru's socialist ideas from the mid-twenties to the time of his death, there are two stages. During the pre-independence period, he was vocal about and firm on the content of socialism and was dissatisfied with Gandhi and the Congress for not accepting the full goal of socialism. In the second stage, he started decrying what he called a 'doctrinaire' approach to socialism and emphasised flexibility and pragmatism which led even to the dilution of the essentials of socialism.

Unsuited Tools

Who is responsible for the failure of Nehru's ideals of planning and socialism? The tools employed by Nehru for achieving the socialist goals were the bureaucracy and the Congress Party. Were these the right tools? Were they committed to Socialism or economic planning? For any radical socialist programme, Nehru required the support of a well-organised political party. Without strong political support, he could not have achieved his objectives. What was the character of the party of which Nehru was the leader? The Congress is a 'coalition of interests', a united front of all kinds of social interests and classes. Big businessmen and big landlords control it by making huge contributions to its election funds. In a parliamentary democracy, with a strong capitalist class, the Congress had to depend on it for finances. With the present membership of the Congress, and with its dependence on capitalists for finances, and with powerful Congress bosses not convinced about socialism, it would have been a miracle for Nehru or any other leader to get effective political support for any radical programme.

The critics, however, say that if such support was not forthcoming, he should have resigned from the party and formed a new one. After all Nehru was most popular leader among the masses. Instead of becoming leader of a party which by and large had no faith in socialism, he should have mobilised the masses to form a new party. Why did he not do it?

There are two answers. First, it was too much to expect Nehru (or any other leader) to sever relations with an organisation with which he had life-long association and loyalty.

Second, instead of leaving the party, he chose to make sincere and herculean efforts to convert the largest political organisation to the ideas of socialism. Even in pre-independence days, he had been making such efforts. He continued these efforts till the end of his life. Nehru's belief was that if the Congress Party could commit itself to socialism, it would be very difficult either for his successors or the party to give up socialism and economic planning. He was trying to make socialism a national goal, and for this he was educating the masses and converting party men. His faith was that progress towards the goal through his methods might be slow but it would be steady and firm. Perhaps the poor performance of the Opposition socialist parties in the elections made Nehru stick to the Congress and try to convert it. Nehru believed that the revolution could not be made to order.

Nehru believed that if a revolutionary idea (socialism) could capture the imagination of the people, it would become a material force. People inspired by great ideas are capable of great deeds. He tried to imbue Indians with great ideas so that they could perform great deeds. It is alleged that the Congress Party is responsible for Nehru having been not able to lay the foundation of a socialist society in India. It is further alleged that so-called conversion of the Congress Party was doomed to failure, in view of its class character.

Bureaucracy

His failure is also ascribed to his reliance on the bureaucracy. Nehru believed that with the help of the state machinery, he would be able to achieve his targets. But the administrative apparatus inherited by independent India was hardly suited for the tasks of social reconstruction and economic development. It is surprising that Nehru who had been so critical of the bureaucracy in the pre-independence period, should have accepted it as an instrument for the establishment of a socialist society. The Nehru of post-independence India not only protected the rights and interests of the ICS but also relied on them for achieving his social objectives. For the modernisation of the country, economic growth had to be accelerated, the backwardness of centuries had to be removed in decades. How could this be achieved by the slow-moving, procedure-bound bureaucracy? Further, modernisation did not mean only industrialisation but also transformation in the way of living of the people.

Could the bureaucracy, with its snobbishness and exclusiveness, reach the masses and influence their way of living and thinking? A new system of economic production creates new relationships in society and changes the way of living of the people. But the new system of economic production—the use of machines and technology—has to be accepted by the people who were using antiquated methods of agricultural production. Who was to create this awareness among the masses? Did the bureaucracy have the social attitude necessary to perform the gigantic task of creating a social revolution simultaneously with the economic revolution? Were our civil servants so public-spirited? An absolutely different kind of bureaucracy was required to fulfill the tasks which Nehru wanted to perform. Career seekers and mercenaries were hardly fit for the new tasks.

Basic Mistake

It may be argued that Nehru should have deployed Congress Party workers for creating a social awakening among the masses. But the faction-ridden Congressmen interested in capturing power for personal gain were neither competent nor to be trusted for this job. This job has been done in other countries by political parties organised on strong well-knit ideological foundations. Russia was a backward country. It had to be industrialised and modernised, and the pace of modernisation had to be accelerated. Devoted and dedicated cadres of the Communist Party were given the task of conveying to the people the new message of educating them in socialism. Nehru admired Russia and its economic development. But one of the important things which could have been learnt by him from the Russian experience was that without a cadre of political workers devoted to socialist ideology, the masses could not be awakened. Nehru failed to create 'soldiers of socialism'. It must be stated that he did his best to spread the ideology of socialism in India. It is also a fact that the establishment of democratic institutions and periodic general elections created awakening in the masses. These were no mean achievements. But talking to and trying to educate an unorganised and amorphous mass of people has limited utility. It should have been supplemented by creating a band of political activists who would have taken Nehru's message to the far-flung areas of the country. They would have obtained strength from Nehru and would have sustained Nehruism much better than the Congress Party or the bureaucracy.

Lack of Austerity

Much of the failure of Nehru's plans has been attributed to his reliance on the Congress Party and the bureaucracy. It may be worthwhile to examine some of his personal feelings also.

Much should not be made of his petty bourgeois background but one effect of this background was obvious, i.e., Nehru did not set any standard of austerity or simplicity or Swadeshi before the people. The Gandhian tradition of 'simple living', instead of being strengthened, was abandoned. If a backward economy was to be transformed and a new social order was to be created, austere living was essential. When Nehru talked of 'sacrifices' for a better future, the common man did not respond. In India, the common man looks to the top leadership for setting social standards. When Nehru failed to set any social standard, people started copying the way of living of the richer classes. Nehru's India saw the erosion of social and moral values. His own living did not show that he was the leader of a poor country. Congressmen and capitalists were adding to their wealth. The common man had hot been given any values by the leader.

Poor Organiser

Nehru was not a great organiser. He gave excellent ideas, but could not give proper institutional and organisational expression to those ideas. Although he was the most important leader of the party, he did not do anything to reorganise it for socialistic objectives. Except under the Kamaraj Plan, there was no weeding of undesirables. What kind of structural changes were required to make the Congress an effective instrument of modernisation and socialism? Nehru did not concern himself with these questions of party organisation. In the field of administration under Nehru's Prime Ministership, no radical reorganisation was affected. India inherited a system of administration suitable for a law-and-order state. After independence, the administration had to perform social welfare functions. A different kind of administrative set-up was needed to achieve socialistic objectives. But Nehru never gave enough thought to the reforms needed in the administrative structure.

The Nehru era will be known as that of 'revolution from the top'. The reverberations were not felt by the common people. Parties, leaders, movements all remained in the background as long as Nehru was alive. True, this was not his fault. But the fact that the Opposition parties and leaders could not play their role during the Nehru period, resulted in a sense of complacency in the people. Many felt that Nehru would do the job; those who were not satisfied with Nehru's achievements, became frustrated and cynical. India got both, the best and the worst of the 'revolution from the top'.

Power Structure

The successful functioning of parliamentary democracy in India will depend, among many other things, on how far and how quickly a new social order based on industrialisation, economic planning and socialism is created. If India could achieve socialism and destroy the foundations of the acquisitive society through democratic means, and without violent class conflict, Nehru will go down in history as a path-finder. He would have been more successful if he had paid attention to required reforms in the traditional system of parliamentary democracy, and thought about devices for adapting and adjusting the form of democracy to the new tasks which it will have to perform in India. If parliamentary democracy becomes the defender of the status quo and the vested interests, it will be challenged by the exploited but emerging and conscious new working class. If parliamentary democracy becomes the vehicle of a new social order and an instrument for the devesting of vested interests, the latter may try to subvert it, resulting in clashes and conflicts. Nehru's belief that parliamentary democracy is suitable for Indian requirements, remains open to question.

Stability and Peace

This critical analysis should lead us to the pinponting of his singular contributions. Nehru's greatest contribution is the importance that he attached to science and technology. He was convinced that India cannot make progress without industrialisation. This was why in the Five-Year Plans he gave great importance to the development of basic and key industries. He was convinced that planning would take the country to self-generating growth by the end of the Fifth Plan. For this political stability was essential. His very important contribution was the provision of political stability. Once the economy becomes self-generating, he thought, India would be able to face any storm.

For economic development of the country, peace was very essential. His clear understanding of international forces convinced him that India could progress only if she kept away from 'Cold War' and 'bloc' politics. Any involvement in bloc politics would endanger India's economic development. The policy of non-alignment, peace, and emphasis on negotiations for the settlement of international disputes were the essential conditions for socialism in India. Nehru strove hard to achieve this. He was emphatic that a strong industrial base was essential even for the defence of the country. The Chinese aggression of 1962 was a shattering blow to his dreams because the demands of defence would hamper the pace of economic development. The Chinese aggression in fact provided an excellent opportunity to the militarists and communalists in India to attack Nehru's policies of peace, non-alignment, co-existence and socialism. Nehru had a world perspective, and had a clear understanding of the relationship between the problems of the country in the context of world happenings and events. He brought before his countrymen the implications of the Nuclear Age.

Nehru was a fighter against the main currents of socio-cultural life in the country. He never concealed his opposition to moth-eaten traditions and superstitions. He believed that industrialisation and economic development were prerequisites for the successful operation of secularism. He emphasised the importance of the 'scientific outlook' and, thus, was truly a Renaissance leader. He had a coherent picture of the tasks facing the country. Secularism, democracy, economic planning, modernisation and socialism were all an integrated approach to the problems of a communal, backward and agricultural society. If we are to live in the modem world as an independent country, with the power to take decisions independently, a modern way of life and modern techniques of economic development have to be employed. This was Nehru's vision of modern India: where science and not superstition, reason and not blind faith, humanism and not religious bigotry will reign supreme. This is the unfinished task left by Nehru to us. This is his message.

Nehru and Nation-Building

During the struggle for freedom, Nehru was spreading the message of his value-beliefs among the masses of India. After Independence he got an opportunity to translate his social and political ideas into practice with the help of state power. It is worthwhile to examine how far Nehru succeeded in achieving his goals and objectives.

Before attempting an evaluation of Nehru, it is appropriate to describe in brief the tasks that Nehru had set for himself. In pre-independence days, Nehru had repeatedly said that he was a republican and a socialist. In his presidential address at the Lahore Session of the Congress (December, 1929), he stated:

> "The philosophy of socialism has gradually permeated the entire structure of the society the world over. And almost the only point in dispute is the pace and methods of advance to its full realisation. India will have to go that way too, if she seeks to end her poverty and inequality, though she may evolve her own methods and may adopt the ideal to the genius of her race."

Thus, socialism, equality, freedom for the individual, and democracy were the cherished goals of Nehru. Further, he stood for secularism, a scientific attitude towards life and industrialisation of the country. He was clear in his mind that only industrialisation would liberate the Indian masses from the shackles of mediaevalism and poverty born out of colonial domination. Thus, quintessence of Nehruism can be stated as:

> "It is based upon a secular rather than a sacred view of human relations, a rational outlook, an acceptance of the substance and spirit of the scientific approach, a vigorous application of an expanding technology, an industrialised organisation of production, and a generally humanistic and popularistic set of values for political life."

The institutional arrangement created by Nehru to achieve these values, was a Constitution, an elected Parliament, a Planning Commission, and an expanding Public Sector. Democratic Parliament and economic Planning (with its system of institutional arrangement) were the main pillars of Nehru's efforts at nation-building.

The question that arises is: Did this value structure and institutional arrangement become an accepted philosophy of a large number of people in the country? Is this legacy of Nehru safe in the post-Nehru India? The answer to these questions will determine the success or failure of Nehru in nation-building.

Nehru's values and institutional arrangements for the management of national affairs evoked different responses from different segments of the Indian elite. His philosophy of economic planning was attacked by the Rightists as encouraging statism, leading to a progressive diminution of individual freedom and private initiative. According to them, planning stifled the spirit of individual enterprise. On the other hand, the Leftists appreciated the role of 'public enterprise' but criticised the Public Sector undertakings for being bureaucratically managed institutions, which in actual working went against the spirit of socialism. Further, economic planning in the country helped the rich and the disparities between the classes in the country went on increasing during the period of Nehru's economic planning. Economic Planning in India helped the growth of monopolies and the concentration of wealth in a few hands. Economic Planning instead of establishing a socialist society strengthened capitalism in India. Thus, Nehru was criticised by both, the Left and the Right though for different reasons.

His another pillar of nation-building was political democracy in the form of periodic elections, adult franchise, etc. Nehru believed that in building modern India, people's active support and popular participation were essential. Not only this, through the medium of these elections and adult franchise, Nehru wanted to create consciousness among the people also regarding their role in the processes of nation-building. Again among the elite, there is a difference of opinion regarding the effectiveness of democracy as established by Nehru in India. The response of the elite to the functioning of democracy is mainly of three kinds.

First, opposition has come from a section of the elite who believe that Nehru imposed Western ideas and institutions on a society whose soil is quite unsuitable for the functioning of such institutions. It is argued that Western type of party democracy does not suit the genius of India. Hence, we should have a communitarian type of democracy, with the place of pride given to the village panchayats. These critics of Nehru betray romantic clinging to the past, to an imaginary golden age which they would like to come back. It was suggested that the issue is the management of diversity and unity, more specially the need to relate the parochial and the universal, to fuse basic components of the indigenous culture with the standards and practices to the modern world. Nehru was criticised for ignoring the past, on whose basis only the present and the future could be built.

Second, opposition has come from the capitalists who say that democracy has created great social conflicts in the country and that sectional demands have assumed greater importance than the desire to add to the size of the national cake by producing more wealth. Democracy is being viewed as the anti-thesis to the economic development of the country. It is argued that the worst casualty of Indian democracy has been economic production.

The third and the last attack on Nehru has come from the socialists who allege that democracy in India is a tool in the hands of the capitalists. The entrenched classes are using it for their own benefit.

If both the Rightists and the Leftists are unhappy with Nehru, then the question arises: where exactly did Nehru fail? His failure lay at three different levels:

(a) He could not create any 'symbols' around which the masses of India could rally. He described the Bhakhra Dam and the Bhillai Steel Plant as 'New Temples' but they did not replace the old symbols which were ingrained in the minds of the Indians during the past thousands of years. He wanted to change the attitudes and ways of thinking of the masses, but he could not establish concrete alternatives to the images cherished by the people. Thus, modernisation, scientific temper, secularism—all remained paper slogans.

(b) His values did not percolate down to the masses. What to say of the masses, even his partymen and cabinet colleagues remained unconvinced about the validity of many of Nehru's ideas. The almost unceremonious farewell to the policy of 'Independence and non-alignment', given by the successors of Nehru illustrates this point. Thus, compeers and compatriots shed no tears on the demise of India's foreign policy.

(c) Nehru did not build any political movement or party for the preservation or perpetuation of his values. The Congress Party, as it is constituted, could hardly act as the defender of Nehru's ideology. Nehru was a keen student of world history. He knew it very well that ideas can shake the world if they become part of a movement. He admired Lenin, but did not learn anything from him. He acknowledged it in the *Discovery of India* that: "A study of Marx and Lenin produced a powerful effect on my mind and helped me to see history and current affairs in a new light." But Marx had also said that the time had come to change history. This could only be achieved by a strong political movement committed to the ideology of change.

Nehru's strategy of nation-building was defective. In the absence of a cadre of committed party workers, and a network of media of communication, the message of ideology cannot spread. Those leaders who live from hand to mouth, who simply concern themselves with the problems of today, and who have no vision of tomorrow, can afford to ignore the importance of party workers. But Nehru was different. With all his faults, he had a clear vision of the future of India. He laid the foundations of modernisation and industrialisation. Perhaps it would be difficult to reverse this process. But there is a chance element in it. Democracy may be subverted if the entrenched classes fear the challenge of the emerging classes. Socialism and economic planning have already been devalued in the country. Nehru made no attempt to create soldiers of socialism and defenders of democracy. Here, lies the greatest failure of Nehru.

On the ideological plane also, Nehru's attempt to follow a middle path between Western liberalism and Marxian socialism created a situation where his ideology is not a part of the inheritance of any party or movement. His attempt to adapt socialism to the Indian genius ended in a confused kind of pragmatism.

This ideological confusion in Nehru becomes clear, when in his *The Basic Approach* a stand is taken that the distinction between Capitalism and Socialism is wearing thinner and thinner. He writes: "Socialism is basically a different approach from that of Capitalism, though I think it is true that the wide gap between them tends to lessen because many of the ideas of Socialism are gradually incorporated even in the Capitalist structure."

It is not surprising that even in the Left Movement in the country, Nehru's impact is insignificant, though his contribution to the making of modern India is generally admired and appreciated by the Left.

Parliamentary Democracy: Nehru's Perspective

The basic goal of India's struggle for freedom was to establish democracy in the country, and the Indian masses were mobilised against British imperialism by the national leadership for achieving the goals of free and democratic India. After the transfer of power on August 15, 1947, it fell on the shoulders of Nehru and his other colleagues of the national movement to nurture and nourish the experiment of democracy in India. After independence of the country from foreign rule, many negative and hostile forces were at work against the experiment of democracy in India, and the Indian leadership had to fight against communal and feudal elements in the country to safeguard democracy. Nehru was very conscious of anti-democracy forces in the country, and he struggled against them by making the masses conscious of the enemies of democracy.

Nehru's strategy to fight against the opponents of democracy had many essential components. First, Nehru recognised the role of leadership in struggle against feudalism and communalism, the twin threats to democracy, and he used his political and administrative power in his fight against enemies of democracy. While Nehru recognised the potentialities of leadership role in generating positive ideas in the country, he was fully aware of its limitations and inadequacies. To supplement his efforts of building democracy, he vigorously worked for mass mobilisation through adult franchise.

Nehru's second strategy of strengthening Indian democracy was directed towards the masses. Apathetic and inactive people cannot safeguard democracy. Masses should be made politically very conscious to confront challenges and threats to democracy. Three general elections of 1952, 1957 and 1962 were utilised by him to educate the people in the merits of democracy.

Third, Nehru was aware of that a lip service would be paid to democracy, if its institutions were not strong enough to check the ruler's arbitrariness. Democracy can be a formal thing if its institutions are incapable to exercise effective control, with proper checks and balances, on people in the government. History knows many instances of democratically legitimised authoritarianism, and no one was more aware of this fact than Nehru himself. Hence, he made every effort to strengthen Indian Parliament. Nehru wanted Parliament to become the focus of national power. Hence, he attached great significance to Parliamentary debate and discussions. It is only democratically elected Parliament which can ventilate people's grievances and evolve appropriate programmes for people's uplift. If Parliament is strong, it can hold the cabinet accountable and project people's demands effectively

But Parliament cannot be strong, if party system is weak and if one leader is supreme in the nation. Parliament would be weak and ineffective in the face of an extremely powerful leader who would use it as a rubber stamp. Nehru strengthened the institutions of Parliamentary democracy in India by focusing attention on the central role of Parliament in the governance of the country.

Fourth, Nehru recognised the need of collective and coalitional leadership in the Congress Party to safeguard Parliamentary democracy against very powerful and authoritarian leader. Nehru had many conflicts with his comrades and party colleagues, and he involved himself in democratic struggles against his opponents in the party. This is a very important strategy to strengthen democracy in a country, where serious challenges and threats to democracy exist. Nehru believed that if a leader cannot tolerate opposition and criticism of his own party, he would not tolerate and accept the criticism of opposition parties. Authoritarianism starts by purges within the party and then cleaning process is extended to all the parties. A leader who cannot stand criticism of party colleagues and political opponents, cannot also manage parliamentary democracy. Nehru was competent to manage parliamentary democracy because he showed tolerance towards the opposition, and involved himself in debate and discussion with his critics.

Nehru's strategies of safeguarding Parliamentary democracy in India were based on a firm belief that as a tender plant, it has to be consciously nurtured, and its institutions have to be strengthened, and challenges have to be faced by extending democracy and debate, and not by circumventing democratic debates in the country. Nehru recognised that Parliament is safe only in a country where free press exists because Parliamentary debate should be reported and commented upon. Parliament can perform its vital role of governance of the country, if the masses know the inside story of Parliament. A free press is an essential component of Parliamentary democracy, and Nehru attached a great significance to it.

Nehru believed that Parliamentary democracy was a vehicle of gradual and peaceful social transition in India and through Parliament, challenges of poverty and social inequality would be met. Parliament would represent the collective will of the nation, and its power would be used to eradicate poverty and establish social justice in India.

In Nehru's perspective, Parliamentary democracy was essential for bringing social transformation in India. Nehru never said that he failed because opposition was creating problems or Parliament was more powerful than the Prime Minister. Nehru would have felt amused, if he was told that Parliamentary democracy was obstructing the programmes of gradual social transformation. On the contrary, Nehru's firm belief in Parliamentary democracy was based on the fact that gradual social change in India is possible on the basis of national consensus, and parliamentary debates help in arriving at national consensus.

Nehru and Adult Franchise

A few historians of modern India maintain that parliamentary democracy is a gift of the British to our country. Nothing can be farther from truth than this kind of interpretation of our history in the modern period. A fundamental pillar of democracy is universal adult franchise, because it is an institutional mechanism for the people's participation in the governance of a country. Universal adult franchise in India was resisted by the British rulers, and the national movement in India had struggled to achieve it. Thus, democracy is not a gift of the British but it is the result of India's struggle in which millions of people participated and made sacrifices.

A relevant question is: What is the significance of adult franchise for nation-building in India? A related question is: What was Nehru's contribution to the functioning of adult franchise, with which democracy is intimately related, during the first decades of Independence?

The post-Independence phase was a formative period for strengthening the institutional arrangement for democratic governance and the functioning of adult franchise in India. Nehru played an active role in the first three general elections of India, held in 1952, 1957 and 1962. All these three elections were significant for strengthening the base of Indian democracy.

A few aspects of the actual functioning of adult franchise in India during the Nehru phase may be highlighted to understand its proper significance in a critical manner.

The most significant implication of the introduction of adult franchise in India was felt in remote lakhs of villages in the country. The masses of rural India were politically apathetic, and the colonial rule and their local collaborators, i.e. the feudal landlords had left the rural masses under their political control. Adult franchise demanded that political parties would mobilise voters to elect their representatives. Such a large-scale mobilisation of the rural voters during the elections helped in raising their political consciousness. While it is a fact that caste, community and linguistic loyalties influenced voters in their voting decision, and many a times 'vote banks' operated under the guidance of traditionally established rural leadership, the other aspect of electoral mobilisation and campaigning is that the voters ask questions and evaluate governmental performance. The introduction of adult franchise raised the level of awareness of people about their political environment, and farms, factories and families-became centres of political debate.

Nehru's contribution in raising the level of political consciousness of the Indian masses was pre-eminent during his marathon election campaigning of 1952, 1957 and 1962. He acted as a great teacher, and educated the people in the meaning of democracy. His very well-attended election meetings were an occasion for the masses to pay their respect and regard for their beloved leader, and also slowly and gradually imbibe the message of the leader who asked them to shed their apathy and participate in governance.

Further, adult franchise helped in making politics a competitive activity. To begin with, competition among various political parties was marginal, and Nehru and the Congress party dominated the national political scene. But political competition increased with every new election. Voters were subjected to competitive political education. The process of political competition also helped in increasing the level of political consciousness among the voters of India. Intensification of political competition alters the quality of political debate in the country. When a voter is presented with different viewpoints, he develops a sense of discrimination. It is a slow process, but all fundamental transformations in any society take their own time.

Adult franchise and the growing involvement of masses in the political process of India created a new situation in which the old socio-economic order started showing strains and stresses. It was a logical development, and Nehru had recognised this. Voters cannot be satisfied with an empty right of vote. With growing political consciousness, they demand new rights, and government has to respond to them. Nehru's election speeches always emphasised the new tasks of government, and he linked adult franchise with economic and social transformation of the country. Mobilisation of voters, slowly and gradually, created a new situation in the country, where demands on government increased and the status quo was threatened.

While the elections are constituency-centred, the results of elections are relevant beyond the boundaries of a constituency. The dynamics of adult franchise helped in the creation of national image of government among the voters, and Nehru in his election campaigns emphasised on national goals, national priorities and national tasks. India has to be welded into a nation so that its diversities find their fulfillment in national unity. National integration of India is a continuing task, and those who are responsible for nation-building should consciously do it. Nehru was conscious of this great task of nation-building, and in this he recognised the significance of creating a sense of national identity among the Indians who were plagued with many primordial loyalties. Adult franchise is a mechanism which links local loyalties with regional and national centres of power. Localism has to be transcended, and new loyalty structures have to be created. Such a creation of new loyalties cannot be commanded. It has to be a slow process in historically old societies. Adult franchise generated a new awareness in India about the significance of Parliament, Cabinet, Prime Minister, etc. Nehru's great attachment to Parliament was not a formality. He was really devoted to Parliament because of his faith in adult franchise.

How has the adult franchise operated in the post-Nehru phase? Has adult franchise taken deeproots in the country? What has been the record of the system established by Nehru?

In the post-Nehru phase, two serious challenges emerged on the scene by groups and individuals who were anti-adult franchise. The first opponent of the adult franchise was infantile Left in India which debunked elections as a bourgeois luxury. Elections were boycotted, and violence was adopted to achieve political goals. Infantile Left, which glorified violence did not succeed in this country because its theory and practice was wrong. The people of India have opted for adult franchise, and they are its defenders. Hence, the Naxalite movement could not become a part of Indian mainstream. It is bound to be a fringe movement in Indian politics because its understanding of Indian history and political culture is faulty. Adult franchise and Parliament gets its support, strength and sustenance from the masses, and it is not just a superimposed superstructure.

The second attack on adult franchise and Parliament was launched by adventurists in polities who did not want to hold the elections. Political adventurists also did not understand the political evolution of India. Hence, on the first opportunity in February-March 1977, the people of India reaffirmed and reasserted their faith in adult franchise, and proved that Nehru's efforts along with many others were not a waste. Political analysts are still debating the reasons for the holding of elections in March 1977. Whatever may be the reasons for such a decision, the result was astounding, and democracy was restored in this country.

What is the moral of the experience of adult franchise during the last 33 years? The moral is very clear and it may be summed up as follows:

(a) The people of India would not accept infringement of adult franchise and Parliament.

(b) Adult franchise has awakened the masses who are now struggling against the 'status quo'. Both these struggles are interconnected.

(c) The most important institutional safeguard for democracy in India is adult franchise. The leaders of India's national movement had recognised this; and those leaders, who wanted to tinker with it, were taught a lesson. The people of India defeated its Prime Minister because they identified her as an opponent of Parliament and adult franchise. The lessons of 1977 elections should be clear to all political leaders and groups. In a way, "Nehru's success was experienced only after his death, i.e. in March 1977.

2

Indira Gandhi: The Consolidational Phase

Nehru was under attack from 1962 to 1964 because his powerful opponents, within the Congress party, had viciously targeted him on his China policy especially when China launched a border war in 1962. A section of Indian and foreign commentators also began a speculation on After Nehru: Who? Because Nehru's legacy was considered as weak and his successors were not considered to be worthy of defending the challenges faced by democratic India. The speculation of After Nehru: Who? was laid to rest when Lal Bahadur Shastri, a Minister in the Nehru cabinet, was elected as successor, on June 9, 1964 and he continued as Prime Minister till his death on January 11, 1966. Gulzari Lal Nanda became a stopgap Prime Minister from May 27 to June 9, 1966, the Congress party elected Shastri as the leader of the government in place of Nehru. Nehru had also been accused of establishing a 'dynastic rule' in India and this propaganda got its legitimacy, when Indira Gandhi became the President of the Congress party during Nehru's lifetime. This propaganda died down only when Shastri succeeded Nehru and Indira Gandhi was nowhere in the reckoning for the office of the Prime Ministership of India. Lai Bahadur Shastri's untimely death re-opened the issue of finding a successor and the Congress party elected Indira Gandhi as its leader, in preference to Morarji Desai who believed himself to be a successor of Shastri. Indira Gandhi occupied the office of Prime Minister from January 24, 1966 to March 24, 1977 and after a break of about two and a half years, she came back to power from January 14, 1980 to October 31, 1984. Indira Gandhi's years-in-power as Prime Minister were not only historic but also most controversial and her term of office ended with her assassination on October 31, 1984. Unlike Nehru, Indira Gandhi's years of power brought glory as well as infamy to India and this is the reason that all evaluations of Indira are based either on admiration or hatred for her. Indira showed immense personal courage while leading the country and also while facing great personal difficulties during her years of power. A catalogue of her achievements, as prepared by commentators on her years of power, deserves to be stated here. Indira was elected by the Congress party with a view that she could lead the party during the Lok Sabha and State Assembly elections of 1967. The election results proved disastrous for the Congress party and it was for the first time, in post-Independence India, that one party dominance of the Congress party had been challenged by conglomerate of parties. The Congress organisational leadership lost their faith in Indira's capacity to win an election and factional conflicts between Indira and a powerful section of party organisational leadership became public and this factionalism within the Congress got intensified on the nomination of party's candidate for the office of President of India. Zakir Hussein's untimely death in 1969 created a situation for group and factional leaders to promote the candidature of their factional loyalists for the Office of the President of India. The factional leaders like S. Nijalingappa, the Congress party President, K. Kamaraj *et al.* succeeded in nominating their loyalist N. Sanjeeva Reddy as a party candidate for the Presidency of India. Indira Gandhi reacted by sponsoring V.V. Giri, as her own nominee and in a highly contested election V.V. Giri defeated N. Sanjeeva Reddy and the Congress 'split' in 1969 between Congress (Indira) and Congress (Organisation). Indira Gandhi as a Prime Minister took steps like Nationalisation of Banks, abolition of Privy Purses of the erstwhile princely rulers and these actions were opposed by her critics within the Congress. The Congress 'split' of 1969 reduced Indira Gandhi's support in the Lok Sabha and she gradually started moving towards the direction of a fresh Lok Sabha elections. Indira contested the Lok Sabha elections of 1971 on the slogan of *'Garibi Hatao'* (Eradicate Poverty) and she secured two-third majority in the Lok Sabha. The Lok Sabha elections of 1971 made Indira politically secure and extremely assertive. Another occasion, which made Indira an undisputed leader, was provided by the Bangladesh war of 1971 because she could stand against American imperialism. Indira also showed statesmanship at the Shimla Conference and refused to humiliate the defeated Pakistani army in Bangladesh. The famous Shimla Agreement, between Indira and Zulfiqar Ali Bhutto of Pakistan, brought peace to both the countries. Indira's nationalist assertion also showed her militarist aggressive attitude which was revealed in 1974, when India exploded nuclear bomb at Pokharan. Social discontent in India was increasing during 1973 and 1974, and instead of tackling the causes of growing social discontent, she ruthlessly suppressed the Railway Employees strike of 1974. This restlessness gave birth to anti-Indira movement led by Jayaprakash Narayan and during 1974-75, people were mobilised against Indira and her discomfiture increased, when Justice Sinha of Allahabad High Court declared her own election to the Lok Sabha as 'illegal'. The events moved very fast and Indira decided to impose the Emergency on June 25-26, 1975 and the country was put under an authoritarian regime. The Emergency Rule ended in March 1977, when Indira Gandhi was decisively defeated in the Lok Sabha elections and a Janata Party government was formed with Morarji Desai as the Prime Minister. The Janata Party ruled from 1977 to 1979 and in this brief period, the party was 'split' by Charan Singh who became the Prime Minister for six months. Indira 'split' the Congress party again in 1978. The Lok Sabha elections were held at the end of 1979 and Indira Gandhi came back to power as Prime

Minister in 1980 and her second term in office began on January 14, 1980 and came to a tragic end by her assassination on October 31, 1984.

How does one evaluate Indira Gandhi's acts of omission and commission as Prime Minister for fourteen years, beginning from 1966 to 1977 and from 1980 to 1984? Indira's imposition of the Emergency Rule in 1975 had completely alienated middle class intellectuals, who accused her of destroying democracy in India. The Sikh community was completely alienated, when she decided to launch military action against the Golden Temple on June 6, 1984. The Blue Star Operation hurt the Sikh community who held her responsible for inflicting the great humiliation on the community by violating the sanctity of the Golden Temple at Amristar. The Assam Movement, which was launched by all Assam Student Union for the 'detection, deletion and deportation' of 'outsiders' who had illegally occupied Assam also brought brickbats, and Indira was at her tenterhooks while dealing with the Assam Movement in 1979-80. The Communist parties which had supported Indira for her actions in 1969 to 1971, also turned against her during the Emergency and they also opposed her decision to ask for a mega loan of more than 5 billion US dollars from the International Monetary Fund. Indira Gandhi continued to pursue the foreign policy of Non-alignment and India and the Soviet Union concluded a Treaty of Friendship and Co-operation with one another. Indira's positive initiatives on foreign policy paled into insignificance because of her image of a ruthless and authoritarian leader who suppressed movements like the JP Movement, the AASU movement and her democratic credentials were always doubted by her critics and political opponents. Indira left a 'mixed legacy' of achievements and Himalayan blunders and she was a suspect 'democrat'. Every biography which has been written about Indira, conveys the message about her complex personality. Her many contradictory political legacies have been mentioned by her biographers.

Phase of Congress Party

A political party in a democratic system has to adapt and adjust itself with new demands and pressures of the socio-economic system of the country. It is characteristic of a transitional society that old forces and established institutions are replaced and displaced by new forces and institutions and political parties have to grapple with the challenge posed by the old forces and the emerging conflict between the old and the new.

Further, conflict between the old and the new social forces is not a straight affair, it follows a zigzag process of continuity and change, conflict and compromise and counter-revolution and revolution. The basic point is that the Congress Party of India has to grapple with complex social context, and to survive as a party, it has to intervene and mediate either as an instrument of change or status quo or both i.e. change as well as status quo.

The Congress Party leadership has an advantage of learning from India's phase of national movement in which the Congress provided a platform for all segments of society who wanted to involve themselves in struggle against imperialism. The Congress platform was managed by the leadership of the pre-independence era on the basis of reconciliation of contending and conflicting interests, and everything was subordinated to the basic goal of winning freedom for the country.

After winning freedom, the Congress leadership followed the same strategy of reconciliation and consensus in maintaining their supremacy over the public life of India. But the role of Congress in the post-independence phase was essentially different from its role during struggle against imperialism. The Congress Party had to earn its legitimacy by participating in the electoral process which was based on adult universal franchise and political competition with other political forces and groups. The Congress Party evolved an electoral strategy on the basis of open membership and mobilisation of all strata of society irrespective of regions, religions, castes or classes. The basic electoral strategy of the Congress was based on a coalition of diverse groups, and in this way it became an all inclusive party and differentiated itself from exclusivist parties, which were based on any dominant caste or religion or region.

As a party which tried to accommodate many diverse social groups, it played down ideological issues and tried to project itself as a party of ideological pragmatism. The party raised the slogans of achieving socialism in the country, but it was never serious about it because the ideology of socialism would have brought serious splits and divisions in the party. The Congress Party was always interested in extending its social base and not in narrowing down to any single or dominant social interest or group or ideology.

It is not without reason that all important splits in the Congress since 1969 were the result of power struggle in the leadership and no split had any commitment for any fundamental change in public and social policies of the Congress. The Congress splits were around personalities and its result was the clear emergence of personality cult in the party. The Congress Party splits of 1969, or 1977 were on the basis of serious struggle for control over the party, and this has resulted in the establishment of the concept of pre-eminent leader in the Congress. Thus, the Congress has shown continuity of maintaining its broad social base, and a change has occurred within the party by engineering splits to establish personal pre-eminence of the leader. Those Congressmen who left the party in the struggle of 1969 or 1977 were motivated by the same considerations, as those who remained in control of the party.

A basic shift has occurred within the Congress Party from the pre-independence phase and also from the pre-Indira Gandhi's phase of party leadership. Since the Congress Party was a coalition of classes, castes, regions, languages and ideologies, it naturally gave birth to factions and factional leaders or bosses within the party, and all decisions within the party were based on factional considerations and factional pressures. The Congress system of reconciliation was based on the basis of compromise among the factional leaders. This system of factional accommodation continued till the death of Lal Bahadur Shastri. Indira Gandhi emerged on the Congress scene as a compromise among factional leaders, but this did not continue for long and factional leaders came to a headlong collision in 1969 and many heads rolled in the struggle for power within the party.

It must be mentioned here that pre-eminent leadership of Indira Gandhi has not been able to eliminate factional fights within her party. The way Congress Party is constituted, factionalism is inherent in it. The coalition of broad social groups cannot be without factions. Hence, factionalism shows continuity of Congress political dynamics, but the change is the unassailable position of Indira Gandhi as a leader of the party. In the long history of the Congress Party, leadership always belonged to a group of individuals, only exception to the rule is Indira Gandhi.

To sum up, the internal shifts within the Congress reveal continuity and change. The explanation for such a continuity and change is provided by the essential feature of the party i.e. its broad based social character and its basic coalitional strategy. If some groups or individual leaders leave the party, many others walk into it. The Congress closes its doors and also keeps it open. If the rich peasants in some of the north Indian States walked out of the Congress under the leadership of Charan Singh, many other leaders of rich peasantry walked into the party.

The Congress has supplied many leaders and workers to other political parties like the Lok Dal or the Janata, it has also attracted many leaders and workers from the ranks of other political parties. The Congress is both, an open as well as closed party. The openness of the Congress Party is a continuity of its historical tradition, its closeness is related with the emergence of Indira Gandhi as an undisputed leader.

The winning of elections compels political parties to manage their internal affairs in a manner that the voter accepts their credentials. Many things are done by a party with a view to win elections, but the life story of a party cannot be fully understood by concentrating on its internal dynamics and election winning compulsions. A political party is much more than a strategy for electoral purposes. The shifts in the Congress should be analysed by examining its main public policies followed by it as a ruling party in the country. Politics in a country operates at many levels and the reality of a party can be understood by differentiating the levels of politics.

During the last 35 years, the Congress Party has shown a lot of continuity and change in its basic public policies which it has followed as a ruling party of the country. The basic policy framework of the Congress is to build capitalism in the country with active initiative and intervention of the Government. All Five-Year Plans, industrial policy resolutions, agaraian reforms and policy on science and technology are geared around the building of state capitalism in India. In this basic goal of building capitalism in India, two phases of the Congress can be differentiated i.e. the formative phase of the

Nehru era and the consolidation of the capitalist ideology in Indira Gandhi's approach.

In the formative phase of the Nehru era, the capitalist class was important but not strong enough to build capitalism without the support of the state. The Indian state under Nehru's leadership laid down the regulatory framework for the development of the state capitalist sector and the private corporate sector. The Indian private corporate sector could not develop without the Indian state which was the main instrument of development of infrastructure in the field of transport, communication, power and heavy industries which required a lot of capital investment. The private corporate sector did not possess the resources in the 50s and the 60s for the building of huge steel plants or machine tool factories. The Indian state intervened to create an infrastructure for capitalist development, and assisted and regulated the private corporate sector to develop in fields reserved for them.

The Life Insurance business was nationalized by the Nehru government in 1956 because resources for development were needed by the state and their regulated disbursement was made to the private corporate sector. The capitalist development of India was obstructed by obsolete agrarian structure, the Congress Party abolished the absentee landlordism for the modernisation of Indian agriculture. A modernised agrarian sector was essential for the development of industrial capitalism in the country.

Thus, during the Nehru phase, under the compulsions of distorted colonial legacy, a complex network of capitalist state was laid down by the Congress which was basically acceptable to the basic coalition of classes represented by the Congress Party. The abolition of absentee landlordism appealed to the peasant proprietors who extended full support to the Congress and the capitalist class was satisfied because transformation of agrarian structure broadened the Indian market. While the economic planners during the Nehru phase gave slogans of socialism and justice for the poor, the foundations of capitalist state were laid down by Nehru with the agreement of the leading social classes of India. Nehru's phase had an advantage over Indira Gandhi's phase because the contradictions and crisis of capitalist development did not create social protests or great social unrest. Nehru's journey was smooth, and ideological clothing and slogans satisfied the critical middle class intelligentsia and social unrest did not pose any serious challenge to Nehru's policies as the leader of the Congress Party.

Indira Gandhi had learnt from her father that capitalist development in India has to be mystified with socialist slogans to manage left-of-centre policies and this she repeated to her astounding success in the 1969-71 phase of her struggle for leadership within the party. But slowly and gradually the crisis of capitalist development changed the levels of social consciousness of the masses and the rural proletariat and the urban working classes were asserting their demands. The package of policies evolved during 1971-77 could not satisfy the masses because some aspects of Nehru's reformist phase and policies had outlived their utility. The Congress and Indira Gandhi went out of the power in the 1977-79 period, and when she came back to power, she abandoned even the pretension of socialism. The Indira Gandhi government during 1980-83 have been wedded openly to capitalist development with the support of international finance capital. This was a big break between the Nehru and Indira Gandhi's phases of capitalist development. Indira Gandhi's government have opened the Indian market to foreign investors, multinational corporations and a full encouragement is being given to the Indian capitalist class to go in for foreign tie-ups. The external element in Indian capitalist development during the Nehru phase was limited, the Indira phase clearly laid down the foundations of openness to foreign capital. She looked towards the international investors was instruments of capitalist development of India. The Indian capitalist class is hunting for foreign collaboration for captive power plants, hotel industry, car manufacturing and many other consumer industries like the production of shaving blades and electric type-writers.

This gradual integration of Indian capitalism with the world capitalist system needs an explanation. Within the Congress of the post-1977 split, many people have entered the party who are not the product of the Congress history and who are themselves involved in business and trading activities directly. The late Sanjay Gandhi had attracted a group of entrepreneurial class and many of them won the elections. Many of them are committed to capitalist development and they are using their political clout for this purpose. Further, Indira Gandhi recognised that the present crisis cannot be resolved without external help.

The big business in the country also convinced that the fraternity of international capitalist class is the only saviour of the struggling capitalism of India. Thus, leading actors in politics, bureaucracy and economy agreed on the opening of India to the foreigners, and if foreign investors are not coming in the big way to our country, it is not because of our unwillingness.

Conclusion: The Congress Party has been examined from two perspectives, i.e. its internal dynamics and its public policies as a ruling party. The internal dynamics reveals its transformations for party management, but its public policies reveal its class character. The class character of a party can be clearly understood by examining the totality of its public policies, and by demystifying the party reality.

The Congress Party is a coalition of the leading classes of India with a commitment to the building of capitalism in the country, and continuity and change in the Congress can be perceived by understanding its links with the leading classes. The linkage between the leading classes and their political representatives is quite complex and this complexity in the case of the Congress Party has been examined in terms of continuity and change.

The basic class position of the Congress is to build capitalism in India and it evolves many strategies to achieve this basic goal. A distinction should always be maintained between shift of strategies and fixity of goals and any confusion in this, would create a situation where the left forces hailed the nationalization of private banks in 1969 as a great progressive step of Indira Gandhi.

A capitalist state needs controls over resources and nationalization was just a strategy to mobilize resources and help the private capitalists to invest in development. The nationalization of banks in 1969 was not aimed at any structural change in property relations in India and Indira Gandhi is not credited with any structural change in agrarian relations in the country. Unfortunately, the Left played into the hands of Indira Gandhi who was performing a normal function of leader of capitalist state. This is the story of the Congress during its different phases of development.

Protest Movements

The social and cultural environment in India is marked by serious cleavages among different sections of the people and by discontent and even strife. Such an environment frequently leads to grave situations, in which the people affected feel the need to protest against acts of omission and commission by the public authorities. It is, therefore, in the fitness of things that India should adopt political system, in which organised protest and dissent are recognised as legitimate methods of opposing and exposing governmental policies.

An analysis of the protest movements in India is made here with reference to two inter-related questions. First, what kind of issues have provoked protests in the country? Second, what has been the response of the policy makers to the various organised public protests? The touchstone of a truly democratic polity is the quality of the response protest movements evoke.

Total Attack

Broadly speaking India has witnessed intra-system and anti-system protest movements, both, at the micro and at the macro levels. The continental size of the federal polity, the uneven political development of the various regions of the country, the diverse historical experiences and exposures of the people, and the intermixture of the various cultural streams in society are bound to create situations, where a social group launches a total attack on all the major assumptions underlying the political system and struggles for a total replacement of the existing system by an alternative system; or where a specific public policy leads to the organisation of a movement to demand remedial measures. And the strength of a polity lies in its capacity to tackle and make a proper response to both the intra-system and anti-system movements.

India has witnessed many intra-system protest movements directed against specific public policies. The most important examples of such movements are the movement for the reorganisation of States and the movement to oppose the imposition of Hindi as an official language. In 1956, mass movements were organised by the Samyukta Maharashtra Samiti and the Maha Gujarat Janata Parishad for the bifurcation of the then Bombay State into Maharashtra and Gujarat. Similarly, Sant Fateh Singh organised a mass movement under the leadership of the Akali Dal for the creation of a Punjabi Suba consisting of areas, where the Punjabi language was the main spoken language. In 1965, students and political leaders in Tamil Nadu protested vigorously against the imposition of Hindi. All these movements achieved their respective 'one point' goals before they died away.

The most important characteristic of these movements is that they politicised the issues, participated in electoral politics, maintained channels of communication with the political decision-makers, and evolved strategies of protest in conformity with the stated assumptions of the political system. The objectives were achieved by pressure tactics, mass mobilisation, and dialogue with the policy-makers. Although there were a few cases of self-immolation, police-firing, and rioting, the protests were basically organised on the basis of non-violence and with full faith in the capacity of parliamentary processes to redress grievances.

The political system responded to these movements by a strategy of 'assimilation, accommodation, and adjustment'. The policy-makers set the highest store by consensus formation in responding to these movements. Such emotionally explosive issues as the demand for a reorganisation of States and official language of the country were tackled with the objective of strengthening national consensus. Indeed, that was the style of the democratic politics of the period. The movements had limited goals and were short-lived; and their leaders got integrated in the political process after the movements withering away.

Naxalite Stir

The most significant anti-system movement to emerge so far has been the Naxalite movement. The Naxalites challenged all the basic assumptions of the political system, denounced its normative beliefs, and repudiated the procedures of Indian politics. They had an entirely different political blueprint for the country. Their strategy was to 'annihilate all the class enemies' through violence and bloodshed. By adopting this strategy, they dramatised the discontent obtaining among the landless labourers and the tribals, and exposed the blatant exploitative character of the rural agrarian structure. For capturing political power, the Naxalites wanted to encircle the 'Centre' by capturing the 'periphery' through violent struggles against the police and the landlords in the rural areas. They thought that their strategy would lead to demoralisation in those wielding the coercive apparatus of State power and that the ruling class would collapse in due course.

The glorification of the cult of violence brought them into direct confrontation with State power; and during 1967-70 many innocent and dedicated persons died or otherwise suffered heavily on account of the adventurist policies of the Naxalites and their faulty assessment of the correlation of social forces in the country. The Indian political system did not collapse like a pack of cards, as the Naxalites had envisaged.

This tragic experience raises important issues for consideration. It is undoubtedly the duty of the State to curb and crush the violent activities of a group of people who want to jeopardise the democratic experiment of social transformation adopted by India. This, however, does not mean that the political leadership can ignore such social issues as are raised by an anti-system movement. A democratic polity can survive only on the basis of positive responses to the social issues raised by the anti-system movements. Did the leaders of the Government of India make • a positive policy response to the problems of the landless labourers and the tribal poor? There is no evidence that any basic structural changes were made in the agrarian set-up in the country. The tyranny of the landlord is still a fact of India's rural life. The discontent on which the Naxalites built their movement continues. This means that India's political leaders have not learnt any positive lesson from the Naxalite movement. An anti-system movement throws a basic challenge, and if the policy-makers ignore it, the challenge re-appears in a different form and threatens the system. It must be stated here that the strengthening of the Youth Congress, the creation of Chhatra Parishads, and the rigging of elections were by no means a response to the social issues raised by the Naxalite movement.

Seeds of Violence

An anti-system movement different from the Naxalite kind is in progress in the north-eastern region, i.e., in Nagaland, Mizoram, etc. Politically, the people have always been outside the mainstream of all-India nationalist politics; and culturally, in the margin of the 'great traditions' of Hinduism. The movement here is, therefore, secessionist and separatist and aims at resisting or annulling integration with the rest of India. The response of the political system is to adopt 'politico-administrative' measures like the creation of new States and to enable the Union Home Ministry and the Governor of the area to provide apt leadership to face the problems thrown up by the process of integration of the 'periphery' with the 'Centre'. Further, extremist organisations like the Mizo National Front and the Underground Federal Government of Nagaland are being isolated and effectively contained. The approach is of a political character and is marked by caution and sympathy. While the general mass of educated public opinion in India is ignorant about the sensitivities of those who are culturally not quite within the pale, the political elite has shown enough finesse in integrating the north-eastern region with the rest of the nation. It is true that the basic economic problems of this region have not been resolved to the satisfaction of the people of the area, but it is a matter of satisfaction that no indecent haste or chauvinism has been shown to achieve the goals of integration.

Unlike the above-mentioned categories of movements, the aim of the movement led by Jayaprakash Narayan (JP) is to restructure the existing political system in accordance with its stated objectives. According to JP, the moral foundations of the existing political system have collapsed because of the growth of corruption in public life, erosion of the legitimacy of the electoral process, expenditure of huge sums of money in the elections, and the irresponsiveness of public representatives after they get elected. With moral anguish in his heart, JP wants to restore the values of integrity, legitimacy of the electoral process, and responsiveness of the people's representatives. These political objectives, coupled with other social and cultural goals, could be achieved by organising and mobilising the people and making them conscious of the basic ills of the polity. The Gujarat movement for the dissolution of the State Assembly and the prevailing discontent in society prompted JP to demand 'correctives'.

The question here is: How has JP conducted his protest movement? And, also, what has been the response of the political leadership in power to the political issues raised by him?

Basic Changes

More than a year has passed since JP started his movement, and yet he has not been able to create his own viable organisation to achieve the goals of his protest movement. Any protest movement which calls upon those who wield power to make basic changes in the polity, must have an effective organisation behind it. Further, if a leader is not on the scene, how can a struggle continue without an organisation committed to the goals? The kind of individuals and political parties who have joined the JP bandwagon, cannot be the trustees of this movement.

When JP fired his first shot against the electoral practices obtaining in India, it was sufficient to unnerve the beneficiaries of the corrupt electoral process. But the ruling political party has since succeeded in involving JP in electoral politics without conceding any basic demand of JP's regarding electoral reforms. JP would be involved in electoral politics on the terms and conditions laid down by the ruling political party. Money would play as decisive a role in the forthcoming elections as in the previous ones. It is indeed surprising that JP should have accepted the challenge of the ruling political party to participate in the elections, when these elections are to be fought in the same old corrupt manner as in the previous five general elections. If the vote is vitiated by the role of big money, it is all the more reason not to participate in the corrupt practice. Would it not be logical for JP to give a national call for the boycott of such elections? Would it not serve the cause better to campaign against the corruption rampant in politics by organising a mass boycott of elections? It seems to us that Mahatma Gandhi would have organised such a boycott. He would have non-cooperated with the evil and exposed it. JP has made a fundamental compromise with his position by agreeing to participate in the elections. The JP movement would at best end up as electoral confrontation between the ruling political party and a so-called Janata Front of a few opposition parties. Is it not an anti-climax?

As far as the response of the ruling political party to the JP movement is concerned, it has been one of fighting it politically. Some insiders of the ruling political party want a dialogue with JP, but the strategy of the leaders is to have a confrontation with JP on the political plane. These leaders know how weak JP's organisation is, and they intend to exploit it fully. The political strategy adopted by Mrs Indira Gandhi seems to be paying her dividends by involving JP in electoral battles, and by embarrassing him about his political company made up of a motley crowd of politicians from diverse political parties, all with a past. Mrs Indira Gandhi has placed JP in the trap of elections without conceding anything to him and no one can predict how and in what direction JP would move from there.

New Leadership

Here, it is pertinent to ask: What has been the impact of these protest movements on the body-politic of India, and what are the directions of future development? The most significant impact of these protest movements has been mobilisation and politicisation of sections of community which were insulated from, or indifferent to the political processes. Protest movements have articulated public grievances and compelled the public policy-makers to respond to them. In a democratic system, alternation of leadership and recruitment of new leaders are essential to make the system operate without serious breakdowns. Protest movements have acted as forums for the recruitment and training of new leadership, especially at the middle level of the polity. Many student leaders, who spearheaded the movement for the dissolution of the Gujarat State Assembly, are now contesting the elections. And this is no mean achievement on the part of the protest movements.

As far as response of the ruling political party to the protest movements demanding basic structural changes in the polity is concerned, the response has been negative. The main reason for the failure of the political leadership to respond positively to the basic issues raised by the protest movements is that they do not have clear 'policy perspectives' for socio-economic transformation of the society. Protest movements demand improvement in the living conditions of the landless and the tribals. But the present government has no package of policies to respond to this demand. Further, if a protest movement demands eradication of corruption, the ruling party's vested interest in corruption comes in the way of initiating any remedial measures against corruption.

This lack of response to the issues raised by protest movements may lead to serious anti-system movements. If proper remedial measures are not initiated by the leadership, the country may witness the emergence of protest movements committed to violent ways. The soil is now very fertile for such movements. And the present style of politics, which is conspicuously lacking in well-defined goals and well-formulated plans for action is bound to create a social situation which may throw up violent movements. Recently, we have seen students involving themselves in all sorts of movements, from JP's *sangharsh* to the Naxalite movement. Frustration of the youth can be exploited by any kind of anarchic movement. Bold policies are needed for a basic socio-economic transformation of society that would safeguard the functioning of democratic institutions in India.

Challenges to Indira Gandhi

On January 19, 1966 the Congress Parliamentary Party elected Mrs Indira Gandhi to be the third Prime Minister of India. A profile of a person who has completed nine years in the highest office during some very difficult years for the country, needs to be prepared to assess her achievements and failures, as well as her prospects.

The task which Mrs Gandhi assigned to herself was to build the nation on the foundations laid by Jawaharlal Nehru. Thus, the expectation was that she would provide continuity and bring about the changes in the overall perspective of her social and political inheritance. She was expected to provide content and flesh to the goals of democracy, socialism, and secularism. To that end, she was expected to evolve new strategies of development and provide policy perspectives which would strengthen national unity, cement serious social cleavages, and channelise national energies for the strengthening of democratic institutions. Her programmatic platform of *garibi hatao* meant that political activity would be directed towards achieving goals, that the political system would be geared to performance, and that political power would be used to 'push' this country towards 'further' development.

Vital Questions

The questions that arise are: What concrete policies have been adopted by the Prime Minister to achieve the goals that she set for herself? Has she made any institutional and structural changes to make the political system performance-oriented? And has her style of politics been in consonance with her goals? If there seems to be a serious gap between the two, what is the explanation for it?

The first important challenge to her policies came from protest movements of the organised working class and the articulate political opinion for the dissolution of the State legislative assemblies, which were reflective of the serious political corruption obtaining in the country. India had never before witnessed such organised and persistent protest movements in the post-Independence era. The manner, in which a leader responds to a protest movement in a democracy, reveals how real his capacity is to face situations and draw correct meaning from such protests. Such crises situations in the history of a nation compel the leadership to think seriously about their performance. But this depends on how the leadership views the protest movements.

Mrs Gandhi has always read negative meanings in the protest movements; and, in the process, she has not come out with any policy or programmatic alternative to ensure that these protest situations are not repeated. She dismissed the railwaymen's strike as an attempt of the organised working class to hold the society to ransom. The implicit meaning of this approach was that governmental policies and failures were not responsible for sky-rocketing inflation; that the railwaymen were being adventurists; and that they needed to be disciplined. And the question asked was: What about the poor living in the Indian villages? Were not the urban working class better off than the landless peasantry?

The response to the protest movements launched against political corruption also went on the same lines. These movements, said Mrs Gandhi, are being sustained by the urban middle class; the rural poor are not with the movement. She, therefore, decided to discipline the urban middle class by a huge expenditure on the law-and-order machinery for the defence of democracy in Bihar. The assumption behind this attitude was that the rural people and the poor were not involved in these protests and that these protests were, therefore, to be dealt with as a law-and-order problem. Instead of responding to the issues raised by those protest movements, the Prime Minister was more concerned about the individuals who were raising such issues. The protest movements were dismissed as urban 'delinquency' and it was felt that no reformulation of governmental policies was needed.

Black Money

Another concrete issue which confronted Gandhi was the erosion of the autonomy of the political system owing to the involvement of money in the elections. For the first time, the legitimacy of the political process was seriously questioned—What was Mrs Gandhi's response to that?

To answer this question, it is necessary to recount, albeit briefly, the events and processes of the last 27 years. The founding fathers of the democratic political system knew very well that an interaction exists between the political process and the socio-economic structures of society. In this interaction, if conscious steps are not taken, the political system will become subservient to the powerful pressure groups. Periodical elections on the basis of adult franchise, conscious attempts at politicisation of the apolitical sections of this vast society, and legal safeguards against the penetration of 'money power' were some of the steps taken to safeguard the autonomy of the political system. It was further expected that on the basis of experience, the political leadership would innovate and create further safeguards to insulate the political system from the illegitimate pressures of other existing social structures. It is a continuing responsibility of the political leadership in a democratic polity to diffuse the various pressures and 'mediate' in social issues with reasonable impartiality and neutrality.

Party Bosses

When the Congress split of 1969 occurred, and Mrs Gandhi became the leader of the New Congress, the widespread impression in India and elsewhere was that she was releasing the party from the pressures of the party bosses. These bosses had been functioning as the fund-raising instruments of the Congress Party, and by virtue of their ability to raise funds, they had managed to acquire undue importance in the decision-making institutions of the party and the Government. The 'Congress split' signified that Mrs Gandhi would go to the root of the problem and initiate structural changes to restore legitimacy to the political institutions that had been vitiated by the role of money in elections.

Mrs Gandhi has also confronted another factor in the States. In spite of the fact that the Congress Party got a large chunk of rural votes, the State legislatures were cornered by the rich peasant. And power in the Indian States is used by the rich peasant to get concessions and financial subsidies from the Government. This political reality—namely that the State Congress parties were pocket boroughs of the rich rural gentry meant that if the *garibi hatao* programme had to be implemented, there should be structural changes in the rural sector.

Powerless with Power

If Mrs Gandhi wanted to give a new direction to development in India, the political role of money and the rich peasant had to be attacked. Unfortunately, she did nothing in this direction.

She allowed the 'dual social structure' to persist. Land reforms were essential to liberate the State governments from the pressures of the rich peasant and harness the energy of the huge masses of rural people in nation building activities. The Union Home Ministry pointed out in 1969 that the situation in the rural areas was quite explosive. It found that it is 'agitations for distribution of land to the landless which have elicited the maximum response and have also had a wide geographical spread.' Since land is unevenly distributed and since more than eight million households (in 1960-61 of the NSS data) are landless agricultural labour, this results in serious social and political tensions.

Basic Step

Mrs Gandhi, with her massive mandate of 1971 and with her new electoral strategy, could have taken the basic step of social change in rural India by implementing the land reforms to which the Congress Party is committed. Implementation of land reforms would have brought in rich political dividends. The State governments are immobilised by rich peasants who derive all the benefits of the new technology and the subsidies; and in return, refuse to pay anything to the State exchequer for social welfare activities. Rural credit institutions like land development banks were cornered by the rich peasant. A recent study (1974) conducted by the National Council of Applied Economic Research points out that the small farmers are the least important category of loanees in Gujarat, Haryana, Madhya Pradesh, Maharashtra and Rajasthan from the land development bank. The existing hold of the rich peasant, strengthened by the traditional loyalties of caste and kinship which is at present the basis of rural electoral politics—would collapse, if meaningful land reforms were instituted.

Mrs Gandhi did not bring about any structural changes in the rural sector to liberate politics as an activity from the stranglehold of the rich peasant. Her New Congress adopted the old electoral strategy of winning over the suppport of the 'influential' people in the rural areas, who operated 'vote banks' in the return for State favours.

As far as money for elections was concerned, no safeguards were evolved and political competition was reduced to a competition in resources.

The challenges to Mrs Gandhi have failed to evoke any responsse; not a single policy initiative has been taken from the top to remedy the situation. The Prime Minister is drawing wrong conclusions from the protest movements. She has not positively responded to the issues raised by such movements in the past few years. She is following the old electoral strategies whose social and political costs are very heavy for the political system.

Is she suffering from any constraints? Nehru used to complain that the Congress party was not a fit instrument for achieving his goals. He, too, cared for his old loyalties and did not disturb the party structure. As a leader laying the foundation of the political system, he attached great importance to 'consensus' in the party. Mrs Gandhi cannot make such complaints after the mandate of 1971. She had difficulties in the party between 1966 and 1969. In 1969, the initial problems created by the in-fighting over the issue of her leadership were over. Her authority in the party today is unchallenged and unquestioned. The manner in which she shifts her senior Cabinet colleagues and inducts individuals in the corridors of power show her pre-eminent position both, in the party and in the Government.

No Constraints

Now she cannot complain of any party bosses obstructing her from doing the right thing. She is the boss, she has now only those contraints, which in a parliamentary system any prime minister would be subjected to. There is no other political or governmental hindrance to initiatives, if she wants to take. In the international sphere, India never had such a favourable situation, as obtains today. She has definitely made a contribution in tilting the superpower balance in favour of India; and 'bilateralism' in foreign affairs is paying rich dividends to her.

In such a situation, how one is to explain the immobilism of the Prime Minister?

Further, no Prime Minister of India has been, so well-equipped with secretarial staff assistance as the present one. The Prime Minister's Secretariat has the country's experts at its beck and call. In spite of her anti-urban middle class attitude, the country's intellectuals are at her disposal. She is not short of the services of the talented.

Dead End

If the constellation of forces, domestic as well as external, is in her favour why is she at a dead end with regard to policies for nation-building? The present situation is paradoxical in that it is a situation illustrating the powerlessness of the powerful. Mrs Gandhi does not hesitate to remove well-entrenched Chief Ministers and to replace them by her own trusted colleagues; but she fears to put her full weight behind land reforms and to de-link State politics from the rich peasant. In the party, she does not fear to change individuals; but she hesitates to abandon the well-known path of winning elections on the basis of money and the support of the rich peasant and the caste and community support of the scheduled castes and Muslims. She knows that the panchayati raj institutions and the rural credit co-operative societies have been cornered by the rural rich; but she fears to disturb them because she is not sure about its political implications for the electoral battles of the Congress party.

Nehru became prime minister after an active role in politics in the struggles and protests of the people, for about three decades. He led the people in their struggles. And in this process, he developed an understanding of the masses. Mrs Gandhi's life history is different. She became aware of the complex processes of India's politics only in the sixties. She is unsure about herself, and she perhaps thinks that basic social changes can prove politically very costly to her.

Gunnar Myrdal's description aptly sums up Mrs Gandhi's responses to the Indian situation. Myrdal said: 'In India, an intellectual and moral conversion tends to be advanced as a panacea for all kinds of ill. But to change attitudes without changing social institutions is a rather hopeless quest. This remains the basic dilemma and challenge of Indian politics.

Dilemma of Indian Polity

Powerlessness of the Powerful

A section of middle class intelligentsia under the influence of Gandhism and romantic egalitarianism, regional and communal political parties like the Akali Dal, the DMK and the AIADMK, and 'ruralists' like Charan Singh have been demanding a fundamental restructuring of the existing balance of power between the Centre and state governments with a view to decentralising governmental power in the country.

This motley group of 'anti-centralists' argues that diverse and specific problems of Indian society cannot be properly tackled by a powerful central government. It advocates creation of multiple centres of decision-making, which requires transfer of more financial resources and economic powers to state governments.

This plea goes against the experience of other federal political systems in industrialised countries. All of them have become highly centralised. In all old federal countries like the U.S., Canada and Australia, a gradual transfer of powers has taken place from autonomous provinces or states to central governments in response to pressures and demands generated by industrialisation and the growing interaction between the states.

The logic of centralisation of power has been different in the case of the communist countries. They have resorted to centralised planning to overcome economic backwardness. But the result has been the same in both, capitalist and communist countries.

Colonial rule cannot become an integrative factor in a society. Thus, it was only in 1920s, 1930s and 1940s that the Indian people moved towards nationhood, as they identified themselves with Mahatma Gandhi and Pandit Jawaharlal Nehru. India began to emerge as a nation as result of mass mobilisation by national leadership against colonial rule. Even today, India has not fully become a nation-state. It s a nation-state in the making. Many cleavages remain to be eradicated which can be done only if we create a national culture.

Further, India has to develop a modern productive system with emphasis on the national market. India, plagued with conflicts of internal sovereignties, cannot establish a modern economy. This does not mean that diversities have to be ignored. But the problem of under-development in certain regimes can be tackled only in a proper national framework. This calls for a strong modern state with the necessary strength to mediate in situations of domestic conflict. A legitimate central authority which implements positive programmes of nation-building can alone promote national integration.

Some people argue that the pre-eminent position accorded to the Central government in the Indian federal system has not proved beneficial to the development of India. Even after thirty years of centralised economic planning, the Central government has not been able to make any dent in the condition of backward regions of the country. The sixth five-year plan document (1980-85) admits that even in 1971, around 27.5 per cent of the employment in manufacturing was concentrated in nine towns in the country. It also admits that the 'new seed-fertiliser technology has probably accentuated regional imbalances which are reflected in the large differences between states in the percentage of population below the national poverty line.

The advocates of decentralisation contend that development of backward regions is possible only on the basis of a reallocation of powers between the Centre and the State governments. In their support, they cite the fact that resource-rich states like Madhya Pradesh and Bihar have remained very poor.

Be as it may, the legitimacy of Central government in a federal polity gets eroded, if it employs extra-constitutional methods to contain healthy political competition. A democratic federal polity has to work on the basis of the consensus that the rules of the game would be followed and the mandate of the people would be respected by allowing different political parties to run Central and State governments.

While in the U.S.A. and Canada, the federal and state governments run by different political parties get along smoothly, in India, serious difficulties have been experienced in this regard. Thus, the CPM has been in serious conflict with Mrs Gandhi's government at the Centre.

Confrontation

The CPM maintains that Mrs Gandhi does not believe in fair political competition, and instead of following this path, she, according to it, follows the path of political confrontation and might not hesitate to dismiss a duly elected state government. That is presumably, why the CPM demands transfer of powers from the Centre to States.

Another argument of the party is that the present tilt in favour of the Central government discourages healthy political competition, and that the future of Indian federal system is tied up with the future of democracy. Therefore, in its view, democracy and the federal system can be defended only if the Central government ceases to enjoy extra-ordinary power under the Constitution.

Thus, those who want to correct regional imbalances, view the present division of powers between the Centre and the states as an important bottleneck. The communist parties, want to be assured that they would be allowed to run state governments, if they are elected.

While these issues have been debated for the last three decades, a qualitatively new situation has emerged, which demands serious analysis and responses.

The collapse of the Congress party and the absence of a viable national party system have thrown the whole democratic process out of gear. It should be a matter of grave concern that the Prime Minister has to visit state capitals to review the performance of state governments and pull up chief ministers. It is a sign of the weakness of the political system that state governments are not capable of managing their affairs.

But it is also simplistic to suggest that Mrs Gandhi is managing a highly centralised political system in India. In the absence of a viable political party and multiple levels of leadership, she is managing a highly fragmented and weak political system with the help of bureaucrats.

The evidence of weaknesses of the system is overwhelming. Mrs Gandhi's government has proved ineffective in controlling rich peasants and black marketeers. Her reliance on the bureaucracy in the absence of an organised political party is also a sign of weakness, not of strength.

Blameworthy

Many leaders have contributed to the breakdown of the party system and the weakening of democratic institutions. For example, Jayaprakash Narayan broke the rules of the game, when he spearheaded the movement for the dissolution of the state assembly in Bihar. Morarji Desai did the same, when he undertook a fast unto death in 1975 to seek early elections in Gujarat. Mrs Gandhi violated the national consensus, when she proclaimed the emergency. The dissolution of state assemblies in April/ May 1977 by the Janata and then by Mrs Gandhi in April/May 1980 fall in the same category.

The serious weakness of Indian democratic process was dramatised in Assam, when students did not allow elections to the Lok Sabha. Thus, the circle was complete, and from total revolution to emergency and to the successful boycott of elections in Assam revealed the serious decline of democracy in the country.

The crisis of Indian federalism is quite deep, The effectiveness of the modern state depends on a strong party system. Erosion of parties must help divisive tendencies. An effective bureaucracy can create a national market. But the politics of integration has to precede economic and social transformation of the Indian society.

Mrs Gandhi represents the phenomenon of the 'powerlessness of the powerful'. She is the undisputed leader of the country, but her policies and programmes do not work even in the states ruled by her own party. She centralises political authority but that cannot amount to much, when state governments are unstable and chief ministers do not have any political weight of their own. The Indian federal system was strong under Nehru because it was supported by chief ministers like Dr B.C. Roy, G.B. Pant and K. Kamaraj. Indian federalism has developed big cracks, because Mrs Gandhi has to depend on weak chief ministers. The modern state in India should centralise authority with proper support from grass-roots leadership. The most important source of strength for a federal system is a sound party system. The collapse of the Indian party system has weakened both, the Central and the state governments.

Prolonged Phase of Coalitions: 1977

Politics is a conscious and purposeful activity to develop society, and the leadership performs a crucial and critical role in defining the direction of national development. In the present state of transitional politics, a pre-eminent leader like Jawaharlal Nehru is not available. Nehru had laid down the foundations of Indian democracy by gently nourishing and nurturing an imported model of governance. It would have been a healthy development for the political system, if Nehru had been replaced by 'coalitional leadership'. But this did not happen. Mrs Indira Gandhi struggled hard to become pre-eminent leader, and in this process she sacrificed collective decision-making and democratic debate among senior cabinet ministers.

During her eleven years of power, the emphasis was on personal supremacy. After Mrs Gandhi's defeat it was expected that the new leaders of the Janata Party would recognise the role of collective thinking and decision-making in national affairs. The three stalwarts of the Janata Party had many common points. All the three, i.e. Morarji Desai, Jagjivan Ram and Charan

Singh were the products of 'Congress Culture', and were broadly committed to the national goals of secularism, democracy and social justice. All the three had participated in the national struggle for freedom, and consciously opted for a common platform to fight for the restoration of democracy in India. Moreover, all these three leaders and their followers had regard for Jaya Prakash Narayan's advice, who had occupied the position of an elder statesman in the affairs of the Janata Party. What has led to the failure of the emergence of coalitional political leadership in the country?

The Janata Party experiment failed because its major constituent elements were involved in creating one political party on the pattern of the Congress Party of India which the Janata had replaced after the general elections of 1977. This was a wrong attempt to make. The collapse of the Congress Party in the elections of 1977 meant the end of 'one party dominance system' in India. The Janata Party leaders did not recognise the significance of this fact. The failure of the Congress Party to provide governments at the Centre and the States would lead to coalitional political arrangements. The Janata Party leadership did not accept the logic of coalitional form of government.

The result is that after two years of struggle to maintain unity in the Janata Party, the three stalwarts have parted company.

In one way, the new developments of June 1979 are healthy. An attempt should now be made to forge an honest coalition to manage public affairs. India has entered the stage of political transition from 'one party dominance system' to the era of coalitional governments. In this transitional stage, India would witness political instability and phenomenon of minority governments. Other countries also went through the same process of political transition. When the Labour Party was challenging the Liberal Party in England; coalitions and minority governments were installed many a times, in the first decades of the twentieth century. In Canada, Social Democrats are slowly emerging to challenge the well-established two political parties i.e. the Liberals and the Progressive Conservatives. Canada has experienced minority governments and coalition cabinets. Italy, West Germany and France are the classical examples of political instability caused by coalitional governments. It must be stated here that India has entered a new stage of politics after witnessing three decades of stability.

A few features of this new stage should be highlighted. They are:

(1) Politics of coalitions would succeed, if partners in the government do not compete to establish hegemonic position in relation to one another. Since India has to live with 'coalition governments' for a long time, it must be clearly understood that the success of a coalition depends on an honest acceptance of strength of numbers by the various constituents in the coalition.

(2) Coalition governments would succeed only when leaders of constituents accept a position of equality. The Prime Minister would have to be the first among equals in a coalition, and

decision-making would have to be collective.

(3) Coalition governments would succeed, if minimum programmes are accepted by the members. The Janata Party failed because there was no agreement on minimum programmes. It is only consensus around goals of nation-building which would provide unity in fragmented coalition governments. Politics based on issues is the only substitute for personality-oriented politics. The Janata experiment collapsed because of maladjusted leadership and diversity of social outlooks on national issues like secularism. Political mobilisation in India depends on issues and not on personalities.

Politics, in India, has entered a new phase of coalitions and collective leadership. For some time, the country would pass through political instability and quick succession of cabinets. The nation would have to adjust to this new political milieu. In this phase, two contradictory trends might be noticed. First, governments would be called to resolve serious social conflicts which are developing in the country. In India, people expect effective intervention by the government to deal with conflict situations. Governments would be under great contradictory pulls and pressures. Second, while people's demands on government would be increasing, the capacity of the coalition governments to meet contradictory demands, would be limited. Since coalitions would be formed around minimum programmes, they would not be able to deliver maximum goods. Recognition of this fact is essential to appreciate political developments in the country.

To sum up, alarmists in India and abroad are busy in writing obituaries of Indian democracy and they are longing for the revival of authoritarianism in the country. Fear of political instability is being created even by well-meaning public leaders. Liberal democracy in India has entered the phase of extended transition because of the collapse of the one party system. Survival of the country depends on the capacity of coalitions to work on the basis of goal-oriented politics around minimum programmes. If this takes place, other problems can be tackled.

Politics gets meanings only around social issues. The Indians had first-hand experience of this kind of politics under Nehru. The sharpening of social issues is essential to expose misdeeds of politicians. One cannot ignore the capacity of political manipulators to use political issues for self-aggrandisement. But the only path to clean politics is through ideologies and values. Political activists in India should direct their attention to the restoration of goals of secularism, social justice and democracy. Only this would ensure a bright future for the country.

3

Congress: Rajiv Gandhi

The story of Indian politics beginning from October 31, 1984 to 2004-06 can be narrated by focusing attention on the ups and downs faced by the Congress during these twenty years. The rationale behind this approach is that the Congress, except for a brief period of 1977 to 1979, had dictated the agenda of Indian politics by occupying a dominant position in post-Independence India. Today, the Congress is a pale shadow of its former self and Rajiv Gandhi was the last Prime Minister of the party with a majority support in Lok Sabha who completed his term beginning from October 31, 1984 to December 2,1989. It has been suggested that Rajiv Gandhi won the Lok Sabha elections of 1984 only because of 'sympathy wave' which was created by the assassination of Indira Gandhi. Hence, it was an 'abnormal' election and every other Lok Sabha election of 1989, 1991, 1996,1998 and 2004 were normal elections and the voters of India did not give any clear verdict in favour of any party or group during the elections. The Congress could not get a clear majority in the Lok Sabha election of 1991 in spite of the fact that an attempt was made by the party to win over the sympathy of voters because of the assassination of Rajiv Gandhi in 1991. Further, the Congress party vacated its pre-eminent space which it had occupied from 1947 to 1989, its replacements were also not able to win over a clear majority in the Lok Sabha elections. The 'decline' of the Congress party led to the phenomenon of the formation of 'coalition governments' at the Centre beginning with V.P. Singh in 1989 to Manmohan Singh in 2004. V.P. Singh was the Prime Minister from December 9, 1989 to November 10, 1990, Chandrashekhar from November 10, 1990 to June 21, 1991, H.D. Deve Gowda from June 1,1996 to April 21, 1997, Inder Kumar Gujral from April 21, 1997 to March 19, 1998 and Atal Bihari Vajpayee from March 19, 1998 to May 22, 2004. The only exception was P.V. Narasimha Rao who could manipulate to remain in office from June 21,1991 to May 16,1996. India entered a new phase of coalitional politics at the centre and consequently, coalition governments have been either unstable or stable and it is very difficult to make any generalisation about the longevity of coalition governments in India. Why is it that the story of twenty years of Indian politics from 1989 to 2004-2006 is built around the

Congress? The Congress has been an important pl ayer even when it has been in power or in opposition from 1989 to 2004-2006. The V.P. Singh government followed by Chandrashekhar or H.D. Deve Gowda or Inder Kumar Gujral could form their short-lived coalition governments at the centre with the 'outside' support of the Congress, which was the major opposition party, when not in power. The Congress party played the role of 'opposition' and did not extend any support to the BJP-led government of Atal Bihari Vajpayee from 1998-2004. Congress has remained a critical factor in Indian politics from 1989-2006 and this was the reason that politics of these years revolved around the Congress. V.P. Singh or Chandrashekhar or H.D. Deve Gowda or Inder Kumar Gujral were stopgap and purely temporary Prime Ministers and the only notable achievement of V.P. Singh, for which he is remembered, is the announcement in August 1990 of the forgotten report of Mandal Commission for reservations of the backward castes. V.P. Singh felt politically threatened from his own supporters and he played a trick and announced the implementation of Mandal Commission but in spite of this, he could not save his position as Prime Minister of India. V.P. Singh survived in office from December 9, 1989 to November 10, 1990 on the basis of a full-fledged support of the BJP, when the Sangh Parivar withdrew its support to V.P. Singh. L.K. Advani was the only beneficiary of political tricks played by V.P. Singh on Mandal Commission, and he launched the most infamous Yatra from Somnath to Ayodhya for the construction of Ram Temple by destroying the Babri Mosque.

The decade of the 1990s can be described as the phase of Divide and Rule in Indian politics. V.P. Singh laid the foundations of caste driven politics and the BJP succeeded in dividing Hindus and Muslims, and elections were won or lost on the basis of targeting of caste versus caste and religion versus religion. A full-fledged caste-based and religion-based politics emerged in the 1990s and the socially cohesive agenda of the Congress party completely failed to checkmate the casteist and communalist politics which dominated the political scene of India. The post Nehru-Indira and Rajiv-Congress became just one of the player among multiple contenders of caste-based and religion-based competitions in electoral politics. Not only this, even with P.V. Narasimha Rao's projection of "liberalisation, privatisation, globalisation and structural adjustment" could not become an alternative package for the voters in village India. It has been suggested that during 1991 Lok Sabha elections the Congress, could emerge as the single largest party with 232 seats only because of 'sympathy factor' as a fallant of Rajiv Gandhi's assassination.

The Table 3.1 is helpful in understanding the growing erosion of the strength of the Congress and emergence of the party of Hindutva.

Table 3.1: Vote Share and Seats: Congress and BJP (1952-2004)

Sl. No.	*Year of Election*	*Total Seats*	*INC*		*BJS/BJP*	
			Seats	*% of Vote*	*Seats*	*% of Vote*
1.	1952	489	364	45.0	3	3.1
2.	1957	494	371	47.8	4	5.9
3.	1962	494	361	44.7	14	6.4
4.	1967	520	283	40.8	35	9.4
5.	1971	518	352	43.7	22	7.4
6.	1977	542	154	34.5	—	—
7.	1980	542	353	42.7	—	—
8.	1984	542	415	48.1	2	7.4
9.	1989	543	197	39.5	86	11.5
10.	1991	543	232	36.5	120	20.1
11.	1996	543	140	28.8	161	20.3
12.	1998	543	141	25.8	182	25.6
13.	1999	543	111	28.3	182	23.8
14.	2004	543	145	26.69	138	22.16

The Table 3.2 clearly shows that the dominance of Congress over national politics came to an end and the vacuum created by the decline of Congress has been filled by the BJP and other regional parties.

Table 3.2: Electoral Performance of Pan-Indian, Hindu Revivalist and Other Ethnic Parties: Share of Valid Vote (percentage wise) Election Year-wise

Party	*1952*	*1957*	*1962*	*1967*	*1971*	*1977*	*1980*	*1984*	*1989*	*1991*	*1996*
Congress	45.0	47.8	44.7	40.8	43.7	34.5	42.7	48.1	39.5	36.4	28.5
Others All	22.1	23.0	29.7	28.2	32.0	—	—	26.3	30.8	26.5	25.9
Pan-Indian Parties	67.1	70.7	74.5	69.0	75.7	—	—	74.4	70.3	62.9	54.4
Hindu Revivalist Parties	5.9	7.2	7.7	9.4	7.4	—	—	7.5	11.6	21.0	21.4
Other Ethnic	5.6	4.2	6.6	7.8	7.0	8.1	6.5	10.0	12.9	12.6	13.5
Ethnic Parties	11.5	11.3	14.3	17.1.	14.4	—	—	17.5	24.5	33.6	34.9

Notes:

(1) The Congress denotes the Indian National Congress for 1952-69, Congress in 1971 and 1977, and Congress (I) thereafter.

(2) The main Hindu revivalist party, the Bharatiya Jan Sangh, merged with some Congress offshoots to form the Janata party in 1977 and remained part of it until after the 1980 elections. The Bharatiya Jan Sangh poll as many votes as all other ethnic parties combined from 1957 to 1971, the Janata Party won in 1977 and was the second strongest party in 1980. So, it is difficult to distinguish the share of the Pan-Indian parties from that of the Hindu revivalists for 1977 and 1980.

Table 3.3: National, State and Registered Parties Since 1989 (Cumulative seats and vote percentage)

Year of Election	*No. of National Parties*	*No. of State Parties*	*Registered Parties*	*Total*
9th Lok Sabha 1989	6 (471) (78.13)	8 (27) (6.24)	10 (19) (4.16)	24
10th Lok Sabha 1991	7 (470) (80.67)	13 (52) (9.93)	(4) (0.73)	24
11th Lok Sabha 1996	7 (403) (68.98)	19 (127) (18.97)	4 (4) (0.73)	30
12th Lok Sabha 1998	7 (387) (67.10)	20 (101) (17.76)	12 (49) (8.33)	39
13th Lok Sabha 1999	7 (369) (67.10)	23 (158) (23.34)	8 (10) 1.50	38
14th Lok Sabha 2004	6 (364) 62.89%	22 (159) 28.90%	9 (15) 3.96%	37

Indian party system continued its fragmentation and the Table 3.3 clearly shows that the number of political competitors were proliferating and its impact was felt on the process of government formation at the Centre.

What has been the 'agenda of political mobilisation' in post-1989 India? V.P. Singh in 1990 took recourse to Mandal Commission recommendations it led to the emergence of full-fledged phenomenon of caste-based politics and following in the footsteps of V.P. Singh, Sonia Gandhi too Congress-led has taken refuge behind caste-based politics by announcing the policy of reservations in educational institutions for the other Backward Castes in 2006. Caste-based politics is the order of the day and everyone from V.P. Singh to Sonia Gandhi is seen as following the path of mobilisation of caste against caste to establish a specific caste-based vote bank. The BJP, a party of Hindutva, launched a movement which led to the demolition of Babri Mosque at Ayodhya on December 6, 1992 and in this way caste versus caste politics was replaced by religion versus religion politics.

The Congress party from Rajiv Gandhi to Sonia Gandhi has been politically 'reactive' to the challenges posed by religion-based and caste-based political formations. Rajiv Gandhi had announced some new policies for the modernisation of India and his government announced literacy Mission and Missions for the spread of science and technology to rural areas. However, all his new ideas were overshadowed by political events of 1984 to 1989. Rajiv Gandhi had inherited contentious issues like Punjab problem and Assam problem, and he tried to resolve these issues by signing peace accord on Punjab and Assam. Rajiv got involved in political controversies with Zail

Singh, the President of India, and the other famous controversies were on the purchase of Bofors gun from Sweden. Zail Singh, had almost decided to 'dismiss' Rajiv Gandhi and V.P. Singh's campaign against Rajiv on Bofors gun issue had completely paralysed Rajiv's government. Rajiv Gandhi blundered badly on his dealing with the challenges posed by the forces of Hindutva on the issue of Ram Janmabhoomi-Babri Mosque controversy. Not only this, Rajiv had shown great confusion in his responses to the issue of Muslim Personal Law and the result of all this was that Rajiv-led Congress was defeated in 1989 Lok Sabha elections. The Indian Peace Keeping Force sent to Sri Lanka also brought brickbats to his style of foreign policy decisionmaking. Rajiv became leader of the opposition in the Lok Sabha in 1989 and his own erstwhile colleague V.P. Singh, who had walked out of the Congress, became the Prime Minister though for a very short period from December 9, 1989 to November 10, 1990. After the split among the supporters of V.P. Singh, Chandrashekhar assumed the office for a very short period from November 10, 1990 to June 21, 1991. The Congress returned to power and P. V. Narasimha Rao remained in power from June 21,1991 to May 1996. Sonia Gandhi became the President of the Congress party in 1998 and under her leadership, the Congress could form a coalition government at the Centre in 2004.

What is the explanation for the decline of this Grand Old Party of India? Has India bid good-bye to the phenomenon of an all-India national party system? Has 'regional politics' replaced all-India party system? What are the prospects of a party of, by, and for the Hindus to emerge as an all-India alternative to secular all India Congress party?

India in the Twenty-First Century is faced with many open-ended questions in the sphere of politics. The core issue of India for the Twenty-First Century is: How would the centripetal and centrifugal tendencies be managed politically?

The assassination of Rajiv Gandhi on May 21, 1991 is an act of the section of society, which does not believe in the power of ballot. The believers of the politics of bullet have again assaulted Indian democracy at a time when the electoral process was in full swing in the country. The timing of assassination of Rajiv Gandhi is quite significant because the assassins are determined to derail the electoral process in India. A peculiar feature of the centrist parties in India is their dependence on a single leader. If the leader is removed, the party is paralysed. Hence, the assassins have to target the leader to achieve their goal of destroying a party and spreading political confusion in the country.

Rajiv Gandhi entered politics after the death of Sanjay Gandhi. Unlike his brother, Rajiv was quite reluctant to enter politics. When Rajiv Gandhi came to politics, he became the General Secretary of the Congress-I and also an MP in 1980. He began his political journey from the Centre and he had no understanding of the complexities of grassroot politics of the country and also of the Congress party system. Since Mrs. Indira Gandhi presided over the

Congress, Rajiv was inducted to learn the internal dynamics of the party and politics of the country.

After the assassination of Mrs. Indira Gandhi in 1984, the then President of India, Gyani Zail Singh, appointed Rajiv as the Prime Minister of India. Rajiv Gandhi and the Congress won the Lok Sabha elections of 1984 on the basis of "sympathy" factor and he was launched as the elected Prime Minister.

Rajiv started with many assets in 1984. First, he was different from his brother and mother. Both Sanjay and Indira Gandhi were linked with the Emergency regime of 1975-77 and a large section of political class was against the authoritarian politics of Mrs. Gandhi. Rajiv had nothing to do with the Emergency regime and the new Prime Minister in 1984 started with goodwill by the people who viewed him differently than his dominating mother.

Second, he applied a healing touch in the Punjab and Assam. The Rajiv-Longowal Accord of 1985 and the Assam Accord of 1985 were welcomed as a breakthrough in these two troubled States of India.

Mr. Clean

Third, the Indira Gandhi regime was suspected to be very corrupt by a section of the political class, and Rajiv was viewed as 'Clean'.

Fourth, Rajiv's performance as the Congress President was quite refreshing because the Congress under Mrs. Gandhi was a private property of the leader. Rajiv, in his address at the Congress session in Bombay, attacked 'power brokers' within the Congress, and promised to hold elections within the party.

The critics of Mrs. Gandhi and the Congress were quite happy with Rajiv because democratic Congress would safeguard Indian Democracy. If the Congress party does not practise internal democracy, such a party cannot be trusted to defend democracy in the country.

Fifth, Rajiv was young and modern, and his outlook on economic development was welcomed by a section of the elite in India. Rajiv's attempts to liberalise and modernise Indian economy, created a social constituency for Rajiv's economic policies.

Thus, Rajiv's democratic credentials, a clean image and a moderniser became his great assets for the first two years of his becoming the Prime Minister. The Bofors bomb exploded and from 1987 to 1989, the Rajiv regime was on the defensive on the issue of corruption. From Clean to Corrupt was Rajiv's downhill journey in India.

While Rajiv Gandhi's personal integrity was in question, many serious political questions also emerged on the scene. Rajiv and the President of India came to a head-long clash. Rajiv[1] as Prime Minister did not perform his constitutional responsibility of meeting the President. The President wanted to dismiss Rajiv. It would have been a constitutional blunder on the part of President Gyani Zail Singh. Rajiv was vehemently criticised for his childish behaviour vis-a-vis the President.

Rajiv's much promised election within the Congress remained on paper. Neither the elections were held nor the Congress leaders were trusted. A coterie of advisers and friends of Rajiv emerged as managers of politics. Rajiv also showed centralist tendencies of his mother, when he dismissed Surjit Singh Barnala in 1987. A section of the political class disapproved Rajiv's action of dismissal of the Akali Dal government in Punjab in 1987. It was also alleged that the Barnala Ministry was dismissed with a view to influence Haryana elections of 1987. The Congress was badly defeated in the Haryana Assembly elections.

Rajiv was also criticised for compromises with the Muslim fundamentalists on Muslim Personal Law. While Rajiv was welcomed as modern and forward looking leader, his compromise on the Shah Bano case revealed that his commitments to modernity were not deep.

Fragility

Rajiv's assassination has shown the fragility of the largest party of India. The killers have to kill the leader, and the party gets paralysed. The Congress politics is around personality, and the removal of the person can prove disastrous for a party. After Nehru's death, many tall leaders within the Congress were available to lead the party, K. Kamaraj, Morarji Desai, Lal Bahadur Shastri and many others were available to collectively lead the party. Mrs. Gandhi destroyed the collective leadership structure of the Congress. Rajiv promised to restore it, but failed to do it. Other parties should learn a lesson. The building of personality-cult in a party destroys the party in the long run. The democratic process in India cannot be entrusted to tall individuals without strong party organisations and collective leadership structures at all levels within the country.

Congress Party: A Crisis That's an Individual's Doing

The brutal assassination of Rajiv Gandhi on May 21 has paralysed the Congress at a time, when the election process for the Lok Sabha is on. While the National Front, the Left parties and the BJP are actively campaigning for the elections, the Congress organisation is in a shambles. All efforts of the Congress are concentrated on finding a transitory arrangement to meet the current vacuum within the party. Such a deep crisis of the Congress was not witnessed, when Pt. Jawaharlal Nehru died on May 27, 1964. Pt. Nehru was a tall personality whose impact was felt on the national affairs and also on the working of the Congress. After Pt. Nehru's death, the then Congress president K. Kamaraj evolved a consensus in favour of Lal Bahadur Shastri. The untimely death of Lal Bahadur Shastri in 1966 again brought the Congress organisational leadership to elect a successor to Shastri. The central and State leadership of the Congress performed this job by electing Mrs. Indira Gandhi whose candidature was contested by Morarji Desai. Thus, neither Nehru's death nor Shastri's death immobilised the Congress in electing successors either through consensus or through properly contested elections.

Nomination

Mrs. Indira Gandhi's tragic assassination in October 1984, again brought the issue of succession and it was resolved by installing Rajiv Gandhi as Prime Minister of India. The procedure of nominating a successor to Mrs. Gandhi was fundamentally different from the procedures followed by the Congress in the post-Nehru phase. The fundamental characteristic of the post-Nehru Congress was its democratic functioning and procedures for electing the leaders. Mrs. Indira Gandhi slowly and gradually destroyed the Congress democracy and evolved a 'nomination culture' for running the Congress organisation. The result of Mrs. Indira Gandhi and Rajiv Gandhi's 'nomination culture' is pathetic situation within the Congress to find even a temporary successor to Rajiv. The present crisis is quite deep and the processes generated by Mrs. Indira Gandhi and Rajiv Gandhi are solely responsible for paralysis of the party.

The Congress party had a very strong all-India presence because its organisation was visible in all parts of the country. The party organisation was effective because it had built its structure on the basis of democratic elections within the party. The Congress had an army of leaders at the local, state and national levels. Leaders and personalities are very important in politics but the legitimacy of leaders depends on their democratic foundations. The Congress party organisation was based on the city Congress committees, the taluka Congress committees, the district Congress committees, the provincial Congress committees and the All India Congress Committee. The Presidents of all these committees at various levels were elected persons and they carried enormous weight within the party.

The party was always involved in factional and personality politics, but the ultimate resolution of conflicts within the party was resolved democratically. Party democracy nourished the Congress. The Congress evolved a system of High Command whose essence was a collective leadership in the hands of tall Congress party leaders. Differences of opinion and dissent were the hallmark of Congress democracy and personality clashes were not unknown to the Congress. But democracy within the party was not scuttled. After Independence of India, the tall Congress leaders like Pt. Nehru, Sardar Patel, Abul Kalam Azad, Rajendra Prasad and others, managed the Congress with the support of state level leaders who were equally important in their states and regions.

Mrs. Indira Gandhi inherited this kind of Congress party and it was a rich inheritance. Instead of building the Congress, she destroyed its essentials. Mrs. Gandhi inherited the tradition of factionalism and the culture of dissent within the Congress. She fought against factionalism and destroyed the democratic culture of dissent within the Congress. Instead of recognising that factional competition in the Congress, reveals the co-existence of plural tendencies, she suppressed it.

Rich Heritage

The consequence of Mrs. Gandhi's approach to the Congress was the replacement of the collective leadership by the personality cult. Loyalty to leader replaced the spirit of tolerance of multiple leadership. The renewal of the Congress party came to an end because elections within the Congress were not held by Mrs. Gandhi. Instead of elected PCCs and elected PCC Presidents, Mrs. Gandhi started nominating party functionaries.

Cut to Size

The so-called chief ministers ceased to be effective spokesmen of their States because they were the nominees of Mrs. Gandhi and not elected by the party at the State levels. Mrs. Gandhi removed popular leaders who had deep roots in their states and replaced them by rootless leaders by nominating them to the office of the chief minister.

A.R. Antulay in Maharashtra or Abdul Ghafoor in Bihar were nominated as Chief Ministers not because they represented the wishes of the Congress parties of Maharashtra or Bihar. The chief ministers and PCC presidents were not elected democratically but nominated by the leader. Even this practice of Mrs. Gandhi did not succeed in eliminating factionalism in the Congress. Instead of learning lessons in favour of democratic practices for the Congress, Mrs. Gandhi persisted in imposing leaders of her own choice.

Two inter-related issues demand a little probing and analysis. What were the political and personal reasons for Mrs. Gandhi to destroy democracy and collective leadership of the Congress? What were the reasons and explanations for the capitulation of tall leaders before Mrs. Gandhi? The Congress had split in 1969 and 1978. It reveals that many congressmen stood up against Mrs. Gandhi but the current was in her favour and a large number of Congress functionaries always succumbed before Mrs. Gandhi.

Dynasty

Mrs. Gandhi was personally bitter with many Congress leaders whom she thought as obstructionists. Mrs. Gandhi had a concept of prime ministership based on pre-eminence of the leader. Such a pre-eminent role of Mrs. Gandhi was contested by some tall leaders of the Congress from 1966 to 1969. Instead of resolving the issue of the role of Prime Minister, Mrs. Gandhi resolved to eliminate the critics within the Congress. And once some of these leaders of the Congress were marginalised, Mrs. Gandhi emerged as the tallest leader in the country.

Having established her unquestioned authority on the Congress, Mrs. Gandhi could have revived democracy in the party. It should have been clear to Mrs. Gandhi that an all-India party needs capable and acceptable leaders.

Since Mrs. Gandhi did not revive party democracy even after establishing her supreme position, the explanation of her dynastic ambitions assumes credibility. Mrs. Gandhi weakened Congress leadership to pave the way for her children to assume power. Mrs. Gandhi had disposed off all challenges within the party against her family rule.

Further, Mrs. Gandhi became the fountain source of money for the Congress. The congressmen looked towards Mrs. Gandhi for money and electoral victories. The tinpot Congress leaders emerged on the scene who looked towards Mrs. Gandhi for patronage, protection and promotion in politics. Naturally, the vacuum of leadership within the Congress was beneficial for dynastic rule. Hence, the tragic end of dynasty has revealed the tragedy of the party which has no capacity to stand on its own.

If the Congress has not to disintegrate, it will have to reject the Indira-Rajiv Congress traditions. The Congress survival depends on the revival of the democratic traditions of the Congress. It is a big challenge to tinpot leaders of the Congress but they have no options. The Congress stands at the crossroads. The party can either disintegrate or slowly renew itself by following democratic procedures. The Congressmen have to blame themselves for their pathetic situation, where they find themselves as leaderless and rudderless.

4

V.P. Singh: Messiah of Mandal Politics

The politics of V. P. Singh, Laloo Prasad Yadav and Mulayam Singh Yadav, has accelerated and intensified caste confrontations in north India. During the last 47 years, multiple social constituencies have been mobilised on the basis of primordial loyalties. However, the new phase of caste politics is fundamentally different from the early post-Independence political process in India.

First, the Congress evolved a coalition of high caste Hindus, Scheduled Castes and Scheduled Tribes to win elections. The Congress system of a "patron and client" caste coalition did not target castes outside its coalitional politics.

V.P. Singh, and the Yadavs, Laloo Prasad, Mulayam Singh, have mobilised the upwardly mobile backward peasant castes by targeting the upper caste domination which is presented as a historical fact of Indian society. The "new caste politics" is confrontational because it is situated in the philosophy of "undoing the cruelties of history" whose present representatives and custodians are upper caste Hindus, irrespective of their economic status.

Such a mobilisation of caste in politics has been built around "hatred" and the manageable levels of social violence. This has been happening during the last four years of caste politics and is a definite break from the earlier phase of Indian politics.

Second, the Congress system, while winning the elections on the basis of a "caste coalition", did not govern the country on the basis of mere caste factors. A political party mediates and harmonises conflicting and competing social interests after winning elections because the government stands for the whole society.

It is true that such neutral governance is a "pure model" but a ruling party by definition is "relatively autonomous" of its specific social support structure.

The Janata Dals or the Samajvadi Party on the other hand, are not political formations of an autonomous character. They are mere instruments in the hands of the elite of their castes.

This is a casteisation of politics where the upwardly mobile backward peasant castes and the elite of the other dalit castes are not mere voters; they are the rulers. The only yardstick of governmental performance in Uttar Pradesh and Bihar is the successful promotion and protection of specific caste interests.

Laloo Prasad and Mulayam Singh have to show to their caste supporters that their governments are openly practising policies of discrimination against the so-called upper castes.

The current phase of caste politics is a negation of the modernisation and secularisation of Indian society and polity. How can such a reversal of history go unchallenged by the secular and modern intelligentsia of the country? How can maverick caste operators receive intellectual support?

Democratic politics is based on multiple sources of legitimacy. The ongoing casteisation of society and erosion of the secularisation process have great intellectual support in India.

Ram Manohar Lohia, in the fifties, made a powerful intellectual case against Western capitalism and Soviet-type Communism. He evolved a complex model of an Asian path for peasant societies and specifically for India. He pleaded for mobilising the backwaid castes for social change and a peasant model of socialism.

Those who believe in the progressive potential of backward castes in democratic politics in India, can be traced to Lohia's "Asian model", Many caste reform movements have been in existence in India and they have exercised great influence over social change in various regions of the country. But caste mobilisation for elections to change peasant India for egalitarianism was Lohia's contribution.

It is not without reason that Mulayam Singh Yadav claims legitimacy from Lohia in spite of the fact that so-called socialists like Sharad Yadav, Ram Vilas Paswan, Laloo Prasad or Mulayam Singh have caricatured Lohia by ignoring his complex social philosophy that too without answering some important questions about the serious limhations of the Lohia model.

First Lohia was extremely marginal in Indian politics because the Congress' caste coalition was more successful in gradually changing Indian society. Second, many progressive socialist contemporaries of Lohia, did not accept Lohia's diagnosis or analysis as relevant for India.

Lohia's claim that the backward peasant castes have the potential of causing progressive change in India was a non-starter even when he was alive. Charan Singh, the most conscious caste and class leader of the upwardly mobile peasants, never practised caste exclusivism. The current caste leaders cannot appropriate even the politics of Charan Singh because he imbibed some values of the national movement and dissociated himself from Lohia.

A section of academics led by Rajni Kothari has projected the role of caste in politics as a secularisation of society. Kothari, in his numerous writings on caste in Indian politics, has maintained that, "in reality, the consequences of caste-politics interactions are just the reverse of what is usually stated. It is not politics that gets caste-ridden, it is caste that gets politicised" and in the process, India will move towards modernity on the basis of traditionalisation process.

It is not without reason that Kothari was excited by V. P. Singh's acceptance of the Mandal Commission report. If intellectuals like him have any commitment to modernisation in India, a visit to the villages and towns of Uttar Pradesh and Bihar will suffice to find out that not only is modernisation in a mess but its very element has been eroded by casteism.

Caste relations have always been oppositional and conflictual. The caste system is based on an ideology which determines the world view, beliefs and value structures of every *jati* and *sub-jati* in India. Caste is a system of social organisation with a view to hierarchically organise society on the basis of *"do's* and *dont 's"* for every *jati.*

Rajni Kothari escapes by taking an easy way and saying Indian modernisation will proceed by involving traditional social categories in the new democratic process. The real issue is to weaken caste loyalties by making people transcend the local and attain the cosmopolitan.

Politics has to play a crucial and critical role in the process of modernisation. Caste loyalties have to be weakened before they are replaced by new reference points which are secular. Jawaharlal Nehru had this vision because he linked his modernisation enterprise with nation-building.

Politics of goals was the tool of mobilisation. Gradually, socially weaker sections were changing their social status and politics consciously, followed policies of social accommodation.

Caste politics minus that of nation-building is the current reality and caste competition has been deliberately accentuated *son* that V. P. Singh or Laloo Prasad or Mulayam Singh do not have to answer questions regarding their governmental performance.

It will be helpful to intellectuals like Rajni Kothari to listen to the warning of Paul Brass in his *Ethnicity and Nationalism* (1991): "Political and economic elites who make use of ethnic group attributes are constrained by the beliefs and values which exist within the group and which limit the kinds of appeals which can be made".

Ethnic politics in India has the same dangers as caste politics. Leaders strengthen ethnicism and casteism because their universe is limited and only confrontations can bring political dividends. In the process, neither is caste weakened nor can it be used for social harmony and governance.

Mandal has Devoured its Marxist Messiahs

A powerful intellectual support to the practitioners of low caste politics has come from the radical secular intelligentsia because the former leaders have talked of the same social goals of egalitarianism, as the latter have claimed to believe in V.P. Singh, Mulayam Singh Yadav and Laloo Prasad Yadav are the new messiahs of social justice and the radical intelligentsia has actively supported their caste politics.

In politics, excellent slogans have been coined by dictators and even power-seekers in a democracy. Rural India cannot have growth with equity without land reforms and appropriate institutional answers for land and wage contradictions.

What is the track record of the current practitioners of caste politics in rural restructuring?

The nature of contradiction in the most backward states of Uttar Pradesh and Bihar is on the "land question" and the "wage question". The social class which is led by V.P. Singh, Mulayam Singh and Laloo Prasad in the real villain along with other dominant groups.

The radical intelligentsia should see the record of these two States Governments and seek the so-called qualitative differences between the earlier regimes in U.P. and Bihar and the present political formations.

If political rhetoric makes leaders radical and acceptable to the progressive intelligentsia, these new legitimisers are fully responsible for the atmosphere of caste hatred in the villages and towns of UP. and Bihar.

Marxist analysis of caste in India was linked with the overall materialistic interpretation of history and its concrete application to the social reality of India. D.D. Kosambi, an important Marxist historian, analysed caste as an arrangement where India achieved social stability without large scale violence. Thus, European societies were formed on the basis of violence.

Caste's negative consequence was that Indian forces of production and relation of production remained backward and the crisis in feudalism did not lead to the resolution of contradiction since caste, as a stabilisation factor, operated in full strength. Thus, caste in India, played a highly negative and regressive role.

E.M.S. Namboodiripad and many other Marxist intellectuals maintain that caste in India, played a class role because it was a social arrangement for the appropriation of surplus value by determining the social status of the Scheduled Castes as labouring classes. Thus, the "twice-born" and the Shudra were related in such a manner that the Shudra was an Indian variant of the slave.

Contemporary India beginning, with the late 19th century has been involved in a new economics, where, with all its weakness, distortion and fault, the capitalist system of production has come to stay.

In spite of the fact that caste may have played a class role, in contemporary India, caste is a relic of the backward, feudal past. India is burdened by history and the new India has to struggle against many inherited categories and loyalty structures.

Caste belongs to the past social arrangements and it has to be opposed. Only then can class consciousness emerge in India. Caste limits and divides; class consciousness is based on a larger solidarity where members of a class transcend every local loyalty, including their status in their own factory or farm.

It must be a great surprise to even V.P. Singh, Mulayam Singh and Laloo Prasad that a rich reservoir of Marxist intellectuals see them as revolutionaries and liberators of the downtrodden. The Marxists are not worried that caste politics in U.P. and Bihar has completely pushed them away even from their traditional areas of strength. Trade unionists in Bihar and kisan leaders in UP. have become ciphers in the face of assertive backward casteism.

Marxists are committed to an "alternative politics" which requires strengthening of the ongoing democratic revolution in India. India is a society of many contradictions but it is the democratic process which has made people assertive.

Mass struggles have to be launched to deepen the. forces of democratic revolution. Will intensification of caste divisions strengthen the forces of united mass struggles?

Casteisation of trade unions and *kisan sabhas* cannot be stopped, if the caste discourse becomes the dominant ideology of politics. The caste ideology is a historical specificity of India. It is involved in an antagonistic contradiction with the class ideology. Class mobilisation is fundamentally different from caste mobilisation. Mobilisation of textile or steel or workers is different from the mobilisation of Yadavs, Kurmis and Koeris.

Folly of Reservations

The Constitution (Amendment) Bill which provides for 33 per cent of reserved seats for women in the Legislatures has not been openly opposed by any political party or group because everyone wants to be branded as progressive by empowering the effectively disenfranchised women of India. The only opposition to the Bill has come from caste and community leaders who by joining the bandwagon of reservations want that such reservations should be on the basis of caste and religion of the women. Thus, these leaders want the casteisation and communalisation of the Legislatures.

If one follows the yardsticks of the political class of the 1990s, the makers of the Indian Constitution would be dubbed as social reactionaries because they showed great caution in dealing with the whole social project of affirmative action for safeguarding the rights and interests of sections who were inheritors of historically determined social discriminations. It is essential to mention that the Constitution tried to reconcile many irreconcilables by adopting a balanced middle path while dealing with the complex and contradictory social realities.

If, on one hand, a bold experiment was launched by adopting the principle of universal adult franchise, on the other, reservation of seats in Legislatures was provided for the Scheduled Castes and Scheduled Tribes. It was a powerful intervention by the Constitution to empower the most under-privileged and discriminated sections of Indian society. The authors of the Constitution did not go berserk on the policy of reservation of seats in Legislatures because they clearly rejected the demand for communal representation. Not only this, the reservation of seats for the Scheduled Castes, Tribes and for Anglo-Indians was also for a temporary period only and it was to be reviewed after ten years of the commencement of the Constitution.

By various amendments of the Constitution, especially the Constitution (Forty-fifth Amendment) Act of 1980 and the Constitution (Sixty-second Amendment) Act of 1989, it is proposed to extend it upto 2000 AD only. This cautious attitude of the Founders of the Indian Republic is also clearly reflected in adopting a policy of reservation of seats in public services for the deprived strata of society. If, on one hand, every citizen was guaranteed equality of opportunity, on the other, reservation of seats for the Scheduled Castes and Scheduled Tribes was provided to take care of the inherited social disabilities of sections of society who were to be protected against the unregulated principle of abstract equality.

Further, even these reservations in public services were to be consistent with "the maintenance of efficiency of administration." Many a times, the Supreme Court has applied correctives in reminding the policy makers about the limits of the policy of reservations in public services. The Supreme Court in 1951 in the Venkataramana V. State of Madras case held that a person could not be kept out of public services because he was a Brahmin or again in the Balaji V. State of Mysore case in 1963, observed that reservations made "under Article 16(4) beyond the permissible and legitimate limits would be liable to be challenged as a fraud on the Constitution."

When Mr. V. P. Singh, a self-appointed messiah of social justice, found the recommendations made by Mandal Commission on reservations as a profitable political commodity, he created a stir by suddenly announcing the acceptance of the Mandal report on August 7,1990. This raw politics of reservations was played by Mr. V. P. Singh and others without any holds barred and the Supreme Court again intervened to tell the adventurist political class that reservations in services cannot go beyond 50 per cent and that the policy of reservations in public services shall exclude the "creamy layers" of the reserved social categories.

By abandoning the note of caution administered by the Constitution, the new messiahs of reservations in Legislatures and public services have completely fragmented and factionalised the already divided society. Politics is not just a mirror reflection of social reality. It is equally concerned with changing the inherited social categories and identities. The political class, by following a reckless policy of reservations, has encouraged social antagonisms based on caste versus caste, sub-caste versus sub-caste and now it is wanting to bring this division among the women in India.

India has inherited a very complex caste system, but the policy of reservations has solidified and institutionalised caste divisions and caste identities. Politics of reservations generates and stimulates caste, community and gender consciousness and every group in India is involved in targeting the other group as villain of the piece. Social deprivations are not attributed to the Himalayan failures of the economic path of development, followed by the country. The political class does not want to become a target of the deprived people and by following a policy of reservations, politicians have successfully created a situation, where different social groups are targeting each other for their deprivations.

The journey of casteism began with Forward Castes versus Backward Castes and it has reached a stage where every sub-caste is against every other sub-caste. Tamil Nadu has witnessed violence by backward castes against the Scheduled Castes and the rural population of Uttar Pradesh and Bihar is actually involved in a violent caste war. Has the policy of reservations brought social justice for the really deprived groups in society? The answer to this question is a big No.

If the unending system of reservations has promoted serious social cleavages, it has also displaced from public controversy the serious agenda of economic growth with justice. While Mr. Mulayam Singh Yadav, Mr. Laloo Prasad Yadav, Mr. Kanshi Ram, Miss Mayawati and future women representatives in the State Legislatures have created assured social and sectarian constituencies for winning an election, they have completely failed to evolve socio-economic programmes for the real empowerment of the Dalits. Mr. Laloo Prasad Yadav is electorally invincible because of the electoral support of Muslims and Yadavs of Bihar, but the landless agricultural workers of Bihar have to migrate in distress to search for their livelihood to Haryana and Punjab. All political factions which are masquerading as champions of the Dalits have not undertaken a single real step which can empower people living below the poverty line.

The Constitution favoured limited reservations because it was believed that gradually the need for reservations will not be felt because the successful implementation of the programmes of socio-economic development will create new opportunities for the development of the whole of India. Not only has India badly messed up its developmental agenda, the self-appointed guardians of caste, community and gender reservations do not have any agenda for the social and economic development of the country. Mr. Laloo Prasad Yadav, Mr. Mulayam Singh Yadav, Mr. Kanshi Ram, Miss Mayawati, who are the product of casteisation of Indian politics, have failed to pull out their states from the existing stage of poverty and under-development.

The politics of Forward Caste versus Backward Caste, or Hindu versus Muslim or Male versus Female had succeeded not only in dividing the society, but also it has legitimised the idea of politics for the sake of power alone. The believers in the policy of reservations have reduced social justice to a meaningless slogan. The unfinished task of land reforms has not been implemented by the practitioners of social justice and the landless agricultural workers have not escaped from the continuing tyrannies of the landowning castes.

Every political party has become a victim of the aimless politics of reservations. The Communist Parties resisted and very reluctantly fell in line with Mr. V. P. Singh's politics of Mandal. The BJP's Hindutva has no answer to the politics of caste versus caste among the so-called Hindus, whom the BJP claims to represent. The growing decline and decay of the Congress can be attributed to its failure to respond to sectarian politics of the votaries of reservations. Fragmented society has also fragmented politics. Since the 1990s the Central Government has become weak, unstable and vulnerable to domestic and foreign pressures because the electoral verdict is fragmented.

The upshot is that the policies of reservations are mere rhetoric because the real flesh and blood of empowerment and social justice is conspicuous by its absence in the agenda of the champions of reservations. This policy is socially disastrous because it has generated the feelings of social distancing. The political parties, which emerged as champions of reservations, have failed to provide stable governments because the electoral verdict has been fragmented as a result of sectional reservations. There is no evidence that political empowerment of Dalits has brought any change in the life of the Dalits. Similarly, political empowerment of women will not bring any benefit to the landless agricultural women of India.

Empowerment of Dalits Civilization

An analysis of the Lok Sabha elections of 1998 has shown that the voter turnout of the Dalit social groups has increased. Further, these groups are asserting their autonomous Dalit-Bahujan identity and are also active participants in the making of a new agenda. A few facts may be mentioned here to substantiate the argument that the Bahujan Samaj is a powerful force in the politics of the 1990s and their demands have to be on the centrestage of the political agenda. First, the BJP has been compelled to respond to the new assertion of the Dalit-Bahujan Samaj by appropriating even the Mandal formula, which was vehemently opposed by it in the 1990s. In spite of serious opposition by the entrenched high castes in UP. BJP politics, Kalyan Singh is not expendable because he represents the other backward castes and the party of high caste Hindus has to show that it cares for the interests of the OBCs and Dalits.

Out of the 179 Lok Sabha seats, won by the BJP, it won 24 from the Scheduled Caste constituencies and 14 from the Scheduled Tribe reserve constituencies. The BJP won the majority of its Scheduled Caste reserve seats in the Hindi heartland like 4 in Bihar, 5 in Madhya Pradesh and 11 in Uttar Pradesh. The Jan Sangh/BJP before the middle of the 1980s was not at all sensitive to the Dalit-Bahujan phenomenon and it is making every effort to reach these hitherto underclass of the high caste Hindu society. Thus, the emergence of Dalit-Bahujan phenomena has made a Hindu socially conservative party to shift its public agenda to win the elections.

Second, an important explanation for the growing decline of the Congress lies in its failure to continue with the Indira Gandhi model of social coalition, in which the Muslim minority and the Dalits had a significant position. The Dalits looked towards Mrs. Gandhi as 'Mother' who would care for their interests. This protective umbrella role of the Congress collapsed because the Rajiv Gandhi Government was identified with the emerging "yuppie" class and the Narasimha Rao Government because of its new economic policy got projected as 'pro-rich' and 'anti-poor.'

While these facts only prove that Dalit politics has come to occupy a central position in the 1980s and 1990s, a further analysis may be made to understand the complex and contradictory inside story of Dalit-Bahujan politics. The Hindi heartland came face-to-face with the new challenge of Dalit social forces because of land reforms and the constitutional provisions for the reservation of seats in every public institution for Scheduled Castes and Scheduled Tribes. The beneficiaries of land reforms in U.P., Bihar, etc., were the middle peasant backward castes and reservations in public institutions gave birth to a Dalit elite who were upwardly mobile. While the post-Mrs. Gandhi Congress leadership failed to respond to this silent social transformation, independent leaders from backward-Dalit social formations emerged and formed their own political parties. Mulayam Singh Yadav, Laloo Prasad Yadav, Ram Vilas Paswan and others floated all kinds of Janata Dals while the Kanshi Ram-Mayawati established a separate party for the Bahujan Samaj because social contradictions in India are not only between the high castes and the others, but also very much present between the other backward castes, the Dalits and the real Dalits.

This development of backward-Dalit Bahujan politics in north India has revealed that the two largest States of the Hindi region are witnessing the elimination of an umbrella party like the Congress and its replacement by caste and sub-caste formations and leaders. U.P. and Bihar are witnessing only caste politics and caste competition around caste leaders and caste-based parties. The BSP cannot align with Mulayam Singh Yadav in U.P. or Laloo Prasad Yadav and Ram Vilas Paswan in Bihar because there is a fundamental antagonism among the multiple fragmented Dalit-Bahujan groups and leaders of the intermediate castes who promote interests, which directly hurt the interests of those sections of the Dalits who are represented by the Yadavs or Paswans, etc. While the Dalit Bahujan Samaj has emerged to fight against caste oppression and caste exploitation and the villages of U.P. and Bihar, the real Dalits or Jatavs are oppressed by the middle peasant backward castes like Yadavs or Jats in western Uttar Pradesh.

At the end of the 1990s, Mulayam Singh or Laloo Prasad or Kanshi Ram feel helpless because a fragmented Dalit-Bahujan Samaj cannot win the majority of the State Assembly and the Lok Sabha seats on their own. Caste politics has not brought political dividends to Dalit-Bahujan leaders, because it has fragmented every caste group including the Dalit-Bahujan Samaj. If, on one hand, the party of the Hindu Brahminical social order has woken up to the reality of conscious Dalit-Bahujans, on the other hand, pure Dalit-Bahujan political parties are struggling to establish their dominant position in the politics of U.P. and Bihar. Caste exclusion in politics is a multi-edged weapon which makes every sub-caste project its exclusive identity. The Yadavs of U.P. cannot complaint, if the Jatav also parade their separate Dalit caste identity and compete for political power.

The politics of Dalit-Bahujan Samaj tells a different story in other parts of India compared to the Hindu region since anti-Brahmin social reform movements preceded the politicisation of Dalit-Bahujan politics. E. V. Ramaswamy Naicker led a renaissance movement based on an anti-temple, anti-God social platform to awaken the oppressed castes from the influence of Brahmins and priests. Similarly, in Maharashtra, social reform preceded political activisation of the Dalits. Dalit poetry and drama and Dalit education emerged as the platform for Dalit awakening. Such efforts of Dalit social reformists in Maharashtra created a level of awakening so that the Dalits maintained a distance from the Congress because Maharashtra Congress was identified with the Brahminical leadership of Bal Gangadhar Tilak.

The story of Dalit reform in Tamil Nadu and Maharashtra has a lesson for all Dalit-Bahujan parties. Political assertion of the Dalits is a necessary but not sufficient condition for Dalit-Bahujan emancipation. It is a flawed political agenda of the Dalit-Bahujan leaders that political empowerment will necessarily lead to their social and economic empowerment. Politics in democracy is an important activity for securing the rights of equality as a citizen but Dalit-Bahujan Samaj cannot achieve such equality because a powerful anti-Dalit Hindu Brahminical social order precedes the operation of the universal adult franchise-based democracy.

Dalit-Bahujan parties and leaders should make use of every political and public institution for protecting their rights and social dignity, but along with this, they should launch a renaissance movement with other socially enlightened groups irrespective of their caste affiliations against Adi Shankaracharya's idealist interpretation of society 'which denies the existence of the world as separate from God' and which believes that 'God *(Brahm)* alone exists, that the human soul *(Atma)* is a spark of *Brahm* and all the physical world is a mere illusion *(Maya)*. The Vedanta philosophy of the Hindu social order believes in Liberation *(Moksha)* only after death, when the soul is free from the illusion of the physical world.

This metaphysical view is the foundation of the Brahminical caste society of the Hindus, where *Karma* determines human existence in this world and caste hierarchy is linked with the doctrine of *Karma*. The Brahminical social order of Adi Shankaracharya and other *vedantists* superimposed the principle of caste hierarchy, caste inequality and hence, caste oppression. Unless this world-view, which is the foundation of Ramayan-Mahabharat and other streams of Hindu civilian, is powerfully attacked and the bliss of the 'other world' is challenged as illusory and social existence is accepted as a reality, caste emancipation among the Hindus will not be possible. Caste politics as an agenda of the present Dalit-Bahujan leadership has consolidated casteism in India because caste *per se* has become an identity. The alternative agenda for the real liberation of Dalit Bahujan Samaj has to be based on a *non-Vedic Charvaka* (or *Lokayata)* that 'only this world exists' and that 'this world is only material in nature'.

The crux of the issue is that Brahminical Hinduism does not accept the principle of human equality even in theory. The believers in social equality cannot achieve emancipation from a caste-based social order without intellectually taking up the cause of an alternative social philosophy, which has to be based on the fact that social life is organised by human beings in this world and *Brahm* or Brahman has no role in defining our social status. It is a difficult path because it will have many failure stories like that of Dravidian parties in Tamil Nadu, where God or Goddesses have re-emerged in a big way irrespective of the efforts of Ramaswamy Naiker.

In summation, it may be mentioned that a democratic revolution is going on in the country because the oppressed are also politically conscious, but the fear is that the present leadership may betray them by limiting the agenda of Dalit-Bahujan emancipation to electoral politics alone. Atrocities against Dalits will continue even if Mayawati is Chief Minister unless the material and cultural agenda for Dalits is also taken up in a powerful manner. Dignity, self-respect and equal rights for the Dalit Bahujan Samaj can be ensured only by transforming the mind-set which is prepared to reject that *Brahm* or God has created our unequal social order. B.R. Ambedkar's prescription of religious conversion failed because shifting from one religion to another only perpetuates the world-view dominated by belief in God and its supremacy in determining the human social order. If this is so, Hinduism or Islam or Christianity makes no difference for Dalit-Bahujan groups and they will continue to occupy inferior positions in the society.

5

P.V. Narasimha Rao

The Two White Papers

The demolition of the Babri Mosque at Ayodhya on December 6, 1992 has brought into sharp focus the powers and the role of the Central and State Governments in upholding the fundamental values of the Constitution. The events of Ayodhya compelled the Centre and the BJP to publish their White Papers in February and April 1993. These two White Papers are an attempt to explain to the public the roles played by the Centre and the BJP Government of Uttar Pradesh regarding the events of Ayodhya. The two have made an effort to shift responsibility on each other and the two White Papers conceal the truth and reveal falsehood. The BJP White Paper alleges that the 'mosque-like' structure at Ayodhya was demolished by the karsevaks but the manipulative Prime Minister P.V. Narasimha Rao, disrupted all negotiations and wilfully prevented reference of the dispute to the Supreme Court. How could the BJP Government in U.P. deal with the sentiments of the devoted karsevaks who had felt cheated by the acts of omission and commission of the Prime Minister?

While the BJP White Paper is a testimonial in self-defence, the White Paper of the Centre is a self-admission of the political leadership which failed to provide any direction to the country during its hour of crisis on Ayodhya. The White Paper of the Centre correctly mentions that "a constitutionally elected Government (of Uttar Pradesh) could not discharge its duties..., therein lay the failure, therein the betrayal."

Is the Constitution silent on the crucial issue of the legal and Constitutional responsibilities of the elected Central and State Governments? Does it permit an elected Government to go berserk and violate the law with impunity? The answer is a definite 'No'. The Constitution has established a federal system with a very strong Central Government. During the last 45 years, the theory and practice of Indian federation has clearly established the pre-eminent position of the Central Government in relation to the State Governments. It is precisely because of the overriding powers of the Centre that many political parties and regional movements have demanded restructuring of Indian federalism. In spite of many movements for the reorganisation of the power system, the Centre continues to be in the driver's seat in managing the affairs of the country.

Article 355 of the Constitution clearly states that it is the responsibility of the Centre to ensure that "the Government of a State is carried on with the provisions of the Constitution". The Centre has the power to issue 'directions' to the States. And if a State fails to comply with, or to give effect to, any directions given by the Centre, the President can issue a proclamation under Article 356 and dismiss the State Government concerned because "the Government of the State cannot be carried on in accordance with the provisions of the Constitution". Thus, Articles 355 and 356 of the Constitution are devoted to the defence of the constitutional legality against the illegalities of the elected Governments.

The White Paper of the Centre alleges that the U.P Government 'betrayed' the Constitution on December 6, 1992 at Ayodhya, but the interpretation of the Constitution clearly shows that the Narasimha Rao Government 'betrayed' India by not upholding the values of the Constitution on December 6. The Narasimha Rao Government had legal and Constitutional powers to pre-empt the kar seva on December 6, to dismiss the Kalyan Singh Government on a specific charge of failure to defend the constitutional legality linked with temple-mosque controversy. It is essential to analyse the possible reasons for the failure of the Narasimha Rao Government in dealing firmly with the defiant State Government. It cannot be accepted that Narasimha Rao was concerned with any high moral values in not exercising powers given to the Central Government under Article 356. During the last 45 years, the Congress controlled Central Government has misused and abused Article 356 many a times. The Sarkaria Commission report on Centre-State relations has highlighted the distrust created between the Central and the State Governments by the misuse of Article 356, and has clearly stated that it should be used only under exceptional circumstances. The Congress under Jawaharlal Nehru and Indira Gandhi, the Janata Party under Morarji Desai in 1977, and Janata Dal under V.P. Singh in 1989 have made their own contributions in the distortion of Centre-State relations. While a clause was inserted in Article 356 by the 42nd Amendment, 1978—"the satisfaction of the President... shall be final and conclusive and shall not be questioned on any ground"—it opened the possibility of a judicial review of a Presidential proclamation. The Madhya Pradesh High Court held the Presidential proclamation on the dismissal of the Sunder Lal Patwa Government as not legally valid and the Supreme Court has constituted a full nine Judge Bench to review the legality and validity of Article 356 in the case of the dismissed State Governments of Madhya Pradesh, Himachal Pradesh and Rajasthan. The upshot of the above discussion is that Article 356 has always been in controversy and Narasimha Rao was not unaware of his constitutional powers in dealing with the breakdown of law and order in U.P. in the first week of December 1992.

All major parties, except the BJP, had extended full support to Narasimha Rao to uphold the Constitution in U.P. and many of these parties had never supported Article 356. The Centre was at the strongest wicket because it had the full backing of the major parties in the exercise of its responsibility to defend secular democracy in the country. The federal system works smoothly, if there is a consensus on an issue of national significance. The temple-mosque issue concerns the whole nation because the growing communal divide has weakened the fabric of Indian democracy.

The Narasimha Rao Government should have pre-empted the karseva at Ayodhya and a clear lesson should have been learnt from the experience of the Mulayam Singh Government of U.P. The firing on the karsevaks at Ayodhya on October 30, 1990 made Mulayam Singh the villain of the piece and the so-called defenders *of Hindutva* emerged as martyrs. The Narasimha Rao Government should not have allowed the kar sevaks to assemble at Ayodhya on December 6, 1992. On the basis of open support of the parties, the Centre should have issued a 'direction' to the Kalyan Singh Government to disallow the assembly of kar sevaks at Ayodhya. The failure of the Kalyan Singh Government in implementing this direction should have been fallowed by the proclamation of emergency in U.P. This way the Rao Government would have followed the letter and spirit of the Constitution.

The Rao Government failed to defend the federal principles of the Constitution because it had clear obligation to issue 'directions' and ask the President to dismiss a delinquent State Government. It failed at a time, when every condition was fulfilled for dealing with a berserk State Government. First, the national political consensus existed in favour of defending secular democracy by intervention by the Centre. Second, the judiciary considers harsh action by the Indian State as legitimate if it is in defence of public order. Third, the exercise of Article 356 by the Narasimha Rao Government in pre-empting karseva at Ayodhya would have been the first and foremost legitimate intervention in dealing with a recalcitrant State Government. It is not that the BJP betrayed the Rao Government, it is the Rao Government which betrayed the Indian nation by its failure to uphold the essentials of Indian federalism at the most critical time.

Every country has the Constitutional arrangement for emergency situations and the Indian Constitution had taken advantage of the "experience of other federations in providing for emergency provisions". The Centre's White Paper reveals the total failure of the Rao Government. The Centre showed a lack of awareness about international repercussions of the demolition of the Babri mosque. It is the Central Government which has to defend India in international forums and this responsibility cannot be performed, if the Centre is unable to deal with the illegalities of its own State Government. The Constitution recognises the exceptionally significant role of the Centre in dealing with foreign countries and it cannot offer an alibi that a so-called State Government failed to defend the Babri mosque. India is facing criticism by foreign countries because the Rao Government failed to perform its Constitutional responsibilities in relation to Ayodhya.

Economic Reforms

New Challenges and New Opportunities

The supporters and critics of the new economic policy followed by the Narasimha Rao Government have arrived at clear positions. The supporters want to 'accelerate' the process of economic restructuring and the opponents are con-vinced that economic liberalisation has already deepened the economic crisis of India. The Prime Minister, P.V. Narasimha Rao, observed on August 20 that 'the Government's effort during the last two years was to change the course of economy, 'now it is time to accelerate it'. In opposition to the economic policy of the Rao Government, the major trade unions launched a 'jail bharo' programme on August 19 and this is a prelude to the 'Bharat Bandh' planned for September 9.

The policy statement of Rao and the struggles by the opponents of the policy clearly reveal that the initial hesitations, uncertainties and apprehensions have come to an end and the ideas and goals of the supporters and critics of economic liberalisation have become clear. This is an appropriate occasion to analyse some new and significant challenges being faced by the Government in the process of economic liberalisation. The Government has maintained that economic liberalisation and globalisation is essential for the solution of the problems of poverty in India. This fact has been highlighted by the discussion paper of the Government on economic reforms. The paper states that 'if we are to break the age-old bonds of poverty, which continue to afflict many millions of our people', India requires six to seven per cent rate of economic growth. This is the main rationale and goal of economic restructuring launched by the Rao Government. The Left political parties and their trade unions are involved in opposition to the marketisation and globalisation of the Indian economy because they consider it as 'pro-big business' and 'pro-multinational corporations'. Some of the farmer's organisations have also launched struggles against multinational corporations in Karnataka because they apprehend that under the Dunkel Report, the Indian farmers will lose and multinational corporations will gain profits. Even Gandhians have decided to launch a protest march to Kandla on September 30 against the Government decision to allow Cargill, an American multinational corporation, to manufacture and export salt from India. For Gandhians 'Salt Satyagrah' has historical significance and they want to repeat that protest against Cargill multinational corporation.

The above discussion has clearly revealed that in a functioning and active democracy like India, economic restructuring is openly supported and aggres-sively contested and opposed. Hence any comparison between India and China is highly misplaced. Public policy making in India has been always subjected to multiple and contradictory pulls and pressures. Restructuring of

Indian economy has to be gradual and very accommodative of conflicting and competing interests. This is the logic of an 'open' political system of India as opposed to a 'closed' political system of China. The speed of economic reforms in India is determined and decided by the level of political acceptability of the package of reforms. Indian system cannot brush aside completely the viewpoints of the opponents of public policies. Accommodation and compromises are the essence of the political economy of India and China can afford to impose economic policies from above and decide the speed of their implementation because it is an 'authoritarian' political system. Further, working classes are a very important component of Indian society and a democratically elected government cannot be insensitive to their feelings and demands. A mindless or ruthless 'exit policy' in India is simply out of question.

The above analysis clearly reveals that a 'new opportunity' has emerged for the Rao Government because the trade unions and the Left parties have conceded some of the arguments in favour of the new policy, and they have shown apprehensions about the future of the working classes in the process of implementation of liberalised economy. The central question which the trade unions have posed is: Will unemployment in India increase with the advent of sophis-ticated technology by the multinational corporations? Will the employed workers be declared redundant because the employers are getting liberated from the governmental controls? What will be the ratio of public and private sector in the new industrial policy of India? Will the working classes be left to the vagaries of market forces without governmental intervention? Thus, the Rao Government and the apex employers' organisations like the FICCI, Assocham, and CII should enter into an open dialogue with recognised all-India trade unions to resolve problems perceived by the working classes. Poverty and unemployment breeds insecurity which leads to serious social conflicts. The poor and vulnerable strata of society have a genuine fear of free market forces and the poor always look towards the state for protection. It is the role of the Indian state to evolve new package of development for the poor. It was very important that on August 15 Rao announced the extension of Maharashtra Employment Guarantee Scheme to large areas of India to ensure at least 100 days of employment to the poor unemployed rural people. It is a 'new opportunity' for the Rao Government to win over the support of the poor for its economic policies. The success of economic policies in a democracy depends on the support of important social constituencies and the Rao Government has been able to win it against the 'licence-permit raj' which was dominated by an arrogant bureaucracy. It is not only the large industrialists but also the middle-level entrepreneurs in all parts of India that are firm supporters of the dismantling of the regulatory administered economic regime in India. It must be mentioned that the Rajiv Gandhi Government laid down the foundations of economics liberalisation from 1984 to 1989. But it was confined to high technology areas and sunrise industries, especially in telecommunication and sophisticated consumer goods meant for the upper middle-classes. The liberalisation policies of the Rajiv Gandhi Government were supported by a limited social constituency of high technocrats and upper middle-classes. The Rao Government has won social support from millions of small-scale entrepreneurs who are waiting for the death of the 'inspector raj'. This is a great social asset for the Rao Government and in politics every asset has to be converted into 'new opportunities'. The 'licence-permit raj' and the 'inspector raj' were instruments of harassment and they were hated by everyone who wanted to enter trade or industry whether big or medium or small. The liberalisation of the economy has made all of them as the defenders of the new economic policy.

It is essential to understand that the Rao Government's economic policies cannot have smooth sailing on the basis of traders, industrialists and export-earning rich farmers. The organised working classes and the unorganised landless agricultural workers have not accepted the 'market-friendly' philosophy of the liberalisers. This is a great 'challenge' to the new economic policy of the Rao Government. In the third year of economic policy, the Rao Government has gained new social support and 'new opportunities' to accelerate the process of economic reform, at the same time, a powerful 'new challenge' has crystallised against the restructuring of the Indian economy. The 'jail bharo' of August 9, the proposed 'Bharat bandh' of September 9, and the protest march against Cargill multinational corporation of September 30 are clear signals of emerging social conflicts in India on the path of economic development followed by the Rao Government. If the proliferating entrepreneurial classes are willing support-ers of economic restructuring, the organised working classes and the rural poor are directly challenging the economic agenda of the Government. The task before the Government is to reconcile and harmonise the support of the entrepreneurs and the challenge posed by the working classes of India. Since reconciliation is the essence of political economy of a democratic country, the Government should use new social assets and deal with new demands as crystallised by the working classes.

The third year of the economic policy is also facing a clear challenge on the front of globalisation and integration of India with economies of the devel-oped countries. All developed Western countries had clearly welcomed the opening of the Indian economy and their initial response was very positive. The positive response of the western industrialised countries provided 'new oppor-tunities' to India to overcome its foreign exchange crisis of 1991 and the World Bank and IMF extended full support to the Government for the restructuring of the economy.

The initial euphoria over India has been replaced by 'new conditionalities' imposed by the western industrialised countries. Since India does not belong to any trade block, it has to deal bilaterally with advanced western countries and it has to be quite active in global institutions like the GATT, UNCTAD, the

World Bank, IMF, etc. Since India is not affiliated with any trading block, the leaders of world economy take collective decisions and then they impose them on individual countries. The G-7 countries held a three-day summit in Tokyo on July 6 to 9. It is a summit of the most powerful countries like the US, Japan, Germany, France, Italy, the UK and Canada. While the delegate of the European Commu-nity and the Russian President, Boris Yelstin, were heard with great respect by the G-7 summit leaders, President Suharto of Indonesia as the President of the Non-Aligned Movement could not carry any weight with the summit leaders on behalf of third world countries. India has to face serious challenges from the western aid-giving and foreign capital investing countries. Chancellor Helmut Kohl of Germany has sent a firm communication to Narasimha Rao to further liberalise trade, industrial, technology, labour and financial policies if India wishes to attract investment. A powerful delegation of Japan's industrialists visited India to demand an improvement in the investment climate of the country. The US has its own list of demands from India. While liberalisation policies of India in 1991 were welcomed by the western countries, their demands in 1993 are quite clear that the West wants full 'market-oriented' economy in India before making new investments. Thus, the new economic policy is confronted with new challenges which have emerged both within and outside the country. The scenario of political economy in 1993 is quite different from that of 1991 and this demands new responses from the Rao Government.

Foreign Policy

The Narasimha Rao Government inherited a serious balance of payments crisis and foreign policy which was in a shambles because of neglect and incompetence of the Chandrashekhar and the V.P. Singh Governments. After assuming office in June 1991, the Rao Government had to meet the challenges of economic crisis and it had to evolve an appropriate foreign policy for the pursuit of India's national interests.

Atal Bihari Vajpayee, the BJP leader in the Lok Sabha, has accused the Rao Government for not properly defending India's national interests. Vajpayee has alleged that the Rao Government's foreign policy has led to the *'marginalisation'* of India in the Third World and also in the Non-Aligned Movement. Further, Vajpayee has accused the Rao Government for not taking aggressive stand against Pakistan's interventions in the domestic problems of India especially in Kashmir. According to Vajpayee, the Rao Government does not have any Kashmir policy and the Government has not condemned the new stand of the United State's Government on Kashmir. Vajpayee's own vision of Indian foreign policy is based on an image of *India as a world power*. In reality, Vajpayee and the BJP want an aggressive foreign policy for India especially to dominate the neighbours like Pakistan and Bangladesh. The BJP foreign policy is based on an extension of its *Hindutva* ideology, in which the Hindu State of India through its military might and nuclear teeth deal effectively with Muslim neighbouring countries like Pakistan and Bangladesh. The BJP will communalise Indian society and will pursue a foreign policy based on religious considerations. It is pertinent to refer that Atal Bihari Vajpayee was the foreign minister in the Janata Party Government during 1977 and 1979, and he encouraged Moshe Dayan of Israel to visit India in great secrecy. The pro-Israeli and anti-Arab foreign policy of Atal Bihari Vajpayee is based on religious considerations towards Muslim countries of West Aisa. The BJP foreign policy is conditioned by its *Hindutva* philosophy and it is directed against all Muslim countries and it has a very narrow perspective of the national interests of India.

It will not be out of place to mention here that the BJP critique of Narasimha Rao's foreign policy is a continuation of the Jan Sangh/BJP opposition to the foreign policies pursued by Pt. Nehru, Indira Gandhi and Rajiv Gandhi. The Jan Sangh/BJP leadership had never accepted the pillars of Indian foreign policy of Non-Alignment, world peace, disarmament, Anti-Racialism and Anti-Zionism and independent stand of India during the period of Cold War politics of Power Blocs. Pt. Nehru laid down the foundations of a very activist foreign policy for India because he was aware of that the future of India is integrally linked with world developments. An aggressive and militarised India was not the goal of Nehru's foreign policy. Indian foreign policy during Nehru, Indira Gandhi, Rajiv Gandhi and Narasimha Rao has been built on the basis of extension of the areas of peace and reduction or minimisation of armed solutions in international disputes. This is not the perspective of the BJP leadership. Thus, Vajpayee's critique of Rao's, foreign policy is based on a fundamental clash of perspectives on world affairs.

Further, the Rao Government is dealing with a very different world which has emerged after the end of Second Cold War and the collapse of all erstwhile communist countries of Eastern Europe. An inportant pillar of the foreign policy of India was friendship with Soviet Union. The Iraq-Kuwait dispute in which the western countries militarily intervened against Saddam Hussain of Iraq and its impact on world affairs has not been properly appreciated by the critics of Narasimha Rao's foreign policy.

India has to adapt and adjust itself with a really *new world* and the salient features of present day international relations have to be recognised. First, the Power Bloc Cold War has come to an end and India has to redefine some of the contents of its foreign policy of Non-Alignment. Second, the United States has emerged militarily a very powerful country because of the collapse and disintegration of the erstwhile Soviet Union. Third, along with security and defence components of foreign policy, has emerged the significance of economic factors in foreign policy of every country. Economic interests and considerations will determine the agenda of foreign policies of advanced industrialised countries of the West and developing countries of the South. The Rao Government has rightly recognised that economic goals of India have become central factor in deciding on foreign policy issues during the 1990s.

The IMF, the World Bank, the GATT, the United Nations and multilateral and bilateral economic relations of India with developed and developing countries and global institutions become the priority areas of the foreign policy of India. While militarily, the United States may be talking of *uni-polar* world, in terms of economic power, the US, the EEC, the Germans and the Japanese are multiple centres of power and India has to deal with militarily *uni-polar* world on the one hand, and multiple economic giants on the other. The Rao Government has formulated its policy while keeping in mind the qualitative and fundamental changes in post-Cold War global situation.

The end of Cold War and the collapse of erstwhile WARSAW Pact countries have made the global situation extremely complicated for the foreign policy-makers of India because the western countries have asserted that the old concept of *national sovereignity* is not acceptable to them in this new stage of international politics. The Rao Government has to renegotiate and continuously bargain with the western countries because they want India to defend its 'human rights' record especially in Punjab and the Kashmir Valley.

The Rao Government has stood against the Western pressures in important contentious areas like the Nuclear Non-Proliferation Treaty and transfer of missile technology. A very important achievement of Narasimha Rao's foreign policy has been a definite improvement in India-China relations. It may be mentioned that the Jan Sangh was very critical of Pt. Nehru's policy towards China. While China betrayed India in 1962 border war, Rajiv Gandhi and Narasimha Rao have opened new vistas of negotiations and confidence-building with China. Atal Bihari Vajpayee has not extended his full support to the Rao Government on its positive steps towards improving relationships between India and China.

India-Pakistan relationships have deteriorated because Pakistan is involved in low intensity war against India by supporting terrorism in Punjab and Kashmir. While the BJP wants a direct confrontation between India and Pakistan, the Rao Government has followed a sophisticated foreign policy by keeping in mind the changing world situation. Rao has asserted that India and Pakistan should involve themselves in bilateral discussions on Kashmir under the provisions of Simla Agreement. At every international forum, the Government of India has exposed Pakistan's direct involvement in promoting terrorism in India and it has also asserted that Simla Agreement is the framework for bilateral disputes between India and Pakistan. The Rao Government has alerted powerful western countries against Pakistan and it has suggested United States to declare Pakistan as a *terrorist State.* Thus on Kashmir, the Rao Government is neither silent nor aggressive and this is the best strategy to defend and promote national interests of India under the new global situation during the 1990s.

While the BJP wants India to emerge as a military power, the Rao Government has followed a foreign policy of winning over our neighbours. It should not be forgotten that small countries always suspect a large neighbouring country. Except Pakistan, the Rao Government has established friendly relations with all neighbouring countries.

Narasimha Rao has followed an 'activist' foreign policy for promoting national interests of India and this is the continuation of Nehru, Indira Gandhi and Rajiv Gandhi tradition. Vajpayee is wrong in asserting that India has been marginalised in world affairs because of failure of Rao's foreign policy. The fact is that Rao has adjusted and adapted India's foreign policy with fast changing global situation and the emerging challenges of 1990s. It is a fact that India is under great pressure from the United States but the Rao Government has correctly followed the policy of bargaining without surrendering essential national goals on nuclear issues or Kashmir.

It is not only the foreign policy of Rao which is important, he also broke with the inherited Economic Model of Development and laid down the foundation of New Economic Policy of 'deregulation, liberalisation and globalisation'. Narasimha Rao is remembered for his New Economic Policy of 1991.

6

Atal Bihari Vajpayee

The Atal Bihari Vajpayee-led coalition governments of 1989-99 and 1999-2000 have enthusiastically followed and implemented 'economic policies' of globalisation, liberalisation and privatisation. The Jana Sangh was always opposed to the policies of economic planning followed by the Nehru-Indira governments which were characterised as 'licence-permit Raj' by the RSS Brotherhood. Economic policies followed by the Vajpayee government are a continuation of IMF-World Bank consensus on India. The global aid-givers have maintained that economic development is obstructed by an interventionist and regulatory State and economic growth can take place, if market is allowed to play its natural role and the State is rolled-back. The Vajpayee government is actively pursuing policies for the opening of economy to foreign private investors in industrial, financial, insurance and trading sectors of the economy. The Vajpayee government has made many new laws which are required to attract foreign investors, especially in the field of insurance and industrial and consumer sectors of the economy. The Vajpayee government is implementing every commitment which it has made with the World Trade Organisation. Yashwant Sinha, the Finance Minister of the Vajpayee government, is focussed on containing fiscal deficit of the Indian government by either cutting some 'subsidies' or by mobilising financial resources by undertaking disinvestment of public sector undertakings. The BJP and Swadeshi Jagran Manch of the Sangh Brotherhood were critical of the economic policies followed by the Congress party under the leadership of P.V. Narasimha Rao during 1991-1996. The BJP, in opposition, critised economic policies, which it has been aggressively implementing while it is in power at the Centre. The Vajpayee government has constituted a very high power 'Economic Advisory Committee', in which members of the political class and leaders of Indian capitalist classes sit together and evolve policies for the capitalist development of India in the age of New Global Capitalism. A real and significant development in the phase of BJP-in-power in the Central Government is the complete integration of the Indian State and the Indian capitalist classes within the country and externally the Indian State is integrating itself with world monopoly capitalism. The Indian capitalist class is now sitting within the Indian State apparatus and it is actively involved in decision-making institutions of the State. The Vajpayee government's path of development was elaborated in the President, K.R. Narayanan's address to the joint sitting of the two Houses of Parliament on October 25, 1999. The President observed:

"Experience, both domestic and international, suggests that rapid and multi-sector growth is possible only by pursuing a bold strategy of economic reforms. The nation's re-oriented strategy of development will have to rest on a *triad,* in which the government provides a strong policy and regulatory leadership, the private sector brings the dynamism and efficiency of the competitive environment, and, local democratic institutions and the civil society brings enthusiastic participation by the people". What is the reality of this rhetoric?

Table 6.1: Foreign Direct Investment in India

Year	*FD Approval*	*Actual Inflows*	*Realisation Rate*
1991	534	351	65.73
1992	3888	675	17.36
1993	8859	1787	20.17
1994	14187	3289	23.18
1995	32072	6820	21.26
1996	36147	10389	28.74
1997	54891	16425	29.92
1998	30814	13340	43.29
1999	28367	16868	59.46

The actual flow of foreign direct investment in India does not match with the enthusiasm of the Vajpayee government. India is not a great destination for foreign investors in spite of the fact that in February 2000, the Vajpayee government placed about all items "under the automatic approval route for FDI and NRI/OCB investment". It was claimed that the Vajpayee governments' new thrust on liberalisation was "aimed towards increasing the present inflow of FDI to an annual figure of $10 billion, which would imply a jump of nearly two and half times from $4.02 billion in January/December 1999". These hopes of the Vajpayee government have not been fulfilled. On the contrary, the policy of liberalisation has distorted economic development of the country because every decision of the government is guided by the need of 250 million middle and upper middle class consumers of India. S. Balakrishnan in his *"FDI or Fast Depleting Independence"*?[1] draws attention to the socially disastrous consequences of economic policies pursued by the Vajpayee government. He observes:

> "A glaring and tragic example comes to mind immediately. The roads are narrow, badly laid and ill-lit", the traffic, as it is, is chaotic and ill-disciplined and the spiralling bill for import of crude eats up a sizable part of our foreign exchange earnings. Yet models after models of new cars, of various sizes and powers, with vaunted new features and accessories, with different price tags, from well-known foreign stables, are hitting the roads everyday." The worst part of the 'opening of economy' to the foreign investors is that India has not gained in getting new technologies from foreign investors. The most telling example of India's failure to get any technological benefits from foreign investors is our Maruti Udyog, where government of India is a partner. Suzuki has neither 'shared with India its steering road technology' nor it has permitted export of Maruti cars with Suzuki identification."

The Ninth Five-Year Plan document of April 1997 was launched on the premise of growth with social justice and equity'. The only beneficiary of social justice oriented governments of H.D. Deve Gowda, Inder Kumar Gujral and Atal Bihari Vajpayee have been government employees, on whom the Central Government spent Rs. 18,000 crore and the State Governments had to spend Rs. 35,266 crore because the Fifth Pay Commission had recommended pay revisions and the governments implemented these recommendations. In the name of 'national security' the Vajpayee government has increased defence expenditure to more than additional Rs. 23,000 crore in the budget of 2000-2001. The 'holy cows' of India, i.e., the political class, the bureaucracy and defence sector are the main culprits for the rising fiscal deficit of the country and this is precisely the social constituency of the forces of Hindutva. The forces of Hindutva are operating the Indian economy for industrial capitalist classes, business classes, middle class professionals, bureaucrats, entrepreneurs and middle and upper middle class urban and rural populations of India. The BJP does not have any economic programme either for rural development or for the generation of employment in a labour-surplus economy. Since the social base of Hindutva is very narrow, it is operating the economy in the interests of its narrow class base. This is the crisis of India. With hardly 20 million income tax payers, the fiscal crisis of the Indian State is the product of social arrangements of a capitalist-landlord controlled society. The appropriators of social surplus with the full support and protection of the Indian State are not ready to share their wealth with the real producers in society. The working classes of India have become victims of increasing income disparities in the phase of liberalisation of Indian economy and the BJP does not have any economic programme for the working classes of India. The BJP at the Centre has followed economic policies, which clearly reflect its class character which primarily lies in traders, merchants, upper and middle class professionals and self-employed rent-seekers. This is the essence of its economic policies. It has no answers for the problems of either the rural or the urban poor and unemployed youth of India.

Foreign and Defence Policies

Jana Sangh/BJP have always advocated a very tough foreign policy against Pakistan and China on the basis of a premise that Pakistan as a Muslim country can never be positive towards a Hindu majority India and China as a communist country is a rival of India in the Asian continent. Anti-Muslim and anti-Communist ideology of the Sangh Brotherhood is fundamental principle of their foreign policy. The Jana Sangh leadership had always opposed India's foreign policy of Non-alignment because they alleged that Indian policy was tilted in favour of Soviet Russia and Atal Bihari Vajpayee as Minister of External Affairs in the Morarji Desai government proclaimed that India would pursue a policy of'genuine non-alignment' without any tilt in favour of any power bloc, western or eastern communist countries. Since Russian system has collapsed and global power equations have changed, anti-Communist foreign policy orientations of the Sangh Brotherhood are now focussed against China. The Jana Sangh/BJP has been consistent supporters of Israel in India because Israel was fighting against the Arab countries and anti-Islamic Sangh Brotherhood viewed Israel as a natural friend of their anti-Muslim ideological and political plank.

Further, the Sangh Brotherhood has always supported the idea of militarily strong Hindu India and a nuclearised India has been always on the agenda of the forces of Hindutva. A militarised and nuclearised India has been the ideal of Indian nationhood among the believers of the RSS and its multiple affiliates. The BJP got an opportunity to follow an anti-Pakistan and anti-China foreign policy and an aggressive military based defence policy, when it came to power at the Centre in 1998. The BJP celebrated as a day of great national achievement, when nuclear device was exploded on May 11, 1998 at Pokharan. The Vajpayee government proclaimed from the house top that India has become a 'Nuclear Power State'. In a confidential letter written by the Vajpayee government to President Clinton of the United States, it was mentioned that India exploded nuclear device because its security was threatened by Pakistan and China. Since the United States' administration decided to leak the contents of the government of India's letter, Indians came to know that BJP's defence and foreign policies were directed against China and Pakistan. Indian jubilations came to an end when at the end of May 1998, Pakistan followed suit and exploded its nuclear device. The United States, European Union and Japan disapproved this action of the Vajpayee government and all of them imposed 'economic sanctions' against nuclearised India. The Government of India in post-Pokharan phase became active in convincing the powerful western countries about its security threat perceptions and the five nuclear power states demanded that India should sign Comprehensive Test Ban Treaty before economic sanctions imposed on India could be withdrawn. The BJP-led coalition government was unable to accept the demand of nuclear power states for signing the Comprehensive Test Ban Treaty because many opposition parties in India did not support the idea of the signing of the CTBT. In the absence of political consensus in India, the Vajpayee government could not have signed the CTBT and the United States would not remove economic sanctions against nuclearised India without it, putting its signatures on the CTBT.

The worst aspect of nuclear explosion was that India announced that Pakistan and China were threats to our security and Pakistan equalised with India by exploding its nuclear device and India's diplomatic relations with China became a serious bone of contention between the two neighbouring countries. Since the United States had declared nuclear South Asia as the 'most dangerous region in the world', the Government of India was under immense global pressure to mend its fences with Pakistan. Since the economic sanctions were like a sword of democles hanging over the head of Indian government, Atal Bihari Vajpayee undertook a visit to Pakistan on February 20, 1999, which is known as Bus Journey to Lahore. It was expected that India and Pakistan would start moving towards peaceful co-existence after the meeting at Lahore between Atal Bihari Vajpayee and Nawaz Sharif. On the contrary, a war broke out at Kargil in Kashmir in May 1999. Under pressure from the government of United States, Pakistan ended its Kargil misadventure and relationship between India and Pakistan was completely frozen. The so-called victory of India in Kargil war became an issue during the Lok Sabha elections of September-October 1999 and BJP asked the voters : "The leader you can trust in War: In Peace-Proven experience or proven inexperience"? Hindutva survives and thrives on anti-Muslim and anti-Pakistan sentiment and Pakistan's misadventure in Kargil gave a great handle to the BJP campaigners during the elections, who successfully projected India's victory in Kargil as an accomplishment of the leadership of Atal Bihari Vajpayee.

Pokharan II, victory in Kargil, shooting down of Pakistan's aircraft Atlantique by the Indian forces at Rann of Kutch on August 22, 1999 were highlighted by the BJP during the election campaign for the Thirteenth Lok Sabha elections. The National Democratic Alliance Manifesto of August 29, 1999 gave a slogan that 'India shall be built by Indians' and on national security, it observed that "The 13 month long Vajpayee government had brought about a paradigm shift in national security,....The NDA promises to allocate adequate funds to "correct the imbalance and budgetary neglect of Defence needs".[2] The B JP-led coalition government congratulated itself on a very successful five days visit of President Bill Clinton of the United States to India from March 20 to 25,2000 A.D. The government of India has proclaimed that "a new page has turned in the US-Indian relationships after the visit of President Bill Clinton." While the Government of India has publicly stated that its foreign policy is operated in the frame-work of a 'multi-polar world' and not a 'unipolar' world dominated by the United States, in reality, the BJP-led government is enthusiastically pursuing a pro-United States foreign policy. The Ministers of the Government of India like Pramod Mahajan of Information Technology or Yashwant Sinha of Finance and others are leading delegations of government officials and business and industrial groups to the United States for securing economic and trade benefits from that country. A news item in the *Economic Times "CII in pursuit of free trade pact with US'* mentioned that in the first week of June 2000, a selected group of Indian industrialists, including Arun Bharat Ram, Narayanan Murthy, Ajay Piramal, K.V. Kamath, Jamshed Godrej and Tarun Das will visit San Francisco and Washington to look at ways to enhance business links. "Heading the road show will be finance minister Yashwant Sinha and PMO secretary N.K. Singh".[3]

Tarun Das, a member of the delegation, observed that the "Lobbying will intensify during their interactions with select Congressmen and senators led by Jim McDermott of the Indian caucus". The ruling classes of India and political class led by the BJP-National Democratic Alliance is making every effort to strongly link India with the United States for the building of Indian economy and national security. On the advice of the United States, the Vajpayee-led government has opened a dialogue with Hurriyat leaders in Jammu & Kashmir. On the one hand, the Sangh Brotherhood is opposed to the economic policies of globalisation, on the other, social classes supporting the BJP and RSS affiliates are working for close alliance with the United States, which is the leader of world capitalism. This is the class reality of BJP and its pro-United States foreign policy is in accord with class interests of its social constituency. This reality was expressed in the *Organiser* of April 30,2000: "A new globally minded yet spiritually based Hindu intelligentsia is the need of the hour to deal with the challenges from the west. One of the great debacles of modern India is that the Marxists captured the intellectual elite of the country and turned them into mouth piece of anti-Hindu attitudes".[4]

To sum up, pillars of India's foreign policy under Atal Bihari Vajpayee are anti-Pakistan and anti-China and pro-United states. Defence buildup for the security of India has been always a policy plank of the forces of Hindutva because they equate a highly militarised and nuclearised India as a real strong point of the Hindu Rashtra. The grandeur of greatness of the Hindu is the mind-set of the Sangh Brotherhood and in this perspective, Hindu state has to be a formidable military power. On the occasion of 'anniversary' of Pokharan II, George Fernandes in a meeting of the National Democratic Alliance observed that "India is strong because of Operation Shakti thanks due to Vajpayee's leadership."[5]

Not to be left behind, Vajpayee observed that: "Our rivals did not hope that India would emerge a global power. But today we have done it. The world has undisputedly accepted India as a global player. Today we are successfully challenging the world in trade, science and technology as well as other fields. There is no doubt, we would come out victorious. The country is transforming into a global power, as there is a definite policy which had made our enemies envious."[6] The *Organiser* paints Pakistan as real villain of the piece and warns Hindus that it is 'Hindu cowardice', which has been responsible for our humiliations at the hand of others and a patriotic Hindu should be ready to fight an 'epic war' as demanded by K.S. Sudarshan of the RSS. The hate campaign against Muslim Pakistan is a staple diet for the Sangh Brotherhood. "There is no system in Pakistan for the news to appear freely. Doordarshan shows music, dance and glamour. Pakistan cannot, owing to the religious construction", proclaims *Organiser.*[7] It is not surprising that after Kargil war of May-July of 1999, the Government of India has stopped any negotiations or dialogue with the Government of Pakistan on the plea that General Parvez Musharraf should first ask the so-called *Jihadis* to stop cross-border terrorism and only then talks between India and Pakistan can be resumed. Many a time in the past, the Government of India had held serious talks after military misadventures by Pakistan. The BJP has a new 'foreign policy doctrine' towards Pakistan and the result is a complete breakdown of any foreign policy dialogue between the two quarrelsome neighbouring countries.

Domestic Governance for Hindutva

The BJP has vigorously pursued its own agenda while leading the coalition governments at the Centre from 1998-99 and 1999-2000. Atal Bihari Vajpayee, while campaigning during the Lok Sabha elections of 1998, proposed a 'Presidential System' instead of the chronic 'instability of parliamentary democracy'. The BJP in the Lok Sabha elections of 1999 made a proposal for the 'Review of Constitution of India' in the Manifesto of National Democratic Alliance, and the Government of India has given top priority to this programme of the NDA by setting up a Constitution Review Commission.

It must be stated here that the RSS had never agreed with the democratic, republican, federal and secular Constitution of India of 1950. The believers of Hindutva had not accepted any of the basic premises of the Indian Constitution. Hensen states that:

> "Political power understood as sovereignty and national strength was, nonetheless, always crucial to Golwalkar's vision of a Hindu nation. In the 1950s, Golwalkar advocated a strong 'Unitary State' and opposed the reorganisation of the Indian states into linguistic units, which he believed would weaken the cohesion of Hindu society and set in motion centrifugal forces. Instead, the country should move toward 'One Country, one State, one Legislature and one Executive' in order to strengthen itself and be able to counter foreign aggression."[8]

The RSS Hindu 'joint family' had always opposed the essential principle of pluralism as enshrined in the Indian Constitution by propagating the ideology of "One people, one culture, one nation". Atal Bihari Vajpayee, L.K. Advani and every important decision-maker of the BJP is firmly committed to the Unitarian doctrine for the governance of Hindu India, as propagated by Guru Golwalkar and this is the reason that the Vajpayee government has appointed an eleven member Constitution Review Commission in 2000. The ultimate source of truth for every member of the Sangh fraternity is Sar Sanghchalak of the RSS and K.S. Sudarshan while taking over the office of Sar Sanghchalak in 2000 from Rajendra Singh observed that:

> "The post of Sar Sanghchalak is like the legendary throne of Vikarmaditya. Whosoever sits on it, is bound to do justice to the cause".[9]

Atal Bihari Vajpayee, L.K. Advani, Murli Manohar Joshi and every important leader of the BJP was trained by Guru Golwalkar and everyone of them is pursuing the goals of Hindu Rashtra as laid down by Golwalkar and successive Sar Sanghchalaks whose authority over the Sangh 'family' is complete. The RSS demands obedience from its members; otherwise, even Balraj Madhok, President of the BJP, was shown the door for differing with the dominant view point of the RSS leadership. The agenda for Constitution Review of the Vajpayee government is in reality the agenda of RSS as laid down by Sar Sanghchalak M.S. Golwalkar and the target of Review of the Constitution is Chapter III of Fundamental Rights of citizens, which guarantees cultural rights to multiple and diverse communities of India. On the eve of Golden Jubilee celebrations of the Republic of India in the Central Hall of Parliament, on January 27,2000 Atal Bihari Vajpayee observed :

> "Our constitution has served the needs of both India's diversity and her innate unity. It has strengthened India's democratic traditions.
>
> "But even in the mightiest fort one has to repair the parapet from time to time, one has to clean the moat and check the banisters. The same is true about our Constitution.
>
> "Five decades after the adoption of the Constitution, India is faced with a new situation. The need for stability both at the centre and in the states has been felt acutely".

This rhetoric of Vajpayee could not conceal the truth because in the name of achieving the so-called political stability, an attempt may be made by 'nominated' members of the Constitution Review Commission to give a seal of approval to the Unitarian and centralised system of governance for India, as desired by the RSS leadership from the times of Sar Sanghchalak M.S. Golwalkar.

K.R. Narayanan, the President of India, in the Central Hall of Parliament on January 27, 2000 observed that:

> "Our recent experience of instability in government is perhaps not sufficient reason to discard the parliamentary system in favour of presidential or any other system."

President Narayanan expressed the viewpoint which was reflected in the philosophy of our Constitution Fathers that India is a unique mosaic of 4,635 communities and 325 languages written in 24 scripts. India is a country of diversities without any parallel and this pluralist democracy with secular and federal system of governance can keep the country together and any attempt to impose Hindu hegemony in India will destroy the unity of the country.

The eleven member Constitution Review Committee 'nominated' by the Vajpayee government consists of Justice M.N. Venkatachaliah as Chairman, and its other members are Justice R.S. Sarkaria, Attorney General Soli Sorabjee, former Attorney General K. Parasaran, former High Court Judge K. Punniah, Journalist C.R. Irani, former diplomat Abid Hussain, former Lok Sabha Secretary General, Subhash Kashyap, former BJP MP Sumitra Kulkarni, former Speaker of the Lok Sabha PA. Sangma, and Justice B.P. Jeevan Reddy. This Constitution Review Commission is handpicked by the Vajpayee government and it is a mixture of former members who have been active in public services and politicians fully acceptable to the BJP including a former BJP MP. This Commission does not have any legitimacy because 'nominees' of the government cannot be accepted as legitimate instrument for the Review of the Constitution, which is a fundamental basic law of the country. In its first meeting on March 23, 2000, 11-member nominated Constitution Review Commission decided the items for scrutiny and they were listed as follows :

(a) Menace of defections;
(b) Constitutional provisions on removal of poverty;
(c) Working of Article 356;
(d) Appointment and removal of governors;
(e) Decentralisation of powers and strengthening of Panchayati Raj;
(f) Enlargement of fundamental Rights,
(g) Effective enforcement of directive principles/fundamental duties; and
(h) Provisions relating to fiscal and monetary policies.

It may be mentioned here that none of the above listed topic for the Review of Constitution deserves a new National Commission because during the last fifty years many Commissions have gone into the working of many aspects of our Constitution and an elected Parliament of India has many a time amended the Constitution and made suitable changes on the basis of democratic principle of legislative debate on the nature of change in the Constitution of India. The spokesman of the Review Commission Justice B.P. Jeevan Reddy has maintained that they "would only review the working of the constitution and not rewrite it completely". It deserves to be mentioned that review of the working of the constitution has been an ongoing process during the last fifty years and there is absolutely no role for a Commission appointed by the Vajpayee government unless its task is to redefine the Constitution for a ' *Unitary Hindu India*", as desired by the RSS founding fathers. The BJP published a 44 page brochure on 'Constitutional Study and Review', in which it maintained that the Constitution has been frequently amended and nothing new is being done by appointing a Constitution Review Commission and "nobody can doubt that the composition of the review panel is broad-based and totally a political and non-partisan in character. It is headed by Justice Venkatachaliah, a former Chief Justice of the Supreme Court and a highly respected authority on legal and constitutional matters."

The ruling classes and political parties are concerned about the growing political instability in India. The Constitution of India is neither responsible for fragmentation of politics nor it can offer any remedies.

The fault does not lie with the Constitution of India. Adolf I Hitler blamed the Weimer Republican Constitution for all the ills and crises of Germany and after burning the Reichstag in February 1933, he forgot about the Constitution and established a fascist government. Hitler had delegitimised the Constitution of Germany by making the people believe that it was the sole source of Germany's crisis and once people had lost their trust on the Republican Constitution, Hitler did not face any difficulty in subverting it. This is the lesson of History. Indian Constitution has been amended on the basis of proper procedures laid down in the Constitution itself and the Vajpayee government is going beyond these constitutionally laid down procedures for demanding its review. Electoral reforms can be undertaken by amending the Constitution on the basis of political consensus. The crucial distinction is between review of Constitution by 'nominees' of the government of India or amendments of the Constitution, as they have happened in the past on the basis of procedures laid down by the Constitution itself. The Sangh fraternity wants to generate a controversy on the viability and suitability and mutability of the Republican Constitution of India for governance of the country on the basis of a report by its nominated 11-member Commission. The so-called inadequacies of the Constitution will become a very contentious issue in India because the Sangh 'joint family' somehow wants to stabilise itself in power by pushing a Review of the Constitution. After all, Atal Bihari Vajpayee has highlighted the issue of political instability and the Review Commission will have to suggest mechanisms so that the BJP-led coalition can remain in power for five years. The Sangh joint family has shown its contempt for democracy by not going to Parliament for any discussion on the Review of Constitution and this has brought the cat out of the bag because the agenda of Hindu Rashtra cannot succeed on the basis of Parliamentary approval in India.

Minority Communities

While the BJP obtained less than 25 per cent of votes during the Lok Sabha elections of 1998 and 1999, the minorities of India have kept themselves away from the BJP. It is for the first time in the history of democratic India that a Prime Minister does not enjoy the confidence of Muslim and Christian communities. Minorities are not feeling safe in India because the BJP-led Central Government and Uttar Pradesh, Gujarat State Governments of the BJP and Odisha coalition government of BJP and Biju Janata Dal have failed to protect the rights and interests of the minorities. The Sangh 'joint family', especially its affiliates like the Vishwa Hindu Parishad and Bajrang Dal have targeted Christian missionaries on the basis of an allegation that these missionaries are actively involved in 'conversion' of poor Hindus, especially Dalits and tribals into Christianity. The Sangh functionaries have spread a 'hate campaign' against Churches and schools maintained by Christian missionaries as a part of their Hindu agenda and a protective umbrella provided by the BJP governments has encouraged the Hindu lumpen organisations to target the Christian minority. A few facts may be mentioned to substantiate the argument that the BJP governments have made minorities feel insecure and unsafe in the country.

Visit by Pope: The Akhil Bharatiya Pratinidhi Sabha of the RSS passed resolutions on the visit of Pope, cow protection, cultural invasion from West, etc. In a resolution on the visit by Pope, it observed that:

> "The ABPS appeals to all Vedic, Jain, Buddhist, Sikh and all other Hindu religious organisations to reach the poor and illiterate people, especially those living in tribal belts and slums, educate them about the 'Church-sponsored conspiracy of evangelism...".[10]

When Pope John Paul II visited India from November 5 to 7, 1999, the Sangh functionaries became very active in propagating that the visit of Pope was linked with the conversion activities of Christian missionaries in India. With the expansion in the strength of Sangh family in the 1990s, the agenda against all institutions of civil society of Christians has become the object of hostile targeting by its functionaries and other affiliates of the Sangh. Educational institutions, Churches and hospitals maintained and managed by the Christian community have been attacked by the workers of Sangh 'joint family' and these institutions of civil society of Christian community have been labelled as the centres for religious conversion. The Sangh leadership has appealed to the Triumala Tirupati Devasthanan that it should use some amount from its annual income of Rs. 400 crore for Hindu uplift, as is done by the Church for welfare of the Hindus. Hindus have to be protected from religious conversion activity undertaken by the church, and Atal Bihari Vajpayee, as Prime Minister of India, has asked for a 'national debate' on the issue of religious conversion indulged in by Christian churches. Since the BJP is in the Government in the Centre and in some States of India, Sangh functionaries and its affiliates feel fully protected while campaigning against Christian minorities and their institutions. The BJP government in Gujarat and the BJP-BJD coalition government in Odisha have not been able to control the hate atmosphere created by the Sangh fraternity against Christian minority and its institutions because Chief Ministers and Ministers of the BJP governments themselves believe that Christian church in India is a great threat to Hinduism because it is successful in converting a section of Hindus into Christianity. Further, the Sangh affiliates have launched a campaign that churches in India are funded from foreign countries for undertaking activities leading to religious conversions. Acharya Giriraj Kishore, senior Vice-President of Vishwa Hindu Parishad observed that "..., the foreign missionaries have brought funds to the tune of Rs. 50,000 crore in the North-East for conversion purpose".[11]

The Sangh Parivar has launched a big campaign against Christian community and its institutions who have been described as 'conspirators' against Hinduism in India and they have been emboldened in undertaking their activity of targeting the Christian institutions because BJP is in the government and the Prime Minister himself desires that the issue of religious conversions indulged in by Church deserves a public discussion. The Sangh 'joint family' has indulged in violence against some members of the Christian community after accusing them of indulging in conversion of tribals in Odisha, Gujarat and North-East India. The Sangh functionaries could take law into their hands because they felt protected by the presence of BJP in the government.

While the Sangh 'joint family' is targeting Christian missionaries for indulging in religious conversions, the 'reconversion' from Christianity to Hinduism is publicly acclaimed and celebrated. In a 'reconversion' ceremony in Odisha on June 18, 2000, the VHP described "...the reconversion as a home coming for the family and added that several families have shown interest to return to Hinduism."[12]

Who has given this license to Hindu organisations to convert Christians into Hinduism ? If the activity of reconversion' of religion is undertaken openly, conversion to another religion should also be considered a legitimate right of any individual citizen of India. Hindu organisations cannot appropriate a right for themselves and level allegations against others on issues concerning religious conversion and reconversion. Since the Sangh 'joint family' has launched a campaign against Indian Christians and their institutions, the All-India Christian Council has catalogued "300-odd incidents of violence against Christians and churches in India in the last two years...". Not only this... In 1998, 400 copies of the Bible were burnt in Rajkot and three dozen churches were burnt in the Dangs. Christian preachers have become target of Sangh functionaries and a kind of All-India anti-Christian movement has emerged during the last two years. The All India Christian Council observed that: "The ominous mass violence is meant to terrorise the Christian community, to stop people coming to Churches, to frighten away students from our schools and the ill, the weak and the marginalised from our outreach programmes."[13]

While the *Organiser* of June 18, 2000 quotes D.B. Thengadi on its front page in bold letters that *'Conversion is anti-national;'* L.K. Advani, the Home Minister of India, has a readymade reply that the Inter-Services Intelligence Agencies of Pakistan are involved in the current anti-Christian activities and he does not see anything wrong with the climate of hatred created by the Sangh 'joint family'. Advani is busy in arming himself with new draconian 'laws' and 'new techniques', which he has learnt from the Israelis, to contain the ISI activities in India but who will contain his own 'Sangh fraternity', from attacking and targeting the minorities.

The BJP has risen to power because of its involvement in Ram Janmabhoomi Movement by targeting the Muslim community, which was made responsible for the construction of a Babri Mosque over Ram Temple by Mughal Emperor Babar. L.K. Advani's Hindu Symbolism of Rath Yatra from Somnath to Ayodhya was a clarion call to Hindus to defend their religion and places of worship from Muslims. When the Sangh Hindu 'joint family' destroyed the Babri Mosque on December 6, 1992, a message was given to the Muslims of India that Hindu Rashtra has avenged its humiliation inflicted by Muslim rulers. The BJP government in Uttar Pradesh had a legal responsibility to defend the Babri Mosque and for its failure to perform its constitutional responsibility, the President of India dismissed the State government under Article 356 of the Constitution of India. The election results of U.P. State Assembly in 1993 surprised the BJP because it had obtained an absolute majority in the elections of 1991 and it could obtain only 175 seats out of 425 in the post-Babri Mosque demolition elections of 1993. The real message of BJP-in-government is that it will not uphold the law of the land in any situation which concerns Muslim minority. Every hero of the VHP connected with Ram Janmabhoomi Movement, like Uma Bharati, Jaibhan Singh Pahwaiya, Vinay Katiyar, Yogi Adityanath, Swami Chinmayanand and others are members of Parliament of India. The believers of Hindu Rashtra are now legislators and Ministers, Chief Ministers, MPs and MLAs, and under their benign protection sometimes Christians are targeted and some other times Muslims are made victims. The Uttar Pradesh BJP government has a new law to regulate 'places of religious worship' and a plea has been made to regulate the construction of religious places because mosques of Muslims have become places of refuge of anti-national agents of Inter-Services Intelligence of Pakistan. The Home Minister of India, L.K. Advani, himself alerts the country every day that the ISI agents are very active in India and the needle of suspicion naturally is against Muslims of India. While participating in the Debate on demand for Grants of the Home Ministry, Advani, said that "Pakistan which suffered humiliating defeat in 1971 had called for a *Jihad against* India and now 'Indian Muslims' should reply to this call".[14] Advani represents a mindset of every member of the Sangh Parivar, which believes that Hindu is separate from Muslims and Muslims of India are expected to *'Reply to Pakistan'*. If a Home Minister of India expects a special role by Muslims as Muslims while dealing with Pakistan, and the U.P. government wants to supervise the construction of every mosque by Muslims, the message and meanings are very clear that under the BJP government Hindus and Muslims and Christians are separate categories on the basis of which BJP governments would treat them either by showing preferences or discriminations.

Neena Vyas in *'Now, a party with difference'* catalogues some important minority community linked events during the 24 party BJP-led government at the Centre.

(a) October-December 1998—Attacks on more than a dozen Churches in the Dangs area of Gujarat. Advani warns against growing attacks on Christian minority;
(b) January 1999—Prime Minister tours the Dangs and gives a call for a national debate on conversions;
(c) January 23, 1999—Missionary Graham Staines and his two young sons are burnt alive in Odisha, allegedly by Dara Singh, a Hindu fanatic;
(d) Attacks on nuns, Christian schools and churches continue through 1999. February 13, 2000—Nityanand Swami, Chairman of the U.P. Legislative Council, warns of a 'check' on 'Convent Schools'.
(e) February 13,2000—Tirade against the visit of the Pope by the VHP and the Organiser.
(f) April 22, 2000—A Gospel team from Hyderabad attacked in Agra.[15]

The above catalogue of incidents clearly establishes that an anti-minority atmosphere has been created during the BJP-led government in India.

Special Patronage for Hindus

BJP-in-government has been engaged in making every government or quasi-government or autonomous cultural organisation of India, like the Indian Council of Social Science, Indian Council of Historical Research, National Book Trust, Sahitya Academies or Indira Gandhi National Centre for Arts as instruments for the promotion of the ideas of Hindu Rashtra as defined by the Rashtriya Swayamsevak Sangh and its affiliates. Further, Brajesh Mishra, of the Prime Ministers Office plays an influential behind-the-scene role for promoting the bureaucrats who have Hindu belief systems or links with the RSS. Keshubhai Patel, the Chief Minister of Gujarat, not only openly attends public functions of the RSS, but also wanted that membership of the RSS should not be a disqualification for public servants. Since the RSS is the fountain source of doctrinaire Hindutva, its members entering the public services will definitely convert the Indian State apparatus as *Hindu State.* Many political parties opposed the idea of BJP state government of Gujarat to allow RSS membership into the public services and because of very stiff opposition of political parties, the state government of Gujarat withdrew its notification for permitting the RSS members to enter the public services. If on the one hand, the Uttar Pradesh state government of BJP wants to enact a law for the Regulation of Public Religious buildings and places of worship especially of the Muslim community, on the other, Hindu places of worship are getting special attention of the government of Hindutva. Since Odisha suffered huge losses because of super-cyclone, the government decided to increase its annual grant to the Lord Jagannath Temple of Puri from Rs. 6.38 crore to Rs. 6.94 crore for the year 2000. *The Hindustan Times* of May 3, 2000 in a news report mentioned that Urban Development Minister, Jagmohan has evolved 'a grand multi-crore project for the development of a residential pilgrim centre near the Laxmi Narayan temple, popularly known as Birla Temple of Delhi". Jagmohan, the Urban Development Minister has been willing to always provide facilities to Hindu pilgrims whether in Vaishno Devi or Delhi from the public exchequer of the Indian State. If on the one hand, the BJP government has frequently announced special financial grants for facilities for Hindu pilgrims attending religious functions, like Kumbh Mela, on the other "Bajrang Dal of the Hindu fraternity attacked Christians in Ahmedabad on May 6, 2000, who were distributing copies of the Bible and other evangelical literature".[16]

The above narration of a few significant events and developments of the last three years of the BJP government at the Centre clearly points out to the emergence of a new tendency in India, where the Indian State is openly tilted in favour of Hindus and it has shown biases and discriminations against minority communities. The BJP governments of Atal Bihari Vajpayee or Ram Prakash Gupta of Uttar Pradesh or Keshubhai Patel of Gujarat are behaving in a partisan manner for the promotion of the concept of Hindu Rashtra, and under BJP governments minorities of India are feeling insecure.

The Vajpayee-led coalition government at the centre has aggressively pursued agenda of the Sangh Parivar both, in domestic and foreign policies. A nuclearised India which can confront hostile Pakistan and China has always been the goal of Sangh 'joint family'. Dr. S.P. Mookerjee of the Jana Sangh had contested against Jawaharlal Nehru's Kashmir policy in the 1950s. Pokharan II, victory of India in Kargil over Pakistan and the strengthening of defences of India have been claimed as great achievements of Vajpayee-led coalition government and Sangh 'joint family' is celebrating the emergence of strong Hindu Rashtra under the BJP leadership. Within the country, Hindus have received special attention by the BJP government and minorities have been shown their place by the Sangh functionaries. Guru Golwalkar had always opposed the Republican Constitution of India, and the Vajpayee government has fulfilled the desire of Sar Sanghchalak by appointing a Constitutional Review Commission. Guru Golwalkar did not believe in the states' reorganisation of India on linguistic basis in the 1950s; the Vajpayee government has begun the exercise of redrawing the boundaries of the Indian states and Bills for the creation of Uttarakhand, Chhattisgarh and Jharkhand are ready to be introduced in the Lok Sabha during 2000. L.K. Advani, Home Minister of India, made a public statement on May 14, 2000 that "the Ayodhya movement retains its relevance in the current political context in terms of its ability to curb caste-driven politics". An integrated and homogenised Hindusim remains the goal of Sangh family and movements for the liberation of Ayodhya or Kashi or Mathura continue to be an integral part of the forces of Hindutva whether within the government or outside the government. This is the essential reality of BJP-in-government. It is for the first time that a Central Government is pursuing policies, which are directed towards the promotion and strengthening of Hindu Rashtra in India.

Explanations for the Growth of BJP in the 1990s

The BJP has witnessed a phenomenal growth during the decade of 1990s. It succeeded in obtaining 89 Lok Sabha seats in the Ninth Lok Sabha elections of 1989,119 seats in the Tenth Lok Sabha elections of 1991,160 seats in the Eleventh Lok Sabha elections of 1996 and 180 seats in the Twelfth Lok Sabha elections of 1998 and repeated the same performance in the Thirteenth Lok Sabha elections of 1999. Further, the party has increased its share of national votes; it peaked in 1998 Lok Sabha elections, when it secured 25 per cent of the national votes and in 1999, 23.4 per cent of the voters opted in favour of the BJP during the Lok Sabha elections.

The BJP formed three coalition governments at the Centre—in 1996 for thirteen days, in 1998 for thirteen months and the BJP-led National Democratic Alliance is continuing in power under the leadership of Atal Bihari Vajpayee. The BJP MPs represent every state of North and Northwestern India, Karnataka and Andhra Pradesh in the South, and even in Assam the party obtained one Lok Sabha seat in 1998 and 2 Lok Sabha seats in the 1999 elections.

It is important to explain the growth of the BJP in the 1990s because in the first Lok Sabha elections of 1952, it obtained only three seats and it was a very marginal player in Indian politics. It seems paradoxical that the party of Hindutva could not get the support of Hindu voters even when the post-Partition Hindu-Muslim divide was quite deep because of post-Partition tragedy of Hindu-Muslim migrations. It looks quite paradoxical that Hindutva has come to occupy a central position in the Indian public life after four decades of Indian Independence at a time, when inter-community relations had improved as compared with the situation of 1947-1950.

Does an Explanation Lie in the Strategies Adopted by the Sangh Joint Family

The Hindu 'joint family' of RSS, VHP, Bajrang Dal, ABVP and others brought the issue *of Hindu identity* in a big way in the 1980s. The Hindu 'joint family' launched mobilisation Hindus on the basis of their religious and cultural symbols, and Hindu saints and seers were involved in motivating Hindus for asserting their Hindu identity. In a multi-religious country, like India, Hindu identity was constructed by targeting other religious communities like Muslims and Christians.

The theme of humiliation of Hindu Rashtra by foreign Muslim invaders was brought in public discourse and symbols of humiliation, like Ram Janmabhoomi or temple at Mathura or Kashi were projected as standing monuments of historical wrongs done against the Hindus by foreign Muslim invaders. The concept of the 'other' is fundamental for the spread of the message of Hindu identity and K.S. Sudarshan, the present Sar Sanghchalak observed in a meeting of Swayamsevak that:

> "the Muslims kept themselves away from the national mainstream because the religious fundamentalists want to keep them isolated".

That every community should be in the national mainstream has a special meaning, when RSS leaders talk about the idea of 'mainstream' because for them Hindu constitutes the mainstream of India.

Sudarshan observed that "....Hindutva was not the name of any community in particular— it is the concept of cultural nationalism. Hindus have always worked for world peace and unity. Only the Hindutva has the capacity to accept, imbibe and absorb all religions". Sudarshan asserts that Hindus are tolerant and he observed "...that India gave permission to Pope John Paul to visit India although Hong Kong and Sri Lanka had refused his visit. Pope came and promoted Christianity".[17]

That Muslims are not joining the Indian mainstream; tolerance is a special virtue of Hindus and Christianity is involved in religious conversions of innocent poor people of India: these are the main talking points of the Hindu 'joint family'. These statements of Sar Sanghchalak create a wall of distance between Hindus, Muslims and Christians. The Sangh 'joint family' has created the image of wounded Mother India (Bharat Mata). It formed a Shri Ram Janmabhoomi Mukti Jagna Samiti (the committee for the liberation of Lord Ram's Birthplace) and from 1984 the RSS, BJP, VHP, Bajrang Dal launched a large-scale mobilisation of Hindu saints and seers for propagating the idea of liberation of the place of Birth of Lord Rama. Dharam Sansad, Sadhu Sammalans and many such movements were launched for the liberation of Ram Janmabhoomi at Ayodhya. Every trick of the trade was played and Yatras in the mould of Hindu religious tradition were organised to purify the bricks with holy water for the Temple at Ayodhya. L.K. Advani in the tradition of old mythical Hindu kings took a Yatra from Somnath to Ayodhya in 1991 and Hindu mobilisation became the major political and religio-cultural activity of Hindu 'joint family' from 1984. Many activists of Ram Janmabhoomi belonging to VHP and Bajrang Dal contested the Lok Sabha elections of 1989 on the basis of nomination by the BJP. On December 6, 1992 L.K. Advani, Murli Manohar Joshi, and every leader of RSS, VHP, Bajrang Dal with a crowd of 200,000 destroyed the Babri Mosque at Ayodhya. An aggressive and militant political Hinduism had announced its arrival on the Indian political scene after the demolition of the Mosque at Ayodhya.

Is Hindu mobilisation launched by the Hindu 'joint family' on Ram Temple an adequate explanation for the expansion of BJP in the 1990s? Why the appeal of Dr. S.P. Mookerjee of the Jana Sangh or V.D. Savarkar of Hindu Mahasabha or leadership of the Ram Rajya Parishad did not cut any ice with the so-called mythical Hindu voter in the Lok Sabha elections of 1952? If an appeal to Hindu sentiment on the basis of history of humiliations suffered by the Hindus is a sufficient cause for Hindu assertion, it should have been an effective instrument for the mobilisation of Hindus in the 1950s. Why has the appeal to Hindu religious symbols succeeded only in the 1990s? Hindu 'joint family' has been consistently taking an aggressive anti-Pakistan stand and it has always projected Muslims as the 'Other', and suddenly they could succeed in these efforts in the 1990s because of Ram Janmabhoomi movement. Hansen observes:

> "The sharpest edge of the entire Ram agitation, which sought to create a collective Hindu subjectivity as it spoke, by exactly in the constant drawing of the external boundaries of the Hindu-community-becoming-nation".[18]

It cannot be denied that the growth of BJP and other members of its 'joint family' in the 1990s can be explained on the basis of Ram Janmabhoomi movement and other related developments among the Hindu community which were exploited by the forces of Hindutva. At the same time, the limitations of this explanation about the growth of BJP and other Hindu organisations in the 1990s also deserve to be noted. First, the BJP state governments of Uttar Pradesh, Madhya Pradesh, Rajasthan and Himachal Pradesh were dismissed in December 1992 after the demolition of Babri Mosque and in the elections of 1993, the BJP got 96 seats out of 200 in Rajasthan, 117 seats out of 320 in Madhya Pradesh and only 175 seats out of 425 in Uttar Pradesh. Why in these elections did the Hindu voter refuse to provide an electoral legitimacy to the party of Hindutva in the State Assemblies?

Second, Hindu religious symbols were employed for the mobilisation of Indians on many occasions during the Twentieth Century, especially during anti-colonial struggles of India. Bal Ganga Dhar Tilak's Ganesh Pooja festival is prominently referred by some scholars that leaders of Indian national movement made use of Hindu religious idiom during the anti-colonial struggle. Some of these facts have led Peter van de Veer to argue that religious language and idiom is crucial in India because it brings together very effectively 'discourse on the religious community and discourse on the nation" and religious nationalism has played a significant role during India's anti-colonial struggles.[19]

Peter van der Veer is making a mechanical relationship between anti-colonial Indian nationalism with religiosity and religious belief system of the people of India. Gandhi launched powerful Non-Cooperation Movement, Salt Satyagrahya-Dandi March, Civil Disobedience Movement, Quit India movement, and mobilised masses in a purely secular manner on the secular issue of anti-colonialism. The essence of Indian nationalism during its anti-colonial phase lies in its contest against purely religious based mobilisation Hindu Mahasabha and Muslim League. Nationalist leaders launched many secular struggles but religious idioms were never used for popular mobilisation. Not only this. Tilak's Ganesh Pooja festival celebration was confined only to Maharashtra and many a time, local leaders of the national movement mobilised people on the basis of local religious traditions but all-India anti-colonial movement mobilisation was always organised on the basis of secular idiom and symbols. While it is not denied that sometimes religious symbols were employed by the nationalist leaders for local mobilisations, the basic thrust of anti-colonial movement was on secular issues through secular slogans of mobilisation.

Does an Explanation Lie in the Strategy of Coalition-Making by the Hindu Party?

Many scholars specially Jafferlot have maintained that the BJP has come to power because it has deftly and intelligently used the strategy of coalition-formation with many secular parties during last four decades and it has been the beneficiary of this strategy of coalition-making with secular leaders and secular parties. A few facts may be mentioned to substantiate the argument that BJP has grown in strength on the basis of its capacity to make alliances with others. First, whenever Indian voters failed to give a clear verdict for a single dominant party either during the Lok Sabha or State Assembly elections, the Bharatiya Jana Sangh and its present Avatar Bharatiya Janata Party was available either to participate in the coalition governments or it supported a party of its own choice by remaining out of power. The BJP participated in the Morarji Desai-led government in 1977 and it supported the V.P. Singh-led government in 1989-90 without sharing power with it. Even when the BJP was supporting the V.P. Singh government by not sharing power with it in a direct manner, the party exercised immense influence over the decisions of the V.P. Singh government. Jagmohan of the BJP was appointed Governor of Jammu & Kashmir by the V.P. Singh government on the basis of a demand from the BJP. The Lok Sabha elections of 1996 again witnessed that no single party had a majority to form the government at the Centre and the President of India invited Atal Bihari Vajpayee to become the Prime Minister because the BJP had obtained 160 seats and it formed a bloc of 194 with the support of Shiva Sena, Akali Dal, Haryana Vikas Party, etc. Vajpayee failed to receive a vote of confidence in the Lok Sabha in 1996 but a point was made that BJP can form coalition government at the Centre and in the States of India. This story was repeated by the BJP in 1998 and 1999 and BJP-led coalition governments were formed at the Centre.

Second, the Hindu 'joint family' of RSS, VHP, Bajrang Dal, Akhil Bharatiya Vidyarthi Parishad have actively participated and supported movements and struggles landed by opposition parties and opposition leaders. Gujarat and Bihar Movements of 1974-75 were openly and enthusiastically supported by the Sangh Fraternity.

Jayaprakash Narayan felt obliged to the RSS during his struggles against Mrs. Indira Gandhi's government in 1974-75 and 'J.P.' publicly proclaimed that

"RSS workers are devoted nationalists". The RSS strategists have never missed any opportunity to participate in any mass movement, whenever an occasion arose from the 1970s to the 1990s.

Third, it has been suggested that the most important asset of the BJP has been its highly committed and motivated RSS cadre. Since BJP is a cadre-based party, this asset of the BJP has been loaned to many parties and leaders either during the elections or whenever they decided to launch any anti-government struggle. Anderson and Damle have devoted full attention to the internal organisation of the BJP and RSS cadre for understanding the strength of the forces of Hindutva.

The BJP has gained in strength because it has successfully practiced the strategy of coalition-making in politics and its devoted and committed cadre has proved a great asset for the survival and expansion of the BJP. While many political parties or groups or leaders have refused to enter into any alliance with the BJP, many others have legitimised it by working together with the BJP. BJP has never considered any party or group or leader as 'untouchable in politics' and every such association with them has brought political dividends to the party.

If strategies of coalition-making followed by the BJP have brought it great political dividends, the Communist parties should not have been left behind by the BJP. BJP and Communists have been great champions of coalition governments but at the end of the Twentieth Century, it is the BJP-led coalition which is in government at the Centre while Communist parties are still struggling to form a viable alternative of Third Front. It is also true that strategies of the Communist parties succeeded in 1989-90 and 1996-98, when Third Front groups could keep away the Congress and BJP from political power in the Central government. This is only one part of the story of coalition-making strategies of the BJP and Communist parties. BJP has expanded its electoral base in India by following the politics of strategic alliances, and it has succeeded thrice in leading a coalition government at the Centre but the Communists have not been able to expand their electoral base in India. Hence, any explanation for the growth of BJP on the basis of its strategies of coalition-making has its own limitations because electoral and political strategies are necessary but not sufficient explanations for the growth or decline of parties.

Explanation for the Growth of Hindutva Lies in the India of 1990s

Craig Baxter (1969), Bruce D. Graham (1990), Walter K. Anderson and Shridhar D. Damle (1987), Christopher Jafferlot (1996), Peter van der Veer (1996) and Thomas Blom Hansen (1999) have in their scholarly studies offered explanations either by looking into the internal organisation and strategies of the BJP and its cadre or they have explained the growth of BJP by linking it with political process and Hindu cultural ethos of India. These scholarly studies provide lot of insights into the internal dynamics of 'Joint Hindu

Family' and they have linked their explanations by bringing out the changing dynamics of Indian politics which has facilitated the growth of BJP.

The focus of any study on the phenomenal growth of BJP and various Hindu religious organisations should be in finding an explanation for the need of Hindus to accept the party of Hindutva in the 1990s. Hindus of India did not show any preference for the Jana Sangh in the 1950s and 1960s, when memories of Partition and post-Partition events were quite fresh within the country. The Jana Sangh, Hindu Mahasabha and Ram Rajya Parishad failed to win public space on the basis of their appeals to Hindus. Hindus were not convinced that they needed a Hindu religion-based party to defend their interests in India.

How could Hindus of the 1980s and the 1990s respond positively and enthusiastically to the appeals of Hindu religion-based party and organisations? Why did Hindus embrace politics of Hindutva in the last decade of the Twentieth Century, when they had earlier rejected it in the 1950s and the 1960s? The so-called Hindu India was not at all threatened by any outside country in the 1980s and 1990s but even in the absence of any threat to the security of India, the Hindu party could create an acceptability for itself by playing on the so-called feelings of insecurity among the Hindus of India. How could a Hindu majority country become a fertile ground for the propagandists of Hindu Rashtra? The idea of Hindu identity suddenly became attractive to the Hindus in the 1990s and the party of Hindus succeeded in positioning itself as a great defender and promoter of Hindu identity. What is the explanation for the search for Hindu identity in a Hindu majority country? The growth of BJP and the expansion of Hindu 'joint family' of organisations in the 1990s can be explained by identifying the causes which have made Hindus assert their 'identity' in a Hindu majority country. Why have the Hindus felt the need for the construction of religious Hindu community national identity? Why have Hindus chosen to identify themselves as Hindus at the close of the Twentieth Century? A community may construct its own identity, if it feels threatened by any other community. Who is a threat to the majority community in India? How have Hindus come to believe that their identity is under threat from other communities? Hansen is the only Western scholar who has attempted an explanation on the growth of BJP in the 1990s by referring to the new aspirations and anxieties of the large middle class and dominant communities' who have been exposed to new 'global cultural and economic flows' at the end of Twentieth Century. Hansen observes that "...it was the desire for recognition with an increasingly global horizon, and the simultaneous anxieties of being encroached upon by the Muslims, the plebeians, and the poor that over the last decade have prompted millions of Hindus to respond to the call for Hindutva at the polls and in the streets, and to embrace Hindu nationalist promises of order, discipline, and collective strength".[20]

Hansen's line of argument about the rise of Hindutva is correct and carries conviction but fault lies in his narrative; he has not been able to properly contextualise the crisis and specific political developments of the decade of the 1990s for properly explaining the linkage between economic globalisation and the politics of Hindu identity. Yogendra Yadav with Sanjay Kumar and Oliver Heath in their very valuable election analysis published in the Frontline (Madras) of November 19, 1999 talk about *'The BJP's New Social Bloc'*. The first important finding of Yogendra Yadav *et al* election Survey of 1999 Lok Sabha is that: "Most of the gains made by the BJP-led front came from the erstwhile United Front and the allies of the Congress (I). But these votes did not flow directly to the BJP : they accrued to its allies".[21] An analysis of Andhra Pradesh elections of 1999 has also mentioned that an election alliance between BJP and Telugu Desam proved beneficial to both the parties and because of this alliance, Congress party in Andhra Pradesh suffered an electoral defeat. The second significant finding of their analysis is that: "It may be an exaggeration to say that the BJP represents the rebellion of the elite, but it is nevertheless true that its rise to political power has been accompanied by the emergence of a new social group that is defined by an overlap of social and economic privileges".[22] Third, Yadav *et al* have shown that a positive correlation exists between 'the poorer the voter, the lower the vote for the BJP', 'Caste and class hierarchy reinforce each other in favour of the BJP' and 'both caste and class converge in BJP's support base'. The authors conclude that:...., the highest chances of voting for the BJP obtain in the group that is both, upper class and upper caste, and the lowest among the lowest class Dalits".[23]

Since India is witnessing a 'Grand Transition', the above findings make an important revelation about the social profile of the BJP inspite of the fact that many distinctions or social categories are blurred and in a state of flux.

A few salient features of politics and economics of the 1990s may be briefly mentioned to show that this was a decade of special crisis for India. First, V.P. Singh was involved in a factional conflict with some leaders of his own party and to divert public attention, he announced the acceptance of the Mandal Commission recommendations on reservations in public services in August, 1990. If on the one hand, the V.P. Singh governments' action on Mandal Commission led to serious caste versus caste conflicts in North India, on the other, the BJP and every member of the Hindu 'joint family' jumped into public activity to protect united Hindus identity by launching mobilisation for Ram Janmabhoomi. The ideologues of Hindu 'joint family' launched a counter offensive against the divisive caste politics of V.P. Singh and other supporters of Mandal Commission by mobilising the Hindu Samaj on a common platform of liberation of Ram Janmabhoomi with a programme for the construction of Ram Temple at Ayodhya.

India of the 1990s witnessed the emergence of powerful struggles on the basis of assertions of identity and manipulative politics of identity occupied central public space in India. V.P. Singh, Mulayam Singh Yadav of Uttar Pradesh, Lalu Prasad Yadav of Bihar mobilised the backward caste peasant classes on the basis of their distinct caste identity, Kanshi Ram and Mrs.

Mayawati of the Bahujan Samaj Party mobilised 'other Dalit castes' on the basis of their Dalit caste identity. Identity versus identity politics was on the run and the forces of Hindutva jumped into the ocean of identities with a goal to protect and project an integrated Hindu identity. Politics of identity is always based on the concept of the 'other' and for the Sangh fraternity, the 'other' was Muslim and Christian and also Hindu caste system. The Hindu organisations were involved in the manipulation of Hindu identity for maintaining the inner unity of Hindus by focussing on their 'other', i.e., Muslims and Christians. Mandal versus Mandir, or Reservations versus Ram occupied pubic space in the beginning of the 1990s.

Second, alongwith these political developments of the 1990s, Indians were caught in serious fiscal crisis in 1991 and India was on the verge of an economic collapse. The fiscal crisis of the Indian state was reflected by the balance-of-payments crisis of 1991, when the P.V. Narasimha Rao government approached the World Bank and International Monetary Fund and Western industrial countries to launch a 'rescue operation for Indian economy'. The Narasimha Rao government announced a New Economic Policy for India whose major components were opening of the economy to foreign investors, and privatisation and deregulation of the highly regulated domestic economic regime. Globalisation, liberalisation and privatisation of Indian economy was undertaken as a response to the serious fiscal crisis faced by the Indian state in 1991. The Indian ruling classes and political and bureaucratic governing classes[24] opted for foreign capital to resolve the fiscal crisis of the Indian State which was the product of many wrong policies, followed by the Indian State from 1950 to 1990. The Indian state and the ruling classes were not ready to learn from their own failures at the domestic economic front; many corrective measures could have been undertaken to resolve the fiscal crisis of the Indian State, if the ruling classes and political and bureaucratic governing classes had agreed to set the house in order. In a country of one Billion people, only 20 million of Indians pay income tax. Many private corporate industrial and trading groups pay 'zero tax' to the State. Further, the Indian state allocates a large share of its annual budgeted expenditure for the salaries and benefits to the members of the political and bureaucratic governing classes. While the ruling classes of India do not contribute to the exchequer of the Indian State, the governing classes take away a lion's share from the limited fiscal resources of the State. Fiscal crisis of the Indian State is a logical product of the class action of accumulators of economic surpluses who are reluctant to be taxed and of the governing classes who act as co-shareholders with the ruling classes in exercising control over the fiscal resources of the state.

India opened its economy to foreign investors in the 1990s to overcome its own crisis and once the economy was opened to the foreign investors and rolling back of the state became the new mantra of international and Indian capitalist classes, a large domestic social constituency of middle and upper middle class Indians extended full support to the idea of free market economy, free foreign investments, competition in market, and production of quality consumer goods. The functionaries of the state, leaders of private corporate sector and opinion-makers joined together to project that India was a big market of 250 million buyers of quality goods. It deserves to be mentioned that professional middle and upper middle classes, the middle class entrepreneur, the managers of service sector of economy and surplus generating middle class peasantry were very important beneficiaries of the post-independence economic development of India. This social group, which is broadly the 'petit-bourgeoisie' of India, enjoys great social status and power within the country and these social groups of society are completely linked with the industrial and agrarian capitalist classes.

The decade of 1990s witnessed serious fiscal crisis of the state and also the emergence of identity politics in a big way. Large social solidarities of workers or peasants were all broken into fragments on the basis of caste versus caste, sub-caste versus sub-caste in the Jati system, religion versus religion and region versus region. Many new social movements took birth in the 1990s dealing with the problems of 'Environment' or 'Child labour' or 'Women questions' but all these movements were focussed on 'single issue programmes' and one movement had no linkage with any other movement and larger issues of society were broken into particular issues for mobilisation. Particularism and fractionalisation of society became a distinctive feature of the politics of the 1990s. Political mobilisation on the basis of caste or religion or region in the 1990s disintegrated and fragmented party system and caste-based parties and religion-based parties on the basis of sectional representation emerged on the scene in politics. The construction of all-India Hindu identity which transcended fragmented caste identities assumed great significance for the BJP, and the Hindu 'joint family' popularly known as *Sangh Parivar* rallied Hindus on the slogan of Hindu unity against Muslims and Christians.

Hindu religion-based politics with a goal to establish a powerful Hindu identity replaced an all-India secular democratic politics in the 1990s because secular parties could not create a powerful united movement of the exploited classes which could be perceived by the people as an alternative to the social goals offered by the believers of Hindu Rashtra or Jati Raj. The quest for Hindu identity in the crisis stage of globalisation succeeded because other secular political parties could not offer any alternative social goal for the poor of India. The decade of 1990s has witnessed the deepening of social and economic disparities in India and neither globalisation nor Hindu or caste identity can offer any solution to the basic problems of the marginalised strata of society. The Hindu 'joint family' has acted as a dream merchant by providing a religion-based slogan for mass mobilisation during the elections. The dream of great and powerful Hindu India has been effectively and successfully sold by the Hindu 'joint family' to the upcoming rural and urban middle and upper middle classes who on the one hand have global aspirations and on the other, they aggressively identify themselves with Hindu rituals, temples, and other religious symbols. Hinduism has been offered to the 'lumpen and unemployed poor' who are mobilised by the Hindu 'joint family' to target the Muslim and Christian minorities. Hindu 'joint family' has given a common social goal to different strata of Hindu society and it has succeeded in rallying Hindu groups for the protection and promotion of Hinduism in India.

Hindu middle classes were attracted towards consumerism and open identification with Hindu religions became obvious in the early 1970s, when two Bombay made movies like 'Bobby' on the one hand and 'Santoshi Ma' on the other became a craze with the viewers. The message of 'Bobby' movie was that dreams for worldly success can be fulfilled and achieved, and 'Santoshi Ma' attracted great attention because worldly success without 'religious feelings of prayers' was inadequate. These two movies gave a message that 'Complete Hindu' is one who is 'successful in life' and who practices Hindu religion for his salvation. Hindus have not turned their back either on the goal of economic success or in their practice of Hindu religion. Coloured television sets were symbols of economic success and television serials of 'Ramayana and Mahabharat' fulfilled the religious need. Karl Marx had clearly alerted us to the powerful appeal of religion for the insecure and the poor masses in a society. While describing religion as an 'Opiate' of the people because it strengthens 'false consciousness' Karl Marx also maintained that it provides 'hope' to the hopeless and frustrated masses: "Religion is the sigh of the oppressed creature, the heart of a heartless world, just as it is that spirit of a spiritless situation. It is the opium of the people".[25]

The Congress party of Indira practiced 'soft Hindutva' while contesting the BJP politics of militant and aggressive Hindutva. V.N. Gadgil, a senior leader of the party, observed that the Congress "depends on the support of Muslims and other minorities and ignores the interests of the majority". When a leader of a secular party, like the Congress is taking cognisance of the Hindu identity, it substantiates our argument that Hindu factor in Indian politics has emerged in a significant manner in the 1990s. The upwardly mobile middle and upper middle class Hindus are economic globalises and supporters of Hindu-religion-based politics because it helps them to reconcile 'consumerism' with 'Hindu religious identity'. Since middle class politicians, bureaucrats, professionals, technocrats, entrepreneurs, intellectuals and articulators of ideas occupy a special position of power and influence in Indian society, their ideological beliefs become the representative ideas of the whole society. The ruling classes of India have taken good care of the economic interests of the middle classes because of obvious reasons. First, the Indian middle class identified itself with the aspirations of property owing exploiting classes and second, the middle class of India is a believer and practitioner of social status quoism which ends up in supporting the ruling classes and ideology of Hindu conservatism. In summation, it may be mentioned that crisis-ridden India is finding answers in the ideology of free market economy and construction of political Hinduism.

Finally, the economic integration of India with global capitalism has sharpened economic disparities within the country. It is instructive for Indians to see social reality in the United States, which is the real centre of global capitalism. Americans are worried about growing inequality in their society." The National Centre of Policy Analysis noted recently.. .that the share of total income to the top 20 per cent of American households is increasing while the share going to the lowest 20 per cent is falling. The Federal Reserve Board has found that, while the median family's net worth rose 17.6 per cent between 1995 and 1998, the richest families reaped most of the gain and the poorest families' wealth actually shrank."[26]

If this is the social consequence of capitalism in the most important capitalist country of the world, in India with the exception of 250 million absolute majority of our people are involved in severe struggle for subsistence and survival. While 'working' America and 'corporate' America is sharply divided on the opening of economy for free trade, Indians have become the champions of free market economy. Global capitalism divides every country because it is concerned only with the buyers of quality consumer goods and the majority of population of every country under the impact of global economic integration is ejected out of the market because their share of income is so low that they cannot participate in the market, which caters to the needs of the prosperous only. The Wretched of the Earth of India have been left to their own resources, if any, and at the mercy of God, if any. The opiate of Hindutva does not provide jobs to the jobless. The International Labour Organisation at its 55th International Labour Conference stated that: The world is "still a long way from universal acceptance of these fundamental principles and rights in practice", and globalisation has not helped in improving the social situation for the working classes. "On the contrary, with the internationalisation of production, the power of collective bargaining has been seriously reduced, as corporations have the capital that gives them the ability to exist, when and where they want". Further, "The labour market is getting segmented with restructurisation of production, technological innovation, the advance of privatisation on a large-scale, and labour markets thus getting segmented, part-time work is increasing. Firms are increasingly sub-constructing to cut costs, therefore workers find it more difficult to organise themselves to fight for their interests. The benefits of globalisation have not benefited everyone and everywhere, and global inequalities are growing and many economics becoming increasingly marginalised,...."[27]

The main victims of globalisation, liberalisation and privatisation are the working masses of India and its real 'beneficiaries' are a minority of Indians who consist of 250 million consumerists and corporate sector. The working classes which were always locked in an unequal class relations have reentered a new relationship, where a united working class struggle for the defence of their rights has been crippled by the penetration of caste versus caste, religion versus religion and region versus region clash of identities in the all-India

Trade Unions and All-India Kisan Sabhas. A report by the Associated Chamber of Commerce (ASSOCHAM) has revealed that the loss of mandays due to strikes/lockouts in 1999 stood at a whopping 24.5 million compared to 22.6 million in 1998. The CITU Secretary, W.R. Varada Rajan observed that : "Privatisation, liberalisation and globalisation—which brings with it retrenchment and sickness/closures in uncompetition units—is inflicting horrendous damage on the quality of life of workers."

The ASSOCHAM's study reveals that the 'wage loss on account of industrial action nearly doubled to Rs. 103.06 crore in 1999 from Rs. 54.14 crore in 1998.

The growing social frustrations of the absolute majority of working India during the 1990s have found an expression in street action by Hindu lumpens represented by the Bajrang Dal and others, and the forces of Hindutva have gained in strength because they have successfully played on the fears of the poor by identifying Muslims and Christians as targets of hatred. L.K. Advani keeps on raising the spectre of 'illegal Bangladeshis' in India and according to him, Muslim Bangladeshis and Pakistani Inter-State Intelligence Agencies are threatening Hindu India's Unity. The Uttar Pradesh state government has a new law so that mosques can be controlled because they have become the headquarters of ISI of Pakistan. Similarly, Christian missionaries have to be targeted because they are involved in religious conversion activities and they are a threat to Hindu India. Hindu India is under 'siege' and it has to be defended from its internal and external enemies. While anniversary celebrations of nuclear explosion of Pokharan II were marked by the assertion of strong India, L.K. Advani is taking care of internal enemies of Hindu India by the Criminal Law Amendment Bill 1995, which is a new version of maligned and completely misused earlier Terrorist and Disruptive (Prevention) Act (TADA) which was allowed to lapse. Advani not only needs a new law to deal with domestic 'enemies' of India, he wants his police force to learn lessons from Israelis who smashed the Palestinians.

The focus of our explanation is on the linkage between the fiscal crisis of the Indian State and the emergence of Hindutva as a strong force in Indian public life in the 1990s. The upshot of our narrative is that Indian society has been sharply divided and fragmented around 'exclusivist identities' and the ruling classes and political and bureaucratic governing classes do not feel compelled to restructure fundamental social and productive arrangements in India because the identity politics of targeting the 'other' has weakened the united working class challenge in the 1990s. The Hindu majoritarian identity politics is a response to the deep social and economic crisis of India. The politics of Hindutva is playing an important social role in the situation of deep crisis of Indian economy.

It is a well known fact of history that any powerful 'ideology' or 'social idea' can become acceptable only when social situation is ripe for it. Hitler and Mussolini found a positive response because in the phase of crisis of German and Italian capitalism, fascist ideology of anti-Semitism could be effectively sold to the insecure poor of these countries. This is actually happening in India. Nehru's socialism provided futuristic 'hope' to the Indians in the 1950s and 1960s and in a contest against Nehruvian goals of nation-building the ideology of Hindutva had no takers. The 1990s have witnessed the collapse of East European communist state system, and Indians have also experienced that the communist and socialist parties could not successfully confront extremely divisive politics of identities, and in this situation of crisis of India, social space was occupied either by Hindu communalist or casteists or regional chauvinists who are very comfortable in each others company. Political bloc of casteists, regionalists and the party of Hindus is a reflection of fragmentation of the ruling classes in crisis ridden India. Identity politics has weakened or destroyed large social solidarities of the working classes who could challenge the exploiting propertied classes of India. This is the social reality of India in the beginning of the Twenty First Century. The growth of Hindutva can be understood and explained by establishing proper linkages between politics of classes and fractions in the age of crisis of capitalism, when exclusivist 'identity' politics is legitimised by the political and intellectual representatives of the exploiting classes. The ruling classes always feel threatened by large social solidarities of the working classes and Hindutva serves class interests by its politics of group versus group, and community versus community.

NOTES AND REFERENCES

1. S. Balakrishnan: "FDI or Depleting Independence?" *The Hindu,* New Delhi, May 24, 2000, p. 21.
2. Manifesto: National Democratic Alliance, April 29, 1999.
3. Indrani Bagchi: "CI 1 in pursuit of free trade pact with us", *The Economic Times* : New Delhi, May 31, 2000.
4. *Organizer,* New Delhi, April 20, 2000, p. 2.
5. "P.M., allies became friends again" *The Hindustan Times,* New Delhi, May 12, 2000, p. 8.
6. A.B. Vajpayee "Spread Indian Culture to Counter Cultural Invasion" *Organizer,* New Delhi, Vol. 1, No. 46, June 4, 2000, p. 20.
7. *Organizer,* New Delhi, Vol. No. 41, April 30, 2000, p. 19.
8. Thomas Bloom Hansen : The Saffron Wave : Democracy and Hindu Nationalism in Modern India. New Delhi, Oxford University Press, 1999, pp. 83-84, quoted from M.S. Golwalkar : Bunch of Thoughts, Bangalore; Jagaran Prakash, 1966, p. 299.
9. *Organizer,* New Delhi, March 19, 2000.
10. *Organizer* : New Delhi, March 26, 2000, p. 9.
11. "Construction of Rama Mandir begins in Jan.: VHP", *The Economic Times,* New Delhi, June 5, 2000, p. 2.
12. "VHP reconverts tribal family in Odisha village" : *The Hindustan Times,* New Delhi, June 19, 2000.

13. "Sangh Parivar behind the hate campaign, says Christian council" : *The Hindustan Times, New* Delhi, June 19, 2000.
14. "Muslims, reply to Pak : Advani",' *The Indian Express,* New Delhi, April 27, 2000, p. 1.
15. Neena Vyas, "Now a Party with difference", *The Hindu,* New Delhi, May 7, 2000, p. 14.
16. Rathen Das, "Treating minorities, Gujarat style", *The Hindustan Times,* New Delhi, May 7, 2000
17. Manik K. Kher, "Muslims should join the mainstream", K.S. Sudarshan. *The Organizer,* New Delhi, June 11, 2000, p. 8.
18. Thomas Bloom Nansen : The Saffron Wave 1999, p. 177.
19. Peter *van der* Veer: Religious Nationalism : Hindus and Muslims in India : Delhi, Oxford, 1996.
20. Thomas Bloom Hansen, 1999, p. 5.
21. Yogendra Yadav et al : "The BJP's New Social Block", *Frontline,* Madras, November 19, 1999, p. 32.
22. *Ibid.,* p. 32.
23. *Ibid.,* p. 38.
24. Note: French Marxist N. Povlantz made an important distinction between the 'ruling classes' and the 'governing classes' in capitalist society. The governing classes manage the class state and they also have a share in the accumulated surpluses.
25. Marx's writing: Contribution to the critique of Hegel's philosophy of Right: Karl Marx and Frederick Engels: On Religion (Second Impression): Moscow, Foreign Languages Publishing House, 1955, p. 42.
26. Geneva Overholser "The unfairness of Income Inequality", *International Herald Tribune,* New York, March 25, 2000, p. 6.
27. Shiela Mathurani, "This bargaining right affected by globalisation, ILO": *The Economic Times,* New Delhi, June 8, 2000.

7

United Progressive Alliance Government: 2004-2009

The Congress-led United Progressive Alliance government at the Centre was formed on May 22, 2004 and it was for the first time that the Congress party formed a coalition government at the Centre. The BJP-led National Democratic Alliance government at the Centre had exercised power for more than six years from 1998 to 2004 and its electoral defeat was welcomed by secular political forces in the country because BJP-in-power at the Centre had assaulted the secular fabric and democratic ethos of plural and diverse society of India. It has been suggested that the replacement and displacement of the BJP-led NDA government by the Congress-led UPA government at the Centre has liberated India from the forces of Hindutva and the votaries of Hindu Rashtra have been ejected from state power. It deserves to be clearly stated that an interpretation of electoral verdict of 2004 Lok Sabha elections cannot be dichotomised or even simplified by asserting that the voters during the elections showed their clear preference in favour of secularism and against the Hindu Rashtravadis. The Congress had mobilised the voters on the plank of 'vote for Hand which stands for *aam admi*[1] and the BJP asked the voters to renew their confidence in the party/government, which had created a 'Shining India'. Can it be stated that the Congress and the BJP were clearly identified by the voters on the basis of their ideology of secularism versus Hindutva, and other issues mentioned in the election manifestos of these two parties did not carry any conviction with the voters? It deserves to be clearly stated that electoral verdict cannot be interpreted on the basis of a single factor, especially when victory and defeat of the two major contenders for power is extremely narrow. The Congress-led UPA government at the Centre has to follow and implement 'secular agenda for governance' because Congress is ideologically committed to 'secularism' and it has replaced the BJP-led government, which is firmly committed to the ideology of Hindu Rashtravad. The only significance of the Lok Sabha elections of 2004 is that a party with an agenda of religion-based politics has vacated the office for a party, which is practitioner of secular-based politics. A government-in-power can not be analysed and evaluated on the basis of just one agenda because multiple and diverse social groups look towards a government for the satisfaction of their specific demands. Not only this. A coalition government at the Centre has to accommodate diverse demands of different groups because partners in a coalition government represent the interests and demands of different social constituencies. The Congress-led UPA government at the Centre has to harmonise the conflicting interests of fourteen groups, which are represented in the government along with the demands of the Communist parties which are 'outside supporters' of the government at the Centre. It was alleged that the Congress would not succeed in managing a coalition government at the Centre because it did not have any experience of working with diverse coalition groups at the Centre. The opponents of the UPA government, especially the BJP, were extremely skeptical about the survival of a coalition government led by the Congress but the Congress has belied the expectations of its critics and opponents and the UPA government has continued to remain in power at the Centre. The UPA government is working on the basis of a National Common Minimum Programme, which has been agreed by all the coalition partners including the Communists, who are the 'outside supporters' of the government. It does not mean that the implementation of the Common Minimum Programme can be a smooth affair because in spite of agreements on the CMP, different coalition partners have different priorities of their own and different groups will like to push their agenda through the government. The upshot of above description is that coalition government at the Centre, whether led by the Congress or the BJP, is always at the tenterhooks because it has to accommodate diverse and competitive demands of its supporters in the government.

The UPA government has evolved a mechanism of Co-ordination Committee for dealing with the issues raised by the Communists who are its 'outside supporters'. It deserves to be clearly stated that the Congress and the Communists have never agreed to share power either at a formal or informal levels and it is for the first time in post-Independence India that Communists are 'supporting' the Congress-led UPA government. The Congress and the Communists represent different social constituencies and interests of different social classes and this is the reason that they have never cooperated with one another in the task of governance of the country. The Communists are supporting the Congress-led UPA government with a view to keep the forces of Hindutva out of governmental power. The Congress is a lesser political evil for the Communists because a full-fledged party of the Hindutva has to be kept out of power with a view to defend the secular fabric of India. Hindutva is the greatest threat to the democratic Republic of India because its ideology of religion-based politics is a complete negation of the philosophy of secularism, which is the foundational philosophical principle of Communists and for this purpose, they are extending support to the Congress at the Centre. Communist parties are extending support to the Congress to keep the BJP miles away from state power, it does not mean that the communists have abandoned their pro-poor ideological baggage in favour of pro-rich economic policies of the Congress party. The Communists have applied pressures on the Congress in every Coordination Committee Meeting with a view to keep it under check so that it does not violate the Common Minimum Programme which is the guiding framework of the UPA government. It is worthwhile to mention a few important differences which have emerged between the Congress and the Communists and both of them have tried to resolve contentious public policy issues on the basis of hard bargaining with a spirit of give and take. Communists and the Congress have been opposed to one another on economic and foreign policy. The Communists have opposed economic liberalisation and pro-American policies of the Congress and many a time, both of them have found themselves at loggerheads and a situation arose when the Communists 'decided to walk out' of the Coordination Committee meetings.

The Congress-led coalition has worked very smoothly, because except the Communists who have public policy differences with the Congress, other regional and sub-regional groups have cooperated with each other and the government has been able to project its United image. It does not mean that fourteen groups do not have inter-group or intra-groups tensions but the functioning of the government has not been adversely affected by inter-group conflicts. The State Assembly elections of 2005 in Bihar witnessed that Lalu Prasad Yadav of the Rashtriya Janata Dal and Ramvilas Paswan of the Lok Jan Shakti party were not able to work together at a common electoral platform in spite of the fact that both these parties are part of the UPA government at the Centre. Not only this. Sonia Gandhi also failed to reconcile the differences between these two groups during Bihar State Assembly elections of 2005. The same story was repeated in 2006 and in Tamil Nadu Vaiko decided to form an electoral alliance with Km. Jayalalitha of the AIADMK against M. Karunanidhi's DMK in spite of the fact that Vaiko and the DMK are present in the UPA government at the Centre. The state level political contradictions do not get resolved in spite of the fact that some political opponents have decided to sit around the table as comrades-in-arm at the Centre.

If the above story of relationship between Communists and the Congress and the Congress and other regional partners of the UPA government leads us to conclude that coalition government at the Centre is an 'alliance of convenience', the problems which exist within the Congress also can not be wished away or put under the carpet. What is the relationship between Sonia Gandhi, the Congress party President, and Manmohan Singh, the Prime Minister of the Congress-led UPA government at the Centre? Manmohan is a nominee of Sonia for the office of Prime Minister of India. Sonia abandoned her claim to accept the office of Prime Minister in spite of the fact that her own party and every alliance partner represented in the UPA had shown a clear preference for Sonia's candidature as Prime Minister. It deserves to be clearly stated that Sonia has revived the Congress party and from 1998 to 2006, the Congress party has been led by Sonia who is an 'unchallenged' leader of the party. Sonia's political opponents, like the BJP had to eat an humble pie because the voters have shown complete confidence by electing and re-electing Sonia for the Lok Sabha. The Lok Sabha elections of 2004 brought back Sonia-led Congress to power because her party could form a coalition government at the Centre. Sonia's pre-eminent position in the Congress has remained intact in spite of the fact that she has not accepted to be the Prime Minister of India. Sonia Gandhi decided to constitute a National Advisory Council under her Chairmanship and the constitution of such a NAC has given rise to a controversy that the UPA government has created 'dual centres of power' because in a parliamentary system, it is the Council of Ministers, which is the real repository of 'executive powers' and Sonia's NAC is either redundant or 'extra-constitutional centre of power'. The fact of the matter is that Sonia shall continue to occupy a 'pre-eminent' position in the UPA government because of the 'pre-eminence' in the Congress party.

How does one evaluate the performance of UPA-in-Government irrespective of the fact that Sonia or Manmohan or both of them occupy equal or more than equal status in relation to one another? The Communist parties have a yardstick for the evaluation of the UPA government and they have maintained that it is a government with 'secular agenda' but its economic and foreign policies are flawed because they are pro-Big Business, Indian and foreign, and pro-America. The role of Communists is to apply 'correctives' and 'brakes' over pro-global capitalist policies of the government. Further, except the Communists, other allies of the Congress in the UPA government, have maintained smooth relationship with one another because every regional partner of the coalition government at the Centre does not have any clear cut ideological agenda of its own. Every group in coalition government is guided by the interest of its own social constituency.

It is not enough to maintain that the UPA government at the Centre is guided by secular ideology because its track record on socio-economic issues facing the country deserves to be clearly scrutinised. A few facts may be mentioned to highlight the essentials of socio-economic challenges faced by India in 2006. The Economic Survey of the Government of India (2005-06) has highlighted the reality of economy of the country. While the government has projected a rosy picture of 'economic growth', the Economic Survey on the basis of National Sample Survey Organisation has mentioned that "The Survey had estimated a reduction in the incidence of poverty from 36 per cent in 1993-1994 to 26.1 per cent during 1999-2000."[2] If one-fourth of the population is still under the poverty line as defined by the government, the UPA government has to play an 'activist' role in attacking directly the issue of mass poverty. Not only this. Agrarian crisis is a reality and marginal farmers have taken recourse to 'suicide' because they cannot face economic distress suffered by them. How can rural poverty be tackled, if investment in agricultural sector has been on the decline? The Economic Survey of the Government of India has itself referred to the basic cause of agrarian crisis.

Capital Formational in India Agriculture

The decline in the share of the agricultural sector's capital formation in GDP from 2.2 per cent in the late 1990s to 1.7 per cent in 2004-05 is a matter of concern. This declining share was mainly due to the stagnation or fall in public investment in irrigation, particularly since the mid-1990s. However, there is indication of a reversal of this trend with public sector investment in agriculture reaching its highest level of Rs. 12,591 crore in 2004-05 since the early nineties. The share of public investment in gross investment increased by over 11 percentage point to reach 29.2 per cent in 2004-05 relative to 1990-2000.

Further, India is facing grave crisis of rising 'unemployment' and in a labour surplus economy, the growth of unemployment gives rise to social conflicts and violence.

The economic thinking in the UPA government is clearly anti-poor and the Economic Survey while dealing with a serious issue, like growing unemployment focuses its attention on reform of 'labour laws' to eject the workers, who are already employed.

Gross Capital Formation in Agriculture*

Year	*Investment in Agriculture (Rs Crore)*			*Share in Agricultural Gross Investment (per cent)*		*Investment in Agriculture as a per cent of GDP at Constant Prices*
1990-91	14836	4395	10441	29.60	70.40	1.92
1995-96	15690	4849	10841	30.90	69.10	1.57
1996-97	16176	4668	11508	28.90	71.10	1.51
1997-98	15942	3979	11963	25.00	75.00	1.43
1998-99	14895	3870	11025	26.00	74.00	1.26
1999-00	17304	4221	13083	24.40	75.00	1.37
		New Series (at 1990-00 (prices)				
1999-00	43473	7754	35719	17.8	82.2	. 2.2
2000-01	38176	7018	31158	18.4	81.6	1.9
2001-02	46744	8529	38215	18.2	81.8	2.2
2002-03	45867	7849	38018	17.1	82.9	2.1
2003-04	47833	12809	35024	26.8	73.2	2.0
2004-05	43123	12591	30532	29.2	70.8	1.7

* Quick Estimates.
* *Source:* CSO.
** *Economy Survey*, 2005-06. pp. 169-70.

"Some salient features of the trend of unemployment rates in the country are:

The unemployment rate went up between 1993-94 to 2004. On the basis of current daily status (unemployed on an average in the reference week), during the reference period, unemployment rate for males increased from 5.6 per cent to 9.0 per cent in rural areas, and from 6.7 per cent to 8.1 per cent in urban areas.

Similarly, unemployment rate for females increased from 5.6 per cent in 1993-94 to 9.3 per cent in 2004 in rural areas and from 10.5 per cent to 11.7 per cent in urban areas.

Furthermore, unemployment rates on the basis of current daily status were much higher than those on the basis of usual status (unemployed on an average in the reference year) implying a high degree of intermittent unemployment. This could be mainly because of the absence of regular employment for many workers.

Urban unemployment rates (current daily status) were higher than rural unemployment rates for both, males and females in 1993-04. However, in 2004, rural unemployment rates for males was higher than that of urban males.

Unemployment rates varied sharply across States. States, where wages are higher than in neighbouring ones because of strong bargains or social security provision, such as high minimum wage; had high incident of unemployment, in general."

Year	*Investment in Agriculture (Rs. Crore)*			*Share in Agricultural Gross Investment (per cent)*		*Investment in Agriculture as a per cent of GDP at Constant Prices*
1990-91	14836	4395	10441	29.60	70.40	1.92
1995-96	15690	4849	10841	30.90	69.10	1.57
1996-97	16176	4668	11508	28.90	71.10	1.51
1997-98	15942	3979	11963	25.00	75.00	1.43
1998-99	14895	3870	11025	26.00	74.00	1.26
1999-00	17304	4221	13083	24.40	75.00	1.37
New Series (at 1990-00 prices)						
1999-00	43473	7754	35719	17.8	82.2	2.2
2000-01	38176	7018	31158	18.4	81.6	1.9
2001-02	46744	8529	38215	18.2	81.8	2.2
2002-03	45867	7849	38018	17.1	82.9	2.1
2003-04	47833	12809	35024	26.8	73.2	2.0
2004-05	43123	12591	30532	29.2	70.8	1.7
** Economic Survey, pp. 207-09						

Indian Labour Laws and Labour Market

"Indian labour market is characterised by a sharp dichotomy. A large number of establishments in the unorganised sector remain outside any regulation, while the organised sector has been regulated fairly stringently. It can be reasonable argued that the organised sector has provided too much of job security for too long, while the unorganised sector has provided too little to too many.

Various studies indicate that Indian labour laws are highly protective of labour, and labour market are relatively inflexible. These laws apply only to the organised sector. Consequently, these laws have restricted labour mobility, have led to capital-intensive methods in the organised sector and adversely affected the sector's long-run demand for labour. Labour being a subject in the concurrent list, State-level labour regulations are also an important determinant of industrial performance. Evidence suggests that States, which have acted more pro-worker regulations, have lost out on industrial production in general.

Perhaps there are lessons to be learnt from China in the area of labour reforms. China, with a history of extreme employment security, has drastically reformed its labour relations and created a new labour market, in which workers are highly mobile. Although there have been mass layoffs and open unemployment, high rates of industrial growth, especially in the coastal regions helped their redeployment. In spite of hardship workers in China seems to have benefited from wage growth, additional job creation and new opportunities for self-employment."

The UPA government at the Centre has become quite aware of the prevailing grave economic crisis in the country and its response has been in the form of National Rural Employment Guarantee Scheme. This is not only the response of the UPA government to resolve the crisis prevailing in the country. The Central Government has decided to 'modernise' paramilitary armed forces to tackle the so-called Naxal problem facing thirteen states of India. Naxalism is a consequence of the prevailing social discontent in the country and the UPA government does not have any strategy to eliminate the causes of social discontent and it has decided to take recourse to police oppression. India has been moving from crisis to crisis and the UPA government, whether Sonia-led or Manmohan-led, has not come forward with any policy package to tackle the prevailing social crisis in India.

The upshot of above description is that India has abandoned National Project for the Development of the whole country and every all-India and regional party represented at the Centre is implementing pro-rich and anti-poor public policies and Sonia Gandhi's Congress is the major carrier of the agenda of globalisation, liberalisation, deregulation and privatisation. The poor masses of India are not in the reckoning in the economic and political agenda, following by the pro-rich liberalisers and it is not surprising that the BJP and the Congress have continued to follow the same economic strategy while in power at the Centre. The UPA government has saved India from the forces of fanatic Hindutva and Narendra Modi could not dare to repeat his performance in Vadodra in 2006 because instead of his protector Atal Bihari Vajpayee, Manmohan Singh is the Prime Minister of India. The UPA has liberated the central government from the stranglehold of Hindu Communal forces, it has not risen to the occasion while dealing with the problems faced by *Wretched of the Earth* of India.

Do We have a Prime Minister?

Parliamentary democracy in England or Canada or Australia has in reality become a prime ministerial government; the office of the PM has evolved from the status of primus inter pares or first among equals to the present position of the leadership of the Cabinet and elected House of Parliament.

The council of ministers is collectively responsible to the elected House of Parliament, but in reality the writ of the PM runs over all the members of his Cabinet. Not only this. The PM can ask for the resignation or even the dismissal of a dissident member of his council of ministers because appointment of a minister is his sole prerogative. The PM can act as an unquestioned leader of his council of ministers, if he enjoys the unquestioned political authority over his own party.

Unfortunately, Manmohan Singh is a PM nominated by Sonia Gandhi, who is the real and unquestioned leader of the Congress Party, which is leading the UPA government at the Centre. Singh is not even a light weight leader of the Congress; the real repository of power is Sonia Gandhi who is the president of the Congress and the chairman of the National Advisory Council. Not only this, every coalition partner of the UPA looks towards her as the final arbiter of disputes or differences between the Congress Party and its coalition partners. The Communist parties, supporting the Congress-led UPA government from outside, look towards Sonia for their coordination with the Singh-led government.

It is noteworthy that Pranab Mukherjee, or P. Chidambaram or Arjun Singh, or Kamal Nath of the Congress Party care for the opinions and wishes of the PM because Sonia Gandhi, the supreme leader of the Congress, is supporting Singh in his present position. The Congress CMs too look towards Sonia Gandhi and not Singh, for guidance, advice, instructions and orders. It is Sonia Gandhi who decides to hold meetings of Congress CMs and they have to explain their record of activities to her and not the nominated PM. A telling example is provided by the manner in which Natwar Singh, the former external affairs minister, was made to 'quit' the Cabinet because Sonia Gandhi had got annoyed with her own favourite minister in the Volcker Affair. Natwar Singh was shown the door not by Singh but by Sonia.

The upshot of the above description is that the PM has no authority or freedom to exercise his real prerogative of either appointing a minister or in asking for his resignation. The Congress party representatives in Singh's

Cabinet can continue at the 'pleasure' of Sonia and not on the basis of choice or goodwill of the PM. The essential point to be noted here is that Singh is shinning in the reflected glory of Sonia. He is in office because of his 'loyalty' to Sonia.

Jawaharlal Nehru or Indira Gandhi or Rajiv Gandhi or Narasimha Rao or Atal Bihari Vajpayee were not only PMs in their own right, but also they controlled the party organisation. Complete support of a party is a precondition for becoming a PM in a parliamentary democracy. It is not without reason that Jawaharlal Nehru threatened to resign from the CWC, if Purushottam Das Tandon continued as party president. The clash and conflict between these two personalities was resolved in favour of the PM and the party president was made to quit his elected office.

Indira Gandhi decided to 'split' the Congress party in 1969, when the party president Nijalingappa had ganged up against her on the choice of the party nominee for the post of President of India. Indira Gandhi again 'split' the party in 1978 because a powerful section within the party was 'hostile' to her. In fact, every Congress PM, except Singh, had been either the unquestioned and unchallenged choice of the party or managed and manipulated party support in his/her favour.

A PM has to 'control' his party for his authority to be fully accepted by every minister in his Cabinet. Indira Gandhi fought against her opponents within the party because her authority as PM would have been completely diluted, even eroded, if she had allowed parallel or 'dual' centres of power. It is not without reason that V.P. Singh or Chandrashekhar or H.D. Deve Gowda or I.K. Gujral could remain PMs only for a very short period because none of them had either firm support of a party or a coalition of parties. Vajpayee could remain PM from 1998 to 2004 because he was fully supported not only by the BJP but also other coalition partners. In other words, a PM is effective only on the basis of his own political strength within the party, of which he is the leader.

Singh is not the leader of the Congress or of the UPA and hence, he cannot lead the council of ministers. It has been observed that every pubic controversy involving the UPA government is resolved by the active intervention of Sonia Gandhi and not the PM. He does not have any role in the party's internal affairs because Sonia has the real power. The functioning of the government is also affected by such an unnatural 'dual control system' because every party or group in the UPA looks towards Sonia for the final word. The Left parties had walked out and boycotted the co-ordination committee meetings in the middle of 2005 because they had developed serious differences with the UPA government on economic policies of liberalisation, globalisation and privatisation and it was Sonia Gandhi's intervention, which bought back the Left to the co-ordination committee meetings. Sonia Gandhi's National Advisory Council carries more weight in decision making than Singh and it had become clear on the issue of National Rural Employment Guarantee Scheme and the Right to Information Act, 2005.

It deserves to be reiterated that the office of the PM in the UPA government has been completely devalued. It is not only that Singh owes his job to Sonia, but also all Congress ministers look towards Sonia for their continuation in office. Sonia has power without responsibility and Sing is shouldering responsibilities without real power.

Parliamentary democracy revolves round the personality and leadership qualities of the Prime Minister, who is nearly always the sole spokesperson of the country's foreign and domestic policies. Manmohan Singh's press conference on February 1 was, therefore, a significant aid to understanding the policies of the UPA Government.

The Prime Minister chose to address the media at a time of sharp divisions within the country not only on the issue of foreign policy, but also on questions being raised regarding his own leadership qualities. It is not surprising that the country is debating the issue of Manmohan Singh's political authority, thanks to the circumstances that made him the Prime Minister in May 2004. The Congress had elected Sonia Gandhi to lead the Government at the Centre after the electoral debacle of the BJP-led NDA in the 2004 Lok Sabha election. Sonia Gandhi, however, 'nominated' Manmohan Singh to lead the coalition Government at the Centre.

Manmohan Singh has been the Prime Minister for 20 months and his press conference was an appropriate forum to clarify the issues that are in people's minds. The crux of the matter is the relationship between Manmohan Singh and Congress president Sonia Gandhi. After all, the UPA Government is led by the Congress, which is fully controlled by her.

Is the Prime Minister leading the Government without any authority? Manmohan Singh dismissed L.K. Advani's allegation of being the 'weakest Prime Minister' by observing: "If I am a weak Prime Minister, then how strong was Advani, when he went to Jinnah's mausoleum and had to resign as party president because the RSS didn't like it?" It was easy for Manmohan Singh to dismiss Advani's charges because the BJP-led NDA Government was dictated to by the RSS.

The BJP is the political front of the Sangh parivar. K.S. Sudarshan, the RSS sanghchalak, not only guided the BJP Government, but also ensured that both, Atal Bihari Vajpayee and Advani were reduced to insignificance after the 2004 Lok Sabha election. It was, therefore, quite easy for Manmohan Singh to tackle the BJP at his press conference. If Sonia Gandhi is perceived as an 'extra-constitutional centre of power', the Vajpayee-led Government too was subservient to the RSS. Also, the Manmohan Singh Government is far more stable than the regimes of V.P. Singh, Chandrashekhar, H.D. Deve Gowda and Inder Kumar Gujral.

The Congress has always provided prime ministers, who have governed the country without any other power centre, thanks to their control over party apparatus. In the current scenario, however, Manmohan Singh is the head of the Government while Sonia Gandhi is the leader of the party. Little wonder, Manmohan Singh observed in the press conference: "She (Sonia Gandhi) is a source of strength for me. I'll probably be less effective in many of the tasks she has to perform as UPA chairperson and Congress president."

Sonia Gandhi is aware of the Congress's culture of backstabbing. The party leaders have perfected the art of duplicity and, to quote Rajiv Gandhi, "They are power brokers." P.V. Narasimha Rao, during his prime ministership, provided enough opportunities to Sonia Gandhi to come to the conclusion that traditional Congress leaders did not have the virtue of loyalty or even political integrity.

During the Rao regime, Arjun Singh and N.D. Tiwari walked out of the Congress to float a new party, the Congress (Tiwari). If party leaders could walk out of the Congress at the behest of Sonia Gandhi and betray Narasimha Rao, they would not hesitate to do the opposite for profit. Manmohan Singh is not like a traditional khadiwala politician. Not surprisingly, Sonia Gandhi trusted him over others in May 2004.

A storm broke out soon after the Prime Minister's press conference, when a television channel showed a series of letters written by the PMO and the Cabinet Secretariat over the past 20 months, pleading the ministers to keep the Prime Minister in the loop about various policy decisions taken by their respective departments. It can be argued that the UPA allies are not following the principle of collective responsibility. Every party or group considers itself as an 'equal partner of the Congress'.

The UPA came into existence to keep the BJP out of power. Except this binding principle, the UPA partners have nothing in common either among themselves or with the Congress. The lack of coordination in the Government, therefore, could easily be attributed to the lack of commonality within the UPA.

On the issue of the PMO letter, BJP president Rajnath Singh observed: "We feel sorry for the Prime Minister's helplessness. It would not be off the mark to say that Manmohan Singh is indeed the weakest Prime Minister our country has ever had." It seems Rajnath Singh has forgotten RSS's interference during Atal Bihari Vajpayee's regime. In fact, Rajnath Singh has succeeded L.K. Advani as BJP president because of the Sangh's disapproval of the latter.

As far as the role of the Leftist parties is concerned, Manmohan Singh said, "I do not think they (the Left parties) will do so (stall policy-making). In the long run, some pressure does perform a useful function in a democracy. We will complete five years and with regard to pressure from Left, it is not unexpected." It is not only Manmohan Singh but also every Prime Minister of a coalition Government, who has to work under 'constraints'.

Parliament holds the Prime Minister responsible for the acts of the Government. Sonia Gandhi and her party cannot pretend on the floor of the House that the Government's authority is not exercised by the Prime Minister. Manmohan Singh is in the seat of the most powerful office of the Government and this role provides him with enough room to exercise discretionary powers. Manmohan Singh is not just primus inter pares in his Council of Ministers; he is also not in the category of other Congress prime ministers, like Jawaharlal Nehru, Indira Gandhi, Rajiv Gandhi and Narasimha Rao. Also, he does not belong to the category of stop-gap prime ministers, like Chandrashekhar, H.D. Deve Gowda and Inder Kumar Gujral.

If Manmohan Singh is constrained by Sonia Gandhi's role in politics and Government, he is only emulating Atal Bihari Vajpayee. After all, Vajpayee too was held in check by the RSS and other outfits of the Sangh parivar.

8

Congress Coalition and Government: 2009-2014

The Budget session of the Lok Sabha is expected to be devoted to serious discussion on issues concerning the fundamentals of economic health. The annual Railway Budget and the Union Budget are not mere statements of income and expenditure, nor are they confined to matters of new taxation for the augmentation of fiscal resources for future investments for developmental and welfare schemes for the country. These budget discussions in Parliament from February to May reveal the real situation of the national economy and future challenges, which lie ahead for the forward march of the country.

Finance Minister Pranab Mukherjee's speech conveyed a message that the Indian economy was on the growth track and in spite of the deteriorating financial and economic situation, especially the European Union crisis, India has managed its economy and fiscal situation quite well. He did not convey even a hint of anxiety on the health of the economy. On a different note, in the second week of May while winding up the budgetary annual exercise, he threw a bombshell by declaring that the rate of growth will slow down because of crisis in the international market and also because of adverse impact of the falling value on exchange rate. Mukherjee observed that the country is faced with the prospect of low rate of growth, like 6 per cent of the GDP only, or deteriorating value of the Indian rupee in the international market, the food-related inflation was becoming uncontrollable and the rising inflationary pressure on the economy was becoming unbearable for the common man. Finally, Mukherjee warned that the country will have to face 'austerity' because of the rising budgetary deficit, which was quite alarming.

Democracy is based on a social contract between the government and the people and it is the duty of the government to take public opinion into confidence on such a serious situation facing the Indian economy, but the UPA government did not deem it fit to inform the public about the country's real problems, except when Pranab Mukherjee threw a shocker in the middle of May 2012 while winding up the annual budgetary exercise in the Parliament. If Mukerjee announced some immediate austerity steps to cut the deficit, the

Prime Minister's Office suddenly came out with proposals to streamline the fast implementation of economic projects of the government. The PMO in the middle of May 2012 enlightened the country, especially business and industrial classes, that the Licence Raj of pre-1990s India has been replaced by a very obstructive and negative system of the 'clearance Raj or regime' because at least 58 clearances were required by public or private sector to launch any developmental or infrastructure project, including power-related projects.

These 58 'clearances', which were to be obtained by public or private investors, required everyone to knock at the door of various ministers at the Centre at the level of state governments. Not to be left behind, some 'clearances' were to be given by Panchayati Raj institutions. The toughest task for an investor was to chase the environmental ministry for clearances and pursue doggedly various government agencies which dealt with issues concerning 'land acquisition' for setting up as project.

This analysis of the working of 'clearance Raj or regime' by the PMO clearly shows that in spite of the fact that international economic and fiscal crisis has adversely impacted India, at the same time, it is the domestic political and administrative decision-making process, which is the real villain of the piece and is becoming a roadblock in the way of acceleration of the rate of growth of the GDP of the economy. A few facts may be mentioned to substantiate the argument that the prevailing economic crisis is a direct consequence of political directionless of leadership and over bureaucratisation of decision-making in the area of economic life of the country.

It is the duty of the government to protect environmental degradation but it is another issue to make environmental clearness an uphill task for investors. Further, the UPA government has adopted a time-consuming strategy of making a Group of Ministers to process each and every proposal of economic ministries, where a policy decision is required. A minister of coal or mines or industry or any other infrastructural development minister or department may evolve a 'proposal' for speedy implementation of projects, which fall under the jurisdiction of a particular minister. But then either the PMO or the GoM sits over the proposals of individual ministers before clearances are given. This is a politico-administrative problem, which directly concerns the actual functioning style of the government which Lakshmi Mittal, a big industrialist, publicly observed is 'a slow moving' government.

Another very important issue is of land acquisition, compensation and rehabilitation, because the anachronistic colonial law of 1894 for land acquisition is completely out of sync with new realities of the 21st century. Land is required for developmental projects, but if a proper policy of land acquisition does not exist, serious disputes are bound to arise between the seller and buyer of land. Indian courts are flooded with cases, where involved parties have complained that either the land was forcibly taken or inadequate compensation was paid or agricultural land was acquired for construction of industries.

The UPA government, which has completed three years of its term, has kept the land acquisition law hanging fire for three years. How can any government keep out of the issue of land acquisition, especially when the distinction between public sector and private economic players is getting completely blurred? During the economic regime of Public-Private Partnership, the government cannot keep itself away from land acquisition processes.

The above narrative based on important facts clearly shows that the economy is slowing down because of purely 'domestic' political situation, where decision-making processes have become quite complicated because so many ministries, departments, bureaucracy are involved in clearing a project. There is no political push or a political will to push the decision for a project or a scheme, which is considered important for growth. If the Supreme Court has laid down a policy of 'auctions' for national resources, it has abrogated the policy-making powers of the political executive, which is dithering and confused.

The crisis of economy is a challenge and an opportunity for the political executive to sit in the 'driver's seat' and resolve domestic deadlocks and delays in decision-making by the government departments. It is only purposeful politics, which can meet the challenge of economic crisis.

Grand Mess All Around

The Congress-led UPA Government is completely encircled by critics including some of its regional allies and, of course, by the Opposition, which has a legitimate a role to expose every act of omission and commission of the Government. The story of attacks on the functioning and malfunctioning of the Union Government does not end here.

A very popular movement against the Government has been led by Anna Hazare and his team of publicity-hungry activists who have succeeded in cornering the Government on the issue of widespread corruption in politics and bureaucracy. Anna Hazare has built up public pressure on a reluctant and hesitant Government to approach the Parliament for the enactment of the Jan Lok Pal Bill.

While campaigning in favour of their Lokpal Bill, Team Anna showed a lot of indecent haste by commanding the Parliament to perform its basic role of law-making within a time-frame laid down by these self-appointed and non-elected individual campaigners.

A legitimate anti-Government movement completely devalued itself by its approach and attitude towards procedures of Parliamentary democracy and other well-established norms of law-making in democracy. Team Anna failed to make a distinction between the Manmohan Singh-led Union Government and the role and responsibilities of elected representatives of the Parliament.

Anna and his team has set a dangerous precedent by downgrading the sanctity of elected representatives, who are solely responsible for law-making according to their own thinking of the issue of corruption in public life. The atmospherics created by Anna Hazare-led agitation helped in the creation of an image of weak and vacillating Government and this opportunity was fully exploited by powerful captains of the industry, who started castigating the Government by addressing open letters to Singh.

On October 11, fourteen 'eminent citizens' led by the likes of Azim Premji, Deepak Parekh *et al.* accused the Government for the "absence of decision-making". The open letter stated that "continuing impasse" has led to "delay in clearing projects". It concluded that the "policy uncertainties and delays in approvals are forcing many large corporate entities to seek out opportunities in other geographies".

If Team Anna has been accused of 'blackmailing' elected political representatives by putting them on 'notice' to legislate or face music, in this atmosphere the leading industrialists are also 'blackmailing' the Government. Premji repeated his warning on November 20, in an open letter, that policy paralysis along with the existence of a "strong nexus among certain corporations, bureaucrats and power-brokers is corroding the fabric of our nation" because in such a situation "large scale corruption in public life has become the order of the day."

Singh has many a time emphasised that India is suffering because of the growth of crony capitalism but he forgets to mention that powerful cronies can turn against its own political and bureaucratic benefactors and patrons. Singh's crony capitalists have prospered under the full patronage of decision-makers, who are either sitting in the corridors of power or those who exercise extra-constitutional authority.

It is not only the unelected Anna Hazare, who has succeeded in dictating Singh's Government. Even the unelected industry captains, who have enough financial resources to directly influence the corridors of power, have a hold on the Government. Americans are always engaged in a public discourse on whether to rein in the power of big corporations. American conservatives and their intellectual collaborators are always targetting the role of state because they view the state as the villain and have pleaded to minimise the role of state appointed market regulators.

Believers in the free market economy like Donald Regan or Margaret Thatcher believe in the ideology of a "lean and thin state and freedom for entrepreneurs". Their ideological and political opponents attack the status occupied by big corporations as the fountain source of all evils in the society and opt for a regulated capitalist economy, where the state should be in the driver's seat.

Indians have also been engaged in this basic debate about the relationship between the Government and business. The Nehru-Indira Gandhi model of state-led economic planning was based on the principle of commanding heights which should be occupied by public institutions including public sector enterprises.

The beginning of 1990's experienced a break with the past. It was suggested by then Prime Minister Narasimha Rao and his Finance Minister Manmohan Singh that the model of planned economy had become completely dysfunctional, and be replaced by a new model of 'retreat of the state'.

From a regulated economy to one that has since been deregulated, liberalised and globalised, India today, is a competitive market economic system. The Union and State Governments in the 1990's and the first decade of the 21st century practiced very enthusiastically the New Economic Policy of free market-led capitalism.

This new euphoria for a deregulated economy brought cheers from politicians, bureaucrats, corporate and the media. But everyone forgot that politicians require financial resources and big businesses favours from the Government. It is surprising that Premji and others are alleging a nexus between politicians and power-brokers, when industry captains themselves are often found in the corridors of power.

Time to Call the Bluff on Economic Policies

The new economic policy of globalisation, privatisation, deregulation and the opening of Indian market to foreign private investors was uncritically implemented by the Congress in 1991 and then, the BJP and other political parties. Two decades after it was first introduced, there is a public debate has over the role of foreign direct investment in various economic sectors of India.

The Manmohan Singh-led Government abruptly announced on November 24 that upto 51 per cent of FDI in multi-brand retail would be allowed in India. All hell broke loose, and soon the Congress was completely isolated on the issue. Not only the Opposition but also allies of the Congress-led UPA chose to dissociate themselves from their new policy. Indeed, the opposition to the UPA's unilateral decision was so strong and widespread that the Government was compelled to beat a hasty retreat.

Yet, the opening of the retail sector to foreign investors is a logical step that follows the opening up of the Indian economy that began in 1991. In fact, at the time it was launched, the so-called New Economic Policy was hailed as the solution to India's balance of payment crisis. Also, it was then rightly argued by the supporters of the new policy that India's rate of economic growth was low because it had a closed economic model of planning. Even the balance of payment crisis faced by the country was because of rigidities in economic management.

Ultimately, the proof of the pudding is in the eating, and there is no doubt that the policy of liberalisation, privatisation and globalisation spurred India's economic growth to such an extent that the country is now noticed globally as an 'emerging economy' along with China. In the past two decades, the success of the policy was considered sufficient to sell it to the masses.

Yet, when the Government announced its decision to allow FDI in multi-brand retail, every erstwhile enthusiastic supporter of Singh's economic regime abandoned ship. In fact, Union Minister for Finance Pranab Mukerjee, while addressing Congress MPs on December 6, even said that, if the Government had not withdrawn the policy, it would have been ousted from power. Moreover, with the spectre of Assembly elections in several States across the country looming, the Government was compelled to abandon its foolhardy decision.

Nonetheless, the fact remains that the issue of FDI in multi-brand retail tradehas sharply divided Indian politics, while also bringing the whole package of economic reforms under political scrutiny and public discourse. The Government of India, after announcing its policy on the opening of retail trade to foreign investors, was to announce the policy of foreign investment in the aviation sector, and in insurance and banking too. The Government has been compelled to halt its whole project of liberalisation and the opening of markets because of stiff opposition by political parties. It often happens in politics that one controversial policy decision about just one aspect of a large public policy opens a Pandora's Box and the whole framework of that policy becomes a target of public scrutiny. This is precisely the situation created by the Government and all political parties.

Several important sections of society have thought it appropriate to critically examine the meanings and consequences of the economic policies followed by India during the last 20 years. It is an extremely positive development in Indian politics because a crucial area of public life, like road to economic development was followed without any serious discussion and debate by major political parties because the so-called rate of growth success story had mesmerised every political party, which started competing against one another on the basis of their economic performance and mega economic and industrial projects, which they brought to their state.

A comic situation has developed during these two decades. Regional parties in power in the States have began competing against one another for attracting investors for the establishment of mega industrial projects without thinking about specific requirements of their own State. The State-based and State co-terminus parties, like TMC or DMK or JD(U) *et al.* have not thought it fit to have a close look at the relevance or irrelevance of their economic choices and their political implications.

Captains of industry like Deepak Parekh, Ashok Ganguly and many others have all supported the Government policy on the opening of multi-brand retail business to foreign investors and multinationals. The small traders have opposed the entry of foreigners in multi-brand trade because kirana stores, operators in local mandis or small and medium traders and shopkeepers cannot 'compete' against foreign retailers. India's domestic trading market is worth $600 billion, and more than 50 million shopkeepers are engaged in the domestic 'trade' business.

The fact is that, FDI in multi-brand retail business directly affects small and medium householders, small farmers, small and medium shopkeepers and traders that sell commodities to the neighbouring shopkeepers.

Rein in the Politicians

Power corrupts and absolute power corrupts absolutely. This old hackneyed description of politics has been replaced by new saying, if power goes into the head of a politician, he behaves like a mentally challenged person. Power has made law minister Salman Khurshid not only arrogant, but also he violated all norms of constitutional legalities by showing complete defiance of the pronouncements of the Election Commission, which is a constitutional body responsible for the conduct of free, fair and fearless elections in the country. It is Khurshid's arrogant defiance of the censure note, which has compelled Chief Election Commissioner SY Quraishi to seek President's intervention for disciplining the defiant minister in the Manmohan Singh government.

It was a mild disapproval of the conduct of the minister, when during the elections, contrary to the spirit of the Electoral Code of Conduct, he announced that a vote for the Congress would ensure nine per cent of reservation of public services for Muslims as a subquota of 27 per cent for the other backward castes. It was expected that Khurshid would get the message and move further after the views expressed by the Election Commission but, as power travels to head, he repeated that 'even if they (Election Commission) hang me', he would continue to ensure reservation for backward Muslims and such an affront to the authority of the Election Commission made it seek the intervention of the President for improper and unlawful action of Khurshid, which could 'vitiate free and fair polls in Uttar Pradesh'. The above episode involving the Election Commission, a minister, the prime minister and the president provides an opportunity to reflect on the larger issue of the role of elections and the Election Commission in a participatory electoral democracy based on the principle of universal adult franchise.

First, the provisions of the Representation of People's Act and the defined powers and functions of the Election Commission for the conduct and management of the Lok Sabha and state assembly elections lay down the broad framework for the conduct of elections, which are held generally after every five years. This legal arrangement is a necessary but not sufficient condition to ensure a fair elections. Politicians want to win at any cost and by any means. Politicians and political parties never hesitate to violate or completely break the laws to win elections.

Second, if the Election Commission is weakened or delegitimised, it would not be able to deal with money or muscle power, which is employed to completely rig and vitiate the electoral process.

Third, politics is a lucrative and profitable business, even rich and criminals participate in elections with the goal of maximising their wealth and power. Only a strong, impartial and effective Election Commission can act as a vigilant watchdog of the sanctity of ballot that is threatened by moneyed people and criminals. The Election Commission has been compelled to engage income tax officials, chartered accountants and others to exercise check the flow of illegal money during the elections. Money power makes elections a contest among unequals. In a democracy, it acts as a game changer because those who spend huge money, make every attempt to earn it back after they are elected. When democracy becomes a playground of money power, it ceases to be people's democracy and becomes an oligarchy or plutocracy.

Fourth, elections in Uttar Pradesh or Bihar have their own specificity and the phenomenon of criminals involved in booth capturing or fraud voting has prevailed on a big scale. It is the vigilant Election Commission that has worked overtime to protect the sanctity of the ballot from the influence of money and muscle power. An innovation has been made in Uttar Pradesh of election coverage by webcasting (through internet) from polling booths. This webcasting from various polling stations ensures that the process takes place as per the rules. This webcast network has linked the Chief Election Commissioner, the Chief Election Commissioner of Uttar Pradesh and the district electoral officers, and this new technology is expected to ensure that the whole election activity is monitored properly.

Fifth, every Chief Election Commissioner has performed their duties quite effectively, TN Sheshan, a maverick Chief Election Commissioner, brought the ills and maladies of elections into the public domain and he projected himself as one-man army for the cleansing of the electoral process of its ills, like booth capturing, money power and the role of criminals. TN seshan became a hero, as citizens considered him a messiah of clean democracy. The moral of the Seshan phenomenon is that Indians want clean elections. They were fed up of the malpractices and illegalities committed by politicians and parties during the elections. That's why, Khurshid does not have public support for his offensive attitude against the Election Commission. Narendra Modi, RSS pracharak and Chief Minister of Guajrat, attacked the interventions by the Chief Election Commissioner JM Lyngdogh by calling him a Christian, in spite of media management by the Sangh Parivar in defence of Modi's insolence, Atal Bihari Vajapyee, the then Prime Minister, had to make a public statement that two constitutional authorities should not get involved in public abuse.

If the ruling party does not defend the autonomy of the pillars of constitution, like the Election Commission or the judiciary or the Comptroller and Auditor General, democracy would end up in anarchy and chaos. Indians need to be reminded that it was only because of the independence of the Election Commission that electoral results against Indira Gandhi, the most powerful prime minster of India, were declared in March 1977 and electoral defeat saw the end of the Emergency regime of Indira Gandhi. India witnessed a big debate, when a one-member Election Commission was converted into multi-member commission. The attempt to have three-member commission was considered an effort on the part of the political executive to plant its own favourites into the Election Commission. The taste of pudding is in the eating; the three-member Election Commission experiment has worked successfully.

The prime minister should restrain his ministers, who are crossing the limits of legality and constitutionality by flouting the Election Commission, which is struggling hard to uphold the Election Code of Conduct. Do Indians want sham and fraudulent elections? Make up your mind. Political parties should take note of the Khurshid episode and add more teeth to the powers of the Election Commission to strengthen its capability to discipline the errant politicians. An amendment of the Constitution for providing more punitive powers to the Election Commission may be more opportune.

It has been often pointed out that the Congress-party led UPA government at the Centre is in the 'intensive care unit' and the country is faced with the crisis of governance, clearly reflected in 'policy paralysis', the country is experiencing today. Nothing seems to be moving forward. If the UPA led central government has shown its complete incompetence to take any new policy initiative on the economic front, the BJP, the other claimant for the role of a national party playing the spoilt sport and is determined to play negative and obstructive role as an opposition party in the Parliament and every economic policy initiative taken by the government has been nullified by the BJP, which has mastered the art of disturbing the every policy move initiated by the government in the Parliament.

The consequence of completely weakened leadership of the Congress-government and the role of a negative role of the BJP, as the key Opposition has only worked as a cog in the wheel for the country's economy. The wheels of government have refused to move forward and every important economic move by the government for the country has been vetoed by the BJP. Are these national parties pursuing any national interest whether in government or in Opposition?

A few facts may be mentioned to substantiate the argument that the prevailing 'deadlock' at the level of governance at the centre can be solely attributed to the present political situation. The regional fragments have to brought "on board" by the government so that they feel a part of the political formation. This will reduce the feeling of alienation and help the government push through its all important bills that are of prime interest to the common man.

The regional parties are not expected to provide 'national perspective' on public policy issues, they have to be led and persuaded by the national parties in power at the Centre. First, it is a lame excuse on the part of Prime Minister Manmohan Singh to publicly suggest that his government is functioning under the constraints of a coalition system of policy-making. Has the Manmohan Singh–Sonia Gandhi Congress conveyed to their allies that compromises will not be made by the major partner on issues, like Food Security Bill or the Land Acquisition and Rehabilitation Act. Has Congress leadership shown any strength while dealing with 'allies' about its own 'nonnegotiable' agenda for governance? After all, Congress has its 207 Lok Sabha MPs. It can well flex its muscles.

In the Atal Bihari Vajpayee-led coalition government (1998-2004), the BJP did not have requisite numbers of its own neither did it have the same number of seats that Congress-led UPA has. Despite the lack of numbers, it had the coalition in control.

The agenda of Hindutva, the core ideology of the Sangh Parivar, was vigorously pursued by the BJP-led coalition from 1998 to 2004. The BJP-led government's coalition allies could not force Vajpayee to give marching orders to Narendra Modi of Gujarat after post-Godhra brutal riots of March 2002 in Ahmedabad and other parts of the state. Coalition compulsion was not an issue, while BJP dealt with Narendra Modi.

The UPA II has not shown any firm commitment on any public issue of national and international importance and has always defended its 'inaction' either by talking about 'compulsions of coalition' or 'blaming the negativism of the BJP-led opposition. Why has the ruling UPA not succeeded in 'isolating' the BJP opposition in the Lok Sabha and aggressively hammering the issue of 'destructive role' of the BJP in the Rajya Sabha?

Second, Pranab Mukherjee, the Finance Minister, while addressing the Bengal Chamber of Commerce and Industry on April 1, 2012, made a brave statement that there was 'no policy paralysis' and mentioned that an initiative had been taken by the government while announcing the New Manufacturing Policy. Mukherjee swallowed his pride and observed 'My mandate is to carry people with me' and 'short-cuts cannot be taken' because 'divergent political views' have to be accommodated. Mukherjee should also have observed that 'diverse groups' have also to accommodate the policy agenda of the largest single party in the Lok Sabha while also has a mandate of the people to govern. Mukherjee admitted that even after third year of power of the government important laws remain in limbo and his statement of deadlocked Bills includes: (a) Goods and Service Tax; b) Direct Tax Code; c) The Insurance Amendment Act; d) the Pension Fund Regulatory Act; and e) Amendments to be Banking Act. Mukherjee on April 1, 2012 was telling the Bengal Chamber of Commerce and Industry that there was 'no policy paralysis' and the UPA government announced on April 3 that fiscal reform agenda in the field of insurance, pension and banking cannot be pursued further because of political compulsions.

Third, it happened only in 2012, and never, before, that Dinesh Trivedi, the railway minister, presented UPA governments Budget in the Lok Sabha and all hell broke out because Mamata Banerjee, the Trinamool Congress chief, not only rejected all proposals announced by the railway minister, she demanded that Dinesh Trivedi of the TMC be replaced by her other party protégé Mukul Roy as railway minister. The Minister, who had prepared and presented the budget in the Lok Sabha, was not permitted to pilot his budgetary proposals in the parliament.

The UPA government became a laughing stock because of political tsunami created by this drama in the Parliament and the country. The 'reformist' railway minister, who got public support from all major railway trade unions, ended up as a political orphan and paid price for his efforts to improve sinking health of the Railway's fiscal situation.

The larger question is that a country is formally governed by a coalition government but in reality every political group, whether a self-appointed national party, like the BJP, or small local state-regional parties in the Lok Sabha have empowered themselves to 'veto' every act of governance by the Congress-led central government. It is interesting to note that 'veto' power is exercised not only by the opposition parties or groups, even supporters of the coalition government apply brakes, whenever it suits them.

The reality behind the above narrated story of the malfunctioning of the Congress-led UPA coalition is not because of its opponents. But the Congress itself has completely failed to show any firm commitment to any programme or policy, which it is ready to own and pursue with firmness.

It has become a ritual for Congress leaders to propose at regular intervals that Rahul Gandhi should play an important role in Government. The latest to join the bandwagon is Union Minister for External Affairs SM Krishna, who suggested on June 27 that Gandhi's entry into Government was necessary to solve the problems faced by the country. Earlier party general secretary Digvijay Singh had talked about Gandhi's leadership skills and how his active participation would save the sinking Government of Prime Minister Manmohan Singh.

But ever since the days of Mrs Indira Gandhi, the Congress has always depended on a leader from the 'family' because none of the other leaders could garner the kind of broad-based acceptability that a member of the Nehru-Gandhi family had.

The question that naturally arises now is, if the Congress is called upon to form a coalition Government in 2014, will Gandhi pick her son to head the new regime? Gandhi's status in the Congress is quite different from the other dynasty successors in Punjab, Uttar Pradesh or even Tamil Nadu.

For instance, Akhilesh Yadav has been crowned Chief Minister of Uttar Pradesh with the full support of the Samajwadi Party that was created by his father, Mulayam Singh Yadav. But political inheritance is a tricky affair. Without the unquestioned loyalty and support of the party organisation, the successor can just be a one time wonder.

Gandhi's father himself could only win only one election in 1984 because that was the only time he could leverage public sympathy in his favour in the aftermath of his mother and the then Prime Minister Indira Gandhi's assassination. Rajiv Gandhi was defeated in 1989 because VP Singh portrayed him as the middle man in the Bofor's scandal. Indeed, the Congress's defeat in 1989 was because Rajiv Gandhi had been de-legitimised.

Between 2004 and 2012, Rajiv Gandhi's son was given the opportunity to prove his political capabilities. The young Gandhi assigned to himself the job of strengthening the party by the democratisation of the party organization and, especially the Youth Congress. So, did he succeed in resurrecting the the grand old party? Not really, Gandhi made some half-hearted efforts to recharge the organisational structure of the party but left his task mid-way.

Additionally, Gandhi's leadership qualities have also failed to make a mark in the Parliament. He did not make any contribution on the floor of the Lok Sabha between 2004 and 2012 that is worthy mention. His record of intervention in Parliament on crucial issues is abysmal. Even when the UPA Government was struggling to save its proposed Lok Pal legislation, Gandhi's absence was conspicuous.

Finally, a political party like the Congress only bows before a leader who can win elections but this has not been the case with Gandhi. He jumped into the electoral battle for the Bihar Legislative Assembly but could not make an impact.

It was then advertised that Gandhi would show his magic in Uttar Pradesh during the Assembly election. But he disappeared from the political scene after the results were announced. The votes were split between the Samajwadi Party and the Bahujan Samaj Party. The Congress had been completely marginalised.

When Mrs Indira Gandhi was asked to explain the secret of her 'unquestioned authority' among Congressmen, she had replied, "I win elections for them". The upshot of the above discussion is that Gandhi has proved a 'bad coin' for the Congress. His leadership is most uninspiring and he has not shown any capacity of new thinking. Gandhi is a non-starter.

Collective Irresponsibility?

The exit of Pranab Mukherjee as finance minister was welcomed by Big Business, which felt that the former finance minister was a real roadblock in the way of profit maximisation of crony business groups. Decisions of the finance ministry greatly impact the day-to-day and long-term business strategies, followed by market players. Powerful multinational corporations and foreign funding agencies also have come to realise that India is a great emerging market for foreign investments and they along with their Indian business collaborators are also celebrating.

This is not the first time that a Prime Minister has filled a vacuum in this important ministry—even Jawaharlal Nehru had to do so. The atmospherics and the response of the media, which reflects the sentiments and feelings of Big Business, is that Manmohan Singh will amend, modify, even reverse some important economic and financial policies. A lot of noise had been made by foreign investors, who had alleged that under Mukherjee, economic and fiscal policies, especially taxation policies, had not only become unpredictable but also sent out a negative signal.

The hostilities against Mukerjee started when on 16 March, during his annual Budget speech, he announced a proposal for 'retroactive tax penalty' of Rs. 11,000 crore to be imposed on Vodafone. All hell broke loose in foreign capital markets because 'the tax returns' of many foreign investors were expected to be 'reopened' by the income tax officials for finding liabilities of such investors with 'retrospective' effect. The Prime Minister, just a day after Mukherjee relinquished office, asked the finance ministry and the Prime Ministers' Office to review problems on the tax front, which need to be addressed and especially make clarifications on the General Anti-Avoidance Rules (GAAR), which had become the bone of contention because Vodafone might get repeated in the case of 'tax liabilities' of other private investors, especially foreign.

The finance ministry also observed on 28 June that the GAAR is at a 'drafting' stage and 'meetings with the stakeholders will be held' before draft rules are finalised by the government. Vodafone executives were pleading for a 'level playing field', Mukherjee stood firm on his 16 March proposal on GAAR. Manmohan Singh is not only open to renew this scheme, but also he is stated to have told finance ministry officials on 27 June, 'reverse the climate of permission ...review the animal spirits in the country's economy.' The Prime Minister positively responded to the sentiments of HDFC Chairperson Deepak Parekh, who observed on 27 June that 'harassment by tax officials and corruption loom large. Things need to be in black and white and not in grey, as they are today'.

An analytical question which needs to be addressed is the nature of collective responsibility of the cabinet led by Prime Minister Manmohan Singh, who is head of the Council of Ministers. A prime minister in parliamentary democracy is not just one among equals in the cabinet, he presides over every cabinet meeting, where policy-making decisions are taken and his opinions carry greater weight than those of any individual cabinet minister.

Further, the Budget is a policy document of the government and after the ministry of finance sifts through all the proposals and suggestions of all the ministers, the finance minister and his officials prepare a fiscal document of income and expenditure estimate of the year.

The speech while presenting the Budget proposals is an announcement of proposals and polices of the government. Has the Indian parliamentary system evolved to a stage, where the prime minister, head of the government, is kept in the dark about major policy proposals of the government? Is the finance minister king of his empire? Why was Mukherjee not told to refrain from following policies, which were slowing economic growth because foreign investors were losing 'trust' over the UPA government?

The Truth seems to be that the Prime Minister of the UPA coalition government at the Centre does not exercise any authority over either the cabinet ministers of his own Congress party or ministers belonging to the coalition partners. Dinesh Trivedi, the railway minister, presented a Railway Budget, which was highly appreciated by the Prime Minister but he was replaced by coalition partner All India Trinamool Congress. The cabinet at the Centre seems to be a like a pack of jokers, who can be reshuffled or kicked out not by the Prime Minister but by regional party chiefs. In such a situation, every minister is a 'law into himself' and the Prime Minister has obvious not adhered to the principle of collective responsibility of the cabinet.

Thus, every principle and practice of parliamentary democracy lies in the dust because Indian coalition system of government is a collective of disparate and disunited individuals, who represent their own regional party and whose loyalty lies not with the Prime Minister but with their own regional leader, who can make or unmake them as ministers. What's worse, Manmohan's writ does not run even over his party colleagues in the cabinet, because all of them, like representatives of individual coalition partners, owe their power to Sonia Gandhi, the real centre of power in the Congress. The source of authority of every minister is not the Prime Minister but party bosses, whether regional or national.

The National Democratic Alliance government of 1998 to 2004 led by Atal Bihari Vajpayee was not at all different from the UPA of 2004-12. The RSS made crucial decisions about the BJP's, role in the coalition government at the Centre and LK Advani, who was clamouring to become deputy prime minister, owed his elevation to the RSS. RSS interfered even in the allocation of portfolios to BJP ministers in the Vajpayee government.

Clearly, the cabinet system has completely deviated from the model of British or Australian or Canadian systems because from 1989 to 2012, except for a brief period of 1991-96, the central government's prime ministerial candidates had to work under extra-constitutional centres of power, like the RSS or Sonia Gandhi. This is the real meaning of the exit of Pranab Mukherjee and the arrival of Manmohan Singh in the finance ministry.

Time for Self-introspection

The Grand Old Party of India is faced with a serious internal crisis. It is feared to pale into insignificance as a political force in the democracy, if it fails to find immediate and appropriate political solutions to the challenges it faces. The Congress leadership cannot pretend that it did not receive timely warnings from its well-wishers.

Time magazine in its 8 July issue quite unfairly described Prime Minister Manmohan Singh, 'an under-achiever', who is 'unwilling to stick his neck out' on economic reforms. The magazine noted that the 'Investors are beginning to get cold feet' and 'India does not need a Prime Minister, who is a man in shadow'.

Visiting Singapore Prime Minister Lee Hsien Loong, last week while discussing the Indian business environment observed that "India has been working on improving the environment, but it is something that big companies pay careful attention to because they come here for the long-term. If you are not from the country, you will look at the prospects and the possibilities".

Not just foreign investors, India Inc too has been complaining of the Manmohan Singh government suffering from a 'policy paralysis' for long. It is quite simplistic to blame Prime Minister Singh's lack of leadership for the delays and deadlocks in decision-making. In a functioning parliamentary democracy, the effectiveness of the political executive also depends heavily on the support provided to it by the party and in this case, it is the Congress. The crisis faced by the UPA-2 government cannot just be attributed to Manmohan Singh and his Council of Ministers. The prime minister and his cabinet ministers are strong or weak, effective or ineffective, if the party-in-government is committed to its own programme and is able to politically mobilise different sections of the society in support of its own government. In a Congress party-led government, if the system is suffering from a 'policy paralysis', it means that either party leadership is applying 'brakes' on the policy initiatives of its own government or party organisation is not in a position to mobilise people's support for its policies.

Last week, Congress leader Salman Khurshid lamented that his party was 'short on direction best provided by party number two', Rahul Gandhi. Though Khurshid later detracted from his statement, his most significant observation was that though the Congress party has no ideology and Rahul has to play an active role not only in articulating its ideological positions, but also to energise the party organisation to spread the message of such an ideology to the people.

When a committed Gandhi-family loyalist, like Khurshid is forced to express his concerns about the internal health of the party in the national media, it is quite plausible that he is expressing the frustrations of his party colleagues also worried about the Congress' downslide, especially keeping in mind the 2014 Lok Sabha election. For party members, it is natural to be concerned about the forthcoming Lok Sabha elections and it is no surprise that they are looking for 'saviours' in Sonia Gandhi and her heir apparent, Rahul Gandhi.

The message from Khurshid and others in the Congress to Sonia and Rahul is to provide an effective, ideological and organisational leadership before it is too late.

Ironically, Rahul Gandhi's leadership did not bear any fruit in the recent Bihar and Uttar Pradesh Assembly elections. And it is not even a question of winning or losing an election in one or two states, on ground, the junior Gandhi completely failed to inspire his party. Unlike his grandmother Indira Gandhi, and Sonia Gandhi, he could not show the Congress in any new light. A close scrutiny of his election speeches during the Assembly elections clearly reveals his ideological bankruptcy, and if the Congress is expecting any miracle from him in the 2014 Lok Sabha elections, one can only pity their expectations. Mother's love for her son is one thing, but Rahul Gandhi has proved a 'non-starter'.

In such a scenario, Sonia Gandhi appears to be the last hope for the Congress and she has proved her leadership capabilities beyond any shadow of doubt. Congress was a sinking ship because of the disastrous leadership of Narasimha Rao, Sitaram Kesari until Sonia revived it. Sonia's 'thinking' was clearly reflected in UPA 1 from 2004 to 2009, when she balanced the high rate of economic growth with progressive legislations like the Right to Information Act, Mahatma Gandhi Rural Employment Guarantee Scheme, Right to Education, Rural Health Programme et al. The Congress-in-government with full backing of Sonia Gandhi, was active and achievement-oriented between 2004 and 2009. Sonia provided leadership from the 'front' and it bore fruit, when Congress party obtained 206 seats out of 543 in the 2009 Lok Sabha election.

But in its second term, Sonia's Congress lost all sense of purpose and directions and started searching for alibis and lame excuses by blaming the opposition parties or its own recalcitrant coalition allies for the government's non-performance. Just like the drowning man clutches a straw, an exhausted Sonia Gandhi is looking at Rahul to lead the party to electoral victories. Sonia as a leader is a better bet for the Congress, against a non-performing and uninspiring Rahul.

It is bad politics to blame everything on the leader of a coalition government or to expect a single leader to change the destiny of a big party, like the Congress. The' well-wishers of the Congress should stop shadow-boxing Manmohan Singh and should actively participate in the party's revival under Sonia Gandhi, the real leader of the party.

Sonia Gandhi: Crisis of Dualism

The UPA government has been blamed for paralysis in decision-making on public policy matters of great significance. Prime Minister Manmohan Singh, in his Independence Day address, observed that the government was unable to spur economic growth because of the lack of political consensus on many issues.

Absence of political support is only part of the explanation for policy immobilism. The other significant factor is Sonia Gandhis role as president of the Congress party and her chairmanship of a parallel centre of authority, the National Advisory Council.

A national newspaper on August 13 reported data provided in response to RTI queries about the formal relationship between the National Advisory Council (NAC) and the government from 2010. Gandhi, as chairman of the NAC, has intervened on policy issues by writing 25 letters to the Prime Minister and 17 letters to various Cabinet ministers during the last two years. Gandhi occupies a super status in the UPA government and the Prime

Minister and Cabinet ministers have to make public policies, as decided and directed by Gandhi.

The theory and practice of parliamentary-Cabinet system of democracy in every western country, without any exception, show that political executive headed by the prime minister and his council of ministers is solely accountable for the making and implementation of the governments policies, and the elected Parliament holds the PM accountable for all acts of omission and commission of the government.

Walter Bagehot observed that prime minister is the hyphen that joins and the buckle that binds the cabinet, and the system revolves around prime minister, who is the kingpin of the government. The real first Labour party government was formed under Lord Attlee as Prime Minister of England. Prof Harold JLaski, who was chairman of the Labour party, asserted his authority vis-à-vis the Prime Minister because it was expected, as a Labour party government, to function according to the polices conveyed by the party chairman. The government was in office because of Labour, whose chairman carried authority of the whole party.

Lord Attlee conveyed to Prof Laski that the head of the Labour party government was accountable only to Parliament and the party chairman should confine himself to the problems of party only.

Jawaharlal Nehru, as Indias first Prime Minister, had to remind Acharya J B Kriplani that the prime minister is constitutionally recognised as the head of government and party president could not exercise any special authority, political or moral, over the prime minister. Another test for Nehru in the early days of post-Independence India came, when Purushottam Das Tandon was elected Congress party president. Nehru wrote that he could not work with Tandon because of serious ideological differences with him, and the result was that Tandon had to resign as party president because the Prime Minister could not work with a socially-conservative person.

Indira Gandhi faced party president S Nijalingappa and some members of the Congress Working Committee, who ignored the Prime Ministers choice of candidate for the president of India. She openly opposed the official candidate, Neelam Sanjiva Reddy, and asked MPs and MLAs for their conscience vote for V.V. Giri, who got elected. Nijalingappa served showcase notice to Indira Gandhi for indiscipline. Indira split the Congress in 1969.

The upshot of above narrative is clear that government-party relationship has to be based on the logic and conventions of Parliament-Cabinet system, where the prime minister is the real centre of power and a parallel centre of authority of the party president is unacceptable and unworkable according to the principle of accountability of the prime minister to the Parliament.

It is factually correct that Sonia Gandhi is the sole architect of the Congress-led UPA government at the Centre and that she, by her own efforts, revived and revitalised the sinking ship of the Congress. If she had continued to focus on the crisis-ridden Congress party organisation and allowed her coalition government to work on its own, asking only for implementation of her partys election manifesto, the present crisis faced by the Manmohan Singh would not have happened.

The situation is complicated by coalition politics, where every coalition member has its own agenda and is not constrained to accept Sonia Gandhi's leadership.

Sonia's NAC produces a social agenda for the government and expects the Prime Minister to implement it. The NAC has particular ideas on food security but these are not shared by Sharad Pawar, the agriculture minister belonging to the NCP. Dualism of the system of governance has crippled the UPA government and its functioning from 2004 to 2012. Sonia should follow parliamentary system and its practices and stop dictating policies to the Prime Minister.

Manmohan's Unfinished Agenda

Prime Minister Manmohan Singh can legitimately take credit for his achievements and his excellent performance in the field of foreign policy. Singh took over the leadership of India's foreign policy after former foreign minister K Natwar Singh was removed from his post in 2005. For eight years of UPA I and II rule, the Prime Minister himself took every initiative in the formulation and implementation of India's foreign policy.

Singh was very keen to establish strong bonds of friendship between India and the United States because he thought that India's national interests would be well served, if a special strategic relationship could be established with the sole global military superpower. It must be stated here that former US president George W Bush and current President Barack Obama very enthusiastically reciprocated India's keenness to have "special relationship" with their country. The best evidence of that was when the US went out of its way to create conditions favourable to India for the signing of the Nuclear Energy Pact in 2008. Without that, Manmohan Singh's dream of getting India an entry in the global club of nuclear suppliers would have remained unfulfilled.

The PM single-handedly pushed the idea that India needed nuclear energy for economic development even though an important section within his own party was not very enthusiastic about the pact. The BJP and the communist parties were completely opposed to the idea of any nuclear energy pact with the US. In such circumstances, it was only Singh, who successfully piloted this idea, leading to the signing of the pact in 2008.

Americans wanted a "special relationship" with India so as to have New Delhi play a counterweight to a rising Beijing in Asia. Foreign policy has necessary elements, and philanthropic considerations do not play any role in foreign policy calculations among the nations, whether at the global, regional or bilateral level. Manmohan succeeded with Americans in getting "special treatment" because the latter considers India a strategic partner in its goal to contain and counter China in Asia. One of Singh's foreign policy plans was to strengthen and solidify India's relationship with the US. His other foreign policy goal was to improve bilateral relationship with neighbouring countries, especially China and Pakistan because without resolving India's longstanding problems with these two countries, New Delhi cannot achieve its goal of playing an important role in Asia, let alone at the international level.

The PM took all policy steps to resolve India-China and India-Pakistan disputes. However, he must be a very disappointed man because he failed in his mission of strengthening ties with Islamabad. Singh spent a lot of time and energy on finding a common settlement with Pakistan on the Kashmir question, which still continues to remain a huge roadblock in the normalisation of bilateral ties between these two neighbours.

The PM can, however, breathe easy on China because Beijing may not go out of the way to show any special warmth toward India. The Chinese realise that India has enough strength to deal with any threat from China. India and China have achieved a level of relationship and mutual understanding on the basis of which they can have a good working relationship without any fear of aggression from one another.

But Pakistan is a different ball game. The country has its own domestic compulsions and militant anti-India groups in Pakistan cannot permit their country's leadership to make any special efforts to negotiate with India. Manmohan negotiated with Pervez Musharraf, Asif Ali Zardari and Nawaz Sharif, but no outcome was in accordance to the satisfaction and expectation of the Indian PM. It is not Pakistan alone, where the Indian Prime Minister appears to have failed on the foreign policy front; a cooling off situation with the US too is visible.

In his second term, Barack Obama has not shown any special interest in India. Americans have not shown any inclination in involving India while dealing with Afghanistan, especially when NATO forces are all set to withdraw from the country. Singh must have been expecting that Americans would hold special negotiations with India about the future of Afghanistan, especially because the entire South Asia would be affected with any destabilising political situation in Kabul. Americans are making extra efforts to stay on in Afghanistan even after the troop withdrawal but they seem to have forgotten that their "special strategic partner", India, also has its own national interests to protect there.

The PM was also not expecting that his sincere efforts in maintaining the 'special strategic partnership' with US will get a rude jolt with the Devyani Khobragade issue, which led to a rise in anti-American sentiments in the country.

It is a pity that Manmohan Singh, who perhaps wished to vacate the office of the Prime Minister with memories of foreign policy successes, is ending his term without leaving behind a legacy. He is completing his ten years in office without improving the India-Pakistan relationship. But the outgoing Prime

Minister can take heart in the fact that he made the best efforts to resolve delicate issues of foreign policy.

Something has gone seriously wrong within the political leadership of the Congress party which, despite winning 206 of the 543 Lok Sabha seats on its own in the 2009 elections, and unlike its own coalition government of 2004-09, seems to have nothing special to offer to the Indian voter. The Congress not only pulled off the India-US nuclear deal but also the National Rural Employment Guarantee Scheme that brought enthusiastic support from the aam aadmi for the party, which was re-elected in 2009. It cannot be denied that from 2004 to 2014, the Congress-led coalition government launched many social and economic welfare schemes and ensured citizens are empowered with certain important rights, like Right to Education, Right to Information *et al.* But why has the same Sonia-Manmohan leadership seemingly failed to make any impact on the Indian voter? The political credibility of the Congress was eroded, when in 2010 its ministers went to an airport to negotiate with the so-called Baba Ramdev who had threatened to launch a mass agitation against the Congress on the issue of black money. This approach of the party clearly showed its political bankruptcy because the message to the common man was that the Congress had something to hide and, hence, felt threatened by a small-town Baba. Congress ministers rushed to Ramlila Maidan in 2011 to negotiate with Anna Hazare who launched a mass movement for the enactment of the Jan Lokpal Bill to curb corruption in public life. The Congress was at the receiving end of Anna Hazare, whose anti-corruption movement, willy nilly, came to be seen as directed against the Congress party. The Congress could not stand against the storm created by anti-corruption crusaders during 2011-12 and an extremely defensive party could not politically seize the initiative and emerge as a champion of an anti-corruption Jan Lokpal Bill. So, the first explanation for the lacklustre performance of the Congress-in-government from 2009 to 2014 is that it completely failed to understand the full implications of the anti-corruption sentiment at a popular mass level. How can it be a party of the aam aadmi, if it cannot appreciate prevailing feelings among the masses That said, during the full term of the 15th Lok Sabha, it was the aggressive and disruptionist Opposition that determined the agenda of the Parliament and succeeded in compelling the government to follow the dictates of the Opposition. It has been suggested by the Congress that it could not pursue its agenda because of hurdles placed in its way by the negativism of the Opposition. It is a strange argument by a government, with clear a majority of its own along with its coalition allies, that it was handicapped because of the tactics of the Opposition! How could a revolutionary welfare law, like the National Food Security Act not be enacted in 2009 instead of 2013. The same story was repeated, when the Right to Fair Compensation and Transparency in Land Acquisition, Rehabilitation and Compensation Act was enacted in 2013, while the difficulties in land acquisition for public and private projects had been brought to the notice of the government by its own ministers involved in developmental activities. The wheels of government were moving slowly and without any welldefined agenda from 2009 to 2014, and it is difficult to swallow that an obstructive Opposition or unreasonable coalition allies happen to be the villain of the piece. It also cannot be argued that the Prime Minister and Cabinet ministers were unable to take required political initiatives in the process of governance because of the existence of dual centres of power in their party because this so-called dual-authority system had worked quite successfully during UPA-I. There is no evidence to believe the Sonia-Manmohan Singh partnership came under strain from 2009 to 2014 while it worked smoothly from 2004 to 2009. The Congress partys political and governmental leadership is solely responsible for its patchy record of governance from 2009 to 2014 because it lacked courage of conviction in dealing with allegations, and a morally weakened leadership cannot lead from the front in politics. If the Bofors gun deal made Rajiv Gandhi morally weak in politics, history seems to be repeating itself, and Sonia and Rahul are facing an electoral defeat, like Rajiv earlier on the issue of corruption in public life, whether proven or not. Election Verdict: 2014

A few salient, even exceptional, features of the 16th Lok Sabha electoral verdict of 2014 deserve to be highlighted for understanding the true meaning and significance of unprecedented voters 'turnout of 66.38 per cent. It has been always maintained by important theorists of electoral political Representative democracy that an exceptional voters' turnout happens only, when elections are held and and voters feel that an extraordinary situation exists in society and because of much a special situation, the voters come out to exercise their right to vote. The first illustration to substantiate this theory of elections is that of the Lok Sabha elections of 1984, when large number of voters rushed towards the polling booths to exercise their right to vote because they all felt that country's security is threatened because even Indira Gandhi, Prime Minister of India, could not be saved from the bullets of the assassins. Post-Indira Gandhi elections took place under extraordinary conditions, when people felt that India was under siege and the need of the hour was to elect a formidable government with a clear majority of seats in the Lok Sabha. Is 2014 a repeat story of the post-Indira Gandhi elections of 1984? If a common voter feels that he cannot sit at home, because his "vote" matters, otherwise the existing crisis will further deeper, if a government-in-power is politically weak and vulnerable to all kinds of competing and conflicting pressures. Did Indians feel that the Manmohan Singh at the Centre was not at all equal to face the challenges of 2014 India? Perhaps the voters in 2014 desired an alternative to the Congress-led UPA government because of their perception that is was only a capable and effective governmental and political leadership that could deliver the goods. The Manmohan Singh government for many reasons was perhaps perceived as incapable and weak to perform its responsibilities of proper governance of the country and hence, its replacement and displacement have an absolute necessity for the present times. Hence, Narendra Modi-led Bharatiya Janata Party was given a clear mandate and for the first time the party received 282 seats in the Lok Sabha of 543 members.

May be, even BJP has been impressed by its robust electoral victory in its history of fighting ninteen Lok Sabha elections beginning from 1952 to 2014.

Table 8.1: BJP's Performance

The Rise and Fall				
Year	*Contested*	*Won*	*Vote Share (in per cent)*	*Votes polled (in crore)*
1989	225	85	11.36	3.42
1991	468	120	20.11	5.53
1996	471	161	20.29	6.79
1998	388	182	25.59	9.43
1999	339	182	23.75	8.66
2004	364	138	22.16	8.64
2009	433	116	18.8	7.84

Source: Indian Express, Delhi, May 19, 2014-06-18.

The Table 8.1 clearly shows that the Atal Bihari Vajpayee-led coalition government at the Centre could get only 182 Lok Sabha seats in 1996 and 1998 and on the basis of support of a large number of coalition partners, it was able to come to power at the centre in 1996 and 1998. This is BJP's past. Its present is quite different not only because it has majority of 282 seats of its own. L.K. Advani, while presiding over BJP's elected MPs on May 20, 2014, observed that this remarkable electoral victory of the party should be attributed to the single handed successful campaigning by Narender Modi and only Modi deserves full credit for winning 282 Lok Sabha seats in 2014. If the winning party itself has recognised the pre-eminent status of Modi, any other evidence is not required to state that the whole electoral battle for 2014 was fought around Modi as a leader.

Further, India has a competitive multi polar-party system, it is essential to mention the percentage of votes polled by other important contestants in 2014.

The Table 8.2 clearly shows that except the BJP and Congress, which polled 31.0 per cent and 19.3 per cent of the total votes polled, all other state level based parties and groups received from 4 per cent to 0.3 per cent of votes polled because of their limited geographical reach and hence support of the voters. Only BJP and Congress are an all-India national parties and all others are limited to particular states of India. If BJP has obtained 282 seats, the congress (44), the ADMK (37), The Biju Janata Dal (20) and Trinamool Congress (34) and all others have limited number of seats in the 16th Lok Sabha. The picture of Lok Sabha elections cannot become clear without briefly referring to the status of once dominant majority party which ruled over India.

Table 8.2: Final Vote-Shares of Major Players—2014

Party	*Vote Share (in %)*
BJP	31.0
Congress	19.3
BSP	4.1
TMC	3.8
SP	3.4
AIADMK	3.3
CPM	3.2
Independents	3.0
TDP	2.5
YSRCP	2.5
AAP	2.0
Shiv Sena	1.9
DMK	1.7
BJD	1.7
NCP	1.6
RJD	1.3
TRS	1.2
JD(U)	1.1
CPI	0.8
JD(S)	0.7

Source: *Indian Express*, New Delhi, May 19, 2014.

Table 8.3: Congress Performance

Elections	*Winning Party*	*Seats Won*	*Total Seats*	*Vote Share*
1957	Congress	371	494	47.8
1962	Congress	361	494	44.7
1967	Congress	283	520	40.8
1971	Congress	352	518	43.7
1977	Janata Party	154	542	34.5
1980	Congress	353	529	42.7
1984-85	Congress	414	541	48.1
2014	Congress	44	543	19.3

Source: *Indian Express*, New Delhi, May 18, 2014.

The once formidable Congress is lying in a shambles with 44 seats and a little more than 19 per cent of the retained votes.

The Table 8.3 gives a glimpse of the given situation in which Congress has fallen from high pedestal to an extremely miserable political status.

Indian Elections are very special because on the basis of 'Registered' and 'Non-registered' categories defined by the Election Commission of India, the present day India has 1,687 parties 'Registered' for the Lok Sabha elections. It does not mean that all Registered or Unregistered parties actually contest the elections, for example, in 2014, 53 parties actually contested and not to be left behind the contestant candidates, many frivolous and absentee, 5000 contested 2014 elections. If BJP has recorded slow and steadily growth, Congress has shown ups and downs during the last sixteen Lok Sabha Elections.

Table 8.4: Congress Decline in Varous States

Congress in power at state level	*States*	*Number of Seats (All India = 543 Seats)*
Congress has not been in power at state level in 25 years	West Bengal, Tamilnadu, Uttar Pradesh, Bihar, Sikkim, Tripura, Nagaland	205
Congress has not been in power at state level for more than 10 years	Gujarat, Odisha, Madhya Pradesh, Chhattisgarh,	87
Less likely that congress will be able to win power in state without an ally	Andhra Pradesh (Telangana and Seemandhara, (Delhi, Jammu & Kashmir, Maharashtra, Jharkhand)	117
Congress still within striking distance of power at state level	Punjab, Himachal, Haryana, Kerala, Karnataka, Assam, Goa, Rajasthan, Northeastern States, Union Territories	134

Congress Performance in Key Elections Since 1977

Lok Sabha Election Year	*Seats Contested*	*Won*	*Number of Seats Fofeited Deposit*	*Vote Share (in %)*
1977	492	154	18	34.5
1989	510	197	5	39.5
1996	529	140	127	28.8
1999	453	114	88	28.3
2009	440	206	71	28.6
2014	464	44	178*	19.3

*Provisional

Source: *Indian Express*, New Delhi, May 20, 2014.

The Table 8.4 clearly shows that Congress has always shown a capacity to revive and reinvent itself. The future will show whether Congress is able to really face the new challenge before itself or remain a pale shadow of its former self.

To conclude the discussion about the meanings of verdict, Modi's contribution deserves to be highlighted. Modi addressed 440 rallies, including185 Vijay Bharat elector rallies. Modi always appropriated Hindu popular symbols, like launching his election campaign after offering prayers at Vaishno Devi Temple with Mata's blessings and addressed his own election rally at Varanasi with a slogan "Holy Ganga Ma has asked" him to come to Varanasi to contest the elections. Hindutva was always his shield and public face. This is an election victory of Modi only.

9

Anna Hazare's Movement

Anna Hazares agitation in defence of his version of the Lokpal Bill seems to have revived public memories of the 1974-75 Jayaprakash Narayan-led anti-corruption mass agitation, especially among the new generation of technology-driven middle class youth in metropolitan towns of India. But can Anna Hazare's anti-corruption crusade become a benchmark comparable with the historical mass mobilisation movements launched by Gandhi from 1920 to 1947 or the one popularly known as the JP movement of 1974-75?

A mass movement has to be distinguished from political mobilisation undertaken by every political party in a competitive democracy because, unlike parties which mobilise their voters and supporters for winning an election, peoples movements are launched for cleansing the system of its fundamental ills. Gandhi prepared Indians to fight the struggle for Independence and for this mass struggle he created a united social bloc of castes, classes, religions, regions and women. The Gandhian movement was socially broad-based and inclusive of all major group identities of the country. The JP movement, unlike Gandhis struggles, had a limited reach, where he raised anti-corruption issues facing India. Further, JP, unlike Gandhi, had no mass base of his own, and he led the movement on the basis of cadre provided by Lohia socialists, the Rashtriya Swayamsevak Sangh (RSS) and the Jan Sangh. Essentially, JP launched a movement on the corruption issue primarily directed against Indira Gandhi as an individual and as a leader of a corrupt party and government. The lesson from the JP movement is that a large-scale mass movement has to be a product of preceding small-scale mobilisations, as Gandhi did from the 1920s to 1947. Anna Hazare's movement has some salient features that are a replication of the JP movement, but it has nothing in common with Gandhian movements. Hazare's movement has spread in towns and cities, especially after his arrest by Delhi Police on August 16 and angry people have come out on the road in support of him. It is a repeat story, because the JP movement had assumed an all-India status only, when the Allahabad High Court judgment of June 1975 set aside the election of Prime Minister Indira Gandhi. This support of the urban middle and lower middle class to Hazare is not only because of his anti-corruption crusade but because it is also an expression of their general frustration with the existing situation, for which the easy whipping boy is the Manmohan Singh government. Further, Hazare himself and many of his supporters on the streets are targeting corrupt politicians, but in reality they are themselves a political, even anti-politics, in their daily life and ideological value system. Hazare has debunked the system of elections by publicly stating that elections are won by bribing the voter and his complete lack of faith in the democratic process of India can be summed up in his oft-repeated statement that the transfer of power after 1947 was from the white to the brown and black Indians and nothing has changed during the last 64 years of India's Independence. Further, unlike Gandhi, Hazare who has no faith in democracy, has adopted fascistic methods to get a seal of approval by the Parliament for his demand. This has nothing to do with Gandhian movements because Gandhi suspended his movements and never feared to negotiate with the colonial rulers. Anna, like JP, has been compelled to depend on the mobilisation machine of the Sangh Parivar and its communal-fascist cadre of the RSS. The BJP within the Parliament and the whole joint family of the Sangh Parivar on the streets are providing the whole structure of support to keep the pot boiling to stigmatise the Congress, its main rival in politics. Gandhi's movements had a long-term impact on Indian public life, Hazare's movement, like the JP movement, has political consequences and its impact will be felt only in electoral politics. The age of large-scale united all-India mass movements has come to an end because a socially and regionally fragmented country will have, and has been, witnessing local/regional movements or caste-based movements. Our national identity, which was created by Gandhian struggles from Kohima to Peshawar, has been pushed to the background by movements launched by fragments on particularist demands of sections of society. Political competition among parties around local grievances has become the reality of democratic India. It is no one's case that politics will be missing from social movements; the only issue, as raised by the German philosopher Habermas, is that every social movement should be critically evaluated on the basis of its leadership, its social base, and the social cause pursued by the leaders. On the basis of the analytical yardstick suggested by Habermas, Hazares movement and the social support generated by it clearly reveals that the communal-fascist Sangh Parivar is the main driver of this movement.

State Response to Movement

The *Seminar* issue of September 2011 is devoted to the problematic of 'Combating Corruption' and contributors, a majority of them from civil society, have offered rich analysis focused on the Anna Hazare's movement of August 2011. There is, however, need for broadening the discussion on the role of social movements in a democracy. Politics is the driving force in every society and it is no one's case that the activity of politics can be caged within the rules of the game, as defined by the constitutional system of a democratic politics. The pillar of politics in democracy is the 'freedoms' that are available to citizens to exercise their right of dissent against the legally constituted institutions of the state. And dissenters and non-conformists define their own boundaries without caring for the limits imposed by the legal-institutional apparatuses of the state. The question is: How does the state respond to social movements launched by public spirited dissenters and diverse kinds of opposition groups?

The Indian state, during the sixty four years of its post-independence journey, has dealt with a large variety of movements, which have emerged on the basis of felt-grievances of different segments and regions of society in a variety of ways. It used its organized and well-equipped armed forces in dealing with the Communist party-led Telangana movement from 1947 to 1950, despite the fact that it was an 'armed' struggle of the peasantry against feudal oppression and exploitation. The state did not address the genuine demands of an oppressed peasantry because it always uses its coercive forces against angry social groups, particularly if they launch an armed struggle against an irresponsive state, which is protecting the interests of the exploiting classes.

The policy of bullet versus bullet has been consistently followed by the Indian state against armed groups, which sought to opt out of India's territorially defined boundaries or against peasants and tribals who took to arms because the state was seen as protecting the oppressor landlords and mafias, who have exploited the poor tribals and their natural resources.

It is not without reason that the managers of the Indian state have publicly observed that 'the Maoist insurgency is the greatest threat to the security of the state' and have sought to crush it. The above narrative clearly shows that our 'democratic' state has little concern for people's struggles, if solutions are demanded by launching armed movements, either by suffering peasants or tribals or groups, which claim to have the right to opt out of the Indian Union. A democratic state on the basis of its claim of moral superiority and democratic sanctions has legitimized its use of coercive power against anti-state armed struggles of groups, who are fighting for their 'rights'.

While this is one facet of the relationship between state and movements, the other is that the functionaries of the state also negotiate with and accommodate the demands made by social movements, which are described as 'normal activity of dissident groups in a competitive electoral democratic political system.' The Jayaprakash Narayan or Anna Hazare-led movements may rhetorically be described as extra-constitutional, but the functionaries of the state go out of their way to negotiate, bargain and accommodate the demands of these so-called social movements of civil society. Every such movement is concerned with the reform of the political system and while the state may resist some demands, it always keeps its doors open for settlement with the leadership of such intra-state reformist movements because they are spearheaded by leaders and social groups, who are not 'outsiders' as far as the state system is concerned.

The JP movement was launched in 1974-75 to 'purify' a corrupted electoral system with a view to cleansing the democratic institutions by limiting the entry of MLAs and MPs accused of electoral malpractices. Jayaprakash Narayan launched his struggle against 'polluted' governmental institutions because those holding the reins had adopted 'foul' means to come to power. He wanted to restore the majesty and legitimacy of democratic institutions through his proposals for electoral reforms. Reforming democracy was the main agenda of the JP movement. Similarly, numerous other movements for the reorganization of state boundaries too have received a 'royal treatment' from negotiators and interlocutors of the government-in-power, by the opposition parties and media, both, print and audio-visual. Anna's movement too was for a 'negotiated settlement' on the issue of an appropriate mechanism to check corruption in public life and public institutions. Anna led a popular struggle for a Jan Lokpal bill and like many other democratic struggles in post-independence India, this movement too achieved its goal on the basis of 'democratic accommodation' by the powers-that-be.

Clearly the state itself decides to adopt different yardsticks while dealing with different movements in a democracy. Depending upon the basic social issues raised by the movement and the methods chosen for achieving its goal, the state decides either to ruthlessly crush the movement or negotiate with its leaders. If on the one hand, the demands of a surplus generating peasantry or rural oligarchy, as articulated by the late Mahendra Singh Tikait's Bharatiya Kisan Union, are negotiated and conceded, struggles launched by landless agricultural labourers, share croppers, marginal farmers and tribals receive a cavalier response, often pushing them into taking up arms against the state.

The Anna Hazare movement too needs to be examined on the basis of its demands, and the support it garnered from the emerging middle classes, who used modern means of communication to spread their message across the country. Is the emergence of the phenomenon of movements, actively supported by upwardly mobile technocratic, professional middle classes, any surprise? Instead of berating a social movement, which may have a broad social base among the rising Indian middle classes, the focus should be on analyzing the ideological driving force of this segment of our society, since middle class activism is here to stay.

By and large this 'moneyed class' is insecure and socially conservative, even status quoist. It is not sympathetically oriented towards movements for the rights of the 'real' poor, the basic classes, and usually supports every state action which, in its judgement, is needed to maintain and protect the existing social order. The mainstream of this 'new class', a product of fast-changing material forces of production, is status'-quoist', right-wing conservative and, in the specific Indian situation, a believer in and practitioner of ritualized religion.

Hence, the upshot is that the rapid, ongoing social change is creating a new strata of society and movements articulating demands, which cannot be dismissed in a contemptuous manner. Social movements should be properly analysed. Further, historical evidence also testifies to the fact that even the essentially 'socially conservative middle class' can become an 'agency' for basic social transformations in society. The Indian middle class, old and new, has revealed its 'two faces' or two tendencies during the different struggles of the 20th century. At one level, every tall leader of the Indian national struggle against British colonial rule, despite different ideological persuasions, came from the middle classes and made every kind of personal sacrifice for the liberation of the country. The Indian middle class has been actively involved both in right of centre or left-of-centre or even full-fledged Communist party-led struggles. It is this complex and contradictory character of the emerging middle classes, which influences both, the goals and directions of the social movement, as also the response of the state.

Lokpal Movement: Whither Public Accountability?

Corruption crusader Anna Hazare's movement elicited public response because people have developed hatred against public functionaries. They perceive them as violators of laws of the land. Every democratic system has an elaborate system of checks and balances to ensure public accountability. India is not an exception. A complex system of institutions has been created to ensure that every public functionary is held accountable.

Legal institutions for governance are a necessary but not sufficient condition to ensure that an 'accountable' functionary of the state implements the rule of law. India has an elaborate structure for holding every public-decision-maker accountable, but the reality is that a majority of 'insiders' are generally able to subvert the formally laiddown governance procedures.

A political executive in a democracy is expected to act as a defender of the rule of law and the Constitution. But the reality is that many of these custodians of the Constitution have been arrested and prosecuted for violations of law even while holding public office. Members of the union council of ministers have been hauled up by investigation agencies for violating laws and later prosecuted after a fair trial. Public servants—be they ministers or bureaucrats—are pillars of the democratic system to ensure that procedures are followed in government.

There is an internal chain of command among them. They are duty-bound to take decisions while dealing with the problems of citizens. However, this system, with a water-tight, built-in structure of control and supervision, has not yielded proper accountability of decision-makers in India.

Why has the formal system of accountability become so dysfunctional that its violators feel confident and subvert the whole system of checks and balances? The key reason is that the system is not foolproof. First, only internal mechanisms of public accountability have been defined.

However, the 'external' dimension of accountability was never integrally linked to the first. An open democracy and open government has never actually operated in India because every activity and decision of the government was 'open' only to a powerful strata of society. But it was 'secret' for a vast majority of citizens, who had to knock at the doors of decision-makers to resolve their problems.

Even today, most people in India do not have any access or information on the rationale or genesis of any public-decision taken by any public functionary that impinges on their day-to-day lives. The Right to Information Act, 2005 and the setting up of Central and State-level Information Commissions has opened the mysterious gates of the offices of decision-makers. This law has extended, to a great extent, the boundaries of accountability in public service.

Politicians or bureaucrats in the higher echelons of governance can 'close ranks' behind the Chinese wall of 'secrecy'. However, if the wall is broken, they will function with a sense of real accountability. Second, a democratic political system should guarantee that citizens will be served by functionaries of the state as a matter of 'right'.

The Grievance Redressal Bill along with a Citizens Charter, such as the RTI Act, will make public servants more accountable. As some social activists have observed, 'getting his bijli, sadak or paani' is far more important for the common man. The Grievance Bill, and not the Lokpal, will empower them to get these basic necessities.

The real innovation in enacting a Public Grievances Bill or Citizen's Charter is that a grievance redressal officer will 'be responsible for redressal of citizens' grievances within 30 days. Else, penal action will be taken against the errant officer.

India is a country that has several laws, including on very complex issues such as anti-corruption. Despite this, citizens often feel helpless while dealing with an 'all powerful bureaucracy' and its consequence is that only powerful and influential persons can get their job done by a willing, compliant and obliging bureaucracy.

Ordinary citizens do not have any mechanism to hold non-performing bureaucrats accountable to any citizen-body that can oversee the actual functioning of public service.

India has continued with the British colonial structure of bureaucracy, where it is taken for granted that a well-knit chain of a command and hierarchical supervision system will keep the government machinery at work according to procedures laid down by the laws of the country. This system has not worked.

Hence, the process of decision-making by public authorities—be it the political executive or a permanent and professional civil servant—should be exposed to public scrutiny. Citizens must have a right to get their job done. The existing system of public accountability is dysfunctional.

It can be 'restored' only, if offices of the government are 'open', not for powerful lobbyists or touts or middlemen, but for any citizen. The Official Secrecy Act should be replaced with a Citizens' Rights Act.

10

Modi Government

It is for the first time in the history of India that the BJP came to power at the Centre on the basis of its individual strength, securing one-third votes and 282 seats in the 543-member Lok Sabha. The yardstick for evaluation of a party-in-government for two years either at the Centre or in states is quite simple, Policies and performance of a government is judged on the basis of its strengths as well as inadequacies in terms of outcome. Hence, "performance" is the criterion for a critical evaluation of a government after two years. However, this tradition-based criterion of "performance" is not applicable in the case of BJP-in-government from 2014 to 2016 because un-like all other multiple democratic, centrist and secular parties of India, the BJP is quite distinct and its ideology is derived from the Hindutva organisation Rashtriya Swayamsevak Sangh. The BJP is not autonomous and is an affiliate of RSS and like all other 44 affiliates of RSS, BJP too is committed to establish a 'Hindu Rashtra' in India and hence, every political action of its government is expected to push forth the agenda of making the Indian state a 'Hindu Rashtra. RSS, the parent organisation of BJP, VHP, Bajrang Dal, ABVP, et al, as a team are ideologically and politically committed Jo strengthening the foundations of making India a "Hindu Republic". RSS and other Hindu ideologies, like V D Savarkar believed at India belongs to Hindus only and exclusively. Narendra Modi and every RSS affiliate focused their primary agenda of Hinduisation of society by targeting Muslims and Christian minority by projecting them as outsiders, as "enemies" of Hindus and anti-India, from whom 'Bharat Mata' has to be protected. Hence, the yardstick for evaluation of ideological politics, policies and programmes pursued by the BJP-in-government from May 2014 to May 2016 is to identify how far it has been able to rush forward its agenda for 'Hinduisation' of Indian Society, culture, education, etc., a task assigned to it by the RSS. The first hurdle in the way of BJP and Sangh Parivar for this project is the republican, democratic, secular Constitution of India. This is the reason that during its two years, the BJP government has tinkered with constitutional institutions, like Parliament and Supreme Court. It has made every effort to bend and break the letter and spirit of constitutional institutions in order to pursue its goals in a ruthless manner, the new government served notice to the Parliament that procedures and norms of parliamentary democracy are dispensable and even disposable. The BJP took no time to convey a clear message that it does not recognise the need for an "opposition" party in a democracy and on a technical basis it rejected the demand for assigning the status of official leader of the opposition.

Ideologically, BJP and RSS do not accept the value of democratic dissent' and 'opposition' because all swayamsevaks of RSS are trained in shakha's to accept and obey the leader without questioning him ever. The concept of opposition and dissent is foreign to BJP legislators and leaders, many of whom are senior RSS pracharaks. To recall, the very first action of the BJP government was to by-pass the Parliament and issue an ordinance to amend the Land Acquisition and Compensation Act, 2013. During its two years in government, the BJP has literally practised an 'Ordinance Raj', the latest being an ordinance to counter the Supreme Court judgement on NEET, all-India common entrance examination for admission to medical colleges. Similarly, the same contempt was shown by the BJP government on the issue of appointment of Supreme Court and High Court judges. A full constitutional bench of the Supreme Court annulled the law on Judicial Appointments Commission and re-stored the existing system of Collegiums of fraternal judges for appointments because the constitutional bench felt that the proposed Judicial Appointment Commission will open the doors for "political appointments" to judiciary, compromising its independence. A senior Cabinet minister reacted against the judgement by making a public statement, "unelected judges are passing judgements on laws passed by the Parliament", forgetting the fact that it is the Constitution that provides the power of judicial re-view to the Supreme Court and it is arrogance of power to call the judges as "unelected". The deadlock on the issue of Collegiums remains and the government still wants "veto power" in appointment of judges, leading to apprehensions of a possibility of political appointments.

Finally, while the BJP government had been talking about "co-operative federalism", it has not hesitated in dismissing state governments in non-BJP states at the drop of a hat. Arunachal Pradesh and Uttarakhand are a case in point. The Harish Ravvat government in Uttarakhand was re-instated on the orders of the High Ccift and the Supreme Court With strictures against the central government, reminding it of the Supreme Court judgement in the Bommai case. Thus, all these prove that the BJP government, led by Modi, in its two years does not care for constitutional nice ties of a democratic republic, whether dealing with the Parliament or with judiciary. It has displayed authoritarian and centralising approach to governance, showing least care for the noble values of federal democracy mentioned in the Constitution. Further, in these two years, the RSS and its affiliates have been "emboldened" to freely implement the "hate-base" agenda against Muslims and Christians. Anti-minority agenda is being openly pursued by every organisation of RSS, as they feel a sense of protection from the BJP-in-government. The RSS, its affiliates and BJP governments both, at the Centre and in the states picked up the issue of "cow slaughter" and Muslims and Christians were targeted as "beef-eaters". The 'beef politics' has gone to occupy the centre-stage of Indian politics since May 26, 2014, when Modi became the Prime Minister. Extra-legal and extra-constitutional Gau Raksha Committees, supported by RSS and Bajrang Dal, hounded suspected Muslims for either eating beef or slaughtering the "holy cow". It is not only the agenda of protection of the "holy cow"; in fact aggressive groups are openly engaged in targeting non-Hindu religious minorities. On 24 May, 2016, Bajrang Dal and VHP were found to be holding training camps in Ayodhya, where Hindu youth were being trained in rifle shooting and use of lathis/sticks in defence against enemies represented through Muslim symbols. Such trainings are being conducted without any fear.

The agenda of a 'Hindu Rashtra' cannot be fulfilled without the propagation of education in this direction and hence control of the same is being seen as crucial by the BJP government and the RSS. They are working over-time to "re-write the whole curriculum" and teaching syllabus so as to Inculcate "Hindu cultural values" and clear the minds of Hindus of "foreign ideas". The Hindu conformist intellectuals are in the forefront as active messengers of the RSS ideology in making universities as centres of Hindu educational system. Intellectual dissenters in universities, like Central University of Hyderabad and Jawaharlal Nehru University are being targeted and declared as "anti-nationals". Thus, the two-year report card of the Modi government reveals that its primary agenda is 'Hinduisation' and to achieve this it has not even hesitated to disrespect the Constitution.

RSS—A Historical Perspective

K.B. Hedgewar would never have imagined in his wildest of dreams that an innocuous Rashtriya Swayamsevak Sangh (RSS), which he established on Vijaya Dashmi day of October 27, 1925 to impart physical training to Hindus so that they could become physically strong enough to defeat their enemies belonging to other 'non-Hindu religions' could in its 90th year become a force to be reckoned with. As much as Mohan Bhagwat becoming so powerful that he would be able to address the whole nation on the RSS day of birth on October 22, 2015. RSS was established by Hedgewar in Nagpur in 1925 to unite fractured and fragmented Hindus so that they could become strong enough to save themselves from their so-called "religious enemies. RSS *shakhas* (branches) have spread in the whole country with 55,000 shakhas, 40 affiliates like Vishwa Hindu Parishad, Bajrang Dal, Durga Vahini, *et al.*

Alongside these, the BJP governments are playing a decisive role in determining and dictating the agenda of national politics and culture for the entire nation. The reach of RSS is felt in remote villages, towns, cities, including the forest dwelling tribal population; with its committed cadre spreading the message of Hinduisation of the whole society, as announced by Mohan Bhagwat that, "All those, born here are Hindus and their DNA is Hindu". It is not only that in 90 years RSS has become organisationally formidable; it is menacingly spreading the message of its ideology of Hindutva throughout the country. It deserves to be clearly mentioned here that ideologically committed RSS is in distinguishable form BJP governments and it is effectively using its governmental power to strengthen and solidify the root of its ideology of Hindutva. It is a 'total' effort on the part of every RSS trained Swayamsevak from prime minister downwards to work for the celebrated ideological goal of establishing Hindu nationhood in this country. This above description is essential to make a point that RSS of today deserves a close scrutiny because it is not the RSS of 1920s or 30s, but it is the RSS of the second decade of the 21st century. It controls the levers of powers of the Indian State, it merits a deeper analysis by asking new questions for understanding the nature of new challenges posed by it.

The RSS of 21st century has become a "centre of power" in Indian society and it is essential to highlight its strategies for transforming plural and secular India into a monolith Hindu rashtra because it is not simply in power but expanding and strengthening its influence over the whole society. A few facts may be mentioned here to situate the new significance of the new RSS.

First, while its ideology has been in the public domain for the past 90 years and their goals too very much clear, it is vital to highlight the strategies adopted by the RSS to achieve its ideological goal because all its strategic goals are linked together and cannot be seen in isolation from their short term goals or limited achievements. The Nehru government had banned the RSS and arrested its leaders/cadres in 1948, when the country's sentiments were against this organisation because of its alleged involvement in the conspiracy to assassinate Mahatma Gandhi on January 30, 1948, MS Golwalkar, the then RSS supremo was not at all disheartened by the Nehru government's decision and he opened the line of communication with Sardar Patel, the then home minister and agreed to have a written constitution for the RSS. This is only one part of the story. The lessons learnt by the RSS leadership from this episode of 1948 were that they needed a political party to spread its ideological message through elections and also act as its defender in parliament. MS Golwalkar converted its adverse situation of 1948 into an opportunity to earn a legal status in Indian democracy. This has been a consistent strategy of the RSS and it has used every opening during every movement-provided by others to legitimise it self and proceed further. The best example is that of the JP movement of 1974, where RSS actively participated in the movement, went to jail during the emergency and benefited by its association with JP and during the elections of 1977. As the RSS-Jansangh combine elect orally emerged as a single powerful force, it became part of governments at the centre as well as some states of India. It has become a running theme with RSS/Jansangh/BJP that it is not a Hindu communal organisation because JP never described it as communal. The meaning of this is quite clear that politically "untouchable" RSS in 1948 became respectable in 1974 and never looked back continuing its march forward.

Second, this strategy of step-by-step planning for moving forward was again repeated in 1990 when BJP and RSS affiliates led by LK Advani launched Ram Temple movement from Somnath to Ayodhya in December 1992 and demolished the Babri mosque. Was the goal of building a Ram temple achieved? It was foolhardy to accept that RSS-BJP were interested in the construction of Ram temple, because the real strategic goal of temple movement of 1990 to 1992 was to demonise the Muslims and polarise Hindu-Muslim community of India so that BJP could gain the status of "sole champion of Hindu causes and self-respect".

Third, the BJP and RSS have used every opportunity to enter the corridors of political power and every 'coalition government', if required BJP's support, it was available. It has always supported 'anti-Congressism' to advance its interests by participating in coalition governments at the centre and state levels beginning with 70s and continuing till 2004. It is only the BJP which came out successful out of every tottering and temporary coalition government because under the protective umbrella of coalition governments beginning with the 1970s, the RSS has been able to expand its shakhas and penetrate within the bureaucratic and security organisations of the Indian State. The upshot of above narrative is that RSS-BJP has used every opportunity, small or big, to its advantage and even during unstable and temporary coalition governments, the BJP as coalition partner tried to implement its own specific agenda. BJP created the fertile ground for the expansion of the RSS. This is the explanation for the formidable presence of RSS in 90 years of its existence and it has followed "strategies" one after the other by keeping in mind its real goal of strengthening itself so that it could spread its ideology of making India a Hindu Rashtra.

It needs to be mentioned that RSS Swayamsevak turned PM Atal Bihari Vajpayee from 1998 to 2004 always presented in public that he was compelled to follow "coalition dharma" and make sacrifices while in government. Is it so? The answer is a big NO. Vajpayee as PM provided opportunities to the RSS and its affiliates to expand their areas of activity because they were fully "protected" by the BJP in power. Narendra Modi, the then chief minister of Gujarat was a beneficiary of this protective umbrella after the post-Godhra riots spread, like wild-fire in 2002. This story of the gradual growth of the RSS has succeeded in bringing Narendra Modi into power at the centre in May 2014. India is now witnessing the real power of the Hindu Rashtravaadis with Mohan Bhagwat stating in public "trust Modi, one loyal Swayamsevak". Modi's cabinet ministers were called by Bhagwat for three days in Delhi to "explain their achievements and performance" in the government and it was left to Modi, who while appearing in this "accountability session" observed in September 2015 that RSS is our "Marg darshak. Further, he stated that RSS has taught "values" to him which he is pursuing. Even Vajpayee during his tenure had pro-claimed his complete loyalty to RSS and this provides us with watertight evidence that RSS and all its affiliates including the BJP are "comrade-in-arms" and provide collective support to one another while achieving the supreme goal of establishing Hindu Rashtra in Indian politics. It is RSS, which is laying down the agenda for Hinduisation of India. Hence, 'Alternative Left Democratic polities' has to confront and challenge this agenda of RSS. India is facing a challenge of Hindutva and organisational network of the Hindu Rashtrawadis is becoming strong. It is imperative to confront these forces politically, ideologically and organisationally. The RSS in its infant stage projected itself as a social movement and its appeal to Hindus that Hindutva requires rejuvenation had attracted small time traders and merchants of small cities and towns in Western India and because of the presence of Arya Samaj in North India, the RSS could reach Hindu minded trading class. This was the social base of RSS and even at the age of 90, it has not abandoned its pro-property ideology and the Hindu private property minded classes have found great hospitality in the ideology of RSS i.e., combination of Hindutva with protector of property rights of the Hindus. This is the material foundation of RSS that the BJP-led government at the centre and the states are able to harmonies their basic ideology of Hindutva with the class interests of Hindu monopoly capitalist class. Ideologies have a material foundation and this is the 'social-material' base of Hindu Sangh Parivar.

Boundaries between RSS and BJP dissolve

Prime Minister Narendra Modi and Cabinet Ministers of the BJP presented their report card of activities as the highest functionaries of the Government of India to the unelected and unaccountable Rashtriya Swayamsevak Sangh's supremo Mohan Bhagwat at a meeting held in Delhi for three days—from September 2 to September 4. Amit Shah, the Bharatiya Janata Party President described it as a "co-ordination meeting" between the elected Chief Executive of the parliamentary-cabinet system of democracy and the RSS, led by Mohan Bhagwat. The obvious purpose was stocktaking of actions and activities of the RSS *Swayamsevaks*, who are in the BJP-led government at the Centre.

The BJP-led NDA government was sub-jected to scrutiny over the border situation in Jammu and Kashmir, the Maoist threat and the "education" agenda of the Education Minister. At the conclusion of the three-days accountability session, Bhagwat observed that he "strongly endorsed the Modi Government", asking the Sangh *Parivar* to repose confidence in its *Swayamsevaks*, who were doing well. He advocated that they (the Government) should be given time. Narendra Modi himself asserted that he looked to the RSS for *margdarshan* (guidance) and "he was proud to be a *Swayamsevak*". It should not be forgotten that Modi was an RSS *pracharak* before entering politics. What is the real significance and unambiguous message of such formal and informal close linkages and interconnections between Modi's

Cabinet Ministers and the leadership of the Sangh *Parivar,* led by Mohan Bhagwat? To characterise the RSS as an "extra-constitutional authority," with remote control over the Modi Government would mean missing the wood for trees. This ignores the fact that the RSS is the BJP and the BJP is an instrument in the hands of the RSS, with a clear mandate to implement the Sangh *Parivar's* programmes while in power at the Centre and in various states. Hence, the BJP ministers have not only to seek concrete policy instructions from the top hierarchy of the RSS, but also have to regularly inform the RSS about the implementation of such policies. If the need arises, the RSS functionaries can suggest "corrections" to individual BJP ministers for efficient implementation of the agenda of Hindu nationhood. It's important to understand the role of the RSS and it's hierarchical organisational structure in the decision-making process of it's approximately 45 affiliates, including the political affiliate, the BJP.

First, Mohan Bhagwat decided to make Nitin Gadkari, the BJP President in 2009, by cajoling LK Advani to make place for a new leader. It was Bhagwat's decision, somewhat reluctantly accepted by the BJR to nominate Narendra Modi as the Chairperson of the Election Campaign Committee of the BJP for the Lok Sabha Elections of 2014. On July 15,2013, Modi made a public statement saying, "I am nationalist, I am a patriot, I am a born Hindu. Nothing is wrong. I am a Hindu nationalist because I am a born Hindu." Modi's statement was a reiteration of Bhagwat's statement made a little later on August 17, 2013 that "Hindustan is a Hindu *Rashtra...Hindutva* is the country's identity." Bhagwat had found his Hindu messenger in Modi, whom he nominated as the BJP prime ministerial candidate for the 2014 Lok Sabha elections. Can anyone doubt the fact that the RSS occupies a supreme position and the BJP is just an affiliate of the RSS, subject to it's ideological and organisational authority? Mohan Bhagwat's supreme position was clearly established before the Indian public, when the government-controlled television channel, Doordarshan, broadcast Bhagwat's address to the nation on October 3, 2014. A private organisation, like the RSS enjoyed the privilege of broadcasting its message of Hindutva. Was Sonia Gandhi, the so-called centre of the extra-Constitutional power over UPA Government, ever found to be holding "public accountability .sessions" of the UPA? The whole ideological structure of the RSS is built around the idea of presenting binaries between "We" the Hindus and the "other" Muslims and Christians. From KB. Hedgewar to Mohan Bhagwat, the RSS has propagated the idea that Hindus are the real natives of *Bharat Mata* and Muslims, Christians and non-Hindus, who do not belong to the Hindu mainstream religions are "outsiders". Such ideas based on the territorial claims of the Hindu community warrant the "other communities" to accept Hindu hegemony and stay as second-class citizens. The RSS and it's cadre have felt free to target non-Hindus. BJP's MPs like Yogi Adityanath and Sakshi Maharaj have organised "hate campaigns" under the pretext of "love jihad," wrongly associated with Muslims.

Conversion of Muslims and Christians to Hinduism has been carried out in what is termed the *shuddhi* movement or *Ghar Wapasi.*

Mohan Bhagwat himself "blessed" the re-conversion of Muslims and Christians to Hinduism, making conversion a public discourse, out of the blue. The Home Minister made a statement in the Parliament in 2014, that if all parties agreed, an all-India conversion Bill could be brought before the Parliament. The *Ghar* Wapasi movement should be seen as the RSS agenda at religious polarisation of a plural society. Education is another means through which the RSS aims to push forward its idea of a Hindu Rashtra. It is not without reason that Bhagwat has repeatedly made calls to the NDA Government to "correct history textbooks" and weed out foreign influences. In fact, the HRD minister Smriti Irani and Education Ministers of states were asked to take "suggestions and share perspectives" with the RSS in October 2014. D.N. Batra, an RSS ideologue, launched a Shiksha Bachao Aandolan and his non-scientific books were prescribed in Gujarat state schools. All cultural activities are being undertaken under the direct supervision of Bhagwat and Smriti Irani is a mere spectator. Many RSS-affiliated bodies are actively participating in the formulation of the new education policy by the HRD Ministry. The focus of the education policy, according to the RSS, has to be on the "ancient Hindu Sanskriti/culture and values" and on teaching *vedic* values to children at school. Schools, especially government schools, have been asked to start the tradition of *Surya Namaskar* and teach Hindu epics, like the *Ramayana* and the *Mahabharata* compulsorily as part of the curriculum. The Chairperson of Central Board of Film Certification had to quit, claiming immense interference by outside agencies in it's functioning.

All these facts prove that the distinction between RSS and BJP is blurred and the boundaries between the two have been broken. This is the larger issue at hand because the Constitutional arrangements of governance have been bid a farewell in the contemporary power arrangements. The Parliamentary Cabinet system in-Indian democracy has become more of a "rubber-stamp" of the RSS organisation.

Threat to Minority Culture

The recent announcement by the Narendra Modi government that Aligarh Muslim University and Jamia Millia Islamia, Delhi established by an act of parliament, cannot be recognised as special "minority institutions' because the secular constitution of India does not permit the government to establish and provide funds to institutions of higher learning, specifically for the promotion of education and culture of religious minority communities. Attorney General of India Mukul Rohtagi while appearing for the central government before the Supreme Court in January 2016 observed, "As the Executive Government at the Centre, we cannot seem as setting up a minority institution in secular India", and hence, AMU cannot be given a 'minority status'. Similarly, Delhi High Court is hearing a case on the question of granting 'minority' status to

Jamia Millia Islamia. The National Commission for Minority Educational Institutions Act (2004) has observed "we have no hesitation in holding that Jamia was founded by the Muslims for the benefit of the Muslims and it never lost its identity as a Muslim minority educational institution". It has also been argued by the advocates of 'minority' status for AMU and JMI that Article 30 of the Indian Constitution states, "All minorities whether based on religion or language shall have the right to establish and administer educational institutions of their choice and the Indian state will provide them with "funds and grants". The Supreme Court had set the record right on January 15, 2015 that "the power to grant minority status to an institution was entirely with the central government which may decide it, based on relevant materials". This is a legislative and formal state of affairs and it is the central government, which has decided not to permit the AMU and JMI, Delhi, the "minority status" and by implication not recognize the "unique" status of these institutions of higher learning. The larger issue is that both, AMU and JMI were established in pre-independence India in special historical circumstances, which prevailed during the British Colonial rule in the country. The Modi government is deciding on this extremely significant educational and cultural issue, which directly impacts the Muslim minority community by completely ignoring the history of institutions and if the context of the establishment of these institutions is ignored, decisions will be taken on the basis of ideological and political benefits of the present central government, which is perceived "anti-minority" by Muslims and Christians of India. The crux of the issue is that "past" is ignored with a view to serve the "present" ideological preferences and beliefs of the Modi government at the Centre.

A few salient facts can be mentioned here to substantiate the argument that the "past" is becoming a victim of the "present". First, Sir Syed Ahmed Khan with a few Muslim leaders established the Mohammedan Anglo-Oriental College, Aligarh in 1880 to impart education to Muslims, especially women and teach English language with a view to bring Muslim community into the mainstream of India. It is later that MAO graduated into AMU and Rs. 30 Lakh collected by Muslims was handed over to the university. The genesis of AMU in imparting education is to promote 'culture' of Muslims for bringing Muslims into the modernisation process of society. Second, while in the 1920s, AMU was getting infected by communal ideology of All-India Muslim League, in response to Mahatma Gandhi's call "to boycott all educational institutions supported or run by the Colonial regime", Jamia as a nationalist institution was established in Aligarh and later on shifted to Delhi as a registered society. Third, the S Radhakrishnan Report on Education, D.S. Kothari report on education in post-independence India had laid great emphasis on the role of higher education in promotion of "culture" and this integral relationship between "universities" and "culture" is a well-recognised pedagogic fundamental philosophical principle and this is precisely the issue that AMU and JMI, Delhi are performing the role of providing education and promoting cultural values and norms of life of minority community.

It deserves to be refered here that Dr. Zakir Hussain, the former President of India, had been Vice-Chancellor of both, minority institutions of Aligarh and Jamia. Further, non-official attempts were made during the colonial period to establish institutions of higher learning like P.T. Madan Mohan Malviya in the 1920s established Kashi Vishwa Vidyalaya which later became Benaras Hindu University and even a temple of Lord Shiva was also established within the premises of this University. Maharishi Rabindranath Tagore established Vishwa Bharati in early 20th Century with a philosophy of education that "repetition is not the purpose of education that can be done by machine". The above narrative clearly shows that public spirited individuals and community leaders had established 'universities' and colleges on their own in pre-independence India to promote values and cultural ethos among students and members of diverse cultural communities, like Muslims, Christians, Brahmo Samaj *et al.* Should history of these institutions be white washed in the name of Constitution and narrow "legalism" to suit the current governments and political dispensation? If the historical context of the establishment of educational institutions of pre-independence India cannot be ignored while dealing with the present situations, the present context where religious minorities, both, Muslims and Christians on the basis of their daily experience, have developed a strong feeling that the BJP-led governments at the Centre and in states, where they are in power are promoting hegemonic sectarian Hindu culture and erasing and completely eradicating minority cultures of a highly diverse and plural society. This fear from the forces of Hindutva, which are in government, has completely unnerved and shaken the minority community on the stand taken by the Modi government on AMU and JMI. The BJP-led state government in Madhya Pradesh has made "Surya Namaskar" and "recitation of Gayatri Mantra" and "Om" as compulsory for every student in schools fully funded by the state exchequer. The BJP-led government in the state of Chhattisgarh has asked all principals of Christian Missionary schools to compulsorily ask their students not to address Principal as Father, but as Acharya. These illustrations can be multiplied and this ongoing Hinduisation of culture in educational institutions by the Modi government was again witnessed, when on January 19, 2016 a high-powered committee headed by Prime Minister himself has been constituted to "identify Yoga Art and Science" for teaching purposes in schools, colleges and universities and Prime Minister Modi's yoga teacher H.R. Narendra is to play an active role in the framing up of curriculum for teaching purposes. There is a genuine apprehension among religious minorities, both, Muslims and Christians, that the Hindu Sangh Parivar is pushing the agenda of Hinduisation through educational institutions and this fear based on facts has made Muslims quite nervous on the stand taken by the Modi government.

Minorities want to "protect" their culture as a matter of their "right" and this "right" of minorities can only be protected by providing special safeguards to their educational institutions. The RSS and the BJP governments are announcing from housetop that inherited British system of education has "polluted" Hindu minds and made them weak nationalists and there is a need to 'promote' Hinduism through new education in India. It is in this context that the present issue of AMU and JMI needs to be seen and the minority cultures need to be protected from the onslaught of Hindu hegemonisation. Education is not "culture-neutral", hence AMU, JMI cannot accept the present approach of the central government as a 'neutral' intervention in minority affairs.

The Rashtriya Swayamsevak Sangh (RSS) held its Akhil Bhartiya Pratinidhi Sabha from March 11 to 13 followed by the BJP's National Executive meeting a week later. Both the meetings affirmed and re-iterated their ideological and political programme for the governance of India under Narendra Modi who is seen as the helmsman both, for the Parivar and for the Indian state. Modi was nominated by the RSS Supremo Mohan Bhagwat because of the great trust which the Sangh Parivar has reposed in its erstwhile Pracharak in faithfully and aggressively implementing the ideological and political agenda of a Hindu Rashtra plus Hindu Raj (State).

It is worthwhile to analyse Modi's track record in achieving the goals of governance as laid down by the Sangh Parivar - to promote 'holy' symbols, like Lord Rama ahd Holy Cow; and to "curb anti-national and anti-social activities at the campuses". This is evident from the arrest of some JNU students under the obnoxious sedition law while Rajnath Singh and Amit Shah repeatedly proclaimed that "anti-national" activities will not be tolerated. The RSS has laid down a clear test which every Indian citizen will have to pass, if he is a nationalist. Mohan Bhagawat has already observed that the "feeling towards your motherland should have been implemented but now-a-days one has to be taught to say Bharat Mata ki jai because voices against this [slogan] are becoming louder." It is not an empty rhetoric, A Maharashtra MLA was abruptly asked by a BJP MLA to chant Bharat Mata ki jai. On his refusal, he was suspended from the assembly on the basis of a vote of disapproval by the BJP, Shiv Sena and the Congress MLAs.

The RSS' standing army and its affiliates along with the new media have commanded everyone to raise that slogan or be ready to be painted as an anti-national. A full-fledged communal party is trying to enforce its idea of Indian nationalism, as defined by the ideologue of Hindutava V.D. Savarkar that Muslim and Christians are not Indians because their religious places of worship and pilgrimage are outside India i.e. Bharat Mata.

It is simplistic to assert that Mohan Bhagwat and Amit Shah are only asking the Muslims to shout Bharat Mata ki jai. Even Hindus have been commanded to prove their loyalty by doing so. Alternative slogans during the national anti-colonial movement like *'Hindustan Zindabad'* and *'Hindustan Amar Rahe'* are not acceptable to the Sangh Parivar. Only Bharat Mata ki jai is the touchstone of patriotism and other slogans do not pass the smell test. Narendra Modi is providing full patronage and protection to the aggressive patriots of the RSS, of which he himself is an integral part. It is not without reason that sadhus and Shankaracharyas, who carry great conviction among many Hindu believers and can influence their political preferences and choices in favour of a Hindu Party, are quite active in BJP and Sangh Parivar politics. Modi has never uttered a word against the anti-Muslim statements of Sakshi Maharaj or Yogi Adityanath because of their proximity to the Sangh Parivar. Bharat Mata ki jai has become a symbol of its anti-nationalism divisive agenda. The holy cow has become a public issue because Muslims slaughter cows while Hindus are expected to protect their "mother' from them. Of late, especially after Modi became Prime Minister, a large number of gau raksha samitis have cropped up. RSS affiliates have been hunting down so-called beefeaters and animal traders. Modi in his address at the BJP's National Executive in March restated that his government is committed to 'vikas' and 'vikas' but Arun Jaitley observed that "the ideology of nationalism guides our belief and philosophy."

Modi fully respects the Sangh Parivar's ideology and political programme which supposedly organically integrates the nation, state, territory and culture into a whole idea of nationhood. The Unitarian idea of one nation, one religion and one language cannot be a construct of a highly diverse and plural India. The RSS selected Modi for the top job to implement this agenda of. Hindu Unitarian nationalism. Mohan Bhagwat detected a great deal of ruthlessness in Modi in implementing the goals of Hindu nationalism. It can be argued that Parliamentary democracy has become a Presidential system.

Modi is a different kind of leader and belongs to the ideological and political school of nationalism, whose integral components are the cult of personality and hero worship. His Gujarat 'model' from 2001-2004 was mainly based on populist appeal. Modi was the sole performer and did not allow any intervention by any other leader or institution. The same model has been replicated at the Centre even if there are multiple checks and balances provided through institutional arrangements. Modi is credited as the sole initiator of programmes, like Jan Dhan Yojana, Swatchh Bharat, Digital India and Skill India. The Ministers have to implement these programmes and bureaucrats regularly monitor their performance.

Modi is not only a centraliser, he is also a polariser. The latest example was his election-time barnstorming in Assam. He played on the emotive and divisive issue of nativity versus the outsiders and promised to native Assamese that "infiltrator" Bangladeshis, meaning a Muslim Bengali, would be deported. The last Lok Sabha election has shown that the BJP does not have a single Muslim MP among its 282 members. The leaders of Kashmir Valley, who are committed to democratic politics, expressed their anger, when their students were targeted for allegedly cooking "beef meat". How can the Kashmiris feel integrated, when Hindu groups target those who venture to the mainland? Such examples can be multiplied to substantiate the argument that Unitarian Hindu India has and will create divisions and situations of violence. Do we want such an India? The answer is a Big NO. The reason is quite clear that plural and diverse India is soul of richness of society. Modi is the greatest danger to this India.

Parivar's Wish: Education for Hinduisation

A common thread which connects the campus disturbances at the Film and Television Institute of Pune, Central Hyderabad University and Jawaharlal Nehru University of Delhi is that all these three educational institutions, along with other 40 Central Universities of India, are managed, controlled and administered directly by heads of institutions and their executive councils appointed by the Central Government. Another special feature of conflicts, which have arisen in these institutions is that many important leaders of the BJP have condemned these student conflicts as "anti-national" activity. This labelling has spread, like wild fire, especially in Case of JNU, Delhi. Beginning with February 9, 2016, when the Home Minister, Rajnath Singh, asked the Delhi Police to arrest a "fringe" element of JNU demonstrators who were alleged to be raising anti-national slogans and slap the charge of "sedition" under the Indian Penal Code against those few who had raised slogans in support of terrorist Afzal Guru.

The story does not end here. The various affiliates of the Hindu RSS, like the ABVE BJP-affiliated lawyers, the BJP sympathisers such as ex-servicemen and widows of soldiers who had sacrificed their lives while defending the attack on the Parliament, in which Afzal Guru was found guilty — were all mobilised against JNU, which had been projected in the public eye by the ministers of the Government and other BJP affiliates as "a centre of anti-nationals." A demand was even made by some BJP activists that the "anti-national" JNU should be shut down.

Civil society was made to believe by BJP activists that JNU is a dangerous anti-national institution and not a single responsible leader of the BJP or the upper echelons of the RSS leadership thought it fit to make a sharp distinction between "fringe elements of demonstrators" and the larger institutions of higher learning. Unfortunately, JNU has been asked to defend its "nationalist" credentials before the RSS-led Sangh Parivar and its affiliates who claim to be the champions of Hindu *Rashtravad* and patriotism. The role of autonomous academic institutions of higher learning have to be examined because the BJP-led Government at the Centre, along with the RSS, has demanded that educational institutions which at present are "under the influence of foreign or external western philosophies of education" should show the "impact" of nationalist education to the Indian youth and instill values of patriotism in students.

A few facts would enable a clear understanding of the ideological belief system of the RSS because universities and the whole educational system in the country is being prepared to act as instruments for spreading the ideological message of the Hindu Sangh Parivar. Firstly, RK Sinha, the biographer of Dr KB Hedgewar, the founder of the RSS, in 1925 has noted that the "RSS is an essence of his life" and "Hedgewar's vision was focused on resurrecting the cultural identity of the nation". Second, the RSS supremo, beginning with Hedgewar to Mohan Ehagwat, is the commander-in-chief of all affiliates of the Sangh Parivar, including the BJP in Government. This is the reason that Mohan Bhagwat's observation of August 17, 2014, on Hindu nationalism needs to be referred to. He observed, "Hindutva is the identity of India and it has the capacity to swallow other identities". Hence, comes the role of "education" as an extension of the nation's interest. In June 21, 2013, he said that, "True education is to develop feeling and dedication for the country". While addressing an eminent group of educationists, including VCs and the UGC Chairperson at Delhi on November 25," 2014, Bhagwat emphasised the need for nationalist education.

Not only this, the RSS asked the HRD Minister Srhriti Irani to "correct" the history taught in schools to "highlight Indian heroes and the role played by Hindu culture in shaping the country" and not the version that the West wanted India to learn. The RSS felt "that Indian children were not familiar with real Indian heroes". Since the Central Government controls all educational institutions publicly funded by the public exchequer, hence all appointments of VCs, executive councils of the universities and other academic bodies are made on the basis of an affiliation or deep commitment to the RSS ideology, for education for Hindutva.

This explains the efforts made by all RSS affiliates and its BJP governments at the Centre and the states, where the BJP is in power, to control every educational institution so that Hindu *Rasthravad* could be promoted through education. The language policy is another tool of control and hence, the emphasis on teaching of Hindi and Sanskrit in recentJimes, so that Hindu scriptures could be taught in these languages. The story does not end here. The whole educational system has to be controlled by the vigilant group of the Sangh Parivar, under the patronage of the BJP in Government.

Sunil Ambedkar of the RSS is in-charge of the Akhil Bhartiya Vidyarthi Parishad, which has a direct link with the RSS and reports to the BJP ministers about the activities at the campuses. Mahendra Kapoor of the Bharatiya Shikshak Mahasangh, Shiv Kumar of Vidya Bharti are some more examples. All these functionaries of the RSS organisations, dealing with education at various levels, have carried weight with functionaries of educational institutions because the BJP is in power. The Sangh Parivar's definition of Hindu nationalism is just one of the definitions of modern nationalism and that too it is socially exclusive and it wants to use universities to propagate this "exclusivism", which is at variance with the true essence of Hinduism that promotes and supports plurality.

Plurality and not homogeneity as the essence of Hindu belief system gets substantiated, if one recalls that in 2012, the Delhi University Academic Council was compelled to delete A.K. Ramanujan's, *"Three Hundred Ramayans: Five examples and three thoughts on translations"*. The RSS has a definitive model of education that wants to wash out all historical memories of cultural diversity of India. It is trying to impose its own model by using Government machinery. Autonomy of education leads to an academic atmosphere of dissent and non-conformism among students and the teaching faculty. The Modi Government wants universities as centres of "conformism".

The Hindutva project of education as defined and interpreted by the ideologues of the Sangh Parivar cannot be pursued under the present university-system, which has been nurtured on the basis of values enshrined in the Constitution of democratic, liberal, secular, Republic of India. Conflicts on the campuses are nothing new. The United States of America witnessed serious polarisation and "anti-Vietnam" war protets in the 1960s and 1970s. The Paris campus in 1968 was in a state of revolt, making philosopher Jean Paul Sartre to observe that campuses will play a transformative role. Neither the US nor the French government declared the students, "anti-national". Democracies grow only in a free atmosphere of debate and dissent but the BJP Government in power does not consider universities as centres of ideas. where a hundred different flowers bloom.

Surrenders before Imperialism

Narendra Modi, prime minister and RSS pracharak, has grown up in the Sangh Parivar ideological training schools as a pro-American and pro-imperialist and its latest example is provided by the Modi government on April 12, 2016, when it declared its commitment to challenge the Chinese growing maritime power by announcing its decision to sign within weeks or 'months' a Logistics Exchange Memorandum of Agreement with US 'to provide supplies and fuel to each other's armed forces from this bases'. This logistics agreement with far reaching consequences has been signed between Indian defence minister Manohar Parikar and US defence secretary Ashtor Carter.

The significance of this logistics agreement is that for the first time in the history of post-independence India, a public declaration has been made by the Modi government on April 12, that India is in the 'camp' of the United States against China. Further, the joint statement on April 12 stated "to continue working toward(s) other facilitating agreement to enhance military co-operation and technology transfer" between the US and India. A bilateral maritime security dialogue between the two countries will be institutionalised with a view "to enhance ongoing navy-to-navy discussions to cover submachine related issues, besides deepening co-operation in the maritime domain awareness by facilitating a White Shipping Agreement".

US defence secretary Carter expressing great satisfaction over India's naval agreement observed 'India is a net security provider' in the region. This-agreement is a game changer because India has never publically positioned itself as anti-China, especially by accepting an alliance of such a nature with the United States of America which is strengthening its naval presence in Asia-Pacific and South China Sea and Indian Ocean directly to confront China.

The UPAI and II from 2004 to 2014 did not agree to the American proposal of logistics exchange because the Manmohan Singh government consciously followed a foreign policy of non-antagonism towards China specially in public and India made every effort to keep China engaged in negotiations on issues of bilateral differences. India-China bilateralism was the keynote of Congress-led governments from 2004 to 2014 and any open and public association with American naval and maritime ambitions by India would have sent a direct signal to China that India is abandoning its 'bilateralism' in favour of an anti-China alliance with the United States. Modi has clearly and unambiguously announced that unlike its predecessor UPA government, his government— Is going to compete and confront China by adding to its maritime power in partnership Wifhthe United States. The logistics agreement of April 12 is a big step forward by the Modi government, which has openly chosen to announce India-US defence partners'up specially to send a message to China.

The objective of ACSA (Acquisition and Cross-Servicing Agreement) is "reciprocal provision of logistic support, supplies and services to the military forces of one party by the other party in return for either cash payment or the reciprocal provision of logistic support, supplies and services to the military forces of the other party". The real significance of Narendra Modi is that he has affected a complete breach with the ' past traditions of India's foreign policy of non-alignment and keeping a safe distance from any alliance politics with the imperialists, as shown by the logistics agreement of April 12. Thjs significance cannot be appreciated without focussing sharp attention on the ideology of State power as defined by the Hindu Sangh Parivar. Modi is a swayamsevak of the RSS and the prime minister of India is engaged in promoting and'pursuing the goals of State power as visualised in the philosophy of Sangh Parivar.

A few facts may be mentioned that Modi's capitulation before IJS imperialism and the strategies followed by his government beginning with 2014 are solely motivated by the idea of great Bharat Mata, which is militarily well-equipped to confront its opponents, like Pakistan and China. A highly militarised and modernised Hindu State can stand up and face the challenges, real or imaginary of its competitors. First, the Modi government has opened up defence sector production to India's monopoly capitalists and foreign monopoly transnational corporations under the category of public-private partnership system.

Second, VD Savarkar, the ideologue of Hindutva and Hindu rashtra had clearly stated "Hinduise India, militarise Hindu". It is not without reason that K.B. Hedgewar, the founder of the RSS in 1925 had emphasised the 'physical training of young Hindus", because "weak Hindus" would not be able to face the external enemies. Hence, the RSS firmly promotes the idea of 'physically strong Hindu' and translated properly, if RSS can capture State power it will make Hindu state a military super-power. The making of a Hindu military supper power is a fundamental ideological commitment of the RSS pracharak prime minister Narendra Modi.

Third, Narendra Modi has completely abandoned the well-established tradition of 'civilian control arid supremacy over armed forces' by openly and unambiguously 'patronising in public the Indian army and symbolically appointing General V.K. Singh, a controversial retired army chief, as a minister in the Modi government. Not only this, the tragic death of a few soldiers at Siachen Glacier in January 2016 was publically celebrated as the highest sign of 'patriotism' to show to'the common man that any sacrifice like that of 'soldiers' for the cause of defence of India was the most precious display of love for motherland and patriotism. Glorification of sacrifices made by soldiers while defending motherland beyond a point can be dangerous because men in uniform try to think themselves as 'special-super patriots'.

Patriotism and nationalism.cannot be projected as 'special' for some because all citizens of India are equally patriotic. The Modi government for the first time has created a hierarchy of patriots with an announcement that defence expenditure of the government of India will have the highest national priority much above welfare schemes for the poor, like expenditure on education, health and national employment guarantee scheme fof the rural poor. These above mentioned facts clearly show that the Modi government has a special ideologically driven defence policy based on the principle that Hindu India needs strong military muscles and financial and political costs of militarisation of Hindu India are irrelevant factors while pursuing the larger goal of making Bharat a super-military power.

The complete surrender to America by the Modi government can be understood only if the larger project of Hindu India is kept in mind because in the scheme of greatness of Bharat, China is perceived as a major threat and this can be countered only by becoming a 'camp follower' of America. Modi does not care even for an elementary fact that America is determined to pursue its own national interests and it finds India as a willing camp follower in spite of the fact that America is supplying all kinds of arms to! Pakistan, considered by Indians as an 'unfriendly country'. While Modi is blindly following American line of action in Asia, Robert Blackwill, former US ambassador to India on April 12 observed that the sale of F-16s by the United States to Pakistan is a 'dramatic eiample of the failure of American foreijgn policy'.

India has been protesting against American policy of 'militarisation of Pakstan' without any impact on the American policy-makers because Americans know that India itself wants to be very 'close' to America. Americans do not take the Modi government's opposition to the sale of F-16s by the US to Pakistan because the Americans know that India of Modi is always knocking at their doors for military co-operation to achieve its misplaced and unachievable goals of becoming a strong military super-power in the South Asian region.

The upshot of above description is quite clear that Modi has surrendered before the Americans and the latest example of logistics exchange between the two countries is not the end of the journey because Americans have found out that Modi's India is ever willing to deepen its bonds with their country in the fond hope of emerging as a super Hindu military State with the goods supplied by Americans and Modi is ready to pay any price to the Americans for achieving his goal of militarisation of Hindu India. Modi is unwise to announce his public identification of China as India's opponent and accepting America's umbrella to confront China.

11

Explaining Indian State: 1947-2017

India had been described as the 'most important jewel in the British Crown', however, the British colonizers by consciously following ruthless policies of economic plunder and exploitation had left behind a legacy of under-development, mass poverty and deprivation and the greatest challenge faced by the post-independence state was to eradicate mass poverty and undertake programmes for economic development of the whole underdeveloped society and regions of this vast country of continental size. Economic under-development of India was not the only legacy of the colonial rulers, the leadership of newly Independent decolonized country was confronted with anarchic and chaotic social situation created by the partition of India and the retreating colonial power had handed over the task of rehabilitation of transfer of populations from India to Pakistan and Pakistan to India and thus, maintaining 'law and order' in highly disturbed society became the first priority of the Indian state after August 15, 1947. The story of challenge faced by India just after independence does not end here because the nationalist leadership had always claimed that it had won freedom on the basis of struggles based on "Non-violence and Satyagraha", the same leadership asked Indian army to fight war-like situations in Jammu and Kashmir and Telangana, where Communist party-led armed struggle of peasant classes was posing a challenge to the newly independent state of India. It is the above mentioned context which explains that the colonial state apparatus, army, civil and police bureaucracy, got legitimized in Independent India and this coercive and governing apparatus created by the colonizers was not only inherited, it was legitimized because of its engagement while dealing with 'armed challenges' to the newly independent state of India. Not only this. If on one hand, the inherited coercive state apparatus has been brought under 'democratic control', on the other, Army, civil and police bureaucracy has strengthened its roots by establishing its pre-eminence as protectors and defenders of the Indian state. India has third or fourth professional standing army in the world and it is well-equipped with all the latest weapon system, which is available to the advanced NATO Country's Army.

Table 11.1: Estimated Strength of Central Government Select Ministries/Departments

Ministry/Depts.	*2015*	*2016*	*2017*	*2018*
Police	10,28,077	10,07,366	10,94,135	11,13,689
Income Tax	46,400	46,236	80,082	80,082
Custom & Excise	50,100	50,638	91,756	91,756
Railways	13,26,437	13,31,433	13,31,433	13,31,433
External Affairs	8,913	9,294	11,373	1,403
I&B	4,141	4,012	6,258	6,258
Cabinet	900	921	1203	1218
Total	**33,05,646**	**32,84,714**	**35,38,016**	**35,67,574**

(All 55 Government departments., excluding three defence forces).

Note: The figures above are strength of the department mentioned as on March 1 of that year. Statistics for 2015 and 2016 are as per actual and for 2017 and 2018 are as estimation.

Source: Union Budget 2017-18.

The central and state governments are the largest employers of civil and police personnel in India and the Central government is also expanding para-military forces, like the Central Reserve Police Force, the Border Security Force, *et al.* for performing functions of armed forces as second line of defence in 'disturbed' areas, like Jammu and Kashmir, or North East, especially Nagaland, Manipur or states and regions which are infected by Left Extremism or Maoism or Naxalism. The 'defence and security' of the state and its territorial boundaries is given a very high priority not only by employing large number of personnel for the Army and para-military armed forces, but also by enacting Special Laws, which curb fundamental rights of citizens, especially Armed Forces Special Protection Act which is in force in areas considered 'disturbed' by the Indian state. Further, the Indian state has acquired 'extraordinary powers' to curb individual or group activities which are considered a 'threat' to the safety and territorial integrity of the country. If on one hand, the Indian state has not repudiated or repealed law on Sedition or Public Safety Act, which it inherited from the colonial state, on the other, during the last seventy years, it has enacted new tough laws, like Preventive Detention Act to Unlawful Activities Anti-Terrorist Act to curb the activities of individuals or groups considered 'dangerous' by the state. The Civil liberty groups and defenders of human rights consider that democratic state of India has many 'undemocratic' features and these 'libertarians' characterize this state as 'coercive' and 'authoritarian'. This approach to the study of Indian state has been followed by some scholars and 'libertarian' groups, who consider that as a continuation of foreign colonial oppressive state, the decolonized India has given more coercive powers to the functionaries of Indian state and during the last seventy years while continuing with the policies of coercion followed by the erstwhile colonisers the Indian state has more resources and power to effectively enforce its coercive laws and curb freedoms of citizens. This approach of 'libertarians' to project the coercive face of the Indian state as the only 'reality' is not only partial presentation of the essence of Indian state after independence, it is quite flawed because while emphasizing 'continuities' of the colonial state, the real significance of the Transfer of Power in 1947 from British colonizers to Indian nationalist leadership is not properly understood. The real meaning of the Transfer of Power in 1947 is that the colonial rulers were forced to quit India because of the pressures built by powerful anti-colonial mass struggle for independence,. The new rulers of the Indian state were patriots, who had not only fought against colonial oppression, they also had a pride in Independent India. The nationalist leadership of the Indian state in 1947 came to power with a commitment to build a new 'democratic, sovereign, secular, Republic of India on the basis of a constitution prepared by the Constituent Assembly of India. The real meaning of the Transfer of Power in 1947 is that India witnessed a 'break with the past' inspite of the fact that some 'continuities' of the colonial oppressive state apparatus can be pointed out but these 'continuities' of the colonial past have to be seen in the context of fundamental 'change', which took place, when foreign rule was replaced by the state of the natives. Continuities with change is the essence of the Transfer of Power of 1947 and its best example is that coercive apparatus of the state came under the full control of the nationalist leadership who unlike the colonial rulers, were democratically elected to govern the country. The Constitution of India prepared by the Constituent Assembly of India placed state power in the hands of 'democratically' elected representatives, who were accountable for governance and every activity of the coercive apparatus of the state, like Army, Civil and police functionaries. The approach to the study of state by these academicians who consider that post- 1947 state is a 'continuity' of the colonial state system is completely flawed and deserves to be rejected because post-independence Indian state, which begins its journey from August 15, 1947 should be studied by one of the following 'approaches', which help in understanding the 'reality' of post-independence state.

Liberal-Democratic-Pluralist Approach

John Locke, John Stuart Mill and many other western scholars and theoreticians of capitalist democracy have approached the study of state by focusing attention on 'individual rights and freedoms' and institutions of governance, which can ensure that human freedoms are protected and promoted. The state according to liberal-democratic-pluralist theoreticians acts as a neutral umpire while dealing with multiple and diverse problems of sections of society and while resolving inter-group or inter-community conflicts in a plural society, the state in a democracy tries to maintain equilibrium among social groups with the sole purpose of providing equal protection to every individual citizen and social group. Liberal theoreticians beginning with John Locke to John Rawls have been engaged in internal debates about the meaning of Individual liberties and rights and inspite of such debates, all liberal-democratic theoreticians have agreed that the right to own private property is fundamental for the enjoyment of individual freedoms. If individual citizens have a right to elect their representatives and hold them accountable while governing human society, such an elected government has a fundamental duty to protect private property owned by individual citizens. Further, liberal democracies have evolved institutional mechanisms of governance, where power is not concentrated in anyone institution and it is shared and divided among many institutions of governance of the state. Western democratic state systems have adopted institutional system for protecting rights and liberties of individual citizens and inspite of different kind of institutions, which have been working in different western democratic state systems, the common factor in all democracies is that the state is considered as protector and guardian of individual liberties and rights and every individual has institutional protection, if his rights are violated by the functionaries of the state. A fundamental criticism of liberal democracy, its theory and praxis, has been put forward by defenders of 'human equality' who have argued that capitalist democracy of liberal theoreticians is like an empty shell because without 'human equality' individual freedoms are like bones without flesh and blood. Capitalism and inequality in human society create conditions, where real freedoms are enjoyed by the owners of means of production for private appropriation and profit and the majority of working and labouring classes are promised liberty, which is empty and without any substance. The idea of individual liberty hangs in the air in capitalist democratic states because rights and freedoms of exploiters cannot be equal to the so-called rights of the exploited majority of citizens. Social corrections have been suggested by those who recognize that inequality in society creates real road blocks and obstacles in the way of individuals who have been guaranteed freedoms but pre-conditions for the enjoyment of freedoms do not exist because the absolute majority of labouring classes do not have any share in the wealth of society. The idea of welfare state has been put forward by those who want to reconcile to some extent the problems created by capitalism in democracy and some capitalist countries have tried to pursue social welfare and social security policies and programmes for creating some essential conditions for everyone to participate in democratic processes of governance and enjoy to some extent freedoms provided by democratic state systems. The welfare state in a capitalist country acts as a midwife by creating some conditions for deprived citizens so that they can enjoy some freedoms. However, the basic issue of liberty in an unequal capitalist society remains unresolved because the fundamental feature of capitalism is that private appropriation for profit by the owners of means of production creates 'inequality' and liberty in an 'unequal' society remains an empty promise for the real producers of wealth, the labouring classes.

Marxist Approach to the Study of State

If liberal theorists of capitalist democracy have advocated the idea of individual freedom and rights as the foundational principle of a democratic state in capitalist societies, Karl Marx had offered a fundamental critique of capitalism by pointing out that the institution of private property in capitalism creates fundamental social inequalities because those who own the means of production by appropriating and accumulating surplus and profits generated by millions of labouring classes, create divisions between the 'exploiter' and the 'exploiting' classes. A capitalist society is divided into 'classes' based on 'unequal social relations', the private owners of the means of production need to control the state for private accumulation of surplus and profits. The state in class-divided capitalist societies is an 'instrument' in the hands of dominant capitalist classes and such a state exercises coercive authority over the sellers of labour so that the interests of private capitalist appropriators are fully protected and safeguarded. The state is an agency of the dominant exploiting classes and its basic function is to serve the interests of the exploiters and also maintain social conditions for the functioning of such an 'unequal' society. An issue which is worth examining is the relationship between democracies, which took strong roots in many advanced capitalist societies of the west, especially during the 20th century and capitalist state which acts as a protector and guardian of the exploiting capitalist classes, which dominate over the whole society under the protective umbrella of the state. If democratically elected governments claim that real power is derived from people's vote and support and because these governments are elected on the basis of universal franchise, they are 'accountable' to the citizens who have elected them. Democratically elected governments claim that power is exercised for the development and welfare of multiple sections of society and because the elected governments are ultimately responsible to the society at large, such elected governments cannot be just an agency or an instrument in the hands of dominant exploiting capitalist classes. While this debate on the relationship between formally elected representative governments and the dominant role played by powerful capitalist classes, which control the state for the advancement of their own class interests continues, one issue which is settled once for all is that in an 'unequal society', which is the logical product of laws of motion of capitalism, power in society is also unequally distributed. The state in an unequal society even in a democracy cannot provide equal services and protection to all the citizens because if society is divided basically on the basis of ownership of the means of production for private appropriation, the state has to 'protect the interests of private property owners' and ensure that conflicts, which may arise in socially unequal society are resolved basically by guaranteeing the rights of dominant capitalist classes. If liberal democratic state system in a capitalist society cannot ensure individual liberties and rights for every citizen, Marx intervenes and argues that these individual liberties can be ensured only in a society based on equality and Marx further argues that capitalism cannot ensure equal enjoyment of rights and liberties for every citizen, its alternative is socialism, where equality and liberty of human beings can be really enjoyed. It is only in socialism according to Karl Marx, the idea of social equality can be harmonized with individual liberty and rights. Such a reconciliation is not possible under capitalism and the state which is an agency of capitalist unequal social order cannot be considered 'neutral' while dealing with social class conflicts.

Special and Salient Features of Indian State: 70 Years

The first and foremost specific feature of the Indian state inspite of its commitment to election based representative democracy is that it has actively promoted Indian capitalism and its direct involvement in laying down firm foundations for the development of capitalism has not stopped inspite of India's transition from the era of economic planning to the launching of New Economic Policy in 1991. India had inherited some indigenous capitalist industries on the eve of Independence, and this process of industrialization had to be accelerated by laying down the foundations of robust infrastructure for economic development of the country. Not only this. The new agenda for the acceleration of processes of industrialization was also linked with the modernization of agriculture because India had to feed its own people by raising the levels of productivity of its agriculture. The system of economic planning and the model of mixed economy, which was followed by post-independence state of India created a situation, where the state was in the centre stage of economic development of agriculture and industry and it was the state which was actively engaged in building public and private sectors of economy. This activist role of the state in every major sector of economy created a social base for its relative autonomy form powerful social classes whether landlords or private owners of industry, commerce and trade. Dominant social classes in post-independence India looked towards the state for performing crucial and critical role for the development of public and private sectors of economy.[1] The state enjoyed relative autonomy with the consent of the dominant classes and from 1947 to 1991, these classes had substantially benefited from state intervention in economy. There was hardly any opposition from the socially dominant classes, when in the beginning of 1990's democratically elected political executive decided to break with the past model of state regulated economy to New Economic Policy of 'deregulation, liberalization, privatization and globalization'. The New Economic Policy beginning with the 1990s showed great preference for free market economy model for domestic capital and this new policy, unlike the past (1947 to 1991) openly welcomed foreign private capital for investment in multiple sectors of Indian economy. India has been fully integrated with world capitalist system and during the last about three decades of the 'opening' of Indian economy to foreign capital has provided an opportunity to Indian capitalists to invests in foreign markets and foreign capital investors to freely operate in Indian market. The New Economic Policy has given birth to a new state, which is openly encouraging Indian private capitalists to collaborate with foreign private capital investors. The Indian state of today is a full-fledged capitalist state and Indian capitalist classes find the state very hospitable because it facilitates capitalist classes to operate in the Indian market and also invest in foreign markets. However, this is only one special feature of the Indian state.

The State in an Unequal Society

Capitalism in India has developed very strong roots during seventy years of post-independence of country's journey and capitalist development has given birth to the emergence of most 'unequal' society. A few salient facts about the prevalence of inequality in India deserve to be mentioned with a view to highlight the social consequences of capitalist development.

I. 'Between one-third and one-fourth of Indians live in absolute, sub-human poverty'.[2]

II. Top concentration of Wealth.[3]
   a) 2000 top 1 per cent hold 37 per cent of the wealth of the country and it has increased to 53 per cent by 2016.
   b) Between 2001 and 2016 top 1 per cent cornered 61 per cent of all the increase in wealth estimated at US$ 2.28 trillion.
   c) Forbes mentions that "US dollar billionaires were only 2 in 1995, however, "extremely high net worth individuals were 46 persons in 2012, 55 persons in 2014".
   d) One hundred top richest in India are all billionaires in US Dollar terms.[4]

III. Along with these billionaires, India has population of 300 to 350 multi-millionaires including rising professional, technocratic middle and upper middle classes. It is based on a credit Suisse Global Wealth Survey.[5]

This survey informs that nearly 250 million of world's poorest people are in India. Further, this survey mentions, referring to 2012, that top 22% of Indians owned 77.6% of wealth and the top one per cent controlled 25%, while the bottom 70% of the population owned just 13.6% of wealth in India. The total wealth in the country is estimated at US$ 3 trillion and just 57 billionaires in India have the same wealth (US$ 216 billion) as that of the bottom 70% of their country. If on one hand, the ruling classes and capitalist state is focused on accelerating the rate of economic growth, on the other, in the absence of any redistribution plan, social inequalities have grown and deepened in India. India was always socially an 'unequal' society, however, it was expected that under democratic pressures the state will follow schemes for redistribution so that concentration of wealth, assets and incomes in the hands of a few owners of means of production would not take place, unfortunately, it has not happened and inequalities have increased in society.[6]

India is faced with serious social challenges arising out of social inequality and regional and sectoral imbalances. If some regions are engaged in insurgency and violent uprisings against the Indian state, the other regions or so-called mainland of India is still seeking solutions through democratic methods of elections and participations in parliamentary democratic politics.

Ideological Shifts in Politics and Society

The state and the ruling classes have to establish their ideological hegemony over every strata of society so that their authority to rule is willingly accepted by everyone. The only test of acceptance of ideological hegemony by every section of society is that citizens accept that this is their own state and this state is their real protector and well-wisher. Liberal-Democratic theorists maintain that by ensuring people's participation through elections in governance of a country a democratic state can create conditions for the willing acceptance of authority of the state. The western democratic states of advanced capitalist countries seem to have established ideological hegemony by strengthening the institutions of democratic participation by voters in regular, free and fair elections. If citizens in a democracy accept this fact that an elected government is their own because it is accountable to them, it has been suggested that one can assume that the state has established its ideological hegemony and the citizens of such a state have come to accept willingly the authority of the state. The story of Indian state is quite different. The British colonial state had established its authority over India by following policies of coercion and suppression of anti-colonial liberation struggles and movements. When the colonial rulers realized especially beginning with 1940s that policies of suppression and coercion were becoming counter-productive and the coercive state apparatus of colonisers was unable to suppress popular feelings for freedom, they decided to quit in 1947. Anti-colonial movements and struggles launched by Indians became very strong from 1920s to 1940s and the British colonial state gradually accepted the fact that their days are numbered and popular struggles for freedom could not be suppressed and policies of coercion followed by the colonisers could not succeed, and hence, the decision to quit India was taken by the British. The idea of nationalist leadership to 'delegitimize' the colonial state in the minds of the people became strong and popular, the British had to quit because they realized that the nationalist leadership had succeeded in mobilizing the mass of peasantry, labouring and middle classes against 'the foreign rule', the British had no option but to quit. The idea that the colonial state is not 'ours' and it is 'foreign' rule made people come on the streets and this mass opposition eroded the foundations of oppressive colonial state. The sum and substance of above narrative is that when a state loses its legitimacy, it either becomes very oppressive and authoritarian or like the illegitimate British colonial state, the option of leaving the colony is exercised. The new independent state of India had 'legitimacy' and 'ideological' acceptability because the mass of people recognized a fact that our independent state is a product of our struggles and sacrifices and it is not something 'foreign' like the British colonial state. The new independent state was accepted as 'ours' and led by the people and the new constitution of India was accepted as our Constitution prepared by our Constituent Assembly, which consisted of our representatives. Thus, Indian nationalism acted as 'legitimizer' of the new state of India. However, during the last seventy years, Indians have witnessed many ideological contests on the basis of which different ideological groups have competed against one another with a view to establish their ideological hegemony over the state.

Idea of Ideological State: Hindu Rashtravad

Traditionally, the state has been studied by following one of the three approaches mentioned above i.e. approach of Libertarians or Liberal-Democratic theories of the state or Karl Marx's approach to the study of state, however, some new social and political developments which have taken place in the Arab Islamic world have led some scholars to study this phenomenon of Islamisation of the state by suggesting that these Islamist states are Ideological as distinguished from other state systems of Asia, Africa or advanced Western capitalist countries. The essence of an Ideological state lies in the fact that while performing traditional law and order and developmental-welfare functions, an ideological state is primarily guided by its dominant ideology of promoting and protecting Islam as enshrined in the Holy Quran by Prophet Mohammad and as interpreted by Mullahs and Maulvis. One of the best example of an ideological state is Iran, where only Ayatullah, a chief Islamic theologian, can rule the country. The Islamists are also trying to revive Caliphate, an anachronism, where pure Islamic ideological state system can be established and the rulers are bound by the dictates of Holy Quran and the teachings of Prophet Mohammad. Mullahs as custodians of Islam and the teachings of Prophet Mohammad shall not only be guided by an ideology, it will implement and enforce all the fundamental principles of Ideology and ensure that every citizen of such a state, without any exception, follows the ideological principles an laid down by Islam. It is only an ideological state, which has strict laws on 'blasphemy' and a person or a group, which is alleged to be breaking the fundamental principles of ideology shall be declared 'blasphemous' and the state shall inflict severe punishment on such a violator of supreme ideology. While every modern state is committed to the implementation of some basic social and human values while governing a society, however, unlike other modern states, the ideological state functions under the umbrella of a supreme ideology and it has to defend 'purity' of its ideological principles and inflict severest punishments on those who deviate from the fundamentals of ideology. The state has to be guided by a supreme ideology and it has to act as a 'guardian' of purity of Ideology just as Islam.

Unislamic activities by a citizen cannot be tolerated by an ideological state and Mullahs and Maulvis as custodians of Islam are expected to decide about 'unislamic activities' and the state as guardian of purity of Ideology will announce punishments. In sum, the state is guided by the principles of a supreme ideology and all its activities are expected to conform with the fundamentals of ideology and any deviation from any fundamental principle shall invite severe punishment.

It is argued here that India is witnessing an ideological shift and the Indian state is gradually moving away from liberal–democratic values enshrined in the Republican Constitution of India and Hindu Rashtravadis represented by Rashtriya Swayamsevak Sangh and its 44 affiliates including its political face—the Bharatiya Janata Party are moving forward to capture the India state with the sole purpose of making it an ideological Hindu state. The sole agenda of BJP-RSS is to capture state power through electoral process and exercise this power to establish a Hindu state. K.B. Hedgewar, M.S. Gowalkar to Mohan Bhagwat as Sarsanghchalak or supremo of the RSS have worked very hard to create a strong paramilitary like disciplined organization of Swayamsevaks (cadre)and Pracharaks of the RSS are deployed to inculcate the ideology of greatness of Hindus of India among the 'young' recruits to the RSS. The aim of such an ideological traning by the RSS is to inculcate great pride among its cadre about the glorious past of the Hindus and the RSS recruits are asked to work hard with dedication and devotion to spread this message of greatness among the Hindus who are expected to revive their own glorious past based on traditions mentioned in Vedas, Mahabharata and Ramayana. Brahmans are very important for the RSS because on the basis of their knowledge of Sanskrit language, they can transmit Hindu values as enshrined in ancient Hindu religious scriptures. The RSS is committed to work for the unity of Hindus so that they can defend Hindu Rashtra from external and internal enemies. Leadership of the BJP is in the hands of RSS Pracharaks, who work under the guidance and instructions of the RSS. RSS and BJP are indistinguishable and BJP-in-government is committed to the implementation of the ideology of Hindu Rashtravad in unity with RSS and its 44 affiliates, like Vishwa Hindu Parishad, Bajrang Dal, Akhil Bharatiya Vidyarthi Parishad et all. BJP-in-government in reality means that India is ruled by the Sangh Parivar Hindu Family.[7]

The Indian state ruled and controlled by the BJP-RSS is an ideological state which is guided by a supreme idea of making India a united Hindu Rashtra for the sole purpose of promoting and protecting Hindus and their holy places or holy animals like cow. The BJP and RSS are committed to protect the 'purity' of Hindu race by preventing Hindu girls from marrying Muslims or Christians. It is a part of ideological role of the Indian state currently under the BJP government at the Centre that vigilante groups are operating without any fear and punshing, even killing, suspected killers of holy cow of the Hindus or punishing Muslims who marry Hindu girls by proclaiming that Muslims have launched a 'Love Jihad' against Hindus. The state is quite indifferent to the activities of gau-rakshaks or Love Jihadis because as a Hindu ideological state, it approves of these actions because they are undertaken to defend Hindu religious beliefs. A normal law-based state committed to the principles of Rule of Law would punish illegal activities of groups, like Bajrang Dal or gau-rakshaks or those who spread hatred against other religious communities but an ideological state of Hindus would not take any punitive action because these groups are performing ideological role of the state.

Dominant Hindu society as interpreted by the rulers is at work and the latesr example is that the Modi-led BJP government is engaged in pursuing this ideology is that on May 23, 2017, a notification was issued by the central government asking all the 29 states and 7 Union Territories of India to implement the regulations of lives stocks market rules framed under the Prevention of Cruelty to Animals Act of 1960 requiring "animal market committees to be formed in every distinct to ensure that the purchaser of the cattle does not further sell the animal for purpose of slaughter'. The detailed rules for the sale and purchase of animals and the list of animals mentioned in this notification in reality attempt to prohibit the sale and purchase of holy cow, mother to a section of high caste Hindus, from falling in the hands of butchers and those who run slaughter houses. BJP-led governments are engaged in protecting the holy cow because it is considered sacred by a section of high caste Hindus. Not only this. Hindus consider River Ganga sacred and in normal circumstances a secular and routine agenda for any government of India but cleaning of holy Ganga river water is an agenda for serving the cause of Hindus, who consider taking a bath in Ganga River water a holy and sacred activity. This is the reason that Hindu ideological state-led by BJP-RSS is concentrating on the cleaning of dirty water flowing in holy Ganga River so that Hindu worshippers can take bath in clean water at the holy river. Yogi Adityanath, BJP Chief Minister of Uttar Pradesh observed on My 21, 2017 that 'the holy river belongs to everyone and a symbol of *Sanatan Sanskriti'* It is everyone's mother and people have to save it. Any insult to the river can never be tolerated and it is equal to 'rashtradroh' (anti-nationals). There are many examples to substantiate the argument that Hindu ideological state, like Islamist state is fundamentally committed to promote and protect religious beliefs either of Hindus or of Muslims. And in reality, the primary goal of these ideological states is to implement religious beliefs of either Hindus or Muslims. Hindu or Islamist states are distinguished from other modern states because for the former state systems religion defines their whole world view and comprehensively lays down the basic functions, which these states have to perform. Hindu Ideological State legitimizes its ban on cow slaughter or construction of Ram Temple at Ayodhya because the Hindu state has to be guided by matters concerning Hindu faith and Hindu sentiments has to be respected by such a state.

Summing Up

I. Indian Capitalism and the State

Social classes are formed in a specific historical context and formation of Indian capitalist classes and its relationship with the state cannot be an exception to this general rule of class formation. Indian trading and business communities and classes struggled very hard to emerge as capitalist classes because British colonial state had followed very negative and obstructionist policies towards indigenous emerging capitalist classes. The colonial context in which new capitalist mode of production was emerging led new capitalists to identify their interests with anti-colonial struggles led by nationalist leadership. After Independence, the state leadership consciously promoted the class interests of private industrial and entrepreneurial classes and in this project of nation-building, the state and capitalist classes worked in harmony with one another, especially because the individual private industrial capitalists had recognized that without the active support and involvement of the state any industrialization of India was just not possible. The state and capital have worked in almost complete harmony during the last seventy years of post-Independence India and because of this closeness between the state and capital, not only resource base of Indian economy has increased, individual capitalists have also joined the ranks of big industrial groups and many of them are monopoly capitalists. India has emerged as a full-fledged capitalist state and Indian capitalist classes with the full support and encouragement of the state have become very powerful and prosperous. This is the first feature of the Indian state which deserves to be noticed and India is a new developed emerging economic power of the countries of the South and the economic resource base of the state and private capitalist industrial and entrepreneurial strata of society has increased to an extent that Indian monopoly capitalists and the state have without any hesitation interpreted themselves with global monopoly finance capital and transnational corporations.

II. Consolidation of Power

A modern state has to ensure safety and security of its citizens and it is expected to create powerful and effective infrastructure and apparatuses of the state to defend its borders and legally defined territorial boundaries. During the last seventy years, the Indian state has fought four wars with Pakistan and Indian army was also engaged in war with China in 1962 on the issue of disputed boundaries. During the last seven decades of post-independence journey, India has strengthened its war machine and also civilian police and paramilitary forces have been strengthened to defend the territorial integrity of the country and maintain domestic law and order.

III. Ideology of the State

The state legitimizes its rule by winning over the loyalty of its citizens and the citizens willingly obey the authority and laws of the state, if they believe that their state is working for their interests. Ideology, thus, plays the legitimizing function and this is the reason that every modern state tries to win over the loyalty of its citizens by establishing institutions which promote values and ideology of the state. Liberal-Democratic states legitimize themselves by promoting the idea of individual freedom as their main ideology and most important social value. The state is guardian and protector of rights and liberties of the citizens and it is the duty of citizens to obey the liberal-democratic state because only such a state can ensure freedom to individuals. This ideological message is given to every citizen through every institution of ideology maintained by the state, the most important role is played by educational institutions and the media.

The Constitution of India has laid down the foundations of the state based on ideology of liberal, pluralist and secular value system. This ideology of liberalism as enshrined in the constitution is not acceptable to the Hindu Sangh Parivar of the Rashtriya Swayamsevak Sangh and Bhartiya Janata Party. India is witnessing great 'ideological contest' between the idea of liberal-democratic state and the idea of Hindu Rashtravad of the RSS. Is India moving away from the ideological framework of liberal, democratic, plural, secular state as mentioned in the Constitution of India or to the making of Hindu ideological state? What is the social base of organizations and leaders desiring to establish a Hindu ideological state for India? Ideological shifts of fundamental character can take place, if some powerful social classes and groups support new ideology. Narendra Modi-led BJP government at the centre and BJP governments in North and North-Western India have obviously come to power with the support of voters during the elections but this is only one part of the explanation in favour of the votaries and believers of the ideology of Hindu state. It is just one observable fact but the real issue is to find out the social support base for Hindutva. Dominant Hindu social groups, like big industrial houses, merchants and traders and the emerging professional, entrepreneurial and technocratic upwardly mobile middle and other middle classes of about 300 to 350 million in the income group of multi-million US dollar are a powerful social constituency, which is aggressively supporting the idea of Hindu ideological state, as propagated by the RSS and BJP. Big or medium or small private property owners in urban India are under the influence of Brahmanical-ritual based Hinduism and these Hindu-religious believers are providing conscious support to the parties of Hindutva. It should not be concluded that every practitioner of some kind of Hindu rituals and believer stands up in support of the BJP-RSS ideology of Hindu State. However, a large number of Hindus across the length and breadth of the country are providing social base to expanding RSS-BJP, which stands for the creation of Hindu State. Hindu trading classes and Brahman castes were always attracted to RSS-BJP's ideology of Hindu state, but from 2017, new social classes and groups have joined the ranks of Hindutva. Incidentally, social soil of India seems to be quite fertile for those forces, movements and leaders who are determined to exploit Hindu religious sentiments and one important reason for the success of appeals in the name of Hindu religion among mass of Hindus is that Hinduism and its different religious sects were never 'attacked' and 'delegitimized' by any powerful group which stood for enlightenment, rationality and humanism and Ramaswamy Naikar in Tamil Nadu had launched a movement against Hindu ritual based religiosity and propagated the idea of 'atheism' but even in Tamil Nadu, the home of anti-Brahman movement, ritual based, temple focused Hindu religion is going strong and BJP-RSS is expanding its roots in that state/region also. The best example of three years of the functioning of ideologically-oriented Hindu state is that Rajasthan, Haryana, Uttar Pradesh, Madhya Pradesh, Gujarat, Maharashtra et al is that the protection of holy cow, which is considered holy by Hindus, especially of the upper castes has emerged as the most important agenda of the forces of Hindutva. Islamist Ideological States punish their citizens on charges of 'blasphemy' if they are found dishonouring Holy Quran. Hindu Ideological State considers protection of holy cow as its priority and inflicts severe punishment on an individual who is suspected of harming the holy cow. India is at the cross roads because such a fundamental 'ideological' shifts in national history has never occurred without 'violence'. Is India witnessing the end of liberal-democratic project launched after independence and its substitution by the establishment of Hindu ideological state?

NOTES

1. Land reforms were not implemented and agrarian social and productive relations were not restructured because the landed classes were an integral part of the ruling class coalition.
2. Amit Bahadur; "Danger Zones of High Economic Growth". *Economic and Political Weekly*, Bombay, October 22, 2016, pp. 14-15.
3. Global Wealth Databook, 2014.
4. Rukmani (2014) "India's staggering Wealth Gap in Five Charts", *Hindu*, Chennai, December 8, 2014.
5. *The Economic Times*, New Delhi, Dcember 15, 2016. p. 4.
6. Also see, Francois Bourguignon: The Globalisation of Inequality. Princeton: 2015. Also see, Joseph Stiglitz: The Price of Inequality: How Today's Divided Society Endangers Our Future: (2012).
7. See Dhirendra K. Jha: Shadow Armies: Fringe Organisations and Foot Soldiers of Hindutva: 2017: New Delhi: Juggernaut.

12

Imperialism-led Globalization

The capitalist mode of production as distinguished from its predecessor the feudal mode of production is 'expansioninst' because 'capital accumulation' begins with the territorial boundaries of a nation-state but capital's great need to 'accumulate' cannot be fulfilled without colonies and unequal trading partners for the assured supply of raw material for constantly 'expanding' markets. This inherent logic in the dynamics of capitalist expansionism has led many scholars to maintain that the new development of capitalist globalization is not a new one. Since capitalism has been always international, current phase of capitalist globalization is not something different from the ongoing process of internationalization of capitalism beginning with 1500 AD to the present decade of the Twenty First century. Even Eric Hobsbawam states that 'Pax Americana,' is an echo of 'Pax Brittanica just as the latter had been an echo of 'Pax Romana'.[1] The ongoing debate on globalization is centred around the validity and relevance of capitalist nation-state systems, which were formally recognized in the Treaty of Westphalia in 1648. It is maintained that the current stage of 'finance capital' which means globalization of finance capital along with its centralization has broken geographical and territorial boundaries of the nation-state system because 'globalization'-cum-'centralization' of capital has completely weakened the 'capacities' of nation-states to control the fast mobility of finance-capital across the whole world. Two fundamentally opposite viewpoints have been expressed about the viability of nation-states to control their national economies in the age of globalized-cum-centralized finance capital. William I. Robinson and Jerry Harris observe: "...globalization involves an 'epochal shift' in the development of the world capitalist system. Specifically, it represents the transition from the nation-state phase to a new transnational phase of capitalism'.[2] George Soros, a self-confessed speculator, proved that the global mobility of capital was much 'faster' than the abilities of the national federal banks and other financial control mechanisms to control and regulate the 'flight' of capital?[3] Eric Hobsbawm, on the other hand, has a much more 'nuanced' understanding of the role of nation-states in the phase of transnationalized finance capital. Hobsbawm observes :

> "We have a globalized economy, we can aspire to a globalized culture, we certainly have a globalized technology and a single global science, but politically speaking, we have a world that remains in reality pluralist and divided into territorial states."[4]

It is a hurried conclusion that national territorial states are things of the past in the present era of globalization. In spite of the fact that nation-states, especially of the South, are under great pressure from the capital and technology exporting states of the North, the local populations look only towards their own states to act as a 'buffer' against interventionist imperialist states and also manage domestic affairs for the satisfaction of domestic populations. Since capitalist crisis is an inherent and integral part of capitalist system of private accumulation and social production, it is the local state which is expected to find solutions to the 'crisis' created by capitalism at the global level, as witnessed by the East Asian capitalist countries from 1997 to 2000. Eric Hobsbawm draws attention to the social dialectics of globalized capital and 'domestic states' while dealing with the 'conflicts' created by global capitalist crisis. He observes : "This brings us back to the great question of the conflict between the forces of capitalism, which are in favour of removing all obstacles, and political forces, which basically operate through nation-states and are either obliged or deliberately choose to regulate these procedures. This is a conflict because the laws of capitalist development are simple : maximize expansion, profit, and the increase of capital. However, the priorities of governments and people organized into societies are different by their very nature, and to some extent they are in conflict."[5]

While the idea of the 'retreat of the state' and autonomy for markets lies burried after the warnings by Hobsbawm and others, it is not to suggest that the state is only a 'regulator' of free market and competitive economy, as desired by the capitalist globalizers.

Another question may be raised here to deepen our understanding of the role of the state under the present phase of globalized-cum-centralized finance capital. Is globalization inevitable and is it not reversible to some extent? This question has to be faced squarely because from the beginning of 1980s, the model of free market economy has been sold in a fundamentalist manner. Hence, globalization in the last decade of the Twentieth Century rests on an ideology of American model of free market capitalism, in which the role of the state is that of a 'facilitator' and 'regulator' of the rules of the game for managing an efficient free market economy. The state has not only to act as an executive agency of its own ruling classes and corporate houses, but it has also to play the role of a good 'host' for transnational capital. The votaries of globalization have maintained that the state is the real villian and it should be ejected from the centrality of position it occupies in the national economy and replaced by a friendly 'host' state for domestic and global capitalism. In the Introduction to the World Bank Policy Research report entitled *'Bureaucrats in Business : The Economics and Politics of government Ownership'*, Michael Bruno, Vice President, Development Economics and Chief Economist of the World Bank, observes :

> "Yet in many countries, particularly the poorest, some parts of the economy have remained stubbornly resistant to reform. This report deals with one of the more important of these : the inefficient, loss-making state-owned enterprises that are a significant burden on government budgets and scarce resources in many countries. These enterprises hinder growth, impede market liberalization, and thus, both, directly and indirectly limit efforts to reduce poverty."[6]

Further, the report points out: "However, we have presented evidence that SOEs are less efficient than the private sector in competitive markets and, with effective regulation of private firms, in monopoly markets as well. Finally, we have shown that large SOE sectors can be a drag on the economy because of the aggregate impact of inefficient operation at the microeconomic level and because large SOE sectors are typically associated with large fiscal and current account deficits, which in turn have negative repercussions on growth."[7] Thus, the ideological recipe of antistatist neo-liberal classical economics is sold to the new liberalizers in the Third World that the post-Independence project of state-led model of economic growth followed by these countries has been completely flawed and the model of free market capitalism of the United States of America is recommended for achieving goals of economic growth, which these countries have missed during the period of interventionist state-led economy.

It deserves to be stated that assumptions underlying the neo-liberal free market ideology, sold by the Americans and global institutions, like the World Bank and IMF controlled by them, have been proved empirically wrong and as Hobsbawm observes : "In theory, economists believe in the complete triumph of the free-market ideology, but in practice no country has ever tried to go all the way down the road, partly because of political impediments.'[8]

Contradictions of this Model of Globalization

Historically, capitalism has developed and expanded internationally with the help of its own national states. Harry Magdoff brings out this aspect :

> "While the expansion of capitalism has always presupposed and indeed required co-operation among its various national components—with respect to transportation facilities, weights and measures, monetary and credit arrangements, etc. —there never has been a time, when these national components ceased to struggle each for its own preferment and advantage.'[9]

Hobsbawm and Magdoff have alerted Third World globalisers that the state still remains the site of social contest both, against local ruling classes and the external imperialist ruling classes. Further, many social conflicts emerge within countries of the South, if they follow policy prescriptions of free market fundamentalists, and it is only the local state which has to deal with social conflicts which are the product of exported global ideology of free competitive market capitalism. Stephen Gill in '*Structural change and global political economy : Globalizing elites and the emerging World Order*' observes :

> "Nonetheless, trends in the ownership, location, and nature of economic activity suggest that the identity and allegiance of firms have taken on a less and less territorial aspect in the 1990s. This indicates potential contradictions between globalizing and more territorially bounded social forces and institutions, and between economics and politics at the global level. The economic system is one of increasingly planetary reach, whereas political authority is still primarily constituted at the national level,... states are being recast into a kind of transmission belt for globalizing forces—a transformation that has been developing since the 1990s, and that accelerated in the 1980s, especially in the third world.'[10]

The most important implication is the birth of a 'new contradiction' between the demands of global finance capital for the restructuration of the state systems to implement the neo-liberal classical economic ideology and the pressures of local populations on their states to fulfill their 'basic demands'. The impoverished majority of masses especially of the South will be involved in struggles against their own states due to failures of these states to meet legitimate demands of their poor citizens. This will weaken the democratic legitimacy of every state under neo-liberal umbrella. Further, socially unstable countries cannot have stable democratic states. Since different fractions and strata of the ruling and non-ruling classes will be differentially impacted by economic arrangements under free market capitalism, society will be seriously fragmented because intra-class, and inter-class struggles will take place to assert their rights over the size of the economic cake and in such an unstable social situation, the state will be continuously involved in fire fighting activities.

In summation, it may be mentioned that the new imperialism-led capitalist globalization will consolidate the 'core' capitalist countries of the North and marginalize and exclude the developing countries of the South on whose shoulders super-capital accumulation is going to take place. It is not without reason that Bukharin characterised the imperialist state as a "robber state."[11] Polanyi had warned that "market mechanism" would "result in the demolition of society".[11]

Politics and Economics of Imperialism-led Global Capitalism

The internationalization of production and globalization of finance has also happened at a time, when Pax Americana had become a reality in the last decade of the Twentieth Century and the beginning of the Twenty First Century. Every countervailing force and every system of balance of power among the nation-states has come to an end with the collapse of socialist state systems and the last decade of the Twentieth Century has witnessed the emergence of a hyper-super economic and military power. The implications of sole super-power-led New Global Order deserve to be mentioned because economics and politics of the new epoch of globalized-cum-centralized finance capital can not be clearly comprehended without analysing the arrival of imperialist America on the world scene. President George Bush Sr. declared that the decade of 1990s has begun with the emergence of a New International Order, which in reality meant unipolar world in place of a post-World War II situation of bipolarity, where space was occupied by two super-powers and the two alliances—North Atlantic Treaty Organization and the Warsaw Pact. The collapse of Soviet Russia provided full space for American hegemony to emerge which was asserted during the American war on Iraq in 1991 on the pretext of liberating Kuwait from Iraq. This caravan of hegemonic America is unstoppable. It has been legitimized by George Bush Jr. by launching his so called global war against terrorism in the form of a response to the terrorist attack on World Trade Centre on September 11, 2001. Americans have changed regimes in Afghanistan and Iraq between 2001 and 2003 on the pretext of fight against global terrorism. Even George Soros, who built his reputation as a great speculator and launched US$ 5 billion project to promote democracy at the global level, observes : "America, under Bush, is a danger to the world'[12], and he has announced he would distribute funds to democratic forces in America for the defeat of George Bush in the forthcoming presidential election.

A very dangerous doctrine has been advanced by neo-conservative forces ruling over America that the post September11, 2001 events of terrorism against America demand a 'pre-emptive' war against any sovereign state suspected to be supporting terrorism against America. This doctrine of 'pre-emptive war' against any country by America means that except the American state, no other state is sovereign and every nation-states' sovereignty is at the mercy of America.

The America's war against Iraq in 2003 was launched under the doctrine of 'pre-emptive' strike against the most dangerous enemy of America. This new threat to the sovereignty of every state in the 1990s deserves a little elaboration. Strobe Talbott, an important policy maker in America, observes : "Along with the expansion and adaptation of international institutions in the Nineties came the establishment of a new principle. It was agreed that there are limits on the sovereignty of the nation-state : national governments are subject to international sanction, if they violate certain basic norms within their own borders,'[13] and hence, war against Bosnia (1995), Ksovo (1999) Afghanistan, (2001/2) Iraq (2003) *et al.* The only exception to the general rule of the end of state sovereignty theory is that America is super-sovereign state and pre-eminent power in the world. It has the license and the responsibility to act as a global policeman and punish the errant nation-states. Not only this. America is above any international obligation and it showed a contempt for the Security Council of the United Nations, when it unilaterally declared pre-emptive war against Saddam Hussein of Iraq in 2003. America has not only shown contempt for the United Nations, but also it has, at its sweet will, refused to be a party to the Kyoto Treaty on Global warming or international treaty 'on Ozone-destroying chemicals' (1989).

The arrogance of power by the sole policeman has been stated by Tabott : "Virtually all previous watersheds in the evolution of the international system had entailed the repudiation of specific empires. Cumulatively, they amounted to a repudiation of imperialism in general. Westphalia marked the end of the Holy Roman Empire, the Congress of Vienna carved up the Napoleonic one, Versailles did the same to the 'Habsburgs' and 'Ottomons'; the 'Romanous' was by then already on the ash heap of history. The allies in the Second World War defeated the Third Reich and the Empire of the Rising Sun, and the sun began to set on the British empire not long after. Throughout the 20th century, the US was an opponent of empire and a champion of decolonization. The fading of the cold war was made possible by the collapse of what was often called the world's last Empire, with Moscow as its metropole. Yet a decade later, in 2001, theoreticians for a new administration in Washington toyed with the idea of imperialism as a model of American foreign and defence policy."[14]

The Bush regime and the American neo-conservatives have made American imperialism not only 'fashionable' but also profitable because wars are profitable for the imperialists. Shripath Ramphal, a former Secretary-General of Commonwealth of Nations, gave a warning that "The ambition for world domination has ever been a global curse. September 11 is not the origin of present dangers. As many understood, and said, at the time, it was an enormously criminal act of terrorism; it was also enormously stupid. What it did was to provide a new imperialism to emerge with plumes of virtue and trumpets of righteousness."[15] Listen to the language of US President Bush in London who "...defended the war not only against Iraq as necessary to confront repression but also for 'effective' multilateral institutions, and for the Global expansion of Democracy".[16] What is the US record while dealing with international democratic obligations? Americans have refused to endorse a) the Kyoto Protocol; b) the International Criminal Court; c) the Anti-Ballistic Missile Treaty; d) the Landmine Treaty; e) the Biological and Toxin Weapons Convention; (f) the UN Agreement to Court Agreement to curb the International Flow of Illicit Small Arms *et al.*

War for Profit

Harry Magdoff has alerted us that the sluggish Japanese economy was the only beneficiary during the Korean war; Korea's misfortune between 1950 and 1955 brought great fortune to the Japanese "first as suppliers of war materials and services for United Nations and after the July 1953 armistice as suppliers of materials needed for the reconstruction of South Korea".[17] The same story of profits from war is repeating in the case of America's war on Iraq.

On the plea of fighting international terrorism in the post-September 11, 2001, the United States, at the end of year, invaded Afghanistan, in early 2003 it attacked Iraq and on May 1, 2003, declared that the war against Saddam Hussein was over.

But there is another side of the story. After destroying polity, economy, and society in wars of 'aggression', American's hearts are bleeding for the economic and political reconstruction of 'destroyed' Afghanistan and Iraq. Incidentally, Osama bin Laden's Al-Qaeda and the Taliban regime in Afghanistan were created and destroyed by America and Saddam Hussein's most dangerous weapons could not be traced in Iraq, and still the aggressive war was launched against these two countries. It is the post-war scenario which has to be brought into sharp focus around a question : Who will be the real beneficiaries of post-war reconstruction in Afghanistan and Iraq. A few facts may be mentioned to substantiate the argument that 'profit' is the driving force of war mongers in America. First, on October 18, 2003, the United States' Congress sanctioned US$ 87 billion for the ongoing reconstruction of Afghanistan and Iraq. Has the American Congress sanctioned more than US$ 80 billion to establish democracy in Afghanistan and Iraq or to control Afghanistan for Central Asian oil resources and Iraq, an oil rich country?

Second, the World Bank was asked to study vital sectors of Iraqi economy, which were to be re-constructed. Americans assembled seventy countries including tiny Sri Lanka to act as 'donors' for the reconstruction of Iraq's economy and the Madrid Conference was held on October 23-24, 2003 to legitimize American game in Iraq. Incidentally, such a *Tamasha* was also enacted in January 2002. A Conference of 'donors' for Afghanistan was held to pledge US$ 5 billion for reconstruction of that country. The Vajpayee government also stood in the queu at both these American-led conferences and made financial contributions for the reconstruction of war destroyed economies. Every important multinational corporation from road builders to hospitals, which is closely linked with the higher echelons of the neo-Conservative lobby of President Bush has been given a lucrative contract for the reconstruction of these two countries. A non-partisan Centre for Public Integrity has maintained in a report in Washington DC on October 31, 2003, that the first US$ 8 billion in contracts have been awarded to 71 companies by the Pentagon, the State Department and the US Agency for International Development. Charles Lewis, while releasing this report in US, said "There is a stench of political favouritism and cronyism" in awarding contracts. Further, it is well known that Bush Administration has strong linkages with private corporate sector, and this is the reason that private sector companies, like Engineering giant Batchel or Halliburton, an oil services and logistic company, formerly led by Vice-President Dick Cheney *et al* are blue-eyed boys for the award of every new lucrative contract. The puppet Iraqi Governing Council in September 2003, on the eve of G-7 meeting in Dubai announced a so-called policy that 'except for oil' foreigners/Americans were welcome. The Council said 'Foreign investors were to be given highly favourable terms in which to take over banks, insurance, pharmaceuticals, health care, power, telecommunications *et al*.'

The 'Business' of America has always been to earn profits even out of every human destruction, especially wars—global or local. Americans have learnt from experience that wars bring huge profits by selling arms for reconstruction in post-war destroyed societies. Marshall Plan President Truman of America for the reconstruction of war devastated Europe paid rich dividends to the American Big Business, after which the Americans have never abandoned such golden opportunities for earning profits. Prof. John K. Galbraith has authoritatively told us that it was not New Deal policies of President Roosevelt which pulled America out of its great economic depression of the 1930s, but the profits earned during the World War II that brought economic boom to the depressed American economy of the 1930s[18] An important lesson was learnt by the American capitalist classes that while capitalism goes through cyclical crisis even leading to economic depression and stagnation, the 'defence production sector' of the capitalist economy will always earn profits and keep the crisis-ridden economy an ongoing activity. USSR collapsed because it could not bear the economic burden of the Warsaw Pact and cold war competition with America. As a result of the uneven and unequal competition between the two super-powers, America emerged as the sole-super-power on the scene in the 1990s and converted a bipolar world into a unipolar New International Order. Both, India and Pakistan have been involved in military competition since independence, and every defence related purchase brings profits to defence sector of the capitalist countries. As late as October 30, 2003. US Assistant Secretary of State Ms. Christina Rocca, while testifying before the House Committee on International Relations Sub-Committee on Asia-Pacific and International Terrorism observed : "Both, India and Pakistan are responsible for the impasse over Kashmir'. American policy of 'equating' dispute-related neighbouring countries has created a situation of 'competition for arms for security'. Every developing country visits Arms Bazar of the Western Capitalist producers and suppliers of arms. Every local war in any region of the world brings 'profits' to the arms industry of the west. It is not without reason that Dwight Eisenhower in his Farewell Address on January 17, 1961, stated:

> "We now stand ten years past the mid point of a century that has witnessed four major wars among great nations... until the last of our

> world conflicts, the United States had no armaments industry.... We annually spend on military security more than the net income of all United States corporations... .
>
> "This conjunction of an immense military establishment and a large arm industry is new in the American experience.
>
> "In the councils of government, we must guard against the acquisition of unwarranted influence, whether sought or unsought, by the military-industrial complex. The potential for the disastrous rise of misplaced power exists and will persist."

Much water has flown down the Atlantic and Pacific, when Eisenhower warned about 'military-industrial complex' influencing the corridors of power. The present establishment of America under President Bush is consciously and actively pursuing the interests of 'military-industrial complex of America' which is earning profits out of every local war and the so-called post-war reconstruction whether in Afghanistan or Iraq or from dispute between India and Pakistan.

India Trapped

The Indian governing classes with the active and enthusiastic approval and consent of the ruling classes have integrated themselves with the American imperialist-led New Global Order. The decade of 1990s was a kind of probationary period for the Indian state and different fractions of the bourgenisie and the capitalist farmers and they slowly and steadily moved towards global integration. The beginning of Twenty First Century has witnessed 'over enthusiasm' in Indian political, administrative, oppressor and exploiting ruling classes because they have willingly joined the 'bandwagon' of George Bush Jr.'s 'alliance of fight against terrorism' after the events of September 11, 2001. India has accepted the right of Americans to launch preventive and pre-emptive wars against any sovereign state on the plea of a fight against terrorism.

A few facts may be mentioned to substantiate the argument that India has abandoned its national project of self-reliant economy led by a relatively autonomous state, both, internally and externally, in favour of a New Economic Policy based on globalization, liberalization and privatization. Not only this. The national project of self-reliant economy was firmly situated on the principle of sovereignty of the nation-state but the project of New Economic Policy of the 1990s is based on the doctrine of subordination of the Indian state to global capitalist-cum-imperialist countries. The whole programme of structural adjustment and control over fiscal deficit has been carried out by the Indian state at the behest of capital exporting countries of the North and the global institutions, like the International Monetary Fund, and World Bank. It is imperative to find out *social explanations* for India becoming a willing candidate for global integration. The leading strata of the

Big Bourgeoisie is actively supporting the New Economic Policy because if transnational corporations are entering the Indian market, the Indian Big Business is also going abroad to launch its own businesses either through investments or acquisitions. Tata Steel is working on mergers and acquisitions in China, South East Asia, Far East for the emerging markets of Rs. 25,000 crore, where demand for steel is potentially possible. "In the next few years, global demand for steel will come mainly from China and the Southeast Asian countries. It is, hence, important for us to establish a presence in these regions.' 'We are not looking at acquiring small units : Tata Steel has already begun [to look] in some of these countries for available opportunities."[19]

If Tatas are going abroad for accumulation and profits, Indians are reciprocating it by allowing foreign investors in its own firms. 'FIIs now own an average of 30% stake in 10 top Indian Corporates, reflecting the growing role of foreign investors in driving investments. Their stake in the top 50 companies is now put at an average of more than 17.5% up from 15% just two years back.' Further, Morgan Stanley informs that foreign institutional investors "have pumped in over US$ 1 billion in mid-cap stocks, allocating nearly 36% of total inflows to the smaller cap companies."[20]

The Tata Motors have also tied up with Daewoo commercial vehicles, Korea, and signed the 'acquisition' of company for US$ 118 million.[21] The Reliance group, the Aditya Birla group, and IT companies, like Wipro and HCL *et al* are scouting for business in foreign markets. It is estimated that Indian Corporate businessmen have invested US$ 1048.78 million (Rs. 4,813 crore) abroad during 2002-2003 as reported by the Reserve Bank of India on September 30, 2003.[22]

The Indian Commerce and Industry Secretary R.R. Shah informed the Indian Economic Summit organized jointly by the World Economic Forum and CII on November 24, 2003 that the 'acquisition' by Indian companies abroad during the last three and half years involved nearly 124 companies. Warning the Indian Big Business, D.S. Brar, Ranbaxy Laboratories CEO&MD, said it means nothing if 'domestic strength' of a company is weak. He said : "In India, we are used to a lot of short cuts to get our work done but such measures would not deliver in other countries. This is one area, where we can stumble in the global market."[23]

Here is a testimonial from a representative of capitalist class that in the age of globalization, 'state and capital' get fully integrated and the corporate houses achieve free entry to the corridors of political and bureaucratic decision-makers, and so, Karl Marx is vindicated that the state is an executive agency of the bourgeoisie including global ruling classes. The Foreign Financial Institutional Investors are full of liquidity and they have pumped Rs. 23,000 crore into Indian Equity market.[24]

A timely warning has been given by T.N. Ninan to globalised India that 'This year's stock market boom has been fuelled essentially by the dramatic increase in FII in flows, a consequence of the excess money sloshing around in the rest of the world. But how many among us understand the drivers of this global liquidity, which determines our stock prices? As the international hedge funds have moved in for the first time, India's stock market could get more volatile. "So, it matters to Indian businessmen and investors what is the rate of recovery in the US,... These changes reflect the changes in the corporate sector. Between a third and a half of the 100 largest American corporations have set up their tents in India; a decade ago, there would have been barely 10 or 15 of the top 100. Our largest companies in some field are now Korean (white and brown goods). All but one or two (crore) companies are foreign-owned. So, when Daewoo goes belly up in Korea, Indians lose their jobs in UP. Insurance, telecommunication and other sectors have been opened up, the international presence is significant, if not dominant."[25]

The implications of global integration of India are clear. Any crisis in the centre of capitalism would have very adverse and serious consequences for India. It should not be forgotten that the much maligned Nehru-Mahalanobis model of planned economy, saved India from 'debt trap' of the 1970s, when 'oil shock' pushed almost every developing country under the burden of 'debt'. A little less globally integrated India escaped the adverse impacts of East Asian crisis of 1997. Globalization has increased the vulnerability of Indian market to external economic crisis. The Mark & Spencer closed its shops in Paris, France, and the French workers employed by Mark & Spencer were shown the door and it was left to the Parisian workers to fend for themselves. Foreign firms can withdraw from the 'host' country without notice. Alongwith Indian big business, new entrepreneurial strata of the bourgeoisie are supporters of global integration of India because it has opened new opportunities for lucrative profits and incomes for them. The upwardly mobile entrepreneurial, and business managerial class, the product of the institutes of technology, the institutes of managements and business, are a very critical social constituency for the integration of India with global capitalism. Not only this.

The entrepreneurial and business managerial strata of the bourgeoisie attitudinally love to imitate American life-styles and socially feel happy to identify themselves with the American material comforts of life. They are socially delinked with the India of artisans, factory or farm workers or daily wage earners, i.e., the Wretched of the Earth of Fanon. While bourgeoisie is going global, the middle class professionals in bureaucracy, media, advertisement and intelligentsia is behaving, like typical 'moneyed middle class' whose sole goal is to maximise incomes. In every Third World country, the middle classes exercise great influence over every level of social power and the rising Indian middle class has abandoned every important social project in preference to 'money making' project including 'voluntary sector' (the NGOs) which has also become profitable for the greedy middle class. Since 'accumulation' has become the sole goal of the lower middle class the petit bourgeoisie and the big bourgeoisie, these sole beneficiaries of globalization are social legitimizers of the global integration of India.[26]

India, Sitting on a Time Bomb

It deserves to be stated that the Indian ruling classes are enthusiastically integrating themselves in world capitalist system from a position of weakness and any weak peripheral capitalist country is certain to become victim of very powerful imperialist exploiters.

The first weakness of the Indian capitalist system lies in its 'under-developed' character which is proved by the limited resource base of the Indian state. The revenue collection from income tax and corporate tax is estimated as Rs. 1,35,000 crore[27] for 2004-2005. The Central Board of Direct Taxes reported that Tax payer base 'is expected to post a 22% growth to touch 5 crore payers in 2004-2005.[28] If 50 million out of a population of one billion are in the tax net of the Central Government of India, its serious fiscal weakness is quite clear. If Income Tax, Excise Tax, Customs Tax and Corporate Tax are not yielding enough fiscal resources for the Indian state, it has direct implications for the state and the national economy. It is not only that the Indian capiatalist state has its serious domestic fiscal weaknesses, in the decade of 1990s, but also it was under great pressure from powerful countries of the North to reduce its tarrif rates and income tax rates. At the India-ASEAN free trade meeting the World Bank directed India to lower its tarrif and remove non-tarrif barriers. The World Bank consultant Garry Pursell observed : "India has to bring down its tarrif drastically before it signs the FTA with ASEAN".[29] India is not only expected to lower its tarrif rates, but also it is not allowed even to raise its Income Tax rates because neo-classical liberal economic policy promoters are for the downward revision of Income Tax, as practiced by George Bush Jr. of the United States. Mukul G. Asher observes: "Globalization and international trends have substantially curtailed the autonomy of the Asian countries to raise income tax rates. Intense competition brought about by excess capacity and deflationary tendencies are likely to restrain profit shares in national income in most Asian countries. This avenue, therefore, also will not be available for mobilising additional resources."[30] In this new globalized regime of fiscal ideology, the Indian State will be always compelled to follow the suit and implement the taxation and tarrif policies as suggested by the capitalist countries of the North.

The second structural weakness of Indian economy is 'demand constraint' because it has not been able to deepen and broaden its market for production and consumption. India remains primarily an agrarian country and if the economic health of rural society is not sound, 'demand constraint' will remain a specific feature of India which will put a brake over its total economy. D.H. Pai Panandikar informs that "Agriculture contributes about 25% to our GDP. This is not so in other emerging economies which have already left agriculture way behind and depend mainly on exports to drive industrial growth."

Panandikar continues : "Since 1996 both, agriculture and industry have lost steam, the first because the demand emanating from the agricultural sector was not enough to support larger industrial production. Agriculture will remain a bottleneck for industrial growth."[31]

Third, the decade of 1990s has witnessed neglect of rural India because gross capital formation in agriculture and Allied sector has declined interestingly in a few years of the 1990s and it is the private investment which has outstripped the public investment in rural capital formation.

Table 12.1: Gross Capital Formation in Agriculture and Allied Sector (at 1993-94 prices)

	Public Sector	*Private Sector*	*Total (Rs. Crore)*
1981-82	7130	6499	14079
1991-92	4346	10589	14965
2000-01	4520	14931	19451
Pre-reform (Average)	6212	8289	14502
Post-reform (Average)	4777	12589	17366

Source : Department of Agriculture and Co-operation, GOI.

The above Table clearly tells us that the situation between 'pre-reform' and 'post-reform' period is different. In 1981-82, public sector investment led private sector in agrarian capital formation, but from 1991-92 to 2000-01, the private sector investments were leading. Such an investment has its own priorities for its own specific needs. While Indian agrarian weaknesses are growing, the doctrine of structural adjustment and control over fiscal deficit is directed against the 'regime of subsidies' at a time when developed capitalist countries practice huge subsidies for their agriculture. The Cancun Conference of the World Trade Organization 2003 brought into sharp focus this aspect of International Farm Economy, where only 3-4 per cent of total European Union–American population is in the farm sector, and these farmers get domestic and export subsidies amounting to US$ 300 billion. Allan Wheatley observes : "Rich countries spend some US$ 300 billion a year on farm subsidies, about six times more than on development aid. The European Union Cow is the most pampered… The United States funnels more than $ 3 billion a year in subsidies to its cotton farmers, three times its aid to Africa."[32] The rice producers of Japan and the cotton producers of America get 700% subsidency in US$ 3 billion subsidy, respectively in a world, where 2.7 billion poor people have to live on an average of US$ 2 a day or less.

Fourth, the inherent logic of the pattern of growth in India under the new globalized capitalist system is leading to alarming levels of social inequality and the minority of the consuming very rich, upper middle class and the petit bourgeoisie live in an island of vast destitute and deprived social setting. The social distinction between the minority population which has control over surpluses and the absolute majority of the labouring classes gets widened, when the state abandons its role of social equalizer, and this reality of great social inequality has emerged with new vengeance. Lijee Philip divides social classes into three categories : "Consuming 'n' very rich, aspirants class and the destitute class", and he maintains that the first two class categories will remain the key focus for consumption of most consumer products. It is maintained that during the financial year 2002, the consuming class contributed to 29% of incomes of Indian household which is set to increase to 40% in financial year 2007. While the climbers class (Rs. 20,000 to Rs. 45,000) will remain stagnant at 40%. The aspirants and the destitute classes see a decline from 16% and 13% to 9% and 8%, respectively. Further, by financial year 2007, income levels of 85 million will be a little more than US$ 5000.[33]

Alongwith growing social inequality and disparity in the regime of free competitive market economy, the employment position for the unskilled workers, who are a majority of the Indian work force is creating serious social discontent in the country. Under the caption 'Demolishing myth' *the Economic Times* made a plea for the need for an increase in public investment in the country : "It is equally, if not more, important that employment opportunities for unskilled workers grow as well. Unfortunately, thanks to policy-induced rigidities in our labour market, liberalization has seen a sharp fall in employment in the organized sector. With the share of agriculture in GDP falling over 20%, this has meant larger and larger numbers becoming dependent on smaller and smaller share of the economic pie. Inevitably, income disparities will grow and with that, social unrest, unless public investment comes to the rescue by creating demand for unskilled labour."[34]

Alas, the state is not listening to these warning signals and 'unemployment related riots' have already begun in the country.[35]

Decade of 1990s: Emergence of Right Wing Politics and Social Violence

The above description clearly validates the argument that a State, which is under dictations from the global capitalists and domestic strata of exploiting classes, has created a social situation which is volatile and violent protests. It is a well known fact that deep economic crisis either leads to the emergence of rightwing fascist/authoritarian politics or anarchic violence by disorganized deprived social groups. The forces of Hindutva have exploited this explosive social situation to win over the 'unemployed' and the street urchins to defend Hinduism against its enemies. If the ideology of Hindutva has found a fertile social soil for growth in a highly discontented society, many disorganized groups are also indulging in politics of bullet.

Social Violence in India

The greatest challenge to the democratic state of India has emerged from powerful individuals, Mafia groups, land grabbers and phoney pretenders of ideologies of religion or communist revolution, who believe that instead of democratic dialogue, disputes will be settled with the power of gun. Any minor dispute between any two communities or between the police forces and a crowd immediately creates a violent situation, as it happened in Bihar on January 3, 2003, when people came on the roads to protest against the killings of three young men by the Bihar police in an alleged "fake encounter". Bihar witnessed large scale violence which was "spontaneous" because people perceived that the so-called democratically elected Government follows "undemocratic" methods to deal with its citizens. L.K. Advani, the Home Minister of India, observed on December 24, 2002, before the BJP Executive that India was facing serious threats from Islamic Terrorism and Left Extremism because both these groups practiced the politics of bullet and pretended to believe in an ideology which justifies the role of violence in society. Trinath Mishra, the Director General of Central Reserve Police Forces, observed on December 26, 2002 that "Leftwing terrorism poses a bigger threat than Islamic terrorism. It has its roots in social and economic issues, and is, therefore, much more difficult to put down. Left wing extremism will only spread and grow." The CRPF D.G. Mishra identified "nine states" like Odisha, Andhra Pradesh, Bihar, Maharashtra, Jharkhand, Chhatisgarh, Madhya Pradesh and West Bengal, where the Left Extremist groups, like the Maoist Communist Centre or People's War Groups are taking recourse to violence while dealing with their perceived "enemies" whether exploiters of the poor or oppressive state functionaries. President A.P.J. Abdul Kalam, while addressing the Governors of the Indian States on January 11, 2003, asked them to play a "*positive role*" in bringing about unity of minds and he asked everyone "to collectively fight and eliminate communal differences and insurgency in the country". Thus, public policy-makers are concerned with the growth of social violence on the basis of ideologies which believe in dividing the society or by groups and individuals, who gain personal benefits in an atmosphere of general and large scale social violence.

An important issue which has emerged in public discourse is about the role of "foreign supported cross-border terrorism" in Jammu and Kashmir or in some other states of India. But we have also to consider "domestic factors" which give birth to serious social discontent, deprivation and alienation and create a hospitable social situation for violent group activity. The Sangh Parivar has identified Pakistan as the "nerve centre of Islamic terrorism" and L.K. Advani, as Home Minister, has committed the Government of India to fight against Pakistan supported violent Islamic activities in our country. This is an unexceptionable position because a neighbouring country's state cannot be allowed to destabilize Indian society by arming violent groups in the name of religion and *Jihad*. Not only this. A complete national consensus exists that Pakistan's inspired cross-border terrorism has to be effectively contained with the help of the Indian security apparatuses. Difficulties arise, when the Sangh Parivar and the BJP governments make the threat of Islamic Terrorism as their single point political agenda because of their own ideological position, where Pakistan's involvement gets equated with anti-Indian Muslim agenda.

An active and persistent involvement of Pakistan's Inter-State Intelligence agencies (ISI) in spreading violence in India is recognized and accepted by every political formation but identifying, without any evidence, the involvement of ISI and Muslim Jihadis in the burning of railway compartment at Godhra on 27 February, 2002 was enough to burn Gujarat. Communal riots were the logical product of Sangh Parivar's statements about "Muslim Community" beginning from February 28, 2002. A country which has a Muslim population of more than 150 million cannot remain peaceful and free from violence, if every activity of the Pakistan State has to be equated with the conduct of Indian Muslims. Why should the Indian Muslims as citizens of this country be accountable for the misdeeds and misconduct of Muslims in any other country, including Pakistan? Why should the Hindus of India be held responsible, if any Hindu violates the law in some other country? The tragic events of Godhra and post-Godhra violence remain relevant for the analysis of Sangh Parivar's attitude towards Indian Muslims because distrust of Muslim community gets extended to violence against the community. Hence, it came as a surprise when the Prime Minister, Atal Bihari Vajapyee, observed on December 16, 2002, while celebrating BJP's electoral victory in Gujarat that "It saddens me that not many from the Muslim community are stepping forward to say that they are repentant for Godhra. Even now no one (from Muslims) is saying that whatever happened was wrong and that we have to live together". If a Prime Minister has such feelings, in spite of the fact that many Muslim organizations had condemned the Godhra tragedy of February 27, 2002, one can imagine the attitude of Bajrang Dal or Vishwa Hindu Parishad or RSS towards the Muslims in Gujarat.

The upshot of above description is that India has become violent society because the foundational principle of Islamic or Hindu fundamentalism is around the politics of targeting the opposite religious community. The Islamic fundamentalists believe in their religious superiority and it is inherent in their logic of religious Puritanism that believers of other religions, like Hindus or Christians have to be taught a lesson because they are "religious enemies". This logic applies also to Hindu fundamentalists who publicly charcterise Muslims as *Jihadis* and enemies of Hindus. Further, Pakistan can create difficulties for India in Jammu and Kashmir or in some other cities, but if the social climate within India is hospitable, inter-religious violence cannot take place. The "external" factor in the creation of violence in Indian society is not sufficient to institutionalize inter-community violence or regular violent confrontations between the security forces of the Indian State and groups which believe in the doctrine of violence. This is true even in Kashmir, where Pakistan is actively involved but no Indian Muslim group has volunteered to be a *Jihadi* in Kashmir. Local discontent is a necessary condition for the success of foreign inspired violent terrorism. Mufti Mohammed Sayeed, who is himself involved in the battle in J&K as Chief Minister, observed on January 8, 2003, that "..., one should not blame the other side always. It is we who have to address the internal dimensions. We have to address the alienation of people. We have to try and win the hearts and minds of the people... 'If the internal discontent was over, no force can ignite the fire from outside." Mrs. Indira Gandhi as Prime Minister had popularized the conspiracy theory of "foreign hand" for every difficult problem of India but it was sheer escapism from domestic challenges to her government.

Moreover, religious-based political ideology is not the only "mother" of social violence. The Naxalite groups, who are openly following the path of violence, are the product of social-economic conditions in the states which have a large discontented "tribal population" or states which have neglected the rural poor. The Naxalite groups (like the MCC or PWG) have not achieved legitimacy in the whole of India. This question has to be answered. It is a well known fact that Bihar has an "unfinished" agenda of land reforms and the oppressor and the oppressed groups and classes are confronting one another with private armies. The state of Bihar is witnessing the phenomenon of emergence of *"State within State"*, where opposite groups are involved in their own violent battles and democratically elected state has been completely marginalized in dealing with the politics of bullet. There is no "foreign hand" or "external factor" in the violence-ridden society of Bihar because Naxal groups are products of pure "Swedeshi" social milieu based on institutionalized system of social injustice. Vinod Mishra, an authentic Naxal leader, made a statement that "violence" cannot bring agrarian transformation and he abandoned the path of violence for the resolution of agrarian restructuring. If in spite of such a realization by a tall Naxal leader, Naxal groups are still busy in confronting the state police forces and indulging in the politics of bullet versus bullet, the explanation lies in the prevailing social inequalities. A mix of law and order approach and social programme for the eradication of poverty of the exploited classes can effectively contain the Naxalite violence. A visit to tribal belts in Odisha or Bastar in Chhattisgarh or in Madhya Pradesh etc. will clearly show that the tribals are victims of a nexus between local politicians, local bureaucrats and contractors and hapeless tribal men and women have become victims at the hands of this powerful Mafia and Naxal groups are able to play on the emotions of the *Wretched of the Earth*.

Further, non-ideological violence in urban areas has increased because every big city has "islands of prosperity" and "ghethoised slum or quasi-slum population". A large scale semi-working class migrant population is an important segment of population of every urban city. It is not *"A Tale of Two Cities"* of *Charles Dickens* but of many cities in each mega city. In such a situation, social discontent is the order of the day. Urban social discontent arising out of growth in the number of poor migrants and "pockets of richness" can be contained if public services are efficient and service-oriented. In the "age" of privatization of public services their "affordability" is the only criterion and in such a situation, the majority of urban poor are left to depend on their own very meager personal and individual resources. It is a socially volcanic situation and any rumour regarding the destruction of a mosque or a Dargah or a Temple or the killing of a cow brings lumpen groups on the streets who express their own frustrations by killing others. Joseph E. Stiglitz in his seminal work on "*Globalization and its Discontents*" (2002) warns governments that "adverse social situation leads to civil strife". Stiglitz observes that : "Civil strife in Africa has been a major factor setting back its development agenda. Studies at the World Bank show that such strife is systematically related to adverse economic factors including unemployment that can be produced by excessive austerity. Moderate inflation may not be ideal for creating an environment for investment but violence and civil strife are even worse".

In summation, it may be suggested that efficient coercive apparatus of the state is not the only answer to the growing levels of multi-dimensional social violence in India, where democratic elections can not be held without large scale presence of para-military forces. It is a warning to the Indian ruling classes that ideologies of religious hatred and social divide have given birth to social violence, and combined with socio-economic discontent prevailing in the country India has become a headquarter of domestic social violence. Religion is a private affair and public services are meant for building a just social order. This is the only recipe for Indians, if they wish to protect democracy from crowd or mob indulging in violence in the name of religion or economic deprivation. Undettered by the right wing authoritarian forces of Hindutva, the Hindu unemployed indulged in a riot against Hindus. India is sitting on a volcano which is already erupting.

Riot of the Unemployed

The self-appointed ideologues of Akhand Bharat, i.e., believers of one culture, one nation and one country, miserably failed to tackle November 2003 violence in Bihar and Assam which was caused by serious public policy actions of the Central government. The Central government completely failed to understand the grave social implications of growing 'unemployment' in the country, when it received more than 70 lakh applications for only 38,000 railway jobs in the 'D' category. The very fact that the railways received 70 lakh applications for limited openings should have alerted any democratic government to realize the gravity of unemployment situation in the country and any competitive examination for such a limited number of opportunities had the potential and possibilities of generating social conflicts and discord among seven million candidates spread over the whole of India. Not only this. The BJP-led central government always makes tall claims about running a coalition government of one major party along with 24 regional parties and groups but it is extremely sad that such a government does not understand the specific serious economic problems of backward states and regions of India and a policy for recruitment is announced without taking political precautions to deal with any inter-regional conflict among the backward regions, where opportunities for jobs are very scarce and limited. Since the Central government did not prepare itself to deal with any abnormal situation which was likely to arise because of very volatile social situation in backward states, the very first test held for 'D' category jobs on November 9, 2003, led to a chain of violence.

A few facts may be mentioned to substantiate the argument that the Indian political class simply failed to rise to the occasion to deal with emotive issues around *'identity'* because the first warning had come on November 9, and it was a Napoleonic blunder of the Indian state that the killings and violence against ethnic groups had continued for three weeks. First, on the very first day at Guwahati 2 lakh candidates from the whole of India, especially Bihar, came to appear for the examination. Since the local unemployed youth thought that the jobs would go out of their hand, if the *'outsiders'* were allowed to grab them, they reacted violently against the outside competitors. Second, the moment violence began the Railways and the Government of India, as guardians of an all-India national labour market, completely failed to protect either the Assamese travelling through Bihar or Bihar candidates who had gone to appear in the examination to Mumbai. While irritated and angry persons who returned from Guwahati to Bihar, ransacked the railway passengers of the North-East in the train, the Shiv Sainiks captured all trains leading to Mumbai and tore away the 'examination letters' of candidates from Bihar and all candidates from Bihar were packed back from Mumbai. It deserves to be stated that neither the Rabri Devi government nor the Gogoi's government are responsible for creating an atmosphere of inter-ethnic hate, but the Shiv Sena, which is a partner of the Vajpayee-led National Democratic Alliance at the centre, directly contributed to Maharashtrian versus Bihari discord on Railway's recruitment. It is for the Prime Minister to answer about his political association with regional chauvinists, like the Shiv Sainiks.

It has been a great achievement that during the last fifty five years of post-independence India Article 16 of the Constitution which guarantees employment rights of every Indian *'irrespective of place of birth'* of any citizen has been gradually implemented. The Supreme Court of India has also put its seal of approval that all-India jobs are for everyone irrespective of region or state or city of birth. It is a great success of Indian democratic national-integration process that in every long distant train, people from different regions are travelling from their homes to distant places for work. Every metropolis, every industrial, commercial and specific commodity production city like diamonds work in Surat or small shopkeepers in Kohima, is an evidence of mixed populations from far off places. Migration always raises difficult issues, because social and cultural 'dissimilarities' lead to social reluctance for mutual acceptability by diverse ethnic groups and India has enough experience of dealing with inter-ethnic conflicts.

Further, regional identity is a real fact of plural and diverse India and national politics has to create hospitable conditions for inter-regional harmony and fraternity. If on the one hand regional chauvinists have been playing the politics of 'sons of the soil', on the other, the national leadership has tried to create a complex network of 'accommodative' federalism. Region and nation in a multi-regional and multicultural country get integrated only if inter-dependencies are strengthened and this is precisely the role of the Central Government of India and whenever social fabric breaks down and a situation of region versus region emerges, it is only the Central Government which has to provide healing touch and intervene positively and effectively in intra-region and inter-regional conflicts. The Vajpayee government totally failed to deal with anti-Bihari violence in Assam. It is sad to mention that neither the Prime Minister nor the Home Minister of India, *the 'political face' of Indian nationhood,* felt the need to visit the troubled and disturbed Assam to give a clear 'political massage' that the whole nation stands behind the victims of ethnic violence.

It is not a new discovery of India that the United Liberation Front of ASOM (ULFA) or National Democratic Front of Bodoland (NDFB) would be happy to fish in any troubled waters, and it is also well known that extreme chauvinists, like ASOM Gana Parishad would also play with fire and it is not surprising to secular national forces that the local BJP of Assam would try to make it Hindu versus Muslim issues and link it with their anti-Bengali and anti-Bangladeshi plank of political platform in Assam. The most shocking statements came from the State Minister of Home Affairs, and the BJP President Venkaiah Naidu that Bangladeshis are involved in current anti-Bihari violence in Assam. Is Bal Thackeray a Bangladeshi who is also creating anti-Bihari sentiments in Maharashtra? It goes to the credit of much maligned Laloo Prasad Yadav who rushed to Guwahati and met migrant workers and addressed intellectuals on November 25, 2003. Laloo Prasad gave a clear political message that in Bihar, the anti-Assamese mischief was curbed in one day, and the Bihari migrant labourers like push-cart pullers, milkmen, masons, barbers, cobblers et al have been serving the Assameee society for generations and all of us are workers. After this appeal, Laloo in Guwahati "...warned for the upteenth time that if violence against Biharis in Assam continued, then the state may have to starve for essential items, as truckers will not come here in fear." The Centre and state government of Assam are busy in mutual blame game, while the need of the hour was for the Centre to understand the special semi-disturbed situation of the Assamee society, where a claustrophobic attitude exists for the 'outsiders' and any trouble spot in Assam has always taken a violent turn.

The All Assam Student Union is continuing with a struggle for the reservation of all-India jobs for the 'locals.' Is it the way to build a nation of great diversities and pluralities? The Sangh Parivar and its political arm, the BJP should get a clear message from the sad and tragic events of November 2003 that their definition of Hindu Rashtra is completely flawed because real Indian nationalism is based on a 'sentiment of living together' by multi-cultural, multi-lingual, multi-religious and multi-regional communities. A government, which does not accept this real definition can not be democratically responsive to diverse needs and sentiments of the peoples of India. The explanation for the complete failure of the Vajpayee government to mediate successfully among people form Bihar, Assam and Maharashtra flows from their understanding that Indians do not have very diverse goals and aspirations which are defined by their specific religion, or region, or language or culture. Globalization, liberalization and privatization of economy during the decade of 1990s has helped in the growth of highly skilled jobs in information technology, automobile industry or other service sector of economics. India of 1990s has failed to create jobs for the unskilled poor workers, because 'public investment' in the areas of economy, which generate jobs for the millions of unskilled labour force has lagged behind the requirements of expanding Indian labour market. In such a grim economic situation, the practitioners of Hindutva will not be able to stop violence by poor Hindus against Hindus whether in Assam or Maharashtra or Bihar.

The only option before the State alongwith the ruling classes, in a situation of serious social turmoil, is either to practice the ideology of Hindutva and play on the insecurities of the majority by making them believe that all social ills are a product of Muslims and Christians of India, as Nazis did by targetting the Jews or tinker with democracy and take course to Draconian laws, like the Prevention of Terrorist Act. India at the beginning of the Twenty First Century is witnessing the rapid growth of anti-democratic social and religious forces as a result of deep social crisis created by the current New Economic Policy regime of the 1990s. The Hindutva has consolidated itself by propagating the ideology of 'hate' against minorities and this ideology of the politics of targeting is always of the ruling classes during the phases of serious social discontent. Its carriers are 'village vagabonds' and 'lumpen' elements of towns and cities who are operating under the protective umbrella of the state. The Bajrang Dal, the Vishwa Hindu Parishad, the Shiv Sainiks have attracted the semi-skilled or unskilled frustrated and unemployed army of aggressive and violent youth who have been given an anti-minority cause by the Sangh Parivar. India of the 1990s has witnessed recurring inter-community riots as a result of the ideology of hatred against the minorities practiced and preached by the Sangh Parivar. The divisive ideology of Hindutva is the mother of violence and it also keeps busy the army of lumpens recruited by the Sangh Parivar.

India is witnessing a social logic of globalized capitalism, where the 'accumulators' have abandoned the poor and the poor have been rejected by the state, controlled by the exploiting classes. Jeremy Seabrook in '*Ironies of history*' observes: "The global defeat of socialism and the victory of 'globalization'—that contemporary *avatar* of capitalism and imperialism—led to the 'liberalization' and 'opening up' of India. Today's young generation is more likely to be studying business studies, a master's in management, personnel or business administration. They have turned away from any sense that the world can, or indeed, needs to be changed, and seek principally personal ambition, their place in an expanding and highly prosperous middle class."[36] In this situation of social Darwinism, it is not surprising that 'the right of the political spectrum' in India has deftly used Hindu religion to pursue their 'antistatist neoliberalism, where state power is meant for controlling social discontent through 'regressive ideology' and brute coercive power of military and para-military forces.

NOTES AND REFERENCES

1. Eric Hobsbawm in converzation with Antonio Polito: *The New Century* : Little Brown and Company, USA, 1999 : Translation Editori Laterza 2000, p. 52.
2. William I. Robinson and Jerry Harris, Towards a Global Ruling Class? Globalization and the Transnational Capitalist class : Science and Society, Vol. 64, No. 1, Spring 2000 : p. 12, See pp. 11-54.
3. See : George Soros, *The Alchemy of Finance : Reading the Mind of the Market,* John Wiley and Sons, New York, 1994.
4. Eric Hobshawm, *The New Century,* 2000, p. 43.
5. Eric Hobsbawm, *The New Century,* op. cit. pp. 77-78.
6. *Bureaucrats in Business* : Oxford University Press, New Delhi, 1995, p. XI.
7. *Bureaucrats in Business* : (1995) p. 50 : SOE means State Owned Enterprises.
8. Eric Hobsbawn, *The New Century,* p. 74.
9. Harry Magdoff, *Essays on Imperialism and Globalization,* Corner stone Publications, Kharagpur, 2002, p. 278.
10. Yoshikazu Sakamoto (Ed.), *Global Transformation : Challenges to the state system,* United Nations University Press, Tokyo, 1994, p. 117, See the Chapter by Stephen Gill, pp. 169-199.
11. Also See : Karl Polanyi, The Great Transformation : The Political and Economic Origins of Our Time: Beacon Boston, 1957, (1994).
12. George Soros , *The Hindustan Times,* New Delhi, November 12, 2003, p. 12.
13. Strobe Talbott, 'An American Ideal I, *The Asian Age,* New Delhi, November 19, 2003, p. 16.
14. Strobe Talbott, *The Asian Age* II, New Delhi, November 20, 2003, p. 16.
15. Sripath Ramphal, *'Rage against the Machine', The Hindustan Times* : New Delhi, November 20, 2003, p. 10.
16. George Bush, *The Hindustan Times,* New Delhi, November 21, 2003, p. 13.
17. Robert C. Angel, *Explaining Economic Policy Failure,* Japan in the 1969-71 International Monetary Crisis, Columbia University Press, New York, 1991, quoted by Harry Magdoff, *Essays on Imperialism and Globalization* 2002, p. 313.
18. See C. P. Bhambhri, *The Indian State Since Independence,* Shipra, New Delhi, 2000.
19. 'TISCO eyes Rs. 25,000 crore sales', *The Business Standard,* New Delhi, November, 12, 2002, p. 1.
20. *The Economic Times,* New Delhi, November 4, 2003, p. 4.
21. Tata sign MOU to buy Daweoo Unit', The Hindustan Times, New Delhi, November 6, 2003.
22. Sabarinath M. Abhinaba Das, '— — *on Takeover spree abroad', The Economic Times,* New Delhi, November 27, 2003, p. 10.

23. Going Global : Indian Multinationals Abroad, The Indian Express, New Delhi, November 25, 2003, p. 10.
24. *The Economic Times,* New Delhi, November 4, 2003, p. 4.
25. T.N. Ninan, *'Globalised India'* : *The Business Standard,* New Delhi ½ November 2003, p. 11.
26. Satish Deshpande, *Contemporary India : A Sociological View,* Vicking, New Delhi, 2003. Especially chapter 'The Centrality of the Middle class. pp. 125-50.
27. One Crore is ten million.
28. *The Economic Times,* New Delhi, October 10, 2003, p. 3.
29. Garry Pursell, *The Indian Express,* New Delhi, October 17, 2003, p. 10.
30. Mukul G. Asher, *'Budgetary Resource Mobilization in Asia : Growing Complexity', Economic and Political Weekly,* Bombay, August 30-September 5, 2003, Vol. XXX VIII No. 35, p. 3642, See pp. 3639-3646.
31. D.H. Pai Panandikar *7% growth may be a one-year wonder, The Hindustan Times,* New Delhi, December 1, 2003, p. 17.
32. Alan Wheatly, *International Farm Economy, The Indian Express,* New Delhi, September 2, 2003, p. 10.
33. Lijee Philip, Consuming 'n' very rich, a class apart in growth, The Economic Times, New Delhi, September 9, 2003, p. 7.
34. *Demolsihing myths, The Economic Times,* New Delhi, December 2, 2003, p. 6.
35. For the tragic consequences of the Reform Period of the 1990s on the labour market, See. Shuji Uchikawa (Ed.), *Labour Market and Institutions in India : 1990 and Beyond,* Manohar Publishers, New Delhi, 2003.
36. Jeremy Seabrook, Ironies of history, *The Statesman,* New Delhi, November 30, 2003, p. 9.

13

Explaining Coalition Politics

Every practitioner of bourgeois democratic political theory in India has suggested, even disserted, that the withering away of the Congress dominance over the whole political system after ruling for forty years of post-Independence phase of democratic politics has brought to an end the system of dominance of any single party over the Centre and the states of India. The Congress phase of political dominance has ended and it has been replaced by a coalition system of governance at the level of central government. It has also been argued that the emergence of the coalition system of governance at the Centre is also integrally linked with the rising assertions and aspirations of regional and sub-regional political groups and regional identities. It deserves to be clearly stated that the Congress itself was a coalition of classes, communities, and multiple socio-cultural identity groups and the cementing factor to this coalition was provided by an all-India Congress party ideology and organizational apparatus. The first short-lived coalitional system of government at the Centre was in 1977 and this experiment came to an end in 1979. The context of 1977-79 coalitional experiment should be kept in mind because it was first time in the history of post-independence India that the Congress party was decisively defeated in the elections and replaced by a coalition government at the Centre. Indira Gandhi's infamous, even notorious, Emergency Regime of 1975-77 was rejected by the voters of India and political parties, groups and leaders, who had opposed such an emergency regime, were brought to power by the voters on an anti-Emergency Regime Platform. The internal disputes and personality clashes among the leaders of 1977-79, Janata government at the centre rocked the boat and the verdict of Lok Sabha elections of 1979 was in favour of Indira Gandhi Congress. Indira came back to power after a brief exile of two years and in 1984 Lok Sabha elections, the Congress secured three-fourth of the Lok Sabha seats. It was surmised that the Congress had come back to occupy old status of dominance over the Indian political system but it proved short-lived because Congress governments remained in office at the Centre from 1980 to 1988 and in the 1989 Lok Sabha elections, the Congress was reduced to the status of single largest minority party and VP Singh with minority support replaced the Congress and he became Prime Minister with the *'Outside'* support of the BJP and the Communists. This 'freak' arrangement made VP Singh proclaim that he was an expert in the 'management of contradictions' and manage the Central Government. VP Singh's so-called self-proclaimed expertise of 'management of contradictions' failed to keep him in power even for one year and this experiment of coalition government collapsed and the Lok Sabha elections of 1991 provided an opportunity to the Congress led by PV Narasimha Rao to form a government with only 220 out of 543 Lok Sabha members. It deserves to be mentioned that short-lived VP Singh-led government 1989-1990 had created and intensified social conflicts and cleavages based on caste versus caste politics, the Narasimha Rao government from 1991 to 1996 had divided the country on 'religious basis' because the government completely failed to face the challenge of Hindu communalism of the Sangh Parivar. VP Singh's Mandal politics, and Narasimha Rao's failure to confront 'Mandir-Masjid' politics of the Sangh Parivar are legacies of weak and vacillating governments which were based on very limited political legitimacy. The VP Singh and the Narasimha Rao governments of 1989-90 and 1991-1996 could not or did not want to face socially divisive demands because their governments had very limited electoral support and legitimacy. A socially divided India of the 1990s began its political journey which has been described by bourgeois practitioners of political democracy as the era of coalition governments at the Centre and the emergence of the phenomenon of regionalization of political process. The coalition phase of politics at the Centre has seen VP Singh, Chandrashekhar, HD Deve Gowda, Inder Kumar Gujral, Atal Bihari Vajpayee and Manmohan Singh as Prime Minister from 1989 to 2009. The forty years of Congress dominance had Jawahar Lal Nehru, Lal Bahadur Shastri, Indira Gandhi, Rajiv Gandhi as Prime Ministers, and the withering away of the Congress dominance over political system gave birth to a galaxy of Prime Ministers some of whom do not have any place in the footnotes of Indian politics.

What is the evaluation of coalitional era of governance at the Centre based on the criteria of governmental performance? The supporters of coalition government at the Centre have argued that the Congress dominance over the country had led to the 'centralisation of power' and the state governments had become mere applicants and supplicants to the Centre, and coalitional system of government has led to the re-federalization and decentralization of power and a proper balance of power has emerged between the Centre and the States. This has been claimed as first positive consequence of the change from Congress dominance to coalition governments at the Centre. The second positive development of coalition system of government has been seen in the process of new consensus making in democracy. It has been suggested by the votaries of coalition system that power sharing by many political parties and groups at the Centre has brought multiple social groups at common platform of decision-making and politics of accommodation has become institutionally possible because many parties and groups sit together to decide about governmental policies. It has been suggested that coalitional system of politics has broadened the social base of democratic decision-making processes in India.

The critics have maintained that multiple groups decide to join a coalitional government with the sole purpose of controlling the levers of power and there is nothing in common which binds diverse heterogeneous groups to come together and from a government. The Vajpayee-led coalitional government at the Centre from 1998 to 2004 had consisted of members of the BJP and practitioners and believers of Hindu Rashtra and this government led by the forces of Hindutva was sustained and maintained from 1998 to 2004. The co-existence of die hard Hindu Communalists and secular pretenders cannot be described as the phenomenon of de-ideologization of Indian politics because Atal Bihari Vajpayee's party in the coalition did not abandon its core ideology of Hindutvan and Hindu Rashtravad. The real explanation is that irrespective of ideological antagonisms, coalition government was formed because diverse groups were interested in the exercise of governmental power for the sake of power. The Manmohan Singh-led coalition government from 2004 to 2009 was maintained and sustained by the 'outside' support of more than sixty members of the Communist parties. This marriage of convenience or inconvenience came to an end when the Communists decided to withdraw their 'outside' support from the Manmohan Singh government on its pro-American foreign policy and Nuclear Agreement between India and the United States. When the Communists withdrew their support, a vote of non-confidence was moved against the government in the Lok Sabha and the Manmohan Singh government survived the vote of non-confidence because the loss of votes of the Communists could not adversely affect the government because Mulayam Singh's Samjavadi party decided to extend its support to the government. The government survived because one supporter withdrew its consent and another new supporter consented to standby the government. The Fifteenth Lok Sabha elections of May 2009 brought rich political dividends to the Congress and its allies and Manmohan Singh became Prime Minister for the second time and formed a coalition government at the Centre in 2009. Congress and its allies have been always engaged in a tug of war from 2004 onwards because every group in the coalition is busy in maximizing benefits for itself, its social constituency, and its leaders in the Lok Sabha. Every groups in the coalition government is involved in pushing its own specific, special and local interests even at the cost of national interests. These are two sides of coalition experiment in India and practitioners of bourgeois democratic political theory have highlighted its positive and negative features but on the whole, they are supportive of coalition system of government at the Centre.

Marxist Perspective

A scientific theory for the study of society provides an important 'key' or an 'entry point' for grappling with complex and contradictory social forces and processes which are at work at a given historical phase of development of society. Marxist Scientific Theory's greatest contribution is that any study of complex an contradictory web of social relations cannot be undertaken without linking social relations with existing material forces of production in the society and any concretization of productive forces is possible only by identifying the nature of property relations which exist in the society. The ownership of private property is then an instrument in the hands of the class of owners to appropriate social surplus value which is produced by the working classes and these class relationships between the ex-proprietors of surplus value created by the toiling working classes determines the reality of power relations in society. A society which is divided into classes of private property owners and the real producers of wealth leads to the concentration of real 'power-social-to-economic-political and cultural' in the hands of private property owners who create institutions for governance and exercise of power over the exploited classes and power to exploit is exercised by the state power which is controlled by the real ruling classes in a society. The struggle for capturing power of the state in democracy is reduced to the struggle between two unequals i.e. the class of appropriators of surplus value and the majority of labouring classes who are the real producers of wealth. Thus, the real issue is: Who controls the State in class-divided societies? Politics as an activity in class-divided societies is an area of struggle between the antagonistic classes and state control by the dominant classes provide them with an opportunity to exercise their power supported by the state for exploitation of the labouring classes.

The contemporary Indian situation is that 'coalition governments' are reflective of political fragmentation of various strata of the exploiting propertied classes whether industrial capitalism or surplus producing peasant classes. The various strata of the exploiting classes are politically organized either around weak all-India parties, like the Congress and the BJP or locally dominant exploiting groups have politically organized their local, regional and sub-regional parties and group sand these diverse and multiple parties and groups, whether all-India or regional/local do not find any difficulty to 'join' together and form a coalition government. The Indian ruling exploiting classes do not feel threatened by any powerful challenge from their antagonistic exploited labouring classes and in such a historical situation, multiple strata of the exploiting classes have a field day to compete among themselves and maximize benefits for themselves by controlling the levers of state power. India is witnessing 'political tensions' among various strata of the ruling classes and these tensions are resolved by fighting elections against one another and form a coalition after the verdict of elections. The Communist parties of India have formed United Left Front to oppose the politics and economics of the ruling classes and the message of their ideological battle against imperialism, capitalism and exploitative landlordism is confined to West Bengal, Kerala and Tripura. The Communists exercise an all-India influence without all-India power. Another challenge to the ruling classes and its every strata has come from Maoist Liberation groups who have taken to armed struggle against the state of the ruling classes. The Indian state has strengthened its armed forces to deal with Maoist Guerilla warfare and the Maoist struggle and state response is just leading to 'deaths' without any social goal.

The Central issue for any Marxist practitioner of politics is to launch people's struggles with a view to transform their 'social consciousness' which is at the present limited by caste-based consciousness or religion-based consciousness or region-local based levels of awareness of social reality. The Indian masses are still tied with pre-modern social-cultural categories, like caste or sub-caste and religion. Every strata of the ruling classes is engaged in solidifying the pre-modern loyalty structures of the struggling masses and in such a situation 'coalition of the exploiting groups' have a field day and they do not feel threatened by any large scale 'mass action' by the millions of deprived in society. This is the class reality of India. The ideological superstructure is influenced, even determined, by the cultural categories of historical past and political battles are fought on the basis of mobilization of caste versus caste or religion versus religion. Divided and disunited labouring classes can not pose any threat to the ruling exploiting classes, and the so-called coalition politics of India has emerged as a successful model of political contest among the exploiting groups. The most telling example of the coalition of multiple strata of the exploiting ruling classes is that a broad consensus on economic path of development and foreign policy has always existed among them. The India of 1990s and the first decade of the Twentieth Century has operated on the basis of broad consensus among the diverse strata of the coalition of exploiting ruling classes by following pro-imperialist, pro-American policies based on the model of free market-led competitive capitalism. The model of economic and pro-imperialist policies followed by the BJP-led coalition from 1998 to 2004 was also followed and full continuity of policies was maintained by the new coalition-led by the Congress from 2004 to 2009. The Communists of India were kept out of coalition of the exploiting ruling classes whether led by the BJP or the Congress because they had stood for an alternative model of independent foreign policy and demanded abandonment of the policies of free market-led competitive capitalism. The Communist parties have remained on the margin of political power system because they had led an opposition to the model of policies pursued by coalitions of the multiple strata of the exploiting classes.

How does one explain the co-existence of broad consensus on policy framework of 'coalition of the ruling classes' from 1990 to the end of the first decade of the Twenty First Century, and at the same time, the existence of fundamental ideological divide between 'secularism' and 'Communalism' in the country? If on the one hand, an important segment of the ruling coalition of classes proclaims an ideological commitment to 'secular model of modernization of society' on the other, an equally significant segment of the ruling exploiting classes openly advocate the establishment of Hindu Rashtravad. The secularist along with Hindu Rashtravadis share common ideas on pro-imperialism and privatization and globalization of Indian economy, on the other, they are poles apart on the basis issue of the role of religion in politics of multi-religious and multi-cultural society.

The upshot of above narrative is that the coalition system of governance at the centre has been studied from different, even opposite, theoretical perspectives and the narrative in this study can be analysed, explained and evaluated by the readers on the basis of their preferred theoretical approaches. The narrative deals with concrete responses of coalition government to specific public issues, which have faced this country.

Cong-led Coalition

Who Rules Us: Bourgeois social science theory has always concerned itself primarily with the investigation of 'visible' and 'observable' faces of party leaders – the political executive and professional bureaucrats are seen to be responsible for policy making. Social scientific theory, primarily devoted to the analysis of only the 'observable' social facts, is quite inadequate in finding explanations for the complex reality of governance. The primary reason for its inadequacy is that it concentrates on the visible shadow of reality at the cost of exploring 'substance', which lies behind and beyond the so-called concrete governing classes, either political or bureaucratic.

Politics is embedded in history, economy, society and culture, and is not insulated from social forces at work beyond the territorial boundaries of a nation-state. How does industrialist Anil Ambani of Reliance ADAG get appointments with key officers of the Prime Minister's Office every Wednesday? Why are retired executives of public sector undertakings and IAS officers employed on lucrative terms by private industrial houses? One illustration may be given to substantiate the argument that state/politics and capital (big industrial and business firms) are intimately connected and involved in 'joint public policy making'. Former Steel Authority of India Ltd. Chairman SK Rungta joined Anil Agarwal's Vedanta Aluminium Ltd as managing director. A comment will clarify the argument that the distinction between the state, elected political representatives, professional bureaucrats and the exploiting ruling and oppressing classes is non-existent. 'While serving senior executives may still be difficult to find, retired PSU chiefs are a big draw. While the private sector gets access to the goodwill and understanding of the bureaucracy that PSU retirees bring to the table, corporate governance experts warn of a potential conflict of interests.' Can capital be classified as public and private, or state and private entrepreneurship? The practitioners of bourgeois social science cannot distinguish between wood and trees because their theory does not equip them to find the real meaning of social facts and concrete reality. Here, Marxist scientific social theory intervenes by focusing attention on the material, productive system of the social structure, which determines social, political and cultural relations in society.

Eric Hobsbawm has elaborated the Marxist theory of state and politics by focusing attention on its evolution from the 1840s to the later stages of Marxist theoretical sophistication. He states that 'the early communist form of Marx's theory of the state' had suggested that 'the essence of the state was political power', an expression of the opposition of classes within bourgeois society, and 'the present system it represented not a general interest of society but the interest of the ruling class (es).'[1] Such an early theorization of the essence of the state is more enlightening for the analysis of the political complexity of India than the liberal democratic theory of the western capitalist societies, beginning from John Locke to John Stuart Mill to John Rawls. The role of politics is central in Marxist theory, however, politics does not hang in the air or functions in a social vacuum, and capitalist society gets divided into 'classes' and if politics of the ruling classes is to control the state in its own service for accumulation of social surplus, the politics of the oppressed, suppressed and exploited 'basic underclasses' is to launch struggles to 'secure itself against its own representatives and officials', in order to avoid 'the transformation of the state and state organs from servants of society into its masters.'[2] To sum up this discussion, bourgeois theorists only see shadows, just the tip of the iceberg of politics, Marxists catch the bull by its horn because for them, politics through class struggle is a prime mover of society for the replacement and displacement of the ruling class(es) from the corridors of state power.

The Indian political and social reality deserves mention for the purpose of explaining the complex and contradictory social forces and processes at work in the country?

First, the Indian capitalist state, fully supported by every fraction of domestic capitalist classes, has integrated itself with global capitalist system, led by crisis-ridden centres of finance-capital, like the United States and European Union. This integrated global capitalist system has further blurred the distinction between the foreign and domestic politics of different societies. India is not only providing hospitality to foreign direct investment and joint ventures of developed capitalist countries, the big industrial houses of India led by the Tatas, Ambanis, Birlas, Mittals *et al.* are also investing in the US, the UK, Africa, West Asia, East Asia, etc. The capitalist state of India is acting as a midwife of foreign investors and also as an agent of big industrialists, who have become global players.

Second, the capitalist path of development followed by India has generated social inequalities among classes and regions, and sharpened rural-urban divisions. While India was always a heterogeneous society, social divisions have become accentuated because of the way the capitalist state has operated its agenda of nation-building.

Third, causes of the rising inequality lie in the role of politics and political formations representing diverse fractions and strata of the bourgeoisie.

Marx always insisted that the working classes should have their own political party to further class struggle. Political parties of the working classes have become marginal because the oppressed perceive themselves in terms of caste, sub-caste, region, religion, etc. and the consequence of all these social factors is that India's working classes have not been able to launch a large-scale mass struggle against either Indian capitalism or its mentors, the western headquarters of finance capital.

If politics is the site of action, the space is available to both capitalists and labour in a parliamentary competitive multipolar party democracy. The social class struggle of India is complex and it encompasses the big bourgeoisie, who are also global operators; middle/regional bourgeoisie, who operate in their specific regions and are supported by regional political formations; and entrepreneurial classes, such as professionals, financiers, bankers and real estate operators, who are an important fraction of the bourgeoisie but with interests slightly different from the big bourgeoisie. The upper-middle and lower-middle classes are the 'moneyed' classes, and they can identify themselves with either the working-class movements and parties or with socially conservative exploiting classes and their political formations. The whole hierarchy of middle classes functions around the goals and values of social security and the social status quo. Ritualized religiosity is practised by the anxiety-ridden and insecure strata of the middle classes, who provide a solid social base to the communal-fascist Sangh Parivar and its political face, the BJP.

It is not without reason that the modern professional upper-middle classes, along with other fractions of middle- and lower-middle classes, wish to get all benefits from the capitalist path of development and also at the same time regularly visit modern temples, like Delhi's Akshardham, built in the 1990s. This India co-exists very uncomfortably with more than 500 million unskilled, uneducated people, described as 'below poverty line'.

How does one substantiate the argument that the interests of fractions of classes are promoted and protected by political parties, whether all-India or regional? How does one explain that the 'unequal democracy' of India is operated and controlled by parties representing the interests of fractions of classes? The American National Association of Manufacturers stated: 'We have been in New York since before the turn of the century (20th century), because we regarded this city as the centre of business and industry. But the thing that affects business most today is government. The inter-relationship of business with business is no longer so important as the interrelationship of business with government. In the last several years that has become very important.[3] Hence, we have shifted to Washington DC.' India is no exception to this general rule and associations of industrialists are located in Delhi and capitalists of every state continuously keep influencing and lobbying governmental decision-makers to promote and protect the interests of industrialists.

The telecommunication industry has been taken over completely by predatory capitalists with the full connivance and sanction of the political executive of the central government. Pranab Mukerjee, while addressing a joint meeting of CEOs of FICCI-CII and Associated Chambers of Commerce and Industry on March 1, 2011 asked, 'I request your support to build consensus. Not only for the constitutional amendments for the Goods and Services Tax, the concurrence of state is essential. If the parties agree, I can get the Bills passed in this session (of Parliament).' He further stated, 'I seek your (India Inc's) support ... as you have influence over state governments you have interactions across the political spectrum of the country'.[4] Do we need any more evidence to substantiate the argument that capital and the state in India have been completely integrated and the state is actively promoting the interests of private capital?

In an article 'Indian Development Trumps (OR TURNS?) Dysfunctional', Jim Yardley observes, 'India is richer than ever, with rising Gilded influence. Yet its development is divisive at home. It is experiencing a Golden Age of nouveau rich billionaires while it is cleaved by inequality and plagued in some states by poverty and malnutrition levels rivaling those of sub-Saharan Africa. The volatile contradictions ricochet daily through Indian life'.[5]

Public data based on official documents lead one to conclude that disparities and social inequalities have deepened in India and the responses of the state are piecemeal because people cannot be ignored in any parliamentary democratic system where elections are held at regular intervals. If Pranab Mukherjee is openly seeking the support of big industrial houses for public policies, the political executive of such a state is essentially exploiting pro-classes and very marginally it is pro-poor or pro-'basic classes'. The picture becomes clear when the operations of capitalists, like the Ambanis or the Tatas are brought out in the open. Hamish McDonald observes: 'Again, Dhirubhai was not unique in cultivating officials. Many companies had their friends in the bureaucracy. Business like to get close to power and officials looked to post-retirement jobs or opportunities for their children.'[6] This led Sunil Bharti Mittal, the chairman of the Bharti group, to observe: 'The government and Mittal industry are working together on forming a coalition to address it', the mutual problems.'[7] The above narrative clearly proves that neo-liberalism, which is a 'project of class hegemony', can face comfortable serious 'crisis situations' by controlling the managers of the state.

Why is the working class not able to challenge class hegemony and the class state? Why is the Left, representing the working class interests, marginalised and proving incapable of exploiting the social crisis situation created by neo-liberal economic polices pursued by India?[8] How is such inequality in absolute terms persisting without a real working class challenge? The Forbes list of world billionaires for 2011 mentions 55 Indian billionaires in 2011, up from 49 in 2010, and it goes on to state further that 'India with its 55 billionaires has the third largest pool of billionaires, after the US and China.[9] A central question that deserves an answer is: Why is the exploitative and oppressive rule by the capitalist state and the exploiting ruling classes not faced with any strong challenge and resistance from the exploited labouring classes of India?

A biographer of Marx, Francies Wheen, says that for Marx 'social consciousness was the fertilizer for revolution'.[10] The crux of the issue is that the exploitative social, economic system is continuing because the labouring classes have not developed a level of social consciousness that can lead them to launch struggles against social oppressors. The social dialectics of India have revealed very contradictory trends. First, universal adult franchise and the competitive party and electoral system have shaken the foundations of the inherited hierarchical, caste and religiously dominated social structure. The urban and rural labouring classes have become conscious of their rights in a bourgeois democracy. India has experienced many social assertions and struggles launched by the marginal strata and socially excluded and deprived strata of society. The lower-middle classes, landless agricultural workers, marginal farmers, and other deprived strata of urban and rural society have become quite 'demanding' in return for their precious right to vote. Electoral battles have become highly competitive and the ordinary 'voter' has come to occupy centre stage in the country's democratic processes. This is the positive side of the social dialectics and the political level of social consciousness of Indian voters has reached a state where the 'demands' of the poor are taken note of by political parties of every fraction and strata of the ruling classes, whether all-India or regional. 'If social consciousness is the fertilizer' of social revolution, Indians have not achieved that level of social consciousness, where they can unitedly, on the basis of common social struggles, pose a real threat to the domination of the ruling classes and political executive of the state.

The ironical situation in India is that transformation in the levels of social consciousness is held hostage to inherited social categories of the pre-capitalist past, like caste- and priestly class-dominated religiosity. The Indian bourgeoisie is not a patron-in-chief of a modern scientific and secular society; on the contrary, they openly patronise superstition and ritual-based religiousity among the masses and industrial and commercial classes, including modern professional entrepreneurial upwardly mobile middle classes, and extend 'full support' to the communal-fascist Sangh Parivar of the Hindu Rashtravadis. The BJP, a political mask of the exclusivist Hindu joint family of the Sangh Parivar, has been legitimised by the big to medium business classes, irrespective of the fact that the Parivar practises divisive politics. It is not only religion-based political and social divisions that have helped in the fragmentation of social consciousness of the Indian masses, the caste system, a relic of the past, has continued to play havoc in society and working class consciousness has been splintered into sub-ideologies. Hence, the social soil is quite fertile for the continuance of rule by the exploiting classes.

UPA Government 2004

The Congress-led United Progressive Alliance government at the Centre was formed on May 22, 2004 and it was for the first time that the Congress party formed a coalition government at the Centre. The BJP-led National Democratic Alliance government at the Centre had exercised power for more than six years from 1998 to 2004 and its electoral defeat was welcomed by secular political forces in the country because BJP-in-power at the Centre had assaulted the secular fabric and democratic ethos of plural and diverse society of India. It has been suggested that the replacement and displacement of the BJP-led NDA government by the Congress-led UPA government at the Centre has liberated India from the forces of Hindutva and the votaries of Hindu Rashtra have been ejected from state power. It deserves to be clearly stated that an interpretation of electoral verdict of 2004 Lok Sabha elections cannot be dichotomized or even simplified by asserting that the voters during the elections showed their clear preference in favour of secularism and against the Hindu Rashtravadis. The Congress had mobilized the voters on the plank of 'vote for Hand, which stands for *aam Admi*[1] and the BJP asked the voters to renew their confidence in the party/government which had created a 'Shining India'. Can it be stated that the Congress and the BJP were clearly identified by the voters on the basis of their ideology of secularism versus Hindutva, and other issues mentioned in the election manifestos of these two parties did not carry any conviction with the voters? It deserves to be clearly stated that electoral verdict cannot be interpreted on the basis of a single factor especially when victory and defeat of the two major contenders for power is extremely narrow. The Congress-led UPA government at the Centre has to follow and implement 'secular agenda for governance' because Congress is ideologically committed to 'secularism' and it has replaced the BJP-led government, which is firmly committed to the ideology of Hindu Rashtravad. The only significance of the Lok Sabha elections of 2004 is that a party with an agenda of religion-based politics has vacated the office for a party which is practitioner of secular-based politics. A government-in-power can not be analysed and evaluated on the basis of just one agenda because multiple and diverse social groups look towards a government for the satisfaction of their specific demands. Not only this. A coalition government at the Centre has to accommodate diverse demands of different groups because partners in a coalition government represent the interests and demands of different social constituencies. The Congress-led UPA government at the Centre has to harmonise the conflicting interests of fourteen groups, which are represented in the government along with the demands of the Communists parties which are 'outside supporters' of the government at the Centre. It was alleged that the

Congress would not succeed in managing a coalition government at the Centre because it did not have any experience of working with diverse coalition groups at the Centre. The opponents of the UPA government, especially the BJP, were extremely skeptical about the survival of a coalition government led by the Congress but the Congress has belled the expectations of its critics and opponents and the UPA government has continued to remain in power at the Centre. The UPA government is working on the basis of a National Common Minimum Programme which has been agreed by all the coalition partners including the Communists, who are the 'outside supporters' of the government. It does not mean that the implementation of the Common Minimum Programme can be a smooth affair because inspite of agreements on the CMP, different coalition partners have different priorities of their own and different groups will like to push their agenda through the government. The upshot of above description is that coalition government at the Centre, whether led by the Congress or the BJP, is always at the tenterhooks because it has to accommodate diverse and competitive demands of its supporters in the government.

The UPA government has evolved a mechanism of Co-ordination Committee for dealing with the issues raised by the Communists who are its 'outside supporters'. It deserves to be clearly stated that the Congress and the Communists have never agreed to share power either at a formal or informal levels and it is for the first time in post-Independence India that Communists are 'supporting' the Congress-led UPA government. The Congress and the Communists represent different social constituencies and interests of different social classes and this is the reason that they have never cooperated with one another in the task of governance of the country. The Communists are supporting the Congress-led UPA government with a view to keep the forces of Hindutva out of governmental power. The Congress is a lesser political evil for the Communists because a full fledged party of the Hindutva has to be kept out of power with a view to defend the secular fabric of India. Hindutva is the greatest threat to the democratic Republic of India because its ideology of religion-based politics is a complete negation of the philosophy of secularism, which is the foundational philosophical principle of Communists and for this purpose, they are extending support to the Congress at the Centre. Communist parties are extending support to the Congress to keep the BJP miles away from state power, it does not mean that the communists have abandoned their pro-poor ideological baggage in favour of pro-rich economic policies of the Congress party. The Communists have applied pressures on the Congress in every Co-ordination Committee Meeting with a view to keep it under check so that it does not violate the Common Minimum Programme which is the guiding framework of the UPA government. It is worthwhile to mention a few important differences which have emerged between the Congress and the Communists and both of them have tried to resolve contentious public policy issues on the basis of hard bargaining with a spirit of give and take. Communists and the Congress have been opposed to one anther on economic and foreign policy. The

Communists have opposed economic liberalization and pro-American policies of the Congress and many a time, both of them have found themselves at loggerheads and a situation arose, when the Communists 'decided to walk out' of the Co-ordination Committee meetings.

The Congress-led coalition has worked very smoothly, because except the Communists who have public policy differences with the Congress, other regional and sub-regional groups have co-operated with each other and the government has been able to project its United image. It does not mean that fourteen groups do not have inter-group or intra-groups tensions but the functioning of the government has not been adversely affected by inter-group conflicts. The State Assembly elections of 2005 in Bihar witnessed that Laloo Prasad Yadav of the Rashtriya Janta Dal and Ramvilas Paswan of the Lok Jan Shakti party were not able to work together at a common electoral platform inspite of the fact that both these parties are part of the UPA government at the Centre. Not only this. Sonia Gandhi also failed to reconcile the differences between these two groups during Bihar State Assembly elections of 2005. The same story was repeated in 2006 and in Tamil Nadu Vaiko decided to form an electoral alliance with Km. Jayalalithaa of the AIADMK against M. Karunanidhi's DMK inspite of the fact that Vaiko and the DMK are present in the UPA government at the Centre. The state level political contradictions do not get resolved inspite of the fact that some political opponents have decided to sit around the table as comrades-in-arm at the Centre.

If the above story of relationship between Communists and the Congress and the Congress and other regional partners of the UPA government leads us to conclude that coalition government at the Centre is an 'alliance of convenience', the problems which exist within the Congress also can not be wished away or put under the carpet. What is the relationship between Sonia Gandhi, the Congress party President, and Manmohan Singh, the Prime Minister of the Congress-led UPA government at the Centre? Manmohan is a nominee of Sonia for the office of Prime Minister of India. Sonia abandoned her claim to accept the office of Prime Minister inspite of the fact that her own party and every alliance partner represented in the UPA had shown a clear preference for Sonia's candidature as Prime Minister. It deserves to be clearly stated that Sonia has revived the Congress party and from 1998 to 2006, the Congress party has been led by Sonia who is an 'unchallenged' leader of the party. Sonia's political opponents like the BJP had to eat an humble pie because the voters have shown complete confidence by electing and re-electing Sonia for the Lok Sabha. The Lok Sabha elections of 2004 brought back Sonia-led Congress to power because her party could form a coalition government at the Centre. Sonia's pre-eminent position in the Congress has remained intact inspite of the fact that she has not accepted to be the Prime Minister of India. Sonia Gandhi decided to constitute a National Advisory Council under her Chairmanship and the constitution of such a NAC has given rise to a controversy that the UPA government has created 'dual centres of power' because in a parliamentary system, it is the Council of Ministers which is the real repository of 'executive powers' and Sonia's NAC is either redundant or 'extra-constitutional centre of power'. The fact of the matter is that Sonia shall continue to occupy a 'pre-eminent' position in the UPA government because of the 'pre-eminence' in the Congress party.

How does one evaluate the performance of UPA-in-Government irrespective of the fact that Sonia or ManMohan or both of them occupy equal or more than equal status in relation to one another? The Communist parties have a yardstick for the evaluation of the UPA government and they have maintained that it is a government with 'secular agenda' but its economic and foreign policies are flawed because they are pro-Big Business, Indian and foreign, and pro-America. The role of Communists is to apply 'correctives' and 'brakes' over pro-global capitalist policies of the government. Further, except the Communists, other allies of the Congress in the UPA government, have maintained smooth relationship with one another because every regional partner of the coalition government at the Centre does not have any clear cut ideological agenda of its own. Every group in coalition government is guided by the interest of its own social constituency.

It is not enough to maintain that the UPA government at the Centre is guided by secular ideology because its track record on socio-economic issues facing the country deserves to be clearly scrutinized. A few facts may be mentioned to highlight the essentials of socio-economic challenges faced by India in 2006. The Economic Survey of the Government of India (2005-06) has highlighted the reality of economy of the country. While the government has projected a rosy picture of 'economic growth', the Economic Survey on the basis of National Sample Survey Organization has mentioned that 'The Survey had estimated a reduction in the incidence of poverty from 36 per cent in 1993-1994 to 26.1 per cent during 1999-2000.'[2] If one-fourth of the population is still under the poverty line as defined by the government, the UPA government has to play an 'activist' role in attacking directly the issue of mass poverty. Not only this. Agrarian crisis is a reality and marginal farmers have taken recourse to 'suicide' because they cannot face economic distress suffered by them. How can rural poverty be tackled, if investment in agricultural sector has been on the decline? The Economic Survey of the Government of India has itself referred to the basic cause of agrarian crisis.

Capital Formational in India Agriculture

The decline in the share of the agricultural sector's capital formation in GDP from 2.2 per cent in the late 1990s to 1.7 per cent in 2004-05 is a matter of concern. This declining share was mainly due to the stagnation or fall in public investment in irrigation, particularly since the mid-1990s. However, there is indication of a reversal of this tend with public sector investment in agriculture reaching its highest level of Rs. 12,591 crore in 2004-05 since the early nineties.

The share of public investment in gross investment increased by over 11 percentage point to reach 29.2 per cent in 2004-05 relative to 1990-2000.

Table 13.1: Gross Capital Formation in Agriculture**

Year	*Investment in Agriculture (Rs. Crore)*			*Share in Agricultural Gross Investment (per cent)*		*Investment in Agriculture as a per cent of GDP at Constant Prices*
1990-19	14836	4395	10441	29.60	70.40	1.92
1995-96	15690	4849	10841	30.90	69.10	1.57
1996-97	16176	4668	11508	28.90	71.10	1.51
1997-98	15942	3979	11963	25.00	75.00	1.43
1998-99	14895	3870	11025	26.00	74.00	1.26
1999-00	17304	4221	13083	24.40	75.00	1.37
		New series (at 1990-00 prices)				
1999-00	43473	7754	35719	17.8	82.2	2.2
2000-01	38176	7018	31158	18.4	81.6	1.9
2001-02	46744	8529	38215	18.2	81.8	2.2
2002-03	45867	7849	38018	17.1	82.9	2.1
2003-04	47833	12809	35024	26.8	73.2	2.0
2004-05	43123	12591	30532	29.2	70.8	1.7

* Quick Estimates

* *Source* : CSO

** Economcy Survey, 2005-06, pp. 169-70

Further, India is facing grave crisis of rising 'unemployment' and in a laobur surplus economy, the growth of unemployment gives rise to social conflicts and violence.

The economic thinking in the UPA government is clearly anti-poor and the Economic Survey while dealing with a serious issue, like growing unemployment focuses its attention on reform of 'labour laws' to eject the workers, who are already employed.

"Some salient features of the trend of unemployment rates in the country are :

> The unemployment rate went up between 1993-94 to 2004. On the basis of current daily status (unemployed on an average in the reference week), during the reference period, unemployment rate for males increased from 5.6 per cent to 9.0 per cent in rural areas, and from 6.7 per cent to 8.1 per cent in urban areas.

Similarly, unemployment rate for females increased from 5.6 per cent in 1993-94 to 9.3 per cent in 2004 in rural areas and from 10.5 per cent to 11.7 per cent in urban areas.

Furthermore, unemployment rates on the basis of current daily status were much higher than those on the basis of usual status (unemployed on an average in the reference year) implying a high degree of intermittent unemployment. This could be mainly because of the absence of regular employment for many workers.

Urban unemployment rates (current daily status) were higher than rural unemployment rates for both, males and females in 1993-04. However, in 2004, rural unemployment rates for males was higher than that of urban males.

Unemployment rates varied sharply across States. States, where wages are higher than in neighbouring ones because of strong bargains or social security provision, such as high minimum wage; had high incident of unemployment, in general."

Table 13.2: Unemployment Rates

Status	*Rural*			*Urban*		
	Male	*Female*	*Total*	*Male*	*Female*	*Total*
Usual principal status	24	22	23	46	89	53
Current weekly status	47	45	46	57	90	64
Current daily status	90	93	91	81	117	88

Source: Economic Survey pp. 207-09

Indian Labour Laws and Labour Market

"Indian labour market is characterized by a sharp dichotomy. A large number of establishments in the unorganized sector remain outside any regulation, while the organized sector has been regulated fairly stringently. It can be reasonable argued that the organised sector has provided too much of job security for too long, while the unorganized sector has provided too little to too many.

Various studies indicate that Indian labour laws are highly protective of labour, and labour market are relatively inflexible. These laws apply only to the organized sector. Consequently, these laws have restricted labour mobility, have led to capital-intensive methods in the organized sector and adversely affected the sector's long-run demand for labour. Labour being a subject in the concurrent list, State-level labour regulations are also an important determinant of industrial performance. Evidence suggests that States, which have acted more pro-worker regulations, have lost out on industrial production in general.

Perhaps there are lessons to be learnt from China in the area of labour reforms. China, with a history of extreme employment security, has drastically reformed its labour relations and created a new labour market, in which workers are highly mobile. Although there have been mass layoffs and open unemployment, high rates of industrial growth, especially in the coastal regions helped their redeployment. Inspite of hardship workers in China seems to have benefited from wage growth, additional job creation and new opportunities for self-employment.[3]"

The UPA government at the Centre has become quite aware of the prevailing grave economic crisis in the country and its response has been in the form of National Rural Employment Guarantee Scheme. This is not only the response of the UPA government to resolve the crisis prevailing in the country. The Central Government has decided to 'modernise' paramilitary armed forces to tackle the so-called Naxal problem facing thirteen states of India. Naxalism is a consequence of the prevailing social discontent in the country and the UPA government does not have any strategy to eliminate the causes of social discontent and it has decided to take recourse to police oppression. India has been moving from crisis to crisis and the UPA government, whether Sonia-led or Manmohan-led, has not come forward with any policy package to tackle the prevailing social crisis in India.

The upshot of above description is that India has abandoned National Project for the Development of the whole country and every all-India and regional party represented at the Centre is implementing pro-rich and anti-poor public policies and Sonia Gandhi's Congress is the major carrier of the agenda of globalization, liberalization, deregulation and privatization. The poor masses of India are not in the reckoning in the economic and political agenda following by the pro-rich liberalizers and it is not surprising that the BJP and the Congress have continued to follow the same economic strategy while in power at the Centre. The UPA government has saved India from the forces of fanatic Hindutva and Narendra Modi could not dare to repeat his performance in Vadodra in 2006 because instead of his protector Atal Bihari Vajpayee, Manmohan Singh is the Prime Minister of India. The UPA has liberated the central government from the stranglehold of Hindu Communal forces, it has not risen to the occasion while dealing with the problems faced by *Wretched of the Earth* of India.

UPA Government II: 2009 to 2014

A concrete social reality can best be studied, interpreted, explained and analysed in a scientific manner if one follows Karl Marx's Class Theory based on Materialist Interpretation of History because this approach leads us to demystify contradictions of a class-divided society by looking at the real historical content which at a given time impacts the course of developments of a particular society at a particular moment in history. Methodologically, social reality cannot be meaningfully explained without making a distinction between "apparent" and the "real" and without identifying the factors, which really lie beyond and behind the seemingly visible social facts, not only the distinction between trees and wood will get blurred, the analysis will end up without really identifying the focus shaping the processes which are at work at a particular historical stage of social development of a specific reality. Moreover, any valid interpretation of concrete reality is possible, if proper interconnections are made among the seemingly contrary and contradictory social facts.

On the basis of above mentioned insights provided by Marx's Class Theory and materialistic interpretation of History, a few salient facts about Indian society may be mentioned with a view to contextualise the social dialectical processes, which are at work in India. India has followed the capitalist path of development and the state and dominant ruling bloc of classes and fractions of property-owning rural and urban groups are all committed to capitalist path where social surplus is accumulated by private appropriators of the main owners of the means of production and social wealth is socially produced and privately appropriated. Hence, the capitalist society of India is completely divided among classes and fractions of private appropriators and this productive system has logically led to the creation of an unequal society and absolute disparities of incomes and wealth have emerged in a big way.

India has become a country inhabited by many countries and a common factor, which unites these many countries is "inequality of wealth and income". Further, the Indian state and every fraction of the capitalist classes is fully "integrated" with world capitalist system and collaboration between Monopoly Big Business Industrial Houses of India and every transnational corporation and financial institutions of every advanced capitalist country around the globe, especially the Western countries, has been institutionalized and the capitalist state of India, which acts as a mid-wife of big Industrial and Business Houses of India. It has become a bridge between the Indian and global capitalism.

The Indian state has ceased to be an "autonomous" centre of power responsible for the management of public affairs for the whole society because of complete convergence which exists between the interest of the dominant exploiting classes and goals pursued by the Indian state. It has been suggested that in the contemporary age of globalisation, it is inter-dependence and not autonomy of national centres of power which has become a reality. It has been argued that in the age of globalisation of Finance—Capital, the state boundaries and concept of territoriality have lost all meaning because financial transactions have become global and investors travel down the whole world for financial investments. This trans-nationalization of finance capital has created transnational market economy leading to the end of any notion of "national economy or national state". The best evidence of this new phenomenon of globalisation was provided by the banking crisis of the United States of America in 2008, when financial crisis created by American banks impacted every country around the world and every country was faced with financial crises which was exported by the recklessness of American Banks. What is the politics of this economics?

Marx and Engels while writing on Capitalism observed its essential role has been "constant revolutionizing of production, uninterrupted disturbance of all social conditions (and) everlasting uncertainty and agitation, in sum, capitalism leads to "creative disruption". Has capitalism played this "historic" role in India by revolutionizing national forces of production? Has it succeeded in disrupting the ancient feudal, religion-dominated social order? The answer is a Big No. It deserves to be clearly stated that India had inherited an extremely backward under-developed economy as a direct consequence of colonial plunder of India's resources. The long standing income poverty and income and wealth inequality and disparities were inherited as aptly noted by Adam Smith, the founder of Modern Political Economy in his classic 'The wealth of Nations' (1776) that India in general, particularly Bengal was one of the most prosperous region on the globe and when national productive forces are allowed to remain backward, even primitive social productive relations continue to remain archaic and a backward economic structure and primitive social life and institutions remain stagnant.

Indian capitalism has succeeded upto a great extent in bringing qualitative changes in the material forces of production and politics has played an "activist" role in bringing many important break-throughs in national productive system of the country. History of societies has provided a lot of evidence to prove that development of new capitalist material forces may not keep pace with social changes at a particular stage of historical change in society.

Indian society has not kept pace with the changes brought by the new material forces which are at work in productive system and many new ways of social living co-exist with the "old" inherited past. Politics has to grapple with this "New" and its inter-play with the "past" and the best example is that every political party, whether all-India, like Congress or BJP or other regional-state based parties, are compelled to make all kind of compromises with inherited social and cultural categories like that of "Identity" or "religion" or "language" et al. Further, competitive politics of Representative Electoral Democracy has provided enough evidence that all parties, groups and leaders make all kind of compromises and adjustments with categories, like caste system or localism or religions, as they are practiced by common man who are still under the shadow of priestly class and rituals sanctioned in the name of religion by visiting Temples, or Mosques or Churches or Gurudwaras. Political leaders who are laying down the foundations of modern science and technology based economy also visit temples, mosques, churches and gurudwaras, especially at the time of elections. The best evidence is provided by the fact that all political parties, whether all-India like congress and BJP and every regional party and group are working on the basis of complete consensus on New Economic Policy framework of privatisation, deregulation, and every Prime Minister and Chief Minster, irrespective of party nomenclature, is standing in a queue to welcome with open hands foreign investors and transnational monopoly corporations from advanced capitalist countries of the West. Every political party is responsible for implementing policies of free market capitalism and every party is responsible for the deepening of disparities of income and wealth in society, a logical product of these policies followed by the Indian capitalist state. Every party represents the interests of dominant and exploiting classes and their fractions and this commonality of class-base of parties is an explanation for the march of capitalism and its integration with global capitalism and every party is willing to barter away the state sovereignty and even "relative anatonomy" at the altar of exploiting dominant ruling classes of India.

Every class-party has followed a path which has led to rising unemployment, especially among the Dalits and Tribal communities and as Marx told that this reserve army of the unemployed leads to the depressing of wages of the under classes and it helps the property-owning classes to maximise their profits by paying extremely low wages. The ruling exploiting classes of India have to undertake some 'social welfare steps' to maintain their power over the exploited strata of society and this is the reason that the United Progressive Alliance government at the Centre led by Manmohan Singh and Sonia Gandhi got Mahatma Gandhi National Rural Employment Guarantee Scheme, the Food Security Act, along with Right to Education Act et al. It is an imperative need for the exploiting classes, 'specially in a country, like India, where voters after regular and competitive elections can punish political parties and leaders who are perceived to be anti-poor and anti-people because of lack of performance.

The Manmohan Singh-Sonia led UPA Coalition was inflicted a humiliating punishment by angry voters and on May 16, 2014, when election results of the Sixteenth Lok Sabha were declared, the Congress party obtained only 44 seats and with 19 per cent of votes polled by this party. The UPA and Congress were replaced and displaced by BJP, which obtained an absolute majority of its own by winning 282 Lok Sabha seats and 31 per cent of votes were polled by the party. The new political dispensation led by Narendra Modi is committed to rigorously pursue politics of global integration of Indian capitalist classes and Modi has neither offered any alternative model to that pursued by Congress nor it has shown any new commitment to eradicate the sufferings of either people living under poverty line as defined by the Government of India nor it has any recipe for tackling the accentuation of social cleavages because of growing poverty and persistence of income and wealth disparities in society. The BJP like its predecessors does not have any agenda for tackling the virus of acute social inequalities, which have emerged because of the logic of the Laws of Motion of Capitalism.

The Narendra Modi-BJP-led government at the Centre like all other BJP State governments of Rajasthan, Madhya Pradesh, Chhattisgarh, and Gujarat has a distinct agenda of solidifying the foundations of *Hindu Rashtravad* where Hindus are first-class-citizens and minority religious communities, like

Muslims and Christians are expected to live like second-class-citizens. The Rashtriya Swayamsevak Sangh led, guided and controlled every organization of Hindu joint family including the BJP, a political outfit or face of Hindu Sangh Parivar, is expected to aggressively implement the Hinduisation of society with the help of state apparatus and functionaries of the government, whether at the centre or the states. The power of Indian state in the hands of Hindu Joint Family including BJP will be ruthlessly exercised by the Narendra Modi government to consolidate the forces of Hindutva in society. If on the one hand, the BJP-led governments are committed to pursue economic policies for the capitalist development of an unequal India, on the other, the Sangh Parivar and the BJP will consolidate Hindutva on the basis of its control over the levers of government powers. The "two faces" of BJP and Sangh Parivar-in-government will be clearly visible during the Narendra Modi-BJP-led Central Government. The Sangh Parivar's ideology of Hindu, Hindi and Hindustan, or one country, one Nation and one culture is at work in the BJP-controlled states of India and the same story will be replicated by Modi at the helm of affairs in the country.

NOTES

1. Eric Hobsbawam, How to Change the World , *Tales of Marx and Marxism 1840-2011*, UK, Little Brown, 2011, p. 52.
2. Quoted by Hobsbawam, p. 57.
3. *Politics and Society*, Vol. 38, Number 2, June 2010, quoted by Hcker and Pierson, p. 176.
4. *Indian Express*, New Delhi, March 2, 2011, p. 1.
5. Jim Yardley, *The New York Times* (in the *Asian Age*-New Delhi) July 2, 2011, p. 2.
6. Manish McDonlad, *Ambani and Sons: The Making of the World's Richest Brothers and their Feud*, New Delhi, Lotus Collection, Roli Books, 2010, p. 88.
7. *The Economic Times*, New Delhi, August 2, 2011, p. 13.
8. Also Leo Panitch, Greg Albo and Vivek Chibber, (Eds.) *Socialist Register*, 2011 *The Crisis This Time*, New Delhi, Leftword Books, 2010, p. 323.
9. *The Hindustan Times*, New Delhi, March 10, 2011, p. 25.
10. Francies Wheen, *Max's Das Capital: A Biogrpahy*, Bhopal, Manjul Publishing House Pvt. Ltd., 2009.
11. Party claimed to stand for the cause of Common Man/Woman.
12. Economic Survey (2005-06) Government of India, Ministry of Finance, Delhi, p. 17.
13. Economy Survey, p. 209

14

Explaining Bharatiya Janata Party and Hindutva

It is a truism to suggest that a meaningful explanation for the growth of any powerful social-ideological tendency at a particular stage in the development of any human society has to be located within the total dynamics of that particular society. A powerful social-political ideological movement, emerges from the social soil of a particular society and it gains momentum when the social support for such an idea and movement exists in society and new ideas, ideologies and movements emerge, when important social groups feel a need for such an alternative ideology at a given moment in their historical development. Further, erstwhile colonies of Asia, Africa and Latin America were structurally integrated with capitalist-imperialist countries and even after their decolonisation politics of such erstwhile colonies can not be explained by focussing attention on endogenous factors only because exogenous factors, like New Global Capitalism exercise deep influence on the ongoing social development of peripheral capitalist states and societies of the Third World. Politics of peripheral capitalist countries which are still in the early process of capitalist development can not be explained by focussing attention on only the so-called "domestic" without logically linking the "domestic" with global capitalism, which is not an "external" factor in the politics of peripheral developing capitalist societies. This methodological approach which logically and structurally links the so-called "internal social processes" with Global Capitalism is valid for identifying the reasons for the phenomenal development of any powerful social tendency including the ongoing Hindu right-wing shift in Indian society, economy and polity. A minimum consensus exists among social scientists that a Rightist "political party or group consists of members who support social traditional values and the institution of private property and free market economy". The forces of Hindutva represented by every group of the Sangh Parivar (i.e. Hindu Joint Family) fulfill the criterion of Indian Hindu Right-Wing social tendency as defined minimally by social scientists. At the same time, Hindutva in India is much more than a mere right-wing movement because it has a world-view which is similar to the racist right-wing movements in capitalist countries and Islamic movements, like the Taliban of Afghanistan.

Modernity-Anti-Modernity Theoretical Perspective

Many western scholars have devoted great attention to the growth of right-wing extremism in western capitalist countries and the challenges posed by the phenomenon of so-called Islamic Fundamentalism, which inspired Samuel Hunington to write a book on "The Clash of Civilizations". The western bourgeois social scientists have been analysing politics and society of Third World countries on the basis of a theoretical framework of Tradition-Modernity continuum and they have no difficulty in studying right-wing religious movements in the Third World on the basis of Modernity versus anti-Modernity problematic. While this theoretical approach only grapples with the "appearances" and "observable" features of right-wing religious movements, it is worth examining this approach to understand the growth of forces of Hindutva because the absolute majority of Indian social scientists operate under the umbrella of theoretical apparatus provided by the western scholars. In "The Renewal of the Radical Right" Michael Minkenberg observes : "....right-wing radicalism is defined as a political ideology, the core element of which is a myth of a homogenous nation, a romantic and populist ultranationalism which is directed against the concept of liberal and pluralistic democracy and its underlying principles of individualism and universalism. The contemporary radical right wants government by the people, but in terms of ethnocracy instead of democracy. This definition focuses explicitly on the idea of the nation, which is situated somewhere between the poles of *demos* and *ethnos*. The nationalistic myth, as the core of radical right-wing thinking, is characterised by the effort to construct an idea of nation and national belonging by radicalizing ethnic, religious, cultural and political criteria of exclusion and to condense the idea of nation into an image of extreme collective homogeneity."[1]

The salient features of right-wing extremism in Europe have been identified as 'extreme nationalism', 'anti-communism', 'a law-and-order mentality' and 'anti-Americanism'; and on the basis of Nationalism and Modernization Theory, Right-wing extremism in Europe has been explained in terms of 'normal psychological condition of anxiety faced by the people under the stress of modern-technological societies and Right-wing extremism thrives on insecurities and psychological anxieties of the common man or woman. The western scholars have dichotomized the phenomenon of right-wing nationalism or Islamic Fundamentalism as a contest between "politics of recognizing differences" versus "politics of inclusion" or consociational Nationalism versus Islamic Fundamentalism and the suggested prescription is "multi-culturalism" or as Charles Taylor puts it in "Politics of Recognition".[2]

A very complex issue of the right-wing religious extremism, which is epiphenomenal because deep association of religions with politics of Hindutva as defined and practiced by V.D. Savarkar to Atal Bihari Vajpayee can not be explained on the basis of psychological anxieties experienced by Hindu majority community in India, and this argument also is valid for the growth of Islamic Fundamentalist movements in some socially backward Muslim societies. Religious-based politics may have all the features associated with European right-wing extremism but in societies, where religion plays the role of deciding the meanings of politics and the essential content of state power, modernity versus anti-modernity theoretical approach is unhelpful in identifying explanations for the growth of Hindutva. At a symbolic level, Atal Bihari Vajpayee, as Prime Minister of India, fits in with the main elements of right-wing European extremism as defined by the western scholars. On 15 August, 2000, in his speech on the Independence Day of India, Atal Bihari Vajpayee observed: "Kargil has earned us international respect. India's international standing has been enhanced. Our voice is being heard attentively in the capitals of the world".[3]

The themes concerning Hindu national glory, or dignity for Hindus, and the recognition of great importance of India by the United States of America and other related issues linked with the pride and glory of Hindus have emerged as the main political and cultural discourse in India during the BJP-led central government. Not only this. The concept of the "Other", which is the mainstay of the forces of Hindutva is now practiced by the Sangh Parivar (Hindu Joint Family) with great missionary zeal because of the protective umbrella provided by the BJP-led central government.

The American Academy of Arts and Sciences alongwith the University of Chicago Press, Chicago, has brought out multiple volumes in the 1990s on *Major Religious Fundamentalisms,* and in the first volume on *Fundamentalisms Observed,* Martin E. Marty and R. Scott Appleby, as editors have claimed that religious fundamentalism is preferred over "traditionalism", "conservatism" or "orthodoxy" and "orthopraxis" because they are not appropriate to understand this new phenomenon and hence "fundamentalism" is here to stay. The essence of "fundamentalism" as described by the editors of *Fundamentalisms Observed* is found in the ideology and praxis of the Sangh Parivar (Hindu Joint Family). Martin and Appleby observe :

> "These essays make clear a feature which in our inquiries to date have struck us with surprising force and have appeared with astonishing frequency : fundamentalists begin as traditionalists, who perceive some challenge or threat to their core identity, both, social and personal. They are not frivolous, nor do they deal with peripheral assaults. If they lose on the central issues, they believe they lose everything. They react, they fight back with great innovative power."[4]

The above mentioned description of "Fundamentalism" provides a comprehensive picture of Hindutva in India. The Rashtriya Swayamsevak

Sangh (RSS), the parent organization of the Sangh Parivar, was established in 1925 by Dr. Hedgewar to "unite Hindus" and make "Hindus" strong enough to stand against three enemies identified by the Sangh Parivar i.e. Muslims, Christians and communists. Hindu Youth is trained in shakhas (branches) for the defence of Hindu motherland. Daniel Gold observes :

> "Members of the RSS would realize their vision of a Hindu Nation by serving as an active nucleus for it."[5]

For members of the RSS and other members of Hindu Joint Family, the "Other" has been identified quite unambiguously by M.S. Golwalkar, the Sarsanghchalak of the RSS : a Muslim "has a choice in a person of his individual life. For the rest, he must be one with the national current."[6]

It is not without reason that the "Muslim Others" were targeted by the Sangh Parivar on the issue of so-called Ram Temple at Ayodhaya on the basis of a specious argument that Mughal King Babar destroyed the Temple and constructed a Mosque which came to be known as the Babri Mosque. The essence of Hindu mobilization against the Muslims and for the last few years militant Hindu targeting of Christians lies in projecting the image of a threatened Hindu by religious believers, whose religions were not born in India. Hence, Muslims and Christians are a threat to Hindus and according to Savarkar "a Hindu means a person who regards this land of Bharatvarsha from the Indus to the Seas, as his Fatherland as well as his Holyland."[7]

In a very competent study on *"Organized Hindusims : From Vedic Truth to Hindu Nation"* in *Fundamentalisms Observed,* Daniel Gold does not answer the question : How have the forces of Hindutva become powerful during the decades of 1980 and 1990 while they were always marginal during the 1950s and 1960s and even in the 1970s?

Marxist Perspective and the Phenomena of Hindutva

Karl Marx in his *"On the Jewish Question"* had alerted scholars that Judaism was not a theological issue in countries, where a state has been politically formed and he had suggested that the Unites States of America was a fully politically formed state. Similarly, a close association between Hindu religion and politics during the last two decades should be explained by looking very closely at the level of political process of India. Politics is a conscious activity of social groups who are involved either in the defence of the existing social order or who are struggling to create a new social order. Politics is the site of struggle among contending and competing social groups and the role of politician has been aptly defined by Antonio Gramsci. Gramsci observes : "The active politician is a creator, an initiator [who] bases himself on effective reality...on a relation of forces in continuous motion and shift in equilibrium. If one applies one's will to the creation of a new equilibrium among the forces which really exist and are operative-basing oneself on the particular force which one believes to be progressive and strengthening it to help it to victory-one still moves on the terrain of reality, but does so in order to dominate and transcend it."[8] Similarly Karl Marx in "*Communist Manifesto*" observed that class struggle in history has "ended in a revolutionary construction of society at large or in common ruin of the contending classes".

Thus, Marxists believe that politics is an active intervention in society at a given time to create a new society and politics is a contest among the contending social classes. A few distinctive features of politics of India may be stated for the purpose of finding an appropriate relationship between the emerging forces of Hindutva and the social soil, on which Hindutva is currently thriving. The most significant feature of the current phase of politics of India is that the major contesting classes belong to the different fractions of the dominant exploiting classes and this contest among the fragments and fractions of the ruling classes is taking place at a time, when the exploited classes are not in a position to effectively challenge the agrarian and the industrial exploiting classes. Since the fractions of the ruling classes are competing against one another for a share in the surpluses of economy, they need to capture the state power to achieve their goal of ensuring a lion's share in the economic surplus. This political competition is quite severe and fierce because without capturing the state apparatus no segment of the ruling classes is able to corner a greater share of economic surpluses than other fractions of the exploiting classes. The explanation for competition among the factions of the bourgeoisie lies in a fact that while Indian bourgeoisie was not a hegemonic class even during the struggle against colonial rule, the Congress party effectively hegemonized the society during Indian national struggle for independence. Indian historiography has been engaged in the evaluation of the Indian bourgeoisie in the colonial setting of India and evaluations of historians have fundamental differences because an important School of Indian National History writing maintains that because of the colonial setting, the Indian bourgeoisie alongwith very powerful Indian National Congress was ideologically quite advanced in their critique of colonialism and in their picture of future independent India. The "subaltern school" of historiography as launched by Ranjit Guha maintain that the Indian bourgeoisie claimed to speak for the nation, but in reality the Indian bourgeoisie failed to speak for the nation because according to Guha, "There were vast areas in the life and consciousness of the people which were never integrated into their hegemony."[9]

Irrespective of the interpretation of the subaltern historians led by Ranjit Guha, sufficient historical evidence is available to maintain that the Indian National Congress had emerged as "Sole Spokesman of India" during the crucial negotiations for the Transfer of Power in 1947, and the Indian bourgeoisie had established a very strong position through the Indian National Congress. The essence of Indian National Congress was that though its social positions were bourgeois and class interests of the Indian bourgeoisie converged with the ideological positions of the Congress, it had a 'relative autonomy' of its own from the dominant exploiting classes. Hence, Nehru phase of Indian politics from 1947 to 1964 witnessed the development of Indian capitalism with agrarian reforms, which were led by a relatively autonomous capitalist state of India. Congress as a party of dominant exploiting classes maintained its political dominance by winning the elections which helped it to manage the State in a relatively "autonomous" position vis-a-vis the ruling-dominant classes. The factions of the bourgeoisie and the landlord-peasant classes competed for their share of economic surplus within the Congress and gradual decline of the Congress political umbrella began with the withdrawal of some factions of the exploiting classes from the Congress. The factions of classes and formations of separate faction-specific political parties and groups begins in India after the fourth general elections of 1967. It must be stated at the outset that the disintegration/ decline of the Congress as a 'grand coalition of classes" from 1967 to 2000 is not a process of re-alignment of politics as maintained by the bourgeois social scientists and this process should not be confused with the phenomena of an "alternative politics" because contest and competition is among the factions of the dominant classes and different political groups representing faction-class interests have not abandoned the "capitalist path of development", which remains the goal of every political group represented in power at the central government. Not only this. The left-of-centre politics of the Congress, in the process of splits of class-factions, has matured into a full-fledged right-wing politics. The consolidation of rightist political forces begins with the crisis periods of 1967-75, when peasantry started walking out of the Congress-led coalition of classes on the issue of the "Terms of Trade", which were accentuated during the years of drought and oil price shock and this crisis situation was very fertile for contest among the factions of ruling classes because every class-faction was suffering because of the crisis of capital accumulation. While some factions of the exploiting classes supported the Jaya Prakash Narayan Movement, a few others accepted the leadership of Mrs. Indira Gandhi's Congress. The middle of 1970s is the beginning of polarization between full-fledged 'right-wing' coalition led by Jaya Prakash Narayan confronting the 'authoritarian' political coalition led by Mrs. Indira Gandhi. This polarization in politics as represented by social forces represented by 'JP' and "Mrs. Gandhi", has become the reality because Congress has been pushed out of the leadership and social factions have shifted to the Bharatiya Janta Party which is supported by backward caste middle peasant caste-based political formations, and Hindu communalism is the ideological framework of right-wing politics, which is supported by caste-communal parties.

Further, the right-ward shift in politics has taken place along with the New Economic Policy of the 1990s, and both, politics and economics of the decade of 1990s is a definite break with the four decades of post-independence politics of India. Instead of building a national productive economic system (capitalist) on the basis of self-reliance and relative autonomy of the state from global capitalism, the politics and economics of the 1990s has made a decisive right-wing shift by accepting that without global capitalist investments Indian economy can not grow to the extent that a reasonable share of surpluses gets generated to satisfy the multiple factions of the ruling classes. Politics of liberalisation, privatization and globalization of the 1990s is a product of the crisis of accumulation of capital which is commonly talked as fiscal deficit or fiscal crisis of the State. The ideology of Hindutva has grown in the 1990s in the context of serious social discontent in the country because of the crisis of capital accumulation and in this socially turbulent situation, right-wing Hindutva has emerged as an answer to the problems facing the people of the country.

The growth of the BJP and other members of the Joint Hindu family can be explained by the social base of Hindutva, which has expanded beyond its original "Bania-Brahman" social constituency. The post-independence capitalist development of India, with all its infirmities, distortions and weaknesses, has expanded the strata of owners of private property throughout the country and the social base for globalisation and Hindutva has emerged from these beneficiary classes and strata of Indian society. While the Indian State and Capital (all factions of industrial and agrarian capitalist classes) have been fully integrated with one another and the so-called "Partnership" between the state apparatus, its functionaries and the capitalist groups has been fully cemented, this phenomenon has created a situation, where big Bourgeoisie, upwardly mobile entrepreneurial and professional large middle classes and agrarian capitalist farmer and upwardly mobile agrarian backward castes and Dalits along with political and bureaucratic groups have come to occupy a large space in society and this is "quasi-hegemonic power-bloc" of India. This ruling-bloc has its internal conflicts but it has successfully ejected from every centre of social and political power 350 million people who are living "below-poverty line" and about 400 million people who are involved in daily struggle for survival. Such a social situation is a logical consequence of peripheral capitalism of a backward developing country, where bourgeoisie has limited capacities to undertake the task of leading democratic revolution for the transformation of the whole society in capitalist direction.

The failure of capitalist classes of peripheral capitalist society to transform the whole society has resulted in the creation of *many Indias*, in which people are living with social relations and cultural attitudes beginning with the most backward pre-capitalist social relations and productive system alongwith a large middle class which is linked directly with capitalism and the State which is building capitalism in India. In society, where many modes of production are existing in an uneasy stage of social equilibrium and the capitalist mode of production is the dominant one heterogeneities of multi-structural society are significant social realities. Further, the ongoing process of globalisation has not only accentuated the domestic social disparities, the relative autonomy of the nation-state and national bourgeois productive system is getting gradually eroded. This is the setting in which, on the one hand, Hindutva has flourished because it is creating a dream world of strong Hindu India, and on the other economically prosperous India by opening Indian economy to the foreign investors, which will usher the era of economic prosperity for the country.

Since every faction of the ruling classes and every political formation of the factions of classes is a supporter of free market economy and global penetration of capital into the country, political mobilization of the masses cannot take place on the basis of the ideology of free market economy or globalization of Indian capitalism. Political formations have to invent ideological slogans for political mobilization because masses can not be enthused by the slogans of free market economy. Hence, identity politics has come to play a big role to fill up the vacuum created by the ideological collapse of liberalisers. India is witnessing a competition on the basis of identity politics because political groups can make "identity" as an emotive issue to gain political support from the masses. Hindutva has emerged as a natural candidate in the stage, where political struggles are being launched around identities. Identity politics appeals to the "false consciousness" of the people because they get attracted towards social and cultural categories on the basis of which their social existence has been defined. The growth of Hindutva is linked with the crisis situation created by the distorted path of capitalist development followed by India and because of its incompleteness and inadequacies old identities determining social relationships continue to holed their sway over the consciousness of the mass of people because either new capitalist social relationships create new levels of social consciousness or the old reference points continue to persist. This is the concrete social situation of India, where a riot of "identities" is taking place and Hindutva is one of the important candidates in this competition of identity politics. Since India is a multi-religious, multi-cultural, multi-lingual and multi-identity country, Hindu construction of identity by the Sangh Parivar is divisive and based on violence and coercion because its ideology is fundamentally opposed to the reality of India which is a country where "unity" exists among "diversities".

To sum up Hindutva is an instrument in the hands of Sangh Parivar (Hindu Joint Family) to capture political power and gain political legitimacy in a democratic political system. The BJP without Hindutva is a hollow and rotten shell. Political ideology of Hindutva can not become the foundational principle of the modern Indian nation-state because its inherent logic will lead to divisions, social violence and mini civil wars.

Hindutva: A Challenge to Democracy

The Bharatiya Janata Party, whether in government or in opposition, cannot be discussed, understood and analysed without keeping in mind the Hindutva ideology of the Sangh Parivar. The BJP is just a political face of the Rashtriya Swaymsevak Sangh and other sister organisations established by the RSS for the promotion of the ideology of Hindutva. The real meaning of state power for the BJP and the Sangh Parivar can be understood, only if attention is sharply focused on the project of Hindutva. The Vajpayee-led coalition government at the Centre and the BJP governments in Gujarat or Himachal Pradesh or Uttar Pradesh are acting as a government of the Hindus, for the Hindus and by the Hindus.

This study of Hindutva : A Challenge to Multicultural Democracy is an attempt to prove that BJP-in government along with the Hindu Joint Family has used its governmental power to divide Indian citizens on the basis of their religious identity. A fundamental principle of multi-cultural democracy is that the universal right of citizenship has to be reconciled with special rights of multiple cultural groups. Every multi-cultural democracy has been involved in a struggle to find a proper equilibrium between equality of citizens and special rights for diverse cultural groups. The plurality of cultural groups has to be recognised, respected and protected in a democracy and the ideology of Hindutva is fundamentally opposed to the idea of special group rights for minorities. It is not without reason that the Vajpayee government appointed a National Constitutional Review Commission to rewrite the secular and democratic Constitution of India. The Republican Constitution of India has harmonised the universal right of every individual citizen with special rights for cultural minority groups. How can such a Constitution be acceptable to the believers of Hindu Rashtra?

The Sangh Parivar views Muslims as opponents of Hindutva and Pakistan being a Muslim country is considered as a natural enemy by the Vajpayee government. The study brings out clearly that the targeting of minorities has been the main plank of the Sangh Parivar, which has operated under the protective umbrella of the BJP-led Central Government and if any evidence were needed to prove that the Sangh Parivar felt encouraged to launch its anti-Muslim and anti-Christian tirade the state of Gujarat has amply proved it. The Narendra Modi government in Gujarat has achieved kind of a record of persecution of unprotected Muslim minority.

The study of Hindutva: A Challenge to Multi-cultural Democracy is a description and analysis of the record of governance of the party of the Hindus and also the activities of the Sangh Parivar with special reference to its linkages with other political formations, like the opposition parties. The BJP style of governance, and its various acts of ommission and commission have been highlighted with a view that it is not a party "with a difference" as claimed by its leadership. It is party with a "difference" as shown in its study because the practice of its ideology has created Hindu-Muslim divide.

Western Democratic theory and praxis "is a historical product" (Sartori) and its evolutionary character can be understood by referring to John Locke's "*Two Treatises of Government*" (1689/80), John Stuart Mill's "*On Liberty*" (1859), "*Considerations on Representative Government*" (1861) and finally a seminal contribution by John Rawls' "*A Theory of Justice*" (1971). These classics by Locke, Mill and Rawls have conveyed a message that democracies have evolved from the earlier system of "social exclusivism" of large segments of society from political participation to the present system of "all inclusive" participation by all citizens of regimes, which are practicising liberal competitive democracy. Democracies have gradually extended the meaning of representation and participation and after establishing the principle of universal adult franchise, democracies are now moving towards the goal of establishing 'gender neutral', 'race neutral' and 'religion neutral' political and social order. Further, Marxist social and political theory's claims launched a frontal attack against John Locke or John Stuart Mill or John Rawls' liberal theory of free and independent citizen enjoying universal privileges by raising the issue of social equality, which was a logical consequence of 'the unequal distribution of resources in society.' J.S. Mill's *On Liberty* has been criticised because it completely ignores that the social membership and social participation of individuals in politics is determined and decided by social relations of individuals and groups in the overall productive system of society. It has led Bryan S. Turner to observe that "...definition of citizenship places the concept squarely in the debate about inequality, power differences and social class, because citizenship is inevitably and necessarily bound up with the problem of the unequal distribution of resources in society".[1] While recognizing that equality and its reconciliation with liberal principles of political democracy is problematic, Sartori observes that "The principle of social equality, instead, remains a characteristically democratic pre-occupation. Liberalism does not reject it out of hand, but is not very sensitive about this problem".[2] Sartori continues to struggle with 'liberalism', 'democracy' and 'social equality' and maintains that "....., liberalism is the theory and practice of individual liberty, juridical defense and the constitutional state"[3], and 'democracy' is a political system which strives for the creation and establishment of equality. Many Western scholars have argued that in democracies the underclass or the nineteenth century characterisation of the underclass as lumpen proletariat are protected by welfare state, which has facilitated the creation of social conditions for full participation of citizens in public life. With the emergence of New Right in the West, any quest for social equality in participatory democracy has been completely pushed back by the ideologues of "free market economy" and non-regulatory democratic state.

Many western writers, who are not Marxists, are also concerned with "neo-liberal classical" market-led societies and the emergence of "new underclass" in these societies under the impact of Reagan-Thatcher-Chirac led New Right regimes. Bart Van Steenbergen comments: "Tolerating the existence of such an underclass, however, betrays the basic values of citizenship. Therefore, its mere existence poses a challenge to the moral foundations of our society".[4] While believers of liberal democracy dismiss the problems of socially exploited under-privileged strata of society as their "moral dilemmas", Marxist Social Theory takes the bull by its horns by attacking the foundational principles of capitalist democracy because liberal democratic theory and praxis, with all its variations and modifications, is not able to answer a basic question : How can a citizen freely participate in governance in a society, which is absolutely unequal and unjust? The high priest of democratic theory, Robert A. Dahl concludes his work on *Democracy And Its Critics*: that democratic journey from 'city–state' to 'nation–state' in "Tomorrow's World" has taken us to global and transnational institutions for governance. While Dahl expresses his satisfaction that, "equal rights of citizenship have been extended to virtually all adults", the closing decades of twentieth century have created a new situation because of the emergence of 'global decision-makers' and Dahl characterises it as 'the third-transformation' of democracy from city-state to national state to internationalisation of rule making and decision making. How do democracies cope with the challenges of the twenty-first century? Dahl concludes that "This emerging possibility means that in order to maintain the vitality of the democratic process, democratic institutions within countries would need to be improved. For one thing, stronger democratic institutions would provide whatever democratic control may be possible over the authority delegated to transnational decision makers. Democratic controls will help to prevent delegation from becoming alienation".[5] Samuel J. Huntington is talking of "fourth democratic transformation" by suggesting that democracy equated with good governance is a global phenomena and every country is wanting to establish western type of liberal competitive democratic institutions; and the collapse of erstwhile Russian and East European Communist regimes in the decade of 1990s is a testimony, according to Huntington, that "every country is wanting western type of democratic institutions for governance". It is a triumph of western democracies over every other model of governance. For Huntington, this is the meaning of the beginning of 21st century.

While modern democratic political systems in western capitalist countries suffer from many infirmities and deficiencies, a few important rights have been secured by the citizens in democratic countries. When Thomas Jefferson observed in 1776 that "all men are created equal", blacks and women did not have any rights and the American Twentieth Century has ended with the "inclusion" of all previously "excluded" social groups and democratic rights have been won by the erstwhile deprived, disenfranchised and disempowered groups on the basis of their own struggles against social discriminations. Even until the Twenties or Thirties social theories of "scientific racism" were in circulation in the west and fascism and Nazism practiced such a "racist science". It does not mean that universal democratic rights of the citizens have become real in the west. Liberal democracy in the west has established "necessary conditions" for citizens to participate in social struggles for converting "formal democratic rights" into "substantive human freedoms." What has been achieved in western democracies is the result of human struggles and such struggles are still continuing to expand the areas of freedom in western societies?

While democracies are nowhere safe and constant vigilance has to be exercised by citizens for the defence of their rights, democracy in India is in danger because the Sangh Parivar (Hindu Joint Family) does not accept, even in principle, the idea of equal democratic citizenship for all Indians irrespective of their religion, caste, creed, sex or language. What is the definition of India given by the believers and practitioners of what is popularly known as *Hindutva*? If the foundational principle of democratic political system is rule of law and equality of every citizen, the fundamental belief of the ideologues of *Hindutva* is that India is a Hindu country and Hindus have a right to demand "loyalty from other minority groups, like Muslims and Christians". If democratic government accords full recognition to all plural and diverse social and cultural groups, *Hindutva* is committed to the establishment of "One Country, One Culture and One nation" in India. If democratic institutions for governance in every plural society are organised on the basis of juridically guaranteed opportunities for equal and active participation of all citizens in governance, the Sangh Parivar is extremely hostile to the idea of guaranteed rights for all groups in society. Equality of citizens is not acceptable to the forces of *Hindutva*. The Sangh Parivar is engaged in the establishment of *Hindu Rashtra* (Hindu Nation) and *Hindu Raj* (Hindu State) by rejecting and liquidating plural cultural traditions of the country. The Constitution of republican, democratic and secular India is not acceptable to the practitioners of *Hindutva* because they reject the principle of equal citizenship and believe in the doctrine of equal status to Muslims and Christians, whose Holy places are outside India. India belongs to Hindus and other minority cultural groups are expected to win over the goodwill of the majority community and also willingly accept their 'minority status". *Hindutva* and democracy are involved in an antagonistic contradiction and there is no meeting point between the two. Pralay Kanungo, while describing the mission of RSS observes : "Its ideologues explain that Keshav Baliram Hedgewar (18880-1940) founded the organisation with the objective to unify and revitalise the Hindu community and to establish India as a Hindu Rashtra. M.S. Golwalkar, the second Chief of the RSS (committed himself) to achieve 'the all-round glory and greatness of our Hindu Rashtra".[6]

The goal of *Hindu Rashtra* cannot be achieved without capturing state power and the whole energy of RSS 'family' is devoted for spreading its anti-pluralist, anti-democratic and anti-secular message with a view to mobilise "awakened Hindus" for bringing a party of the Hindus, for the Hindus and by the Hindus into the corridors of power. In their multi-volume study on *Fundamentalisms* Martin E. Marty and R. Scott Appleby (eds) have brought into sharp focus that "all religious mobilizations are inevitably political"[7]. Every member of the Sangh Parivar has been actively promoting exclusivist Hindu identity and the state power under BJP governments is exercised for consolidating exclusivist and specially privileged Hindu community. It deserves to be clearly mentioned that the "quest of Sangh Parivar" to establish "Pure Hindu Nation-State" is based on a well-developed concept of the "Other" and "enemies" and logically, it is socially divisive and based on violence in society. Lahouari Addi writes :

> "A political community that is held together solely by nationalist ideology will never enjoy lasting peace. There will always be ...a purer than thou dynamic that claims a monopoly over pure nationalism".[8]

A pure Hindu state shall mean total destruction of culturally pluralist and diverse society of India and the forces of *Hindutva* will not be able to achieve their goal of establishing a Hindu nation-state without violent civil war in the country. Many a time, the growth of the Sangh Parivar in the decade of 1990s has been explained by observing the Right-wing shifts in society, polity and economy of the country and it has been suggested that the shift in India is closely linked with the emergence of Sangh Parivar, which is full fledged Hindu Rightist organisation and ideology. In a limited sense, it can be maintained that the rise of Sangh Parivar is reflective of the emergence of Hindu Right-wing forces in society because any right wing force practices inequalitarianism and the believers of *Hindu Rashtra* do not believe in the equality of Indian citizens. The Sangh Parivar is much more than the traditional Rightists in politics, like Donald Reagon of America or Margaret Thatcher of England or Jacques Chirac of France. What were the electoral promises of President Chirac's Centre-Right platform during the June 2002 elections in France? President Chirac's centrist and rightist allies promised to crack down on crime, reform the lumbering administration and placate business leaders by lowering income tax rates. Traditional Right in Europe is business friendly, and American or British or French governments under the Right wing parties also protect and promote interests of the business classes in their countries, when Right is in power. Jonathan Freedland commenting on "George Bush Jr.'s 100 days in power" commented under the caption "Presidency of dunces" that "It is an appalling record, assembled in less than 14 weeks. What it amounts to is the wish list of the wealthy wing of the Republican party granted in full Big business does not just have influence over this administration—it is the administration."[9]

Similarly, Ambani and other leaders of Big Business in India can walk into the corridors of power and the obliging BJP, as a party of propertied classes, is ready to willingly exercise state power for the benefits of the property owning classes. In this respect, BJP is a 'Right-wing' party like the American Republican or British Conservative parties. But the BJP is much more than the traditional Right-wing platform in politics. A section of French voters were led by La Pen who contested the French elections of March 2002 on racist anti-immigration platform. Similarly, the British National Party won three seats in the election of June 2001 on the basis of racist anti-immigration ideology. France's National Front or the British National Party or the Danish People's Party or the Austrian Freedom Party or the Italian National Alliance and the Northern League are all, like BJP and the commonality is that these parties are racist right wingers and the BJP is Hindu majority Right-wing party. While the extreme rightists of Europe indulge in hate campaign against "foreigners" the BJP targets Muslims and Christians in India.

Hindutva integrates Hindu religion-based culture with political power to create a polarised society based on the concept of the "Other" and "social exclusivism". Hence, *Hindutva* is a total negation of democracy and Indian Constitution.[10] German philosopher Hebermas alerted everyone about the dangers of the "project of cultural identity" by suggesting that human brings are being taken for a ride in the name of glorious cultural past. People should critically accept or reject traditions. It deserves to be clearly stated that the Sangh Parivar (Hindu Joint family) is a well-knit ideological front to promote Hindu cultural/religious values and BJP is just a political branch of the RSS controlled Parivar. Jana Krishnamurthy, the erstwhile BJP President, enlightened us about the inner-relationship among the various sub-organisations established by the *Rashtriya Swayamsevak Sangh*. He stated that: "There can be honest difference of opinion within Parivar, the BJP is the only organisation in the political field. All the other organisations have their own specialised field. So, one can understand if their approach is different because they view things from outside the political field." He continued further: "There is no tension. There may be occasional friction. It is expected in any family. But then family is a family, and family ties do not get broken by friction"[11]. *Rashtriya Swayamsevak Sangh* (the RSS) is the hyphen that joins and the buckle that binds all branches of the Parivar. The RSS is the creator of every outfit of the Parivar. The present RSS *Pramukh Sarsangh Chalak*, K.S. Sudarshan, acted as the 'watchdog' of the BJP government and he appointed Madan Das Devi, the Joint General Secretary of the RSS, as a co-ordinator between the RSS and the BJP-in-Government. L.K. Advani, while deposing before the Liberhan Commission of inquiry observed: "BJP and RSS shared historic ties and the ban imposed by the Janata Party on Jan Sangh members not to associate themselves with RSS saw the birth of BJP." [12] He further continued: "We were part of the Janata party till 1980. In that year a resolution was passed by the party that none of its members could have any affiliation with RSS. This is what made us launch BJP. This is the historic nexus that BJP has with RSS."[12] Since RSS is the creator and controller of the BJP ideology, the belief system of every member of the BJP whether 'in government or in party' is conditioned by *Brahamanical, Vedic,* Sanskrit definition of Hinduism. K.B. Hedgewar, M.S. Golwalkar and V.D. Savarkar as official translators of Brahamanical Hindu social philosophy have conditioned the thinking and praxis of every BJP functionary. Murli Manohar Joshi, the Minister of Education, is promoting the project of fictionalised interpretation of history with a view to substantiate, a historically false claim, that Aryan Hindus are the indigenous and original inhabitants of India, *i.e. Bharat Varsh.* The purpose of making a claim that Aryan Hindus are the real Indians is to project Muslim and Christian communities as non-Indian outsiders. The prosecution of Hindus as "insiders" by Muslims and Christians, who are "outsiders", is a cornerstone of the ideology of *Hindutva* and political project of this ideology is to "cleanse" Hindu India from the influences of "outsider" Muslims and Christians. M.S. Golwalkar rejects the idea of territorial plural nationalism and he states that "there was a full-fledged ancient nation of the Hindus, and the various other communities, the Jews and Parsis, the Muslims and Christians, which were living in the country were here either as guests or invaders[13]."

The task of BJP-in-government is to faithfully implement the ideology of Hindu cultural nationalism, as propounded by the *Sarsangchaalk* whom the RSS *Swayamsevaks* including Atal Bihari Vajpayee, L.K. Advani, Murli Manohar Joshi and other *Swayamsevaks* of the BJP government pay their obeisance. The tragic happenings in the Gujarat state under the BJP government can be explained by linking Hindu anti-minority agenda pursued by Chief Minister Narendra Modi. To sum it up, the Sangh Parivar is fully engaged in exercising state power for the purposes of establishing *Hindu Rashtra.* It is not without reason that the BJP government appointed a so-called National Commission for the Review of Constitution because the Republican Secular constitution of India is not in conformity with the ideology of the practitioners of *Hindu Raj* (Hindu State).

What is the explanation for the growth of the forces of *Hindutva* in the country? How has the ideology of *Hindutva* based on 'social exclusivism' of the majority Hindus from minority communities captured the minds of different social strata of the Hindu community? The practitioners of *Hindutva* believe that Hindus are 'first class citizens' and Muslim and Christian minorities are 'second class citizens' in Hindu India. How has this completely 'undemocratic' belief system come to influence the so-called Hindus in a Hindu majority country?

A social system (whole) is much more than the sum total of its various parts. Aristotle alerted us that various parts of a social system can not be equated with the total system because 'system' has great power of integrating all its components into a very powerful social whole. Apart from warning about the complexity of social system, Aristotle defined the task of political science in a very modest manner. Aristotle noted that the "actions which political science investigates, admit of such variety and fluctuation....we must be content, then in speaking of such subjects....to indicate the truth roughly and in outline ....for it is the mark of an educated man to look for precision in each class of things just so far as the nature of the subject admits."[14] If social system is much more than the sum-total of its parts and, following Aristotle, if political science explanations are intended "to indicate the truth roughly and in outline....", an attempt may be made to offer a few inter-connected explanations for the growth of political Hinduism in the decade of 1990s.

A few salient facts may be mentioned to properly contextualise the phenomena of the growth of Hindu majoirtarian fanatics during the 1990s. First, the decade of 1990s witnessed a break with the past forty years of post-independence India not only because 'one party domination of the Congress' over country's politics came to an end, and the whole philosophy of economic planning for growth with distribution was given a goodbye in the 1990s. Second, if on the one hand, unstable and unprincipled coalition governments have been formed at the central government level during the 1990s, on the other, whole society of India has been fed on the rhetoric of globalisation, liberalisation and privatisation. The Indian state has retreated or rolled back not only from the management of Indian economy, the leaders of the Indian state have not been able to project any large social and cultural goals for the whole society. Third, in the absence of any alternative large social goals, the upwardly mobile middle class has successfully projected the social goals of consumerism, individualism, economic competition and freedoms for the market oriented economic transactions and activities. Not only this. The upwardly middle classes have publicly identified themselves with *Brahamanical* ritualised Hindu religion and the Hindu masses have begun to exhibit their active and enthusiastic public participation in ritualised Hindu festivals. A public display of Hindu religious rituals and festivals, like *yatras* has become an order of the day. In this atmosphere of heightened Hindu religious assertion the RSS, the VHP, Bajrang Dal *et al* have succeeded in linking activised Hindu religious believers with political ideology of Hindu Sangh Parivar. The Indian mass media, print and visual, have contributed to the growth of public exhibition of Hindu ritualised religious festivals.

It is suggested here that assertion of aggressive Hindu identity during the 1990s is a consequence of the absence of any other alternative powerful social goal which could have captured the imagination of Indian citizens. Human beings need a picture of the future. Human beings wish to construct their society on the basis of large social ideals, goals and dreams. India of the 1990s has witnessed that only the manipulators of *Hindutva* have succeeded in mobilising different strata of society including the underclass or lumpen proletariat for the public demonstration of an exclusivist Hindu identity in public life. A goal-oriented and powerful social alternative to the practitioners of ownership of India for the Hindu only has been found completely absent during the 1990s. Hindu fanatics are marching forward because not only their 'ideological appeal' achieved a level of legitimacy among the Hindus, the success of Hindu demagogues is also explainable because of the absence of any powerful alternative social goal in the life of ordinary Indians. Hindu ideologues have succeeded in filling up a social vacuum by spreading the message of 'Hindus for the Hindus' and 'India belongs to Hindus only'. It seems appropriate to refer to Nehru's phase of politics, when Hindu sectarian forces were completely marginalised, even vanquished. Nehru provided a philosophical framework for a newly independent country and he linked goals of national reconstruction by emphasising the overall "objective" of achieving and establishing a just and an equitable social and democratic order. It deserves to be emphasised that the Nehruvian project of modern democratic nation-state made different sections of society extremely enthusiastic for the promised future. India of the 1990s does not offer any promises or hopes for the future to the deprived strata of society and in this stage of social hopelessness, the poor have also become the carriers of the ideology of Hindu upper caste and exploiting classes. The poor and marginalised sections, including the lower middle classes, in the present stage of social pessimism, have been successfully indoctrinated by the promoters of aggressive *Hindutva*, and the Sangh Parivar has succeeded in making Hindu *Rashtrawadis* aggressively take on their "enemies", *i.e.*, Muslims and Christians.

How have the believers and practitioners of aggressive and militant Hinduism succeeded in selling the idea of a need for defence of Hindus from "Enemies"?

The decade of 'globalisation, liberalisation and privatisation" has injected a powerful dose of economic individualism among the propertied classes, and they are also searching for Hindu cultural identity by bringing a meaning to their 'economistic' daily life. The acceptability and respectability of Hindu priestly class has increased among the Hindu propertied castes and classes. Hindu mythological movies, television serials along with aggressive patriotic symbols have come to occupy an important place in the day-to-day life of successful Hindu traders, businessmen, professionals and opinion makers. It is not an accident that retired judges, army, police and other functionaries of the Indian state are actively involved in promoting the ideology of the Sangh Parivar. The Vishwa Hindu Parishad-led *Ram Janmabhoomi* movement has been guided by highly educated and very successful Hindu professional classes. Kar Sevaks of the VHP or Bajrang Dal may belong to poor and deprived social classes but the real leaders of the ideology of aggressive and militant anti-minority *Hindutva* are Hindu propertied classes, who have become extremely prosperous during the last fifty years of post-independence India.

Rural and urban unemployment situation has become quite "grave" in the decade of 1990s and irrespective of statistical sophistry of the government agencies, G.K. Chadha and P.P. Sahu have given a timely warning that the post-reforms (1991-2002) phase of rural economic development has shown "Setbacks in Rural employment.[15] C.P. Chandrasehkhar and Jayanti Ghosh in their evaluation of the "decade of economic reforms" confirm that "rural dynamism" is a myth because of "great slowdowns in the rate of job generation."[16] The Annual Economic Survey (2001-2002) of the government of India admits to the slowdown of economy because of "demand constraints"[17]. If unemployment is increasing and if ordinary wage earners are just struggling to sustain themselves, the demand for goods required for mass consumption will go down. The Indian capitalist market has a narrow social base because more than 500 to 600 million deprived, poor and marginalised population of the country is just not economically capable to sustain a rapid economic growth. Further, public sector employment is on the decline because of new anti-public sector economic policies of the government, and employment in the agricultural sector is also witnessing a decline or extremely slow growth, as testified by the Government of India Economic Survey for 2001-2002. The impact of this crisis-ridden economic situation is felt by the labouring classes. The prevailing 'social pessimism' is a direct result of the deep economic crisis of India, and in such a situation of deep social crisis, either socially revolutionary or socially conservative and 'backward looking' social ideologies are successful in capturing the mind of the struggling masses. This is the meaning of dialectical process in society. The 'backward looking' social forces of *Hindutva* have succeeded by mobilising the large majority of socially depressed strata by creating an imaginary picture of 'monstrous' minority Muslim and Christian communities.

It is not only in India that the ideology of 'targeting specific minority social groups' as social enemies has succeeded in times of 'deep social crisis', European history tells us that racist, anti-Jew and anti-foreigner sentiments have always emerged during the periods of European crisis. Hitler and Mussolini succeeded in establishing the most brutalised regimes during inter-war periods in Germany and Italy because both these societies were in deep crisis and Hitler's goal of the "Germanising" of conquered Europe carried a great emotive appeal with the German society. The goal of Hinduisation of India, the "Germanising" of conquered Europe, and other militarist hate oriented ideologies carry great emotive appeal to the frustrated and depressed large strata of crisis ridden societies. In May 2001, race riots took place in England. Riots of Oldham of May 2001 have been explained on the basis of growing economic crisis in that area. Oldham is North East of Manchester, where cotton mills are closing and unemployment situation has assumed serious proportions. The idea of "enemy" whether racial or religious or foreigner attracts special attention because deep social divide becomes a reality during serious social crisis. *Hindutva* is selling the idea that "...this land is – and always has been, mine". Hitler had also sold the same idea to the Germans and all racist theories are built around "us" against "them". It is not without reason that racist anti-foreigner British National Party won three seats in the general elections of June 2001 and out of these three, two seats were won in the crisis ridden Oldham and the third in Burnely.[18]

The politics of *Rathyatras* in the decade of 1990s should attract special attention for analysis because the ideology of hatred is carried on the shoulders of large majority of disempowered masses. The BJP ruled state of Gujarat witnessed real communal holocaust because the state apparatus was controlled by fanatic Hindus. A party of the Hindus, for the Hindus, and by the Hindus has succeeded in teaching a lesson to the 'hapless' and 'helpless' Muslim minority in Gujarat. The state apparatus was used by the Hindu government (BJP) to either physically liquidate or completely terrorise and marginalise the minority communities. Dr. Praveen Bhai Togadia, VHP International General-Secretary, observed that Godhra carnage reflected the "*Jihadi* mentality of the Muslims, the subsequent events of Gujarat were proof of the Hindu awakening."[19] National Human Right Commission commented on Gujarat that "Despite the measures reportedly taken by the state government, which are recounted in its report of 12 April that report testifies to the increasing numbers who died or were injured or deprived of their liberty and compelled to seek shelter in relief camps. The Commission has, therefore, reached the definite conclusion that there was a comprehensive failure of the state to protect the constitutional rights of the people of Gujarat."[20] Sunder Singh Bhandari, an RSS activist, as a Governor of Gujarat state met the Prime Minister Atal Bihari Vajpayee and Home Minister L. K. Advani with a suggestion to hold elections for the Gujarat State Assembly. When Gujarat state was burning, the Sangh Parivar wanted elections to be held during such a disturbed situation. The Sangh Parivar wanted the 'newly awakened Hindus' of Gujarat to vote for the Hindu party which will keep on teaching lessons to the minorities. The two-days meeting of the VHP Kendriya Margdarshak Mandal warned Muslims that "if they continue to take the country towards partition", they would have to stay in refugee camps, like Gujarat."[21] Mr. Singhal claimed "that the recent communal violence in Gujarat symbolised the first "positive response of Hindus to Muslim fundamentalism in 1,000 years."[22]

John Stuart Mill must have anticipated the capacity of Hindu majoritarianism to subvert democracy, when he observed in his classic *On Liberty* (1859):

> "When society itself is the tyrant-society collectively over the separate individuals who compose it..it practices a social tyranny more formidable than any kinds of political oppression, since.....it leaves fewer means of escape, penetrating much more deeply into the details of life, and enslaving the soul itself. Protection, therefore, against the tyranny of the magistrate is not enough : there needs protection also against the tyranny of prevailing opinion and feeling, against the tendency of society to impose...its own ideas and practices as rules of

> conduct on those who dissent from them ..and to compel all characters to fashion themselves on the model of its own."[23]

The above very perceptive observation of J.S. Mill against Hindu majoritarians helps us in summing up the above discussion that Sangh Parivar is anti-democracy because it is imposing "qualifications" for participation in representative elected Parliament and State assemblies. A certificate or testimonial of loyalty or patriotism is essential for minorities, if they wish to live like "citizens" in Hindu India.

How has the Sangh Parivar won over the loyalties of entrepreneurial, professional and other social groups in support of the project of Hindu India? Hindu petit–bourgeoisie as a "monied" class is exhibiting its new economic and social status by appropriating Hindu religious symbols, rituals and socially conservative belief system. The role of priest in the daily life of the rising Hindu petit-bourgeoisie has assumed great significance and it has become a 'status symbol' with the *nou-veau* rich class to exhibit their identification with all kind of important Hindu gods and godmen. Hindu identity is a status symbol with the upwardly mobile middle and upper middle classes. May 11-13, 1998 was celebrated by Hindu propertied classes as a moment of arrival of nuclear Hindu India. The Sangh Parivar claimed that 'nuclear weapon state status' achieved on May 11-13, 1998 has compelled the powerful countries to take India seriously in world affairs. The Sangh Parivar has played on the fictitious emotions of the socially successful Hindus that Hindu identity is their real benchmark. The new awakening among Hindus about their identity as claimed by the Sangh Parivar is getting support of socially successful Hindus. Aijaz Ahmad narrates the story of BJP-led central government from 1998-2002 and concludes :

> "We are faced with the classic situation of a pre-fascist upheavals. What used to be the political centre has collapsed, with the Congress reduced to a parliamentary minority and all the rest so splintered as to be assimilated into support for the fascist project as small, ineffectual groupings : The BJP rules on the strength of its own inner cohesion and the obedience of those splinters..., the machinery of terror in the hands of fraternal organisations, such as the VHP and the Bajrang Dal,...., a sufficiently large proportion of the state personnel and the privileged professional strata allied with it,...., rapid changes in the social and cultural environment which favour its ideological position, ..., and negatively, isolation and relative weakness of the Left and the labour movement,...."[24]

All this put together has worked in favour of *Hindutva*. Indian democracy is under siege because the ideology of *Hindutva* is total negation of every foundational principle of constitutional democracy established by the post-independence nationalist leadership. The Sangh Parivar is an enemy of Indian democracy because it does not accept the principle of equality of citizenship.

This is the essence of anti-democratic Sangh Parivar. A telling example of Sangh Parivar's total absence of faith in secular democratic Republican Constitution of India is provided by the role of Hindu Shankracharya in resolving the Temple-Mosque dispute. In democracy, it is the task of an elected government to deal with public disputes and it is not at all the concern of Hindu priests to intervene in public dispute.

Conclusion: is BJP Different ?

The Bharatiya Janta Party got a great success by projecting itself as a "party with a difference" because Indian voters were completely disenchanted with corrupt and cynical Congress party which had ruled/misruled over the country for forty years of post-independence India. Rajiv Gandhi revived the confidence of the Indian voter in the Congress by projecting himself as "Mr. Clean" and by publicly denouncing "power brokers" in his party during the centenary celebrations of the Indian National Congress in 1985. An important section of intelligentsia and the leaders of mass media had raised great public hopes by projecting Rajiv Gandhi as a leader who was not brought up in the Congress culture of "corruption". The camels' back was broken, when the controversy on the purchase of "Bofors Gun" from the Swedish company burst in public because it was concluded that Congress could not have "Mr. Clean" and the Congress political culture of corruption and bribes was deeply institutionalised and even Rajiv Gandhi could not rise above the "logic of corruption". Not only this. Indira Gandhi's Emergency Regime of 1975-77 had completely disillusioned democratic public opinion and the Indian voters began to look for "alternative" parties because Indira Gandhi's authoritarian and centralist regime was considered as a great threat to the survival of Indian democracy.

The BJP leadership succeeded in winning over a sizable section of Indian voters including intellectuals by promising an alternative of good governance in the place of Congress party's misgovernance. Can such a claim of the BJP as a *"party and government with a difference"* be sustained and maintained on the basis of some available facts? A few well known facts may be mentioned to refute the party's claim to be *"different"* from the much maligned Congress party. First , the Congress party was always involved in internal factionalism and factional leaders were quite busy in continuous "struggle for power" for the displacement and replacement of congress Chief Ministers or ministers. The BJP has been completely infected by this disease of the Congress. Kalraj Mishra resigned from the Uttar Pradesh BJP Presidentship on June 5, 2002 by publicly stating that the party was involved in "infighting" among top leaders and "indiscipline" prevails in the party. Jana Krishnamurthy, the erstwhile BJP President, observed that he would have to discuss with party's national leadership about "internal dissensions among party leaders in Uttar Pradesh." Ms. Mayawati, as Chief Minister of Uttar Pradesh, has exploited "factionalism" of UPBJP, and thrown away the policy of "quota within quota" for the most backward castes. Lalji Tandon and Om Prakash Singh, as BJP ministers in the Ms. Mayawati coalition government, supported the "reversal" of reservation policy by Mayawati inspite of the fact that this policy of "quota within quota" was proclaimed by their own party Chief Minister Rajnath Singh. The BJP, as an alliance partner of the BSP in Uttar Pradesh, has been a party to an utter nonsensical policy of the Chief Minister who has fixed caste-based percentages for the posting of heads of police stations. Is it BJP's model of *"governance with a difference"*? The BJP along with Mayawati is pursuing a policy of complete *casteisation* of state machinery in U.P. Second, unlike corrupt Congress party governments, the BJP proclaimed its commitment to "corruption free" public life.

While the Tehelka exposure of Bangaru Laxman of the BJP is an old story, Arun Shourie and Parmod Mahajan, two BJP central government ministers, have fought pubic battles on the role of Tatas in the affairs of Videsh Sanchar Nigam Limited. L.K. Advani had to intervene to settle the dispute between his two BJP colleagues in the government. Further, the BJP has not cleared the confusion on VSNL because Arun Shourie has alleged that "disinvestment" decisions by the government are attracting "corporate rivalries" and different business houses are exercising their influence on government decision-making. Arun Shourie had warned the Parliament also about Air India disinvestment controversy because "Corporate rivalry was casting a shadow on the disinvestment process and scaring away bidders." How can corporate houses fight their battles without support of the BJP bigwags? Like congress party, the BJP has also developed a so-called "High Command" to deal with factional rivalries of BJP-led state governments. In Gujarat, the BJP changed three Chief Ministers from Shankar Singh Vaghela to Keshu Bhai Patel to Narendra Modi and in Uttar Pradesh, the same story was repeated, where Kalayan Singh was replaced by an ailing Ram Prakash Gupta but later he was also given marching orders by the "High Command" and Rajnath Singh became the Chief Minister. Even now Kalraj Mishra is alleging that BJP in Uttar Pradesh is a divided house.

While the upshot of above narration is that the BJP-in-government has been in no way different from the Congress party, the claim of the BJP leadership of being "different" than other democratic parties deserves to be validated by shifting the focus from "routine BJP governance" to its *"real agenda for governance."* Since the BJP is not like any other party or political group in India, evaluative yardsticks to understand its "inner dynamics" will have to be clearly spelt out. The real issue is : what does state power mean for the BJP and other affiliates of the Sangh Parivar? Every political party or group has a "definition of state power" and it deserves to be examined while evaluating the reality of BJP. Michel Foucault, French philosopher, alerted us by saying that "power comes from below; that is, there is no binary and all-encompassing opposition between the rulers and the ruled at the root of power relations, and serving as a general matrix-no such duality extending from top down and reacting on more and more limited groups to the very depths of the social body". The real focus of Foucault is that 'power is dispersed through a network of relationships which make up society and is based on discourse." Foucault's insights on power make us analyse BJP's capacities to reach the multitude of Hindu social groups on the basis of a monolith "discourse" for the construction of *Hindu Rashtra* and Hindu identity in a Hindu majority country. It is not accidental that television and radio are considered very powerful visual media for the spread of message of Hindu discourse by the BJP. The Ministry of Information and Broadcasting is always given to a BJP activist in "coalition governments" led by the BJP. Similarly, Ministry of Education is also managed by the BJP for the purpose of spreading the message of *Hindutva* through educational institutions. The BJP always attacks Muslim community's *madarsas*, (Islamic schools) but the Sangh Parivar itself is involved in a very large school education programme for the promotion of *Hindutva* consciousness among the children. While the Sangh Parivar activists target the Muslims visiting Holy Mecca for Haj with the support of public funds, huge public money is spent on Hindu ritualistic festivals. The Sangh Parivar has brought into active public life Sants and Sadhus to spread the message of *Hindutva*. The Vishwa Hindu Parishad and other leaders of the Sangh Parivar have always maintained that every activity regarding the movement for *Ramjanmbhoomi* is decided by Dharam Sansad or Sant Sammelans. During the decade of 1990s, the Sangh Parivar, with the full support and patronage of the BJP governments, has activised all religious and mythologically associated Saints and Sadhus to take the message of *Hindutva* to the masses of India. Shankracharyas have been brought into politics and with the support of the BJP governments distinction between religious/spiritual leadership of Hindu Shankracharyas has been consigned to the dustbin of history and religious leaders have become political messengers. The "discourse" of *Hindutva* and the instruments for the spread of the message of the Parivar's ideology of *Hindutva* has been actively supported by the BJP governments. If the BJP leadership resurrects V.D. Savarkar as a great Hindu nationalist or L.K. Advani uses the opportunity of the so-called historic Sindhu river in Leh to spread the message of great Hindu tradition, the Indian masses are fed everyday on the Hindu symbols of martyrdom and chivalry in struggles against foreign invaders of India. *We, the Hindus* of India, are true custodians of *Hindu Rashtra* and the state power, in the hands of the BJP, is meant to promote this ideology of strong, militant *Hindutva*. BJP is a different party than the other parties because it believes in the purity of its ideology and belief systems and it has gained an opportunity to spread its ideological message with the help of state power. It is true to maintain that state power is an "instrument" in the hands of every party and political group but the BJP, holding the state power has different meanings because it is used as an "instrument" for the promotion of the ideology of One Nation, One Culture and One Country. The tragedy of Gujarat under the leadership of the

Narendra Modi Government has proved the argument that the BJP is different than other political parties. The Muslim minority in Gujarat is convinced that atrocities against the community have been committed with full support of the BJP state government. Dr. Praveen Bhai Togadia, VHP's international general-secretary, maintained at *Purna Ahuti Mahayagna* held at Ayodhya on June 2, 2002 that while Godhra reflected the "Jihadi mentality of the Muslims, the subsequent events in Gujarat were proof of Hindu awakening." Hindu awakening is the agenda of the Sangh Parivar and it can be achieved by polarising India into "*We the Hindus*" and "*the other*", the Muslims and Christians. BJP is a party with a difference because no other party is practitioner of the ideology of polarization of Hindus and Muslims. If Congress is a weak democratic secular party, the other parties are just casteist and regionalist. The BJP is the only alternative party with an alternative ideology to the wishy washy programme of casteist or regionalist parties which are just opportunistic political actors.

In summation, it may be mentioned that BJP has two different faces and there is no meeting ground between the corrupt or faction ridden BJP-in-government and BJP using state power as an instrument for the spread of its ideology of *Hindutva*. BJP-in-government seems to be making opportunistic compromises with its coalition partners, but BJP-in-government has shown no vacillation or ambivalence for using state power for the construction of the imagined reality of *Hindu Rashtra*.

The greatest success of BJP lies in making every secular party to play safe with the so-called Hindu sentiment. The BJP has succeeded in making the myth of hurt Hindu sentiment as a real political issue and in this respect, it is a party with a difference.

BJP-in-Government is pursuing its own agenda of constructing Aryan Hindu history by making myths like "River Saraswati" or Rama of Ramayana look "real" to prove great Hindu ancestry of the real inhabitants of Hindu India. In this project of construction of a non-existing golden age of Hindus of ancient India, the Sangh Parivar has mobilised all kind of Shankracharyas and priests for influencing the gullible Hindus that they had a great past which was destroyed by Muslim invaders, who are the real enemies of great Hindu civilisation.

BJP-in Government is implementing its agenda of *teaching a lesson* to Muslims and Christians by patronising Hindu fanatics who are indulging in destroying Mosques and Churches V.D. Savarkar's definition of *Hindutva* is actually practiced by the BJP-in-Government, whether at the Centre or in the States. The Narendra Modi government presided over the physical liquidation of Muslims for three months. The state of Gujarat simply burnt from March to May 2002 because the state government controlled by the Hindus was not expected to protect the lives and property of the helpless Muslim minority. In 1923, V.D. Savarkar in *Hindutva : Who is a Hindu*? emphasised that "Hindutva is not identical with what is vaguely indicated by the term Hinduism". There is "a clear line of demarcation between the two... Hindutva is not identical with Hindu *Dharma;* nor is Hindu *Dharma* identical with Hinduism". And S.S. Savarkar, the publisher, wrote in the preface : "Veer Savarkar had to coin some new words, such as '*Hindutva*'..." Is it not expected of L. K. Advani as Home minister of the BJP-led central government to sing praises of Savakrar and declare the jail complex in Port Blair as a national memorial in honour of the hero of the forces of *Hindutva*? If on the one hand Tapan Ray Chaudhuri in his essay on *Swami Vivekananda's construction of Hinduism* writes that "he was among the earliest nationalist thinkers to claim the Indo-Islamic past as part of the Indian heritage", on the other, he castigates the forces of *Hindutva* by saying how "the VHP has the audacity to claim him as their own." *Hindutva* as constructed by Sangh Parivar and promoted by BJP-in-government has specific goal of pursuing an anti-Minority project of its own brand. Robert A. Dahl in his book *Democracy And Its Critics (1989)* mentions that democracy had adversarial critics" and "sympathetic critics' and devotes his attention to examine the "adversaries" and "sympathetic critics" of democracy. He concludes the book by commenting on '*Democracy in Tomorrow's World*' and '*Sketches for an Advanced Democratic Country*'. Dahl concludes : "Yet the vision of people governing themselves as political equals, and possessing all the resources and institutions necessary to do so, will, I believe, remain a compelling if always demanding guide in the search for a society, in which people may live together in peace, respect each other's intrinsic equality, and jointly seek the best possible life".[25]

What is the future vision of the Sangh Parivar? Where does 'democracy based on the principle of equality of all citizens' fit into the project of Hindutva? Is democratic political system safe in the hands of committed anti-minority Sangh Parivar? The answer to this question is a Big No. Democratic political system of India is not at all safe from the attack and assaults of committed anti-minority *Hindutva*. BJP-in-Government has an "adversial" relationship with secular, democratic pluralist political system of India. *Hindutva* and Indian democracy can not co-exist because *Hindutva* is ideologically committed to establish Hindu majority state, which is a negation of the very idea of democratic rights of every citizen irrespective of caste, creed, religion, sex and colour.

Interpreting Narendra Modi

Narendra Modi is a democratically elected Chief Political Executive of an extremely mighty the state of India. Narendra Modi as Prime Minister is presiding over apparatuses of the state and he has proved on the basis of his performance as Chief Minister of Gujarat state government from 2001 to 2014 that he can effectively and single handedly preside over all the level of political and administrative powers with the sole purpose of achieving goods solely defined by himself. Modi's background as Chief Minister of Gujarat clearly reveals that he manages public and government affairs on the basis of his priorities and he is capable of pursuing his defined goals with determination and vigour. This is Modi's special personality trait. Arun Shourie, an admirer of Modi, publically stated that the new Prime Minister's style of functioning will be of a "quasi-Presidential" type and not of a Prime Minister of a parliamentary democracy, Modi has highly personalized and centralized style of politics becomes clear, when on October 4, 2014 while campaigning as Prime Minster during state assembly elections of Maharashtra and Haryana told the assembled crowd of voters "How can a government in Delhi" work with someone who shuts the doors on us...someone who does not have a courage to share a platform with me? Walter Anderson, a very serious student of Sangh Parivar; and an observer of Modi, Chief Minister of Gujarat, observes "Modi is not the collegial leader...." Arun Shourie again publically observed in May 2015, after one year of Modi's leadership that Modi, Amit Shah and Arun Jaitley, they work as a team and .... They have frightened not just the allies but their own group—the extended party, etc. On one year anniversary of Modi-in-office, John Elliot, the author of "Implosion: India's Tryst with Reality", observed that Modi: the man who wants his mark to look perfect. "Love is not a word often used for Modi. His autocratic style is said to have upset fellow ministers, MPs of his own party and bureaucrats. He seems to frighten more than inspire.... People are still waiting for his promise of leadership of change to become a reality". The story does not end here. Narendra Modi, the Chief Minister of Gujarat, seems to have frightened his own BJP Prime Minister Atal Bihari Vajpayee, 1998 to 2004, and the telling example of his capacity to checkmate even the Prime Minister of India, is provided by A.P.J. Abdul Kalam, the former President of India, who wanted to visit Gujarat to see for himself the post-Godhra anti-Muslim riots of February to April 2002, where "innocents were killed, families were rendered helpless..." and The then Prime Minister Vajpayee told President Kalam, when he wanted to visit riot victims that "PM Atal Bihari Vajpayee has discomfited by my decision. He asked me, "Do you consider going to Gujarat as this time essential?". Kalam: "I must go and talk to the people as a President. I consider this my first major task". Vajpayee: ".... there was fear that then Chief Minister Narendra Modi will boycott the trip". Authoritarian personality traits of Modi and his fanatic ideological commitments to the Rashtrya Swayamsevak Sangh's goal of establishing Hindu Rashtra or Hindu nation-state have made the persona of Modi like that of a Messiah determined to implement his goals in this case exercise the state power to establish Hindu Rashtra as defined by the Rashtriya Swayamsevak Sangh. Hence, the essential Modi cannot be understood without very briefly mentoring the ideology and organizational structure of the RSS whose one finished product is Modi. RSS is a workshop which recruits young Hindus and indoctrinates them to act as soldiers to defence of Hindu community and religions, which is threatened by non-Indian foreign origin religions, like Islam and Christianity. These inhabitants of India, whose loyalty and reference point to foreign places of worship and Holiness are not only different for Hindu religious believers, whose place of birth is Mother India but they are also source of trouble for Hindus of Bharat. This is the ideological essence of RSS and every recruit to this "military like discipline based organization" is everyday exposed to the teaching imparted by higher functioning who are whole time Pracharaks and Narendra Modi himself was RSS Pracharak. Mohan Bhagwat, the RSS Sar Sangh Chalak from 2009, observed on Modi in 2013 that "Modi is the only one who has remained rooted in the Sangh Parivar" and on the basis of these qualifications the RSS Chief Mohan Bhagwat made BJP to declare Modi as Prime Ministerial candidate in September 2013 for the forthcoming Lok Sabha Elections of 2014. V.D. Savarkar (1969) "Hindutva: Who is a Hindu? M.S. Golwalkar, RSS supremo: We or Our nationhood defined (1939) or Mohan Bhagwat's 2009 statement "The problem is Hindus have started thinking about themselves as minorities. Hindus should have an aggressive, nationalistic stance".

This is the central message of RSS beginning with its founder K.B. Hedgewar from 1925 till today that Hindus have to be trained to defend themselves and a para-military type training with heavy dose of ideological Hindutva has to be imparted by RSS Shakhas or local branches. RSS creates fanatic army of cadre to work for the creation of Hindu Rashtra. This fact was reiterated by Mohan Bhagwat in August 2014 that "Hindutva is the identity of India and it has the capacity to swallow other identities. "We just need to restore those capacities". RSS, its all affiliates including BJP, are working over time to create capacity among Hindus by capturing the state power for the implementation of RSS agenda. Modi as Prime Minister, and RSS Pracharak, is committed to the ideology of RSS as recently in August 2014 reiterated with a view to remind BJP-in-Government that "Hindustan is a Hindu Rashtra.... Hindutva is the country's identity (Mohan Bhagwat). If the goal of RSS from 2014 to 2019 is to expand and establish one lakh RSS Shakhas or local units, it is at work. If in July 2012, it has 34, 761 Shakhas, in 2013, 37,125 shakhas and July 2014 it has increase to establish 39, 376 shakhas. The RSS-BJP, joint stock Company managed by Bhagwat and Modi are pursuing its Hindu agenda of:

(a) conversion of non-India religious believers, like Muslims or Christians, especially poor tribals to Hindu religion nicknamed as "*Ghar Wapsi*, one back to original of Hinduism".
(b) banning cow slaughter because of Hindu beliefs.
(c) Impact education thought institutions, like Ekta Vidyalayas and others which makes Hindus proud of these glorious past and make them read Hindu classics, like Vedas and other books of the past which contain quintessence of all Hindu knowledge.

Go to the past, Hindus had store of knowledge in shastras and it is not surprising that Narendra Modi, a product of RSS workshop, Prime Minister made such statement, "(a) Karna (in the Mahabharat) was not born from his mother's womb. This means genetic science was present at that time. (b) We worship Lord Ganesha. There must have been some plastic surgeon at that time who got an elephant's head on the body of a human being and began the practice of plastic surgery". These and other belief of the followers of Hindu Rashtriya Swayamsevak Sangh raise a larger issue about the scientific methodology for the study of ancient knowledge systems which has existed in ancient times not only in India but also other old societies, like that of China or Arabs. First, the ancient knowledge system of India cannot be declared a copyright of so-called Hindu religion. Second multiple and diverse Hindu traditions cannot be homogenized under the umbrella of a monolithic Hinduism because eminent historians have an agreement on the plurality of Hindu religious traditions and Great Hindu Religious Traditions is a myth and not a scientifically arrived at opinion on the nature and essence of Hinduism which is essentially internally highly differentiated and consists of many multiple sects. Hindus are divided into sects even on the basis of regional variations and gods and goddesses and modes of worship are also region-specific which differentiate Hindus of India of continental size and diversity. Hence, Hindu religious tradition constructed and imagined by the RSS and its ideologies is a fiction and not a fact based on the essential reality of Hinduisms. Hence, the slogan of RSS that "say with pride that we are Hindus" or treat this country is Hindu India is not based on facts. The question deserves to be raised here is that if the inner reality of Hindu religious tradition is its plurality and multiplicity of traditions, the announcements and pronouncements of Hindu RSS leadership and its ideologies that "we are all Hindus" in India and Hindus in India have to be protected by the believers and practitioners of non-Hindus living in this country, the real RSS agenda of Hinduisation of the whole society deserves to be clinically analysed on the basis of scientific method of inquiry and investigations. The real agenda of Hindu Sangh Parivar and all of its affiliates including BJP is "political" and the goal of Sangh Parivar including the BJP is to politically capture the state power and establish Hindu hegemony over all non-Hindus who should accept that either their ancestors were Hindus or they should be "Converted to Hinduism, the religion of Bharat. The reconversion of Muslims and Christians of India by the Hindu Sangh Parivar affiliates is a logical offshoot of RSS ideology and it deserves to be asserted that the current, "reconversion programmes" of the RSS, under the protective umbrella of the Modi government and the state governments controlled by the BJP are not accidental or aberrations, they are sanctioned by Hindu ideologues and governments controlled by the BJP. Mohan Bhagwat stated in 2015 that "...that all those born in India are Hindus. Whether they accept it or not they are culturally, nationally and DNA wise the same" and following this logic reconversion programmes are, all according to RSS logical because it is "*Ghar Wapsi*", the homecoming to Hindu fold by Muslim and Christians. It is not without reason that the highest organizational centre of authority of RSS, the Akhil Bharatiya Pratinidhi Sabha officially stated that "where is '*Ghar Wapsi*' Campaign, it is just home-coming. The upshot of above narrative is quite clear that it is "Political Hinduism or Hindutva and not ancient great Hindu Religious Traditions, which are the subject matter while dealing with the phenomenon of Hindu RSS led movements and governments both, at the centre or the state levels, further, interpretations or misinterpretations of the ancient great Hindu religious traditions is not at all relevant while dealing with the phenomenon of RSS's "Political Hinduism" because it is Hinduism in the service of "politics and the goal of RSS and BJP is to make Hindus to occupy "driver's seat" in politics and all the institutions of the state, whether coercive or ideological, should be politically driven and managed by Hindus only. Political Hinduism of RSS is similar to the political Islamic movements in some countries of Muslims majority populations, the most aggressive and violent is the Iraq-Syria Islamic State. John M. Owen in his book of "Political Islam" observes candidly that "Political Islam matters and it is not going to go away soon. It is a powerful ideology and social movement, running deep within and across most Islamic countries today..." Is Political Hinduism in anyway different from Political Islam of Islamic countries? The answer is a big no. It is relevant here to mention that many eminent scholars justified and suggested that capitalist globalization beginning with the last decade of Twentieth Century and continuing in the Twenty-first Century will weaken, even demolish, nationalism and a new global world order "without borders or territorial boundaries" would replace and displace the idea of Nationalism. Eric Hobsbawm, an eminent Historian (1990) observed "... the Owl of Minerva, which brings wisdom (says Hegel) flies out at dusk; it is a good sign that it is now circling sound nations and nationalism". The main arguments of Hobsbawm (1990) is that "Nationalism will be transitory in an era of globalization. How wrong was eminent historian? Hobsbawm never thought that beginning with 1990 is that political nationalism will see a rebirth in a deadly form, when "religion" Hindus or Islamic will be appropriated by leaders of movements in India and Arab Countries to fight their political battles against other religious traditions or intra-religious traditions, like Hindus versus Muslims in India or Islamic religious political movements confronting Christian America or within the Arab Islamic societies Sunnis versus Shias. Such political religious movements are engaged in a struggle to capture defined "territories for the establishment of Hindu state or purse Islamic states according to Shariah. It is religion in the service of leaders and groups struggling for state power to establish state systems for the implementation of an ideology of Hinduism or Islam as interpreted by them. The challenge to every citizen who accepts the philosophical promises and assumptions of democratic, republican, secular, federalist Constitution of India is to defend it because political Hinduism or practitioners of religion in politics do not accept the basic democratic principle of "equality of every citizen based on the rule of law". M.S. Golwalkar, the author of 'We or Our Nationhood Defined' (1939) and the longest serving Head of the RSS, had clearly opposed the 'federal' feature of Indian Constitution because Hindu ideologies, on the basis of faulty interpretation of Indian history, have always believed and propagated the idea that Hindus suffered defeats and humiliations for more than 1200 years, which they described as Muslim period, not only because Hindu society was fragmented and internally divided, but essentially because India's authority of the state, instead of being located at one centre only, was also divided among various Hindu Rajas and Maharajas. The implication of this kind of flawed history is that India should have "one powerful centre of power" and unitary and not federal idea of governance is acceptable to the RSS leaders. It is not without reason Deen Dayal Upadhayay, an icon of RSS, following in the footsteps of Golwalkars, re-emphasised that India needs a unitary and nota federal state system. The Hindu Sangh Parivar has a clear blueprint for the establishment of a highly centralized Hindu state and re-write the existing democratic and federal Constitution of India. It deserves to be mentioned that Atal Bihari Vajpayee (1998 to 2004) appointed a so-called National Constitution Review Commission to undertake a re-examination of the principles and structures of government underlying the Republican Constitution of 1950. The Narendra Modi government is in power at the centre to push forward the agenda of Hindu Rashtravadis as handed over by the RSS. Narendra Modi and RSS are indistinguishable and as Prime Minster he is presiding over the machinery of government, which is openly or in a clandestine manner doing everything to strengthen the foundations of Hindu Rashtra, where Hindus are "First class-citizens" and Muslim and Christian religious minorities are "second class-citizen". Is it accidental that only Muslims are arrested after every terrorist's attack including Akshardham in Ahmedabad? Is it not a fact that courts have found many arrested Muslims innocent of such terrorist activities? Is not a fact that Muslims and Christians are feeling nervous and insecure under the Hindu state of India? A French scholar Charlotte Thomas (2015) on the basis of a study formed that "Although formally Muslim citizens have the same rights as their Hindu counterparts, in Ahmedabad and even more in *Jhupura*, their ethnicity disqualifies them from an effective focus of citizenship". The one aspect of inter-religious violent conflicts between Hindus and Muslims lead to death and destruction of property, generally of Muslims, the other reality is every riot pushes minorities to seek collective security among their co-religionists. It is well known fact that the process of Muslim ghettoisation has been increasing because of the feeling of "insecurity" among the Muslims. The Modi Government has not done a bit to assure minorities of India that they are secure and fully protected by his government. It is a misleading statement that lunatic fringe elements affiliated and associated with the Hindu RSS are creating "difficulties" for Muslims and Christians, if so, it was not expected of US President Barack Obama, just after his visit to Delhi on Republic day of 2015 write back to Modi "protect the religious minorities" in your country. The upshot of above narrative is Modi as a Prime Minister or Chief Minister of Gujarat (2001 to 2014) or as Pracharak is committed to carry on his own ideology and belief that India is a Hindu country and political power is an instrument to strengthen the foundations of Hindu Rashtravad as defined and interpreted by the Hindu Sangh Parivar. Mohan Bhagwat has authoritatively opined that "Modi is our man" and this RSS loyalist is the Prime Minister of India. Narendra Modi has behind him the whole RSS 'Machine' of 'organization men' to quote Robert Merton, who in a different context talked of 'organization machine' which really matters in a party or an Organization.

The other important agenda of the Modi government is to pursue aggressively the promotion of interests of monopoly capitalist classes of India and further strengthen the links of Indian capitalist classes with monopoly global capitalist system. The monopoly capitalist classes of India and global capitalists are quite satisfied with Modi's performance as an agent of local and foreign capitalism. It deserves to be clearly mentioned here that Indian monopolists are making every effort to integrate with 'finance capital' at a global level, when the real centre of global capitalist market system is in deep crises and the best example of global capitalist crises is provided by the "decline" of American super economic and military states beginning with the end of first decade of the twenty first century. It is surprising that Modi's rating by the United States of America is not only very high and positive, Indians are proud of testimonials given to Modi by Barack Obama and the US *Time Magazine* inspite of the fact that American capitalism itself is facing serious challenges. If the US *Time Magazine* has listed Modi in 100 eminent persons of 2015, Barack Obama, US President while writing on Modi in the *Time Magazine* described Modi as "India's reformer-in-Chief". The United States and Barack Obama as Chief Political Executive of the ruling classes is calling on Modi to push forward the process of "deregulation, liberalization, privatization and globalization" of the Indian market so that American investors along with capitalists of European Union and Japan can reap profits from Indian market. It is not only global capitalist classes and their Chief Political Executives are applauding Modi, the Indian monopolist, the real beneficiaries of Modi's free market economic policies have also lived upto project him as the right man for the right job at a right time.

1. Ratan Tata on April 17-2015 while addressing the convocation of Mumbai International School of Business expressed hope "in the inspirational leadership of Mődi" because "...the country will move forward in the manner that Modi predicted. Ratan Tata advised leaders of Indian Corporate Houses not to lose "patience"...the country will move forward in the manner that Modi predicated.
2. Infosys N.R. Narayana Murthy on May 20, 2015 asked the capitalist classes "to support Modi" because "we have a PM who is enthusiastic and is working hard....people, all parties and oppositions should rally behind him".

3. On May 27, 2015 the World Bank Chief (President) Jim Yong Kim not only congratulated Modi on the completion of his one year of Prime Ministership also observed that .... One year of visionary steps toward ending poverty in India. The world needs more leaders like you. Are the global and Indian monopoly capitalist building a Louis Bonaparte of mid-nineteenth Century, who exercised power over the whole society because he was made of believe that he was above the whole society? A little more needs to be stated here to substantiate the argument that the darling Prime Minister of the ruling classes is not at all interested in solving the problems faced by exploited and suppressed under classes of India. Modi's model of economic development is focused on the prosperity and progress of fractions of the ruling exploiting capitalist classes and agrarian surplus generating fractions of the exploiting strata of society: (a) Below Poverty Line Indian, Rangarajan on July 6, 2014 observed that if poverty line is calculated on the basis of Rupees 32 in rural areas and Rupees 47 in urban areas "new members mean that 363 million world have struggled to survive, if there was no public spending". What has Modi done for these the tore wretched of the East, (b) Gross inequality: A World bank Report "Addressing inequality in South Asia" on January 20, 2015 based on 59 round of NSSO survey, measuring wealth, land, buildings, machinery, financial assets so on observed that "the average net worth of the 10 per cent of the top population in India was 380 times of the bottom 10 per cent. This bottom 10 per cent can be catagorised as: "(a) the poor, (b) the vulnerable(people above the poverty line), and (c) the middle classes". Further, the new world wealth estimate in 2014 put Indians 14, 800, who were with multi-millionaires i.e. worth over US$ 10 millions.
4. Agrarian India: The National Sample Survey office on December 20, 2014 mentions that: (a) Nearly 90 per cent of Indian farmers have less than 2 hectares of land, (b) An average farmhouse earns less than Rupees 6,500 a month from all sources, (c) The Census of 2011 mentions that agricultural labourers are 144.3 million and cultivators 118.7 million and this huge percentage of rural population earns its living 'exclusively' or 'Partially' working as "labourers" only. Has Modi during his One year of Prime Ministership shows any sensitivity to the structural problems of class-based inequalities or rural-urban divide or regional imbalances? Does Modi realize that his tolerant approach for the solution of deep-seated class, caste, region division will perpetuate social status quo? Modi has taken great credit for his Yojanas, like: (a) Jan Dhan Yojana i.e. financial inclusion, (b) Janashree Bima

Yojana, (c) Jan Suraksha Yojana, (d) Atal Pension Yojana. Modi growth model benefits only 20 per cent of the privileged strata of society only and proportionally poor 28 to 80 per cent of the population continue to remain at the 'margins' of social hierarchy.

How does one tie together Modi's leadership of Hindutva and Political Economy of globalized Monopoly capitalism? Is it a puzzle that a RSS Swayamsevak and Pracharak can reconcile 'Political Hinduism' with his enthusiastic commitment to the growth of Indian monopoly capitalism? Ram Madhav, BJP General Secretary in an interview on April 12, 2015 observed that "The RSS Chief categorically told our cadres that we are working because of a historic reason—that India needed a major political transformation...". The Hindu Rashtriya Swayamsevak Sangh openly and unambiguously supported Narendra Modi during the Lok Sabha Elections of 2014 so that Prime Minister of India can aggressively push the political agenda of establishing a Hindu Rashtra and a Hindu nation-state because as a committed RSS Pracharak Modi can be trusted to implement the RSS agenda of solidifying the foundation of Hindu Bharat Desh. If this is the political agenda of Modi, he has also to fulfill the expectations of Big Industrial Houses and monopolists, who openly championed his candidature for Prime Ministership and the Media controlled by the corporate Houses went out of the way to build the atmosphere for the electoral victory of Modi. The United States based *Forbes* Magazine in 2015 observed that "India is home of the world's 2000 largest and most powerful public companies". Further, Mukesh Ambani's Reliance Industries Limited led the pack of the 56 Indian companies mentioned in the *Forbes* list of 2015. Ambani, Advani, Tatas, Birlas, Bharatis, the leaders of monopoly capitalism supported Modi to win the Lok Sabha elections of 2014. Capitalists have only one agenda that the Chief Political Executive of the Indian state as head of the whole state apparatus should create all conditions, which are conducive to the maximisation of profits by the private accumulators. If at the face value it may seem that political agenda of Hinduism as clearly defined by the Hindu RSS may not be able to push forward the agenda of its main allies, the corporate business and industrial houses, because Hinduism as defined by the RSS is a call to 'polarize' and 'divide' society by targeting the minorities to make them the second class states of citizenship which is disruptive of social order in a multi-religious society. Capitalists want social conditions, which will facilitate accumulation of private profit and RSS agenda of Hinduisation in socially contentious, disruptive and is bound to lead to social violent conflicts between believers of non-Hindu religions and the forces of Hindutva is who will threaten their religious identity. Modi has to do a tight rope dancing and while dealing with these "two contradictory agendas", he will have to manage affairs of the state by compromising with the principles of democratic governance of this country. Hindutva and multi-cultural and multi-religious democracy in a situation, where the leaders and managers of the state are determined to push the Hinduisation of India will definitely lead to contests, conflicts and violence. Hindutva and democracy are in antagonistic contradictions. How can Modi disown his Hindu family of the RSS? Modi also cannot dispense with his deep commitment to build and strengthen capitalism in India. This is the crux of the issue while focusing attention on Prime Minister Narendra Modi.

NOTES AND REFERENCES

1. Michael Minkenberg: The Renewal of the Radical Right: Between Modernity and *Anti-Modernity": Government and Opposition:* volume 35, Number 2, pp. 174-175, see pp. 170-188. Also, see Jurgen Falter and Siegfried Schumann *"Affinity Towards right-wing Extremism in Europe"* in Klaus von Be Yme (ed.) Right-Wing *Extremism in Western Europe*, London : Frank Class 1988, pp. 96-110.
2. Charles Taylor: The Politics of Recognition", in A. Gutmann (ed.) *Multi-culturalism*, Princeton, Princeton University Press, 1994.
3. Harish Khare, "Borders can not be redrawn on religious basis: P.M." The Hindu, New Delhi, August 16, 2000, p. 1.
4. Martin E. Marty and R. Scott Appleby (eds.) *Fundamentalisms Observed:* Chicago: Chicago University Press 1991, p. ix
5. Daniel Gold, "Organized Hinduism from Vedic Truth to Hindu Nation" in Martin E. Marty and R. Scott Appleby (eds.) *op. cit.* p. 567).
6. M.S. Golwalkar: Bunch of Thoughts and Spotlight, Bangalore, Vikarma Prakashan, 1966 and Spotlights: Guruji Answers: Bangalore, Sahitya Sindhu, 1974 : Quoted by Daniel Gold, *ibid*, p. 567.
7. V.D. Savarkar: *Hindutva* : Bombay : Veer Savarkar Prakashan 1969, p. 1.
8. Antono Gramsci: *Selections from the Prison Notebook:* edited and translated by Quinton Hoare and Geoffray Nowell Smith: New York: International Publishers: 1971, p. 172.
9. Ranjit Guha: (ed.) *Subaltern Studies:* Delhi: Oxford University Press, 1982, pp. 5-6.
10. Bryan S., Turner: "*Contemporary Problem In the Theory of Citizenship* in Bryan S., Turner (Ed.) *Citizenship and Social Theory*: New Delhi: Sage Publication 1993, p. 3
11. Giovanni Sartori: *Democratic Theory*: New Delhi: Oxford University Press: 1965, p. 335
12. *ibid*, p. 364
13. Bart Van Steenbergen: *The Condition of Citizenship*: New Delhi Sage Publication 1994: p. 4
14. Robert, A. Dahl: *Democracy And Its Critics*: New Haven: Yale University Press 1989, pp. 320-21.
15. Pralay, Kanungo: *RSS Tryst with Politics: From Hedgewar to Sudarshan*: Delhi: Manohar, 2002
16. See Martin E. Marry and R. Scott Appleby (Eds) *Fundamentalisms observed*, vol. I (Chicago: Chicago University Press, 1991 also see other volumes 1992 1993, 1994, 1995)
17. Lahouari, Addi : *"The Failure of Third World Nationalism"* : quoted by Peter Juviler and Sherrill Stroschein : *Political Science Quarterly*, volume 114, Number 3, 1999, pp. 450-51.
18. The *Guardian*: Europe: April 25, 2001, p. 7.
19. Also see Jorge Larrain: Ideology and Cultural Identity: Modernity and the Third World: Polity Press, 1994.
20. Interview of Jana Krishnamurthy, *The Indian Express*: New Delhi: May 29, 2001.

21. L.K. Advani: Statement before Liberahan Commission: The Indian Express: New Delhi: June 13, 2001.
22. M.S. Golwalkar, *Bunch of Thoughts* p. 182, quoted by Kanungo (2002) p. 116.
23. Aristotle quoted by Richard Mecheon: (ed) *The Basic Works of* Aristotle: New York : Random House, 1941, p. 936.
24. G.K. Chadha, P.P. Sahu: *"Post-reform setback in rural employment: Issues that need further serutiny."* Bombay, *Economic Political Weekly*, May 25-31, 2002, vol. XXXVII, no. 21, pp. 1998-2026.
25. C.P. Chandrasekhar and Jayati Ghosh: *The Market that Failed*: *A Decade of Neoliberal Economic Reforms in India* : New Delhi Leftword Books, 2002.
26. *Economic Survey*: 2001-2002: New Delhi: Government of India: March 2002.
27. Gary Younge: "After Burnley and Oldham, there is no such thing as a black British experience: There are several". The Guardian: London, June 28, 2001, p. 7.
28. *Asian Age* : New Delhi June 7, 2002, p. 1
29. *The Statesman*: New Delhi: June 8, 2002, p. 4.
30. Ashok Singhal, VHP leader: *The Hindu*, New Delhi, June 23, 2002, p. 1.
31. *The Hindu*: New Delhi June 23, 2002, p. 1.
32. J.S. Mill quoted by Sartori, *op. cit.* p. 99.
33. Aijaz Ahmad, *"Cry the Beloved Country"* : *Frontline*, Chennai. Vol. 19, no. 13, June 22-July 5, 2002, p. 116.
34. Robert A. Dahl: *Democracy And its Critics* New Haven, Yale University Press, 1989, p. 341.

Index